ROUTLEDGE LIBRARY EDITIONS:
INTERNATIONAL SECURITY STUDIES

Volume 21

WARFARE IN A FRAGILE WORLD

T0382790

WARFARE IN A FRAGILE WORLD
Military Impact on the Human Environment

SIPRI
STOCKHOLM INTERNATIONAL PEACE
RESEARCH INSTITUTE

LONDON AND NEW YORK

First published in 1980 by Taylor & Francis Ltd

This edition first published in 2021
by Routledge
2 Park Square, Milton Park, Abingdon, Oxon OX14 4RN

and by Routledge
52 Vanderbilt Avenue, New York, NY 10017

Routledge is an imprint of the Taylor & Francis Group, an informa business

© 1980 SIPRI

British Library Cataloguing in Publication Data
A catalogue record for this book is available from the British Library

ISBN: 978-0-367-68499-0 (Set)
ISBN: 978-1-00-316169-1 (Set) (ebk)
ISBN: 978-0-367-71465-9 (Volume 21) (hbk)
ISBN: 978-0-367-71472-7 (Volume 21) (pbk)
ISBN: 978-1-00-315220-0 (Volume 21) (ebk)

Publisher's Note
The publisher has gone to great lengths to ensure the quality of this reprint but points out that some imperfections in the original copies may be apparent.

Disclaimer
The publisher has made every effort to trace copyright holders and would welcome correspondence from those they have been unable to trace.

Warfare in a Fragile World

Military Impact on the Human Environment

Stockholm International Peace Research Institute

Taylor & Francis Ltd
London
1980

First published 1980 by Taylor & Francis Ltd
10-14 Macklin Street, London WC2B 5NF

Distributed in the United States of America by
Crane, Russak & Company, Inc.
3 East 44th Street, New York, N.Y. 10017
and in Scandinavia by
Almqvist & Wiksell International
26 Gamla Brogatan
S-101 20 Stockholm, Sweden

British Library Cataloguing in Publication Data

Stockholm International Peace Research Institute
　　Warfare in a fragile world.
　　1. War—Environmental aspects
　　I. Title　II. Westing, Arthur H
　　574.5′222　　　QH545.W26

ISBN 0-85066-187-0

Typeset by Georgia Origination, Liverpool
Printed and bound in the United Kingdom by
Taylor & Francis (Printers) Ltd., Rankine Road,
Basingstoke, Hampshire RG24 0PR

Preface

The military impact on the human environment is a problem of increasing importance. The present study examines how and to what extent warfare damages the environment. It is the third in a series of SIPRI studies relating to the impact of warfare on the environment. The first two, *Ecological Consequences of the Second Indochina War* (1976) and *Weapons of Mass Destruction and the Environment* (1977), examined particular weapons and techniques of war and their ability to disrupt the environment. The present study examines the several major global environments and their vulnerability to military disruption.

A number of multilateral treaties are relevant to the prevention of environmental damage by war. Among those already in force are the Antarctic Treaty of 1959, the Partial Test Ban Treaty of 1963, the Outer Space Treaty of 1967, the World Heritage Convention of 1972, the Environmental Modification Convention of 1977, and the two Geneva Protocols of 1977 additional to the Geneva Conventions of 1949. I hope that this series of studies will contribute to discussion on this issue.

This book was written by Dr Arthur H. Westing while he was a senior research fellow at SIPRI. He is now Professor of Ecology and Dean of the School of Natural Science at Hampshire College in Amherst, Massachusetts, USA.

July 1979

Frank Barnaby
Director

Acknowledgement
The author is pleased to acknowledge Rajesh Kumar for editing the manuscript.

Contents

Tables

Chapter 8. The global ecology

Tables

Conventions and units of measure

As far as possible, the names of plants conform to Lawrence (1951), of the mammals to Walker *et al.* (1975), and of the bacteria to Buchanan & Gibbons (1974). The chemical nomenclature follows that of Windholz *et al.* (1976) or, secondarily, of Weast (1974: sections B and C). All units of measure follow (or are defined in terms of) the *Système Internationale d'Unités* (SI) (National Bureau of Standards, 1977). Conversions to customary US and British units are from Weast (1974: section F: 282–304). The monetary unit employed is the 1975 US dollar (US \$). The geographic authority adopted is *The Times* (1977).

References to publications in the text provide information sufficient to locate the full bibliographic citation in the alphabetical listing of 'References', that is, author and date. Different publications by the same author that were published during the same year are distinguished by the arbitrary assignment of a series of italicized lower-case letters appended to the year of publication.

The units of measure (and prefixes) used in the text follow:

are (a) = 100 square metres = 1 076.39 square feet

centi- (c-) = 0.01 ×

curie (Ci) = 37×10^9 becquerels (Bq) = 37×10^9 disintegrations per second = 2.22×10^{12} disintegrations per minute

day (d) = 86 400 seconds

degree Celsius (°C) = 1 kelvin. To convert temperature in degrees Celsius to temperature in degrees Fahrenheit, multiply by 1.8 and then add 32.

giga- (G-) = 10^9 ×

gram (g) = 10^{-3} kilogram = $2.204 \, 62 \times 10^{-3}$ pound

hectare (ha) = 10^4 square metres = 0.01 square kilometre = 2.471 05 acres

hect(o)- (h-) = 100 ×

hour (h) = 3 600 seconds

joule (J) = 0.238 846 calorie

kilo- (k-) = 10^3 ×

kilogram (kg) = 2.204 62 pounds

kilometre (km) = 10^3 metres = 0.621 371 mile = 0.539 957 nautical mile

kilometre, square (km²) = 100 hectares = 247.105 acres = 0.386 102 square mile

'kiloton' (kT) = 4.187×10^{12} joules, referring to the energy yield of a nuclear bomb (appendix 7.3) litre (l) = 10^{-3} cubic metre = 0.264 172 US gallon = 0.219 969 British gallon

mega- (M-) = $10^6 \times$

'megaton' (MT) = 4.187×10^{15} joules, referring to the energy of a nuclear bomb (appendix 7.3)

metre (m) = 3.280 84 feet = 0.546 807 fathom

metre, cubic (m^3) = 10^3 litres = 264.172 US gallons = 219.969 British gallons = 1.307 95 cubic yards = 138 board feet = 6.289 81 US oil barrels

micro- (μ-) = $10^{-6} \times$

milli- (m-) = $10^{-3} \times$

minute (min) = 60 seconds

mole (mol) = that amount of substance which contains as many elementary entities as there are atoms in 12 grams of carbon-12 (^{12}C), that is, 602.252×10^{21} elementary entities

nano- (n-) = $10^{-9} \times$

pascal (Pa) = $9.869\ 23 \times 10^{-6}$ atmosphere = 145.038×10^{-6} pound per square inch

röntgen (R) = a unit of X or gamma radiation exposure producing a charge of 258×10^{-6} coulomb per kilogram of air; for biota it is numerically equivalent to c. 0.01 gray (Gy) or else to c. 1 rad, a unit of ionizing radiation absorption of 0.01 joule per kilogram of body weight (Arena, 1971: 215–218)

second (s) = the duration of 9 192 631 770 periods of the radiation corresponding to the transition between the two hyperfine levels of the ground state of the caesium-133 (^{133}Cs) atom

tera- (T-) = $10^{12} \times$

'ton' (T) = a measure of nuclear-bomb yield, for which see 'kiloton' or 'megaton' above; it is also a measure of ship size, for which see appendix 7.2

tonne (t) = 10^3 kilograms = 1.102 31 US (short) tons = 0.984 207 British (long) ton

watt (W) = joule per second = $1.340\ 48 \times 10^{-3}$ horsepower

In tables

– = not applicable or information not available

1. The human environment

The tables for this chapter appear on pages 14–29.

I. Introduction

Wars have occurred without substantial if any interruption throughout the long sweep of human history, unequivocally establishing them among the characteristic endeavours of our species. So far in this century alone there have occurred some 16 major wars and more than 10 times as many minor wars (table 1.1). That is to say, a new war of major magnitude has been occurring once every five years, on the average. There is, furthermore, little reason to doubt that the human failing that leads to such activity will persist in the years to come.

Wars result in loss of life and other casualties, in destruction of property, and in social disruption. They additionally lead to environmental damage and ecological disruption—matters of growing concern and the subject of the present work. Damage to the human environment is of growing concern because of the awakening demands of an ever-increasingly over-populated world. The concern for nature has been reinforced, moreover, by the recent military demonstrations of ecological devastation as an intentional strategy of war.

Two recent SIPRI studies have dealt with the impact of warfare upon the environment, both approaching the subject from the standpoint of specific weapons or means of war. The first of these, *Ecological Consequences of the Second Indochina War* (SIPRI, 1976), analysed a particular war and dwelt especially upon the impact of conventional high-explosive munitions, of herbicidal chemical anti-plant agents, and of land-clearing tractors (Rome ploughs). The second, *Weapons of Mass Destruction and the Environment* (SIPRI, 1977), described the effects of nuclear weapons, of chemical and biological anti-personnel agents, and of a number of so-called geophysical weapons. The present work, in contrast, approaches the subject from the standpoint of specific habitats and their vulnerability to military disruption. Such military disruption is discussed for each habitat against a background of its human occupancy and utilization, that is, of its routine civil use and abuse by man.

The present chapter is devoted to brief overviews both of the Earth and its habitats (section III) and of man's use and abuse of the Earth (section IV). These descriptions are preceded by a summary of modern warfare and weaponry in order to suggest the character, level, and frequency with which military activities impinge upon man and nature.

For an annotated bibliography on the impact of military activities on the environment, the reader is referred to Westing & Lumsden (1979).

II. Warfare and weaponry

Wars are by their very nature violent, deadly, and destructive. The present section discusses their nature and frequency with particular reference to the ecological disruption involved.

In an *interstate* war, the military forces of one or more nations attempt to force an enemy nation or nations into submission by a variety of coercive acts; the recipient nation or nations attempt to reciprocate in kind. Some five major (i.e., high-fatality) and many additional minor (i.e., low-fatality) interstate wars have occurred so far during this century (appendix 1.1). In a *colonial* war, a colony or similar possession attempts to attain its independence. Only two major but many minor colonial wars have occurred so far during this century. Relatively few colonies remain, so that this category of war will diminish in the years to come. In a *civil* (intrastate) war, a portion of a nation or other insurgent force attempts to secede from or overthrow the established government, the latter in turn hoping to counter the revolt or insurgency. Again, both sides resort to violent and destructive acts. There have been at least nine major and large numbers of minor civil wars so far during this century.

Nations are highly complex and diverse entities, but for present purposes each can be dissected into a number of major components. To begin with, a nation is composed of *land* and *people*. The people fall into a number of more or less distinct groups: the civil populace (either urban or rural), the armed forces, the government (this last group drawn from either the civil or, more likely, the military groups), and, quite often, a quasi-military insurgent group. The land is conveniently divided into the so-called built-up environment—cities and land devoted to industry and trans-portation– agricultural land, and land that is more or less wild. The wild land consists of grassland (much of it utilized as pasture or range land), forest land (much of it utilized for timber, pulp, and firewood), and numerous lesser categories: desert, tundra, mountain, lake, and so forth (also utilized to some extent).

The destructive acts of war can be directed against any of these human and other components of a nation, either intentionally or incidentally, and, indeed, have been. Armed forces have available a large array of destructive weapons and techniques to carry out such acts. In some instances they can exert additional pressure on an enemy by cutting it off from a necessary outside source of supply of food or fuel or other essential commodity.

Wars can be considered to be ecologically disruptive for any of a number of reasons, as the examples in table 1.2 demonstrate. To begin with, a war is ecologically disruptive if it exerts a substantial impact on the civil populace. Such impact on the human ecology of a nation can be achieved in one or more of several ways. Thus, a significant (major) fraction of the people can be killed or displaced as a result of the hostilities, their source of food denied for extended periods, or their homes or means of livelihood destroyed. Secondly, a war is also ecologically disruptive if it exerts a substantially disruptive impact on more natural portions of a nation. Depending upon local circumstances, such disruption can have a greater or lesser deleterious impact on the populace. Indeed, such disruption may have only a subtle, delayed, marginal, or even non-existent effect on human society.

A particular concern of the present study is the disruption by war of agricultural and wild lands, and thus of the ecosystems these regions support. The weapons and other means of war available to the armed forces of today are increasingly capable of disrupting these natural and semi-natural habitats. Indeed, there has been a discernible tendency for wars to result in ever greater disruption of the environment. Among the factors that contribute to the increasing military violence against nature are the growing technical and logistical abilities of armed forces to devastate large areas on a sustained basis.

It is today possible to devastate the ecology of large areas with nuclear weapons as well as with chemical agents or biological organisms. Soon, moreover, it may be possible to accomplish the same with so-called geophysical weapons. But one need not turn to unconventional or fanciful weapons for such a purpose. New generations of conventional weapons, from primitive times to the present, have exhibited ever greater destructive abilities and promise to continue to do so in the future (Dupuy, 1978–1979; Robinson, 1977). Of even greater importance, the conventional high-explosive fire-power of armed forces has also continued to increase dramatically over the years. By way of example, the USSR has reported on the weight of the salvo that one of its army divisions can deliver against an enemy, a value that followed an exponential increase between 1923 and 1968, the period described (Sidorenko, 1970: 8).

It is also instructive in this regard to compare US actions during its three most recent wars: World War II, the Korean War, and the Second Indochina War. US battle intensity as measured in terms of the monthly number of US combat fatalities dropped progressively from each of these wars to the next, in the ratio of 15:2:1, respectively. (It can be noted, moreover, that this progressive drop remains intact even when the data are adjusted for the differing total US force commitments in the three wars, the adjusted ratio becoming 3:2:1 (Ellender & McClellan, 1972: 163).) Combat fatalities among the forces opposed to the USA followed a remarkably similar trend, also exhibiting a ratio of 15:2:1 (appendix 1.2). Among other things, these parallel ratios suggest no improvement in relative US combat

3

capability to the extent that this is reflected in the proportion of killed enemy soldiers to killed US soldiers. The three wars can also be compared from the standpoint of the resulting numbers of total fatalities experienced by the nations pitted against the USA. Thus, the Axis nations of World War II experienced an overall fatality rate (military plus civil) of five per cent, North Korea one of about six per cent, and the four Indochinese nations together one of perhaps four per cent (appendix 1.3).

In the light of these several comparisons, it becomes remarkable to note that total US munition expenditures during the Second Indochina War exceeded those of the prior two wars combined. In terms of the respective US areas of action involved in these three wars, US munition expenditures were in the approximate ratio of 1:5:7. Alternatively, US munition expenditures per enemy soldier killed were in the even more startling ratio of 1:6:18 (appendix 1.2). It would be risky to draw too many conclusions from the summary data just presented. These three wars differed widely not only in their objectives and in the matching of their adversaries, but also in their durations, the nature of their theatres, and other significant features. For example, the World War II information lumps together two rather different theatres and types of war, the European theatre (accounting for perhaps 80 per cent of the total US munition expenditures) and the Pacific (accounting for the remaining 20 per cent). The Indochina figures are confounded by lumping together South Viet Nam (accounting for 71 per cent of the total US munition expenditures for that war) with the rest of the region.

Nevertheless, one is forced to conclude that the explanation for the anomalous situation of increasing US munition expenditures without a concomitant increase in the level of enemy fatalities lies in the changing nature of the target against which these munitions were directed. That is to say, these data suggest a changing military strategy that calls for high munition expenditures against larger and more ill-defined target areas, and that consequently results in a higher level of environmental damage. In fact, such a surmise is substantiated by available information.

The several summary volumes of the US Strategic Bombing Survey of World War II (D'Olier *et al.*, 1945 *a*; 1945 *b*; 1946; 1947 *b*; Galbraith *et al.*, 1945) suggest that the major Allied air effort during that war was directed against clearly defined military targets on the one hand, and against urban and industrial targets on the other. Specifically, Galbraith *et al.* (1945: 2–5) provide numerical breakdowns which together account for 72 per cent of the European air war (and thus for 58 per cent of the total air war). Based on this sample, one can calculate that only 31 per cent of the World War II air effort took the form of area bombings, and these largely involving urban areas. (No equivalent information seems available for artillery or sea munitions expended during World War II.)

With respect to the Korean War, Cagle & Manson (1957: 278) provide data covering almost two years of that war (from early 1951 up to 1952 inclusive). Restricting themselves to air munitions for the following figures, Cagle & Manson report that 70 per cent of the US Air Force, almost 100 per cent of the US Navy, and 60 per cent of the US Marine Corps expenditures were used for interdiction, that is, directed against ill-defined (usually rural) area targets. An average of these air data, weighted according to the proportions provided by Futrell *et al.* (1961: 645), comes out to be 74 per cent. Although no comparable ground (artillery) data were provided by Cagle & Manson, they do note that 70 per cent of the sea munitions were expended for inland interdiction purposes.

During the Second Indochina War, the proportion of ill-defined area targets rose once again, and these now became almost exclusively rural in nature. Thus, most by far of the air and artillery expenditures by the USA in Indochina were used for purposes of area interdiction or harassment. Indeed, a very high proportion of the targets were nebulously described as "suspected enemy activity", and a considerable fraction of the strikes took the form of totally unobserved fires (that is, against unseen targets). It can be estimated that fully 85 per cent of the profligate US munition expenditures in Indochina were of this sort (Berger, 1977; Dellums, 1972: 16754; Enthoven & Smith, 1971: 305; Kennedy, 1967: 145; Littauer & Uphoff, 1972: 53).

In conclusion, there is no denying that wars are meant to be destructive, that the destructive abilities of armed forces are substantial, and that these abilities continue to improve. The destructive violence associated with warfare disrupts the environment to a greater or lesser extent, either incidentally or deliberately. Environmental disruption of an incidental nature is at least a modest concomitant of most wars of any size. However, in most major wars—that is, in wars of fatality class 6 or greater (see appendix 1.1, note *b*)—it can be expected to attain substantial proportions. The frequency of such wars during this century has been one every five years (table 1.1). Deliberate environmental disruption for hostile purposes has been used as a means of warfare for millennia and there is no reason to believe that it is losing favour (table 1.2). Indeed, indications presented earlier suggest the opposite. The Earth and its habitats—the actual theatres of war subject to disruption—are introduced in the next section.

III. The Earth and its habitats

Several potential theatres of war are distinguished in the present work, the categories being based on climate or geomorphology (Herbertson, 1905; Cloudsley-Thompson, 1975; Heintzelman & Highsmith, 1973). Their responses to military and other disturbances are in some respects similar, but differ in a number of significant ways. The first major distinction recognized here is the one between *terrestrial* habitats (chapters 2–6) and *oceanic* habitats (chapter 7). The terrestrial habitats are discussed under four mutually exclusive categories—temperate (chapter 2), tropical (chapter 3), desert (chapter 4), and arctic (chapter 5)—and a fifth one—island (chapter 6)—that overlaps the others.

Broadly speaking, the temperate habitat occupies much of the land situated between the Arctic Circle and the tropic of Cancer together with that between the tropic of Capricorn and the Antarctic Circle. It is characterized by a seasonal alternation of warm summers and cold winters and by precipitation adequate to permit the development of forest or grassland. The tropical habitat occupies much of the land that straddles the equator, between the tropics of Cancer and Capricorn. It is characterized by frost-free conditions the year round and, again, by precipitation adequate to permit the development of forest or grassland. The desert habitat can occur anywhere between the Arctic and Antarctic Circles in regions experiencing precipitation less than adequate for the development of grassland. The arctic habitat is found north of the Arctic Circle, south of the Antarctic Circle, and at high mountain elevations. It is characterized by sub-freezing temperatures throughout most or all of the year, the somewhat warmer situation permitting the development of tundra.

The total global surface covers some 510 million square kilometres, quite unevenly divided between land (149 million square kilometres) and ocean (361 million square kilometres) (table 1.3). The terrestrial fraction, two-thirds of which is found in the Northern hemisphere, is separated into numerous large and small land masses more or less well isolated from each other by the intervening ocean (table 1.4). The largest land mass of this type is by far Eurasia (52 million square kilometres), followed in turn by Africa (30 million square kilometres), North America (22 million square kilometres), South America (18 million square kilometres), Antarctica (13 million square kilometres), and so forth *ad infinitum*.

The Earth has served as a life-support system continuously for the past several thousand million years. Life on Earth—the global biomass—has been able to survive and even thrive for this immense span of time because several basic requirements have been met: *(a)* the biomass has been provided by the Sun with a continuing input of new energy; *(b)* it has been provided by the Earth with space to live, finite in extent but reused time and again; *(c)* it has been provided by the Earth with a continuing supply of water and nutrients, also finite in amount, but continuously recycled between biomass and geomass; and *(d)* its milieu has not been polluted with substances inimical to life.

The global biomass—almost 2×10^{15} kilograms of it—annually captures perhaps 60×10^{21} joules of light energy (table 1.5). It is the green-plant component of the biomass (representing perhaps 99.9 per cent of the total) that is actually responsible for absorbing and converting this solar light energy into the chemical-bond energy useful as food. The plants themselves use perhaps half of the food they manufacture for their own growth and development. The surplus—known as net primary production—is available to sustain the growth and development of all other life on Earth, man included.

Life on Earth has been able to flourish through the ages because of a complexity of interactions of the biota among themselves and with their non-living environment. An interacting system of this sort, self-contained with the exception of energy, is referred to as an ecosystem. The green plants make up the autotrophic or self-feeding component of the biomass, whereas the animals—both the herbivores and the carnivores—make up its heterotrophic component, this latter one not capable of synthesizing its own food. All of the biota obtain their water and nutrients from the geomass, either directly or indirectly, and in time return it to the geomass via excretion and shedding and, ultimately, via decomposition.

The Earth as a whole, with its interacting living and non-living components, should thus be thought of as one huge integrated life-support system. Wind and ocean currents travel ceaselessly around the globe, laden with matter that is thereby passively distributed and redistributed. Moreover, numerous sorts of living organism actively move between widely divergent and separated ecosystems at different times during their development or during different seasons of the year. All of the countless local ecosystems on Earth share the Sun as their common ultimate source of energy; and, at least potentially, each local ecosystem is connected to all the others by its hydrological, carbon dioxide, oxygen, and other biogeochemical cycles. The continuing and seasonal patterns of wind, precipitation, and temperature—which are interconnected throughout the world—are crucial in determining the character of the local ecosystems.

In short, it is clear that the global ecosystem is, indeed, an interconnected world-wide system, any part of which is more or less sensitive to perturbations anywhere else in the system. Nevertheless, the Earth is a huge and diverse structure, and it is both logical and convenient for present purposes to divide at least the terrestrial habitats of the world—covering some 14 900 million hectares—into a modest number of major biomes. These biomes can be referred to as vegetational types inasmuch as most are dominated by their autotrophic or green-plant component. The character of the vegetation is, in turn, dependent primarily upon a combination of three environmental factors: *(a)* temperature, *(b)* precipitation, and *(c)* human interference.

The basic biomes or vegetational types determined by the above factors are forest, grassland, desert, tundra, and agricultural. A further major type is the so-called built-up environment, where man has built his cities, transportation systems, and so forth. Forest, unless it has been cleared, is found where there is a warm period during at least a portion of the year and where the annual precipitation exceeds roughly 500 millimetres. There exist on

Earth today about 4 200 million hectares of forest (table 1.6). Grassland (also variously referred to as range land, prairie, steppe, pampa, savanna, or veldt) is, unless cleared, found under similar conditions of temperature, but where the annual precipitation falls within the range of roughly 250 to 500 millimetres (although some is maintained by recurring fires even with higher precipitation). World-wide, there exist today about 3 000 million hectares of grassland. Desert is also found under temperature conditions similar to those suited for forest or grassland, but the annual precipitation is less than roughly 250 millimetres, sometimes much less. Such desert covers an estimated 1 800 million hectares. Tundra is found where the growing season is brief and cool and where the subsoil remains frozen the year round, conditions that pertain to a global total of perhaps 800 million hectares. Finally, either forest or grassland can be cleared for agriculture, as can desert if additionally irrigated, and this has occurred on a world-wide total of perhaps 1 500 million hectares.

The several major terrestrial habitats established here differ considerably not only with respect to their biomass, but also as regards their productivity. The temperate habitat, for example, has a plant dry-weight biomass that averages about 118 tonnes per hectare (table 1.7). The annual net primary dry-weight productivity of this biomass averages perhaps 8 tonnes per hectare. Comparable values are somewhat more than twice as high for the tropical habitat, but roughly an order of magnitude lower for the desert and arctic habitats. The specific vegetational types that make up these habitats can, of course, be expected to exhibit wide ranges of biomass and productivity values (table 1.8).

Severe disturbance of a vegetational type sets in motion a more or less orderly, and thus predictable, series of events. This progression—known as ecological succession—involves as a first step the establishment on the site of a new biotic community, one which is quite different from the destroyed one. Over a period of years or decades this colonizing community, or pioneer stage, gives way to a series of more or less distinct replacement communities, known as intermediate stages. Eventually, if all goes according to theory, a community becomes established that perpetuates itself on the site, the so-called climax stage (Odum, 1971: chap. 9; SIPRI, 1976: chap. 6; Spurr & Barnes, 1973: chap. 13–14; Toumey & Korstian, 1947: chap. 18; appendix 2.4).

The reason that the pioneer community is so different from the pre-disturbance community is that the local habitat has been rather drastically altered in a number of important ways. The microclimate has become remarkably different, the site, *inter alia,* now exposed to the direct rays of the Sun, now much windier and thus more highly evaporative, and now experiencing greater extremes and more rapid changes in temperature and moisture. A combination of particulate erosion and nutrient dumping (loss of nutrients in solution) has served greatly to diminish the nutrient levels in the soil, a soil whose structure and water-holding capacity have also deteriorated. Moreover, wildlife food and cover—and thus also the wildlife itself—have been largely eliminated.

Beyond the necessity for their local availability, the colonizing pioneer plants must be photophilic (i.e., those which foresters call intolerant) and able to cope with the whole diversity of newly established site rigours. Once established, these hardy pioneers—by simple virtue of their presence—serve to change the local site conditions. In doing so they make the local habitat relatively more suitable to a new mix of plant species, ones that are somewhat more tolerant (*sensu* forestry). The pioneer species bring about the site changes by providing partial shade to the ground surface, by reducing the ground-level wind velocity, by beginning to hold the soil in place with their roots, by providing the land with the beginnings of a protective litter layer, and so forth. They also provide new niches (i.e., food and shelter) to a limited selection of animal life, both above and below ground.

As mentioned above, this drama of succession unfolds in a relatively predictable fashion, eventually culminating in a climax stage. The nature of this steady-state community differs, of course, from region to region, depending in large measure upon the regional patterns of rainfall and temperature and upon the influence of man. The climax biota maintains a dynamic equilibrium with the soil (which it has helped to shape) and the climate. Presumably this stage approximates the so-called old-growth or primeval situation.

Ecological succession is, of course, a world-wide phenomenon, occurring in all climates in both terrestrial and aquatic habitats. The entire biotic community—indeed, the entire ecosystem—undergoes successional changes, with continuing interplay occurring between plant, animal, and non-living components. It is, however, the plant component of the ecosystem that appears to dominate events and that seemingly relegates the other components to subordinate roles. Thus, animal succession for the most part appears to be dependent directly or indirectly on the vegetational succession (Beckwith, 1954; Diamond, 1974; Johnston & Odum, 1956; Leopold, 1933; Leopold, 1950). The soil, with its originally diminished nutrient levels, reduced structure, and damaged profile, undergoes a concomitant recovery, also more or less in step with the vegetative succession (Lutz & Chandler, 1946: chap. 11).

The length of time required to attain climax is highly dependent upon a number of factors, the most important of which is usually the severity of disturbance which had originally set the changes in motion. Moreover, the regional climate controls not only the vegetational character of the climax community (various types of forest, grassland, etc.), but thereby also the time-span between pioneer and climax. Temperate-zone successional series culminating in some association or another dominated by grasses usually take several decades to run their course, whereas those culminating in tree communities can take several centuries. Moreover, it must be recognized that when one deals with time-spans of the latter magnitude, successional development is likely to be complicated by and confounded with changes in climate and physiography or geomorphology. Furthermore, depending upon its location, the ecosystem is more or less frequently subjected to new disturbances—both natural and anthropogenic—as the years go by. Indeed, such disturbances as fires, hurricanes, floods, insect irruptions or earthquakes have always been factors with which one ecosystem or another has had to cope with greater or lesser frequency.

One of the important trends in the successional development of an ecosystem from pioneer to climax stages is the continuing increase in the variety of the plants and animals, both large and small. And, as species diversity increases, the complexity of the food-chains and other species interactions also increases. Such changes are thought by some to make for ever-increasing ecosystem stability (but cf. Goodman, 1975).

Both erosion and nutrient dumping are arrested early on in succession, and as time goes by, the various nutrient or biogeochemical cycles become ever more closed. Both the biomass and its detritus (the soil litter and other organic matter and their decomposition products) keep increasing, and various forces serve to enrich the nutrient capital of the system. These include dissolution of the rock material dispersed in and beneath the soil, and also transport to the site via wind and water.

When an ecosystem is disrupted by military actions, successional recovery of such ecological set-back is, of course, set in motion. Two levels of site recovery must be distinguished here. On the one hand, there is the establishment of a pioneer stand, and on the other, the eventual return to the pre-disturbance situation—which, of course, may or may not have been pristine to begin with. The first of these—measurable in months or years—arrests the massive damage to the ecosystem occurring from wind and water erosion and from nutrient dumping. The second—measured in years, decades, or even centuries—involves more subtle and intangible aspects of recovery. Discussions of recovery from military actions often fail to distinguish between these two levels of recovery, especially in some of the uncritical literature about the Second Indochina War.

In conclusion, it appears to be inevitable that even severely war-disrupted sites will recover in time. A pioneer ecosystem of some sort becomes established more or less rapidly, that is, in a time-span that is likely to be measured in months. And eventually—in a period of many decades or centuries—an ecosystem resembling the original one can develop.

IV. Use and abuse of the Earth

At present the Earth supports, at least after a fashion, about 4 100 million people (table 1.4). This huge global population is unevenly distributed over six of the seven continents and over many hundreds of islands. The average density of the global population is 27 people per square kilometre of land surface (or 31 if the permanently ice-covered land is excluded). Most by far (89 per cent) of the world's people live in the Northern hemisphere. About 58 per cent of them live in the temperate regions of the world, about 39 per cent in the tropical regions, 2.5 per cent in the desert regions, and only 0.4 per cent in the arctic regions. The islands as a group, if extracted out of the several habitats, support 11 per cent of the world population. Moreover, some 10 per cent of the world population live in cities of one million or more (table 1.9). Unlike the Earth that supports it, the global population is enlarging at the compound growth rate of 1.8 per cent, for a doubling time of 39 years (table 1.4). That is to say, the global population is currently increasing by one million people every five days.

The global land areas and world population are divided among 159 nations (appendix 1.4) and more than two dozen major colonies or similar territories (appendix 1.5). The 159 nations alone account for 89 per cent of the global land area and 99.7 per cent of the global population. Of the 159 nations, 56 are wholly or largely situated in the temperate regions of the world, 80 in the tropical regions, 22 in the desert regions, and the remaining one in the arctic (table 1.10). Moreover, 34 of the world's nations are situated on islands.

The 159 nations comprise a diverse conglomeration of sizes, population densities and growth rates, forms of government, ages, and levels of sophistication. Some are richly endowed with natural resources while others are pathetically poor in this regard; some are highly industrialized while others are largely agrarian (table 1.11). The world's nations, moreover, range from powerful to weak and from belligerent to pacific (table 1.12). Some 42 nations maintain standing armies with a strength of 100 thousand or more, of which 10 are in excess of half a million. Conversely, 59 nations maintain armies with a strength of under 10 thousand, some of these having no armies at all.

Man makes use of the Earth in a multitude of ways—in simplest terms, exploiting it for his living space, air, water, food, shelter, and clothing, and as a waste repository. He thus derives most of his basic needs from among the Earth's limitless or renewable resources. Important among these—beyond the air, soil, and fresh and salt waters—are the products of agriculture, the forest trees, the grassland vegetation, and the marine fishery.

Man's *use* of the Earth can—and does—turn to its *abuse* in a number of ways:

1. A major category of abuse occurs as soon as man's annual harvest of a resource exceeds its speed of regeneration.
2. A related category of abuse occurs when the basis of some exploited resource—such as the soil—is debilitated more rapidly than its speed of natural renewal.

3. A third category of abuse occurs when man's rate of waste disposal—be it into the atmosphere, on to the land and its fresh waters, or into the ocean—exceeds the rate of its dilution or decomposition to insignificance.

4. A fourth category of abuse (a very real though most difficult one to evaluate) occurs when man exploits living space or some other of the global resources at the excessive expense of the other living things with which he shares the Earth.

5. A fifth category of abuse occurs when the Earth and its natural resources are wantonly destroyed or vandalized.

Whereas under-population in no way ensures against man's abuse of the Earth, over-population leads inexorably towards it (Cloudsley-Thompson, 1977 c). Unfortunately, many regions of the Earth, as well as the Earth as a whole, are already seriously over-populated—a situation, moreover, that worsens year by year. It is a difficult, not to say somewhat arbitrary, matter to arrive at a suitable global carrying capacity for humans, and it is not intended to explore this matter in depth here. Nevertheless, the order of magnitude of this value can at least be suggested on the basis of the 27 richest nations of the world (appendix 1.4). These 27 rich nations constitute quite a diverse grouping of states, having in common only a gross national product (GNP) per capita of at least twice the world average for this value.

If the entire world were populated at the density standard established by the world's 27 rich nations, the global population would have to stand at 2 100 million. If it were populated on the basis of their agricultural area per capita, it would be 2 300 million. On the basis of their forest land per capita it would be 2 000 million. On the basis of global cereal production and their per capita consumption it would be 2 400 million. And on the basis of global forest product (timber, pulp, and firewood) production and their per capita consumption it would be 2 000 million.

Thus it can be seen that the Earth already has almost twice as many people as it should have in order for all to have a standard of living comparable to that enjoyed, on average, by the inhabitants of the 27 richest nations. For those who might consider that this group of 27 establishes too high or restrictive a standard, it can be noted that comparable calculations based on an average of the world's 43 nations of average wealth (all those nations whose GNP per capita falls between twice and half the world average; appendix 1.4) lead to world population values of between 2 700 million and 3 300 million. (Conversely, Hulett (1970), employing a somewhat different approach to the problem but using the USA as his standard, arrived at an optimal global population of the order of only 1 000 million.)

With the above data in mind, it is sad to recall that the global population is neither decreasing nor even holding steady, but is instead rapidly increasing. Moreover, it is the worst-off nations that are increasing most rapidly in population and thus exacerbating their existing plight (table 1.10). The level of poverty of the majority of the nations of the world and thus the misery of the bulk of the world's population is hard to grasp (AID, 1977; Ceres, 1975; Clinton, 1977; Harrington, 1977; McHale & McHale, 1978). The attendant use of the world's natural resources at a rate faster than their rate of natural renewal—especially in the poor nations—is by now well documented (Brown, 1978; Eckholm, 1976; Ehrlich *et al.*, 1977).

The final category of global abuse listed earlier—that of senseless environmental destruction—bears reiteration here inasmuch as warfare is the most obvious cause of such vandalism. There are almost 27 million men continuously under arms in the world today (table 1.13). Sad to say, there does not appear to be much chance of their primary training lapsing for want of use. Indeed, as noted earlier, a new major war—and thus one that has a high likelihood of causing substantial environmental disruption—begins once every five years, on the average (table 1.14). These wars are distributed throughout the world, though they occur primarily in the temperate and tropical regions, where they recur with approximately equal frequency.

Man's uses as well as his abuses of the Earth and its resources are seemingly endless in number and have only been touched upon above. However, a portion of each of the succeeding chapters is devoted to elaborations of these uses and abuses—both civil and military—as they pertain to each of the several major habitats of the world.

V. Conclusion

The world is home to more than four thousand million people—four thousand million people who will be increasing to five thousand million people by 1987. This vast and growing human population must share the Earth's ever more limited resources not only among its own members but also with the other living things that inhabit the Earth. Indeed, humans are an intricate and inextricable part of a world-wide ecological system—a system that permits life on Earth to exist and flourish.

This global ecosystem is subject to much and varied abuse, but is fortunately in many ways a self-renewing system. Until recently, these natural powers of recuperation have more than sufficed to counter man's multifarious environmental inroads, except perhaps in some localized situations. But man's increasing numbers, together with his rising expectations, are now combining to tip the balance in the wrong direction.

With the Earth's natural resources already insufficient to provide an adequate standard of living for all, it becomes especially important to reduce to the extent possible all unnecessary depredations of the global environment. One obvious place to do this is with the environmental depredations that are associated with warfare. It is this anti-environmental aspect of warfare, largely overlooked in the past, that is examined and brought into perspective in the chapters that follow.

Table 1.1. Frequency of the major wars of the twentieth century[a]

Fatality class[b]	Number of major wars 1899–1977[c]	Occurring once every:
6	13	6.1 years
7	2	40 years
8	1	–
Total	**16**	**4.9 years**

Sources and notes:
[a]A major war is here considered to be one that falls into fatality class 6 or greater (see below). For the spatial distribution of these wars, see table 1.14.
[b]In order to determine the fatality class into which a war falls here, the base-ten logarithm of the total number of direct fatalities—both military and civil—is taken and then rounded to the nearest whole number. For further details, see appendix 1.1, note *b*.
[c]The number of wars in each fatality class is taken from appendix 1.1. During the same period there additionally occurred about 25 wars in fatality class 5 as well as more than 100 wars in fatality class 4.

Table 1.2. Ecologically disruptive wars: a selection[a]

1. Persian–Scythian War of 512 BC
   (*a*) *Description:* Successful attack by Persia (now Iran) (under Darius the Great) upon Scythia (now part of the USSR)
   (*b*) *Location:* Northern hemisphere: Europe; temperate habitat
   (*c*) *Type and fatality class:*[b] Interstate war; ?
   (*d*) *Ecological disruption:* As the Scythians retreated, they practised a self-inflicted scorched earth policy so as to hinder the Persian advance
   (*e*) *References:* Herodotus (c. 430 BC: IV: 120–123); see also the sources below

2. Peloponnesian War of 431–404 BC
   (*a*) *Description:* Conquest by Sparta of Athens
   (*b*) *Location:* Northern hemisphere; Europe; temperate habitat
   (*c*) *Type and fatality class:* Interstate war; ?
   (*d*) *Ecological disruption:* Annually repeated destruction of the Athenian grain crop by the Spartans
   (*e*) *References:* Thucydides (c. 411 BC: III: 1, 26; IV: 2; VII: 19); see also the sources below

3. Third Punic War of 149–146 BC
   (*a*) *Description:* Successful attack by Rome upon Carthage (almost the present site of Tunis)
   (*b*) *Location:* Northern hemisphere; Africa; temperate habitat
   (*c*) *Type and fatality class:* Interstate war; ?
   (*d*) *Ecological disruption:* After conquering Carthage, the Romans sold the survivors into slavery and razed the city. (A rebuilt Carthage was razed once again in AD 698.)
   (*e*) *References:* Scullard (1961: 307); see also the sources below

14

4. Hunnic incursions of the fourth and fifth centuries AD

   (a) *Description:* Conquest by the Huns (under Attila, *inter alia*) of western Asia and eastern and central Europe

   (b) *Location:* Northern hemisphere; Asia and Europe; temperate habitat

   (c) *Type and fatality class:* Interstate wars; ?

   (d) *Ecological disruption:* Wanton ravaging of the countryside everywhere that resulted, *inter alia,* in great waves of migrations

5. Sacking of Rome of 455

   (a) *Description:* Successful attack by the Vandals (under Gaiseric) upon Rome

   (b) *Location:* Northern hemisphere; Europe; temperate habitat

   (c) *Type and fatality class:* Interstate war; ?

   (d) *Ecological disruption:* Unrestrained pillaging and destruction of Rome

6. Mongolian incursions of c. 1213 to c. 1224

   (a) *Description:* Conquest by the Mongols (under Genghis Khan) of most of Asia and eastern Europe

   (b) *Location:* Northern hemisphere; Asia and Europe; temperate habitat

   (c) *Type and fatality class:* Interstate wars; ?

   (d) *Ecological disruption:* These conquests were characterized by ruthless carnage, including the killing of all captured males, and the annihilation of all unappropriated crops and livestock; in Mesopotamia (now Iraq) took place the deliberate destruction of the major irrigation works of the Tigris River upon which the agriculture of the indigenous civilization depended

   (e) *References:* Carter & Dale (1974: 49); Lamb (1927: 92–93, 159); see also the sources below

7. Thirty Years' War of 1618–1648

   (a) *Description:* Successful war by the Protestant armies of the German states, Sweden, etc., against the Catholic armies of the Holy Roman Empire (now Austria, etc.), most of the action occurring in central Europe

   (b) *Location:* Northern hemisphere; Europe; temperate habitat

   (c) *Type and fatality class:* Interstate war; 7

   (d) *Ecological disruption:* The German states were ravaged during the course of the war, their populations decimated—an estimated loss of 6 million, representing 40 per cent overall, but 65 per cent in several of the states—their agricultural fields widely devastated, and their towns and villages pillaged by the thousand; the population of Bohemia (now part of Czechoslovakia) was reduced by perhaps 75 per cent; the overall death toll of the war from all causes (combat, disease, starvation, etc.) was probably of the order of 10 million

8. Franco–Dutch War of 1672–1678

   (a) *Description:* Successful invasion by France (under Louis XIV) of the Netherlands, carried out for punitive purposes

   (b) *Location:* Northern hemisphere; Europe; temperate habitat

   (c) *Type and fatality class:* Interstate war; 4

   (d) *Ecological disruption:* Self-inflicted large-scale flooding by the Netherlands (creating the so-called Holland water-line) in order to impede the advance of the French forces

   (e) *References:* Baxter (1966: 72–73); Blok (1907: 380–381); SIPRI (1977: 54); see also the sources below

9. Napoleonic Wars of 1796–1815

   (a) *Description:* Wars of aggrandizement by France (under Napoleon I) against a variety of European states; initially successful

   (b) *Location:* Northern hemisphere; Europe; temperate habitat

   (c) *Type and fatality class:* Interstate wars; 7

   (d) *Ecological disruption:* These wars resulted in vast numbers of deaths through battle (more than half a million) and disease (variously estimated at up to 17 million); as the French advanced through Russia during the summer of 1812, the Russians practised a self-inflicted scorched earth policy in order to impede the enemy advance; Moscow was largely destroyed in September, following the French entry

   (e) *References:* Chandler (1966); see also the sources below

10. Tai Ping Rebellion of 1850–1864

(a) *Description:* Unsuccessful attempt by the Tai Ping (Great Peace) movement (under Hung Hsiu-chuan) to overthrow the Chinese government (the Manchu dynasty)

(b) *Location:* Northern hemisphere; Asia; temperate habitat

(c) *Type and fatality class:* Civil war; 7

(d) *Ecological disruption:* The overthrow was attempted with great violence and much pillaging, and was crushed with equal or greater violence; China employed, *inter alia*, large-scale scorched earth tactics in order to starve the rebels into submission; the population of the lower Yangtze River region (Anhwei and portions of surrounding provinces) was devastated and had not yet regained its pre-war level a full century later; the total number of deaths is estimated at between 20 million and 40 million, representing about 7 per cent of China's population at that time

(e) *References:* Ho (1959: 236–247); see also the sources below

11. US–Navaho wars of 1860–1864

(a) *Description:* Conquest by the USA of the Navaho

(b) *Location:* Northern hemisphere; North America; temperate and desert habitats

(c) *Type and fatality class:* Interstate wars; 3

(d) *Ecological disruption:* The USA deliberately destroyed the sheep and other livestock as well as the fruit-tree orchards and other crops of the Navaho as part of its successful strategy of subjugation

(e) *References:* Jett (1974); Josephy (1968: 333); see also the sources below

12. US Civil War of 1861–1865

(a) *Description:* Thwarted secession of 11 Southern states (the Confederate States of America) from the USA (under Lincoln), the Confederacy having wished, *inter alia*, to maintain Black slavery

(b) *Location:* Northern hemisphere; North America; temperate habitat

(c) *Type and fatality class:* Civil war; 6

(d) *Ecological disruption:* A major strategy of the USA was to starve the rebellious states into submission; scorched earth tactics were carried out with special vehemence in Virginia, where the agriculturally rich 700 thousand hectare Shenandoah valley was systematically devastated during September–October 1864, and in Georgia, the Confederate granary, where perhaps 4 million hectares were laid waste during November–December 1864; estimated total fatalities during the war (primarily military) were 530 thousand—almost 2 per cent of the total population

(e) *References:* Gates (1965); Kellogg (1903: chap. 11–12); Liddell-Hart (1929: 331–335); Sheridan (1888: I: 484–488); Stackpole (1961); see also the sources below

13. War of the Triple Alliance of 1864–1870

(a) *Description:* Military provocations by Paraguay (under Francisco Solano López) countered by Brazil, Argentina, and Uruguay

(b) *Location:* Southern hemisphere; South America; temperate habitat

(c) *Type and fatality class:* Interstate war; 6

(d) *Ecological disruption:* The response by the Triple Alliance led to the devastation of Paraguay and the destruction of a large proportion of its population; the population of Paraguay, officially stated to have been 1.3 million—although perhaps as low as 750 thousand—was reduced to an estimated 220 thousand, those killed including most of the adult males.

14. US Indian wars of 1865–1898

(a) *Description:* Conquest by the USA of the Dakota (Sioux), Apache, Comanche, Cheyenne, and other tribes

(b) *Location:* Northern hemisphere; North America; primarily temperate habitat

(c) *Type and fatality class:* Interstate wars; 4

(d) *Ecological disruption:* The US strategy of subduing the Indians included the systematic destruction of their food stores, crops, and game. (The wanton slaughter of bison herds on the Great Plains was for the USA a largely fortuitous contribution to the undermining of the Indians' means of livelihood.)

(e) *References:* Josephy (1968); Russell (1973); see also the sources below

15. Philippine Insurrection of 1899 to c. 1903

(a) *Description:* Thwarted attempt by the Philippines to gain its independence from the USA, the latter having just acquired the Philippines by force from Spain

(b) *Location:* Northern hemisphere; Pacific Ocean islands; tropical habitat

(c) *Type and fatality class:* Colonial war; 6

(d) *Ecological disruption:* A major means utilized by the USA to crush the insurgency was the systematic destruction of the villages, storehouses, crops, and livestock throughout entire rebellious provinces

(e) *References:* Caterini (1977); Cook (1975: 11-15); Francisco (1973: 7-8); Miller (1969-1970); see also the sources below

16. World War I of 1914-1918

(a) *Description:* A complex of several more or less distinct wars that can in simple terms be summarized as an unsuccessful war by the Central Powers—i.e., Germany, Austria–Hungary, Turkey, Bulgaria, etc.—against the Allies—i.e., France, the UK, Russia, Italy, the USA, Belgium, Portugal, Serbia, Montenegro (the latter two now part of Yugoslavia), Greece, Romania, Japan, etc.

(b) *Location:* Primarily Northern hemisphere; primarily Europe (but also Asia, Africa, etc.); primarily temperate habitat

(c) *Type and fatality class:* Interstate war; 7

(d) *Ecological disruption:* Great loss of life, amounting to perhaps 15 million or more and including 24 per cent of the population of Serbia (now part of Yugoslavia), 13 per cent of Turkey, 8 per cent of Romania, 7 per cent of Bulgaria, and 5 per cent of Greece; systematic extermination of Armenians by Turkey, with an estimated 750 thousand thus killed (perhaps 50 per cent of the total remaining alive following the massacres of the prior two decades); large-scale employment of chemical warfare agents; enormous amounts of largely incidental devastation of agricultural and forest lands, especially severe destruction of this kind occurring in France and Belgium

(e) *References:* Bach (1975); Mudge (1969-1970); Ridsdale (1916; 1919a; 1919b; 1919c); see also appendix 2.2.1 and the sources below

17. Second Sino–Japanese War of 1937-1945

(a) *Description:* Japanese invasion of China, eventually repulsed in conjunction with World War II

(b) *Location:* Northern hemisphere; Asia; temperate habitat

(c) *Type and fatality class:* Interstate war; 7

(d) *Ecological disruption:* In order to stop the advance of the Japanese, the Chinese in June 1938 dynamited the Huayuankow dike of the Yellow River, near Chengchow; the ensuing flood waters ravaged major portions of Honan, Anhwei, and Kiangsu provinces; the crops and topsoil of several million hectares were destroyed, as were 11 cities and more than 4 thousand villages; at least several hundred thousand persons drowned and several million more were left homeless; the river was not brought back under control until 1947; the overall war resulted in a large number of fatalities, estimated at more than 250 thousand Japanese and approximately 4.4 million Chinese, the Chinese dead representing perhaps 1 per cent of the population

(e) *References:* Ho (1959: 250-252); SIPRI (1977: 54); see also the references below

18. World War II of 1939-1945

(a) *Description:* A complex of several dozen more or less distinct wars, all more or less closely connected in some supportive or opposing fashion with wars of conquest by Germany and Japan; summarized in its simplest terms as an unsuccessful war of aggrandizement by the Axis—i.e., Germany (under Hitler), Austria (annexed by Germany), Italy, Japan, Hungary, Bulgaria, Romania, Finland, etc.—against the Allies—i.e., France the UK, Poland, the USSR, Belgium, the USA, China, Czechoslovakia, Greece, the Netherlands, Yugoslavia, Norway, etc.

(b) *Location:* Primarily Northern hemisphere; Europe, Asia, Africa, Pacific Ocean islands, Atlantic Ocean islands, etc.; primarily temperate and tropical, but also desert and arctic habitats

(c) *Type and fatality class:* Interstate war; 8

(d) *Ecological disruption:* Great loss of life, amounting to of the order of 50 million people, and including 18 per cent of the population of Poland, 11 per cent of Yugoslavia, 11 per cent of the USSR, 9 per cent of Germany, and 5 per cent of Austria; systematic extermination of both Jews and Gypsies by Germany, an estimated 6 million Jews (perhaps 60 per cent of the

European total) and 500 thousand Gypsies (perhaps 50 per cent of the European total) thus having been killed; enormous amounts of agricultural, forest, and other ecological devastation as well as much destruction of cities; heavy use of high-explosive and incendiary munitions for area bombing of densely populated urban and industrial areas; two cities—Hiroshima and Nagasaki—destroyed by nuclear weapons; numerous tropical Pacific Ocean island ecosystems devastated; some 200 thousand hectares (17 per cent) of Dutch agricultural lands destroyed by Germany through intentional salt-water inundation; at least 1.2 million hectares laid waste by Germany in far northern Norway as an impediment to an expected Soviet advance; profligate utilization of natural resources by many nations

(e) *References:* Aartsen (1946); Baker (1946); Fisher & Baldwin (1946); Liddell-Hart (1970); Lund (1947); Milward (1977); Mudge (1969–1970); see also tables 2.3 and 6.4, appendices 1.2, 1.3.1 and 2.2.2, and the sources below

19. Korean War of 1950–1953

(a) *Description:* Invasion by the Democratic People's Republic of [North] Korea of the Republic of [South] Korea, the former assisted by China and the latter by the USA and 14 other nations under the auspices of the UN, in an unsuccessful attempt by North Korea to reunify the two Koreas

(b) *Location.:* Northern hemisphere; Asia; temperate habitat

(c) *Type and fatality class:* Interstate war; 6

(d) *Ecological disruption:* High level of incidental forest and other wild-land disruption and some severe urban damage (to Pyongyang, etc.); high loss of life, an estimated total of 1.4 million, North Korea losing approximately 6 per cent of its population and South Korea approximately 3 per cent

(e) *References:* See appendices 1.2 and 1.3.2, and also the sources below

20. Algerian War of Independence of 1954–1962

(a) *Description:* Successful attempt by Algeria to gain its independence from France

(b) *Location:* Northern hemisphere; Africa; largely desert habitat

(c) *Type and fatality class:* Colonial war; 6

(d) *Ecological disruption:* Major rural population displacements and destruction of villages, including the displacement of up to two million people; an estimated half million Algerians lost their lives—i.e., almost five per cent of the population

(e) *References:* Horne (1977); see also the sources below

21. Angolan War of Independence of 1961-1975

(a) *Description:* Successful attempt by Angola to gain its independence from Portugal

(b) *Location:* Southern hemisphere; Africa; tropical habitat

(c) *Type and fatality class:* Colonial war; 4

(d) *Ecological disruption:* Major rural harassment, some population displacements, including a substantial exodus to Portugal, and Angolan loss of life estimated at 25 thousand—about 0.5 per cent of the population; the Portuguese tactics included herbicidal crop destruction in villages not under their control

(e) *References:* SIPRI (1971: 210–211); *SIPRI Yearbook 1976:* 53–61; see also the sources below

22. Second Indochina War of 1961–1975

(a) *Description:* A complex of more or less distinct conflicts confounded by massive US involvement, summarized as follows: an unsuccessful attempt by the USA to prevent the Republic of [South] Viet Nam government from being replaced by the Revolutionary Government of South Viet Nam or, eventually, from being annexed by the Democratic Republic of [North] Viet Nam; a further unsuccessful attempt by the USA to maintain in power the former regime in Laos; also an ancillary war by the USA against Cambodia (Kampuchea), followed by an overthrow of the Cambodian government by Communist insurgents (the Khmer Rouge)

(b) *Location:* Northern hemisphere; Asia; tropical habitat

(c) *Type and fatality class:* Interstate war; etc.; 6

(d) *Ecological disruption:* The US strategy involved massive rural area bombing, chemical and mechanical forest destruction, large-scale crop destruction; destruction of food stores, destruction of hospitals and large scale population displacements—in short, the massive intentional disruption of both the natural and the human ecologies; enormous loss of life, estimated at 1.8 million Indochinese, including 5 per cent of the population of South Viet Nam and 4 per cent overall; population displacements totalling perhaps 17 million—i.e., one-third of the regional population

(e) *References:* SIPRI (1976); see also tables 3.2, 3.3 and 3.4, appendices 1.2 and 1.3.3, and the sources below

23. Nigerian Civil War of 1967–1970

(a) *Description:* Unsuccessful attempt by the south-eastern region, known as Biafra, to secede from Nigeria

(b) *Location:* Northern hemisphere; Africa; tropical habitat

(c) *Type and fatality class:* Civil war; 6

(d) *Ecological disruption:* A major strategy employed by Nigeria to suppress the revolt was to blockade and starve into submission food-poor Biafra; the result was that an estimated 1.5 million Biafrans, primarily Ibos, starved to death—i.e., about 18 per cent of the population

(e) *References:* Gans (1969); Mayer (1969); Mayer *et al.* (1969); Western (1969); see also the sources below

24. Bangladesh War of Independence of 1971

(a) *Description:* Successful attempt by Bangladesh, with the aid of India, to secede from Pakistan

(b) *Location:* Northern hemisphere; Asia; tropical habitat

(c) *Type and fatality class:* Civil war (also interstate war); 6

(d) *Ecological disruption:* Enormous upheaval among the inhabitants (Bengalis) of Bangladesh, between 1 and 3 million of whom were killed (over 3 per cent of the population) and another 10 million of whom were displaced (about 14 per cent of the population). (There was much coincidental flood damage as well.)

(e) *References:* Chowdhury & Chen (1977); Payne (1973); see also the sources below

25. East Timor War of 1975–1976

(a) *Description:* Annexation by Indonesia of briefly independent East (formerly Portuguese) Timor. (An insurgent force (Fretilin) hopes to restore independence to East Timor.)

(b) *Location:* Southern hemisphere; Pacific Ocean island; tropical habitat

(c) *Type and fatality class:* Interstate war; 5

(d) *Ecological disruption:* Major disruption of the East Timorese population, involving perhaps as many as 60 thousand fatalities—i.e., about 9 per cent of the population—and another 40 thousand displaced persons (6 per cent of the population)

(e) *References:* Tanter (1976–1977); see also the sources below

26. Kampuchean Insurrections of 1975–1977

(a) *Description:* Unsuccessful attempts by insurgents to revolt against the newly established government, reportedly involving massive repression and massacres by government forces

(b) *Location:* Northern hemisphere; Asia; tropical habitat

(c) *Type and fatality class:* Civil war; 6

(d) *Ecological disruption:* Forced rapid conversion of the society to a primitive agrarian one based on many small co-operatives presumably in response to the legacy of the Second Indochina War, involving *inter alia*, the abolition of cities, any national currency, postal services, telephones, all but one irregular newspaper, public transportation, higher education, and virtually all intercourse with the outside world; the result has been an extraordinary disruption of the human ecology, one that in deaths alone apparently involves several hundred thousand direct fatalities (5 per cent of the population) plus more than 1 million indirect fatalities, from starvation, disease, etc. (12 per cent of the population)

(e) *References:* Casella (1978b); Dobbs (1978); Shawcross (1978-1979); Shawcross (1979); see also the sources below

---

Sources and notes:

[a]In addition to any special sources noted for individual wars, the information presented here has been derived primarily from Dupuy & Dupuy (1977), Harris and Levey (1975), Montross (1960), and Young & Calvert (1977). A number of these wars are further described in table 8.2.

[b]The wars are divided into one of three types: interstate, colonial, or civil (intrastate). Fatality classes are explained in appendix 1.1, note *b*.

Table 1.3. Global surface area[a] 10^3 km^2 (10^5 hectares)

Hemisphere	Land	Ocean	Total
Global surface not continuously ice-covered			
Northern	98 832	146 218	**245 050**
Southern	34 357	206 694	**241 050**
Ice-free total	**133 189**	**352 912**	**486 101**
Global surface continuously ice-covered[b]			
Northern	2 556	7 444	**10 000**
Southern	13 102	898	**14 000**
Ice-covered total	**15 658**	**8 342**	**24 000**
Entire global surface			
Northern	101 388	153 662	**255 050**
Southern	47 459	207 592	**255 050**
Global total	**148 847**	**361 254**	**510 101**

Sources and notes:
[a]Total land and ocean surface areas are from the *Handbook of Chemistry and Physics 1968–1969:* F144. The total hemispheric land areas are from the *UN Demographic Yearbook 1975:* table 3 (1975 data), being the summations of the individual nations and colonies appropriate to each hemisphere (the several missing areas being taken from the *Europa Year Book 1977,* and overlapping territories being apportioned suitably).
[b]Total continuously ice-covered areas are from Kukla & Kukla (1974: 709). The ice-covered land areas are from table 5.1.

Table 1.4. Terrestrial land masses and habitats: areas and demography (1975 data)

Region[a]	Regional area[b] 10^3 km^2 (10^5 ha)	Proportion of global land area *per cent*	Regional population[b] 10^6	Proportion of global population *per cent*	Regional population density *No./km^2*	Annual growth rate[c] *per cent*
Land mass						
North America	21 818	14.7	314.8	7.7	14.4	1.50
South America	17 808	12.0	215.8	5.3	12.1	2.73
Africa	29 654	19.9	391.1	9.6	13.2	2.68
Europe	10 049	6.8	479.5	11.8	47.7	0.67
Asia	41 536	27.9	2 216.2	54.5	53.4	1.79
Australia	7 687	5.2	13.5	0.3	1.8	1.50
Antarctica	13 000	8.7	0	0	0	0
Islands	7 259	4.9	434.1	10.7	59.8	1.77
of Atlantic Ocean	689	0.5	87.6	2.2	127.0	0.71
of Pacific Ocean	3 672	2.5	322.8	7.9	87.9	2.01
of Indian Ocean	661	0.4	23.6	0.6	35.8	2.19
of Arctic Ocean	2 238	1.5	0.1	0.0	0.0	—
Hemisphere						
Northern	101 388	68.1	3 635.7	89.4	35.9	1.69
Southern	47 459	31.9	429.2	10.6	9.0	2.50
Habitat						
Temperate	56 225	37.7	2 359.7	58.1	42.0	1.21
Tropical	42 239	28.4	1 585.7	39.0	37.5	2.49
Desert	26 688	17.9	101.8	2.5	3.8	2.70
Arctic	23 658	15.9	17.7	0.4	0.7	0.46
Global total	**148 847**	**100**	**4 065.0**	**100**	**27.3**[d]	**1.78**

Sources and notes:

[a]The *land masses* are strictly geographic and the continents are exclusive of islands. The division between North and South America is taken to be the eastern border of Panama. The division between Africa and Asia is taken to be the Suez Canal. The division between Europe and Asia is taken to be the crest of the Ural Mountains and the Ural River; the crest of the Caucasus Mountains; and the Dardanelles and the Bosporus. Mediterranean islands are included with Atlantic islands.

The *habitats* are a function primarily of temperature and precipitation. The temperate habitat is characterized by a seasonal alternation of warm summers and cold winters and by precipitation adequate to permit the development of forest or grassland. The tropical habitat is characterized by frost-free conditions the year round and, again, by precipitation adequate to permit the development of forest or grassland. The desert habitat is characterized by a temperature regime similar to either the temperate or the tropical habitat, but receives precipitation that is less than adequate for the development of grassland. The arctic habitat is characterized by sub-freezing temperatures throughout most or all of the year, the somewhat warmer situation permitting the development of tundra.

[b]Areas and populations are from the *UN Demographic Yearbook 1975:* table 3 (1975 data), being the summations of the individual nations and colonies appropriate to each region (the several missing areas being taken from the *Europa Year Book 1977,* the several missing populations being taken from ACDA (1976: table 2; 1975 data), and overlapping territories and populations being apportioned suitably).

[c]Annual growth rates are derived from the *UN Demographic Yearbook 1975:* table 3 (1975 data), being based on summations of one year's actual population increase of the individual nations and colonies appropriate to each region (the several missing growth rates being derived from the data of ACDA (1976: table 2; 1974 to 1975 data), and overlapping populations being apportioned suitably). A growth rate of 1.78 per cent leads to a population doubling time of 39.2 years.

[d]If the continuously ice-covered land surface (table 1.3) is excluded from this calculation, the density value becomes 30.5 persons per square kilometre.

Table 1.5. Global biomass and productivity[a]

Habitat and biota	Total biomass (dry weight)[b] 10^{12} kg	Average biomass (dry weight)[c] 10^3 kg/ha	Total annual net primary production (dry weight)[d] 10^{12} kg	Average annual net primary productivity (dry weight)[c] 10^3 kg/ha
Terrestrial				
Plants	1 837.0	137.924	117.5	8.82
Animals	1.3[e]	0.098	—	—
Land total	**1 838.3**	**138.022**	—	—
Oceanic				
Plants	3.9	0.111	54.0	1.53
Animals	1.0	0.028	—	—
Ocean total	**4.9**	**0.139**	—	—
World-wide				
Plants	1 840.9	37.871	171.5	3.53
Animals	2.3[e]	0.047	—	—
Global total	**1 843.2**	**37.918**	—	—

For sources and notes, see page 22.

Sources and notes:

[a]The data are presented in terms of dry weight (mass). A number of useful conversion factors for the data as presented here follow. The carbon content of dry plant biomass averages 455 g/kg. The energy content of dry plant biomass averages 16.7 MJ/kg (15.2 MJ/kg for terrestrial plants; 19.9 MJ/kg for oceanic plants). For a rough conversion of net primary production to gross primary production, multiply by 2.

[b]Total terrestrial and oceanic plant biomass values from Whittaker & Likens (1975: 306); total terrestrial and oceanic animal biomass values are derived from Whittaker & Likens (1973: 291–295; 1975: 309).

[c]Average biomass and productivity values are based on those global surface areas not continually ice-covered, as presented in table 1.3.

[d]Total terrestrial net production is from Whittaker & Likens (1975: 306); total oceanic net primary production is from table 7.2. (The 'net primary production' of a plant refers to the amount of food it synthesizes less the amount it utilizes for its own growth and development.)

[e]Of this total, the human species—with its 4 065 million individuals (table 1.4) at an average live weight of 40 kilograms and thus a dry weight of 12 kilograms—represents 0.05×10^{12} kilograms. Livestock—1 207 million cattle at a dry weight of 140 kilograms; 1 045 million sheep at 7.5 kilograms; 660 million pigs at 15 kilograms; 66 million horses at 120 kilograms; 41 million asses at 60 kilograms; 14 million mules at 90 kilograms; and 200 million miscellaneous domestic animals (goats, dogs, etc.) at 4 kilograms (*UN Statistical Yearbook 1976*: table 33, 1975 data)—represents 0.20×10^{12} kilograms.

Table 1.6. Terrestrial land masses and habitats: major vegetation types

10^6 hectares $(10^4$ km$^2)$

Region[a]	Forest land[b]	Grass-land[b]	Agricultural land[b]	Other land	Total land[c]
Land mass					
North America	730	320	280	852	2 182
South America	920	450	90	321	1 781
Africa	620	770	180	1 395	2 965
Europe	330	160	300	215	1 005
Asia	1 170	820	560	1 604	4 154
Australia	140	450	50	129	769
Antarctica	0	0	0	1 300	1 300
Islands	250	80	50	346	726
of Atlantic Ocean	10	20	10	29	69
of Pacific Ocean	230	30	40	73	373
of Indian Ocean	10	30	0	20	60
of Arctic Ocean	0	0	0	224	224
Hemisphere					
Northern	2 770	1 780	1 310	4 279	10 139
Southern	1 390	1 270	200	1 886	4 746
Habitat					
Temperate	1 890[d]	1 310	800	1 623	5 623
Tropical	2 080[e]	810	600	734	4 224
Desert[f]	190	920	110	1 449	2 669
Arctic[g]	0	10	0	2 356	2 366
Global total	**4 160**	**3 050**	**1 510**	**6 165**	**14 885**

Sources and notes:

[a]The regions are described in table 1.4, note *a*.

[b]Forest, grass, and agricultural land areas are derived from the *FAO Production Yearbook*

1976: table 1 (1975 data), being the summations of the individual nations and colonies appropriate to each region (overlapping territories being apportioned suitably). The present forest land category is FAO's 'forest' plus 'woodland'; the present grassland category is FAO's 'permanant pasture'; and the present agricultural land category is FAO's 'arable' plus 'permanent crop'. Grassland is also variously referred to as prairie, steppe, pampa, savanna, and veldt; it is also more or less synonymous with the term range land.

[c]Total land areas are from table 1.4.

[d]Of the 1 890 million hectares of temperate forest land, approximately 1 340 million hectares are coniferous (softwood) forest and 550 million hectares dicotyledonous (hardwood) forest.

[e]Of the 2 080 million hectares of tropical forest land, approximately 1 440 million hectares are dense (closed, rain) forest and 640 million hectares are open (clear, seasonal) forest.

[f]The global extent of the desert vegetation type *(sensu stricto)* is of the order of 1 800 million hectares, in the present table included within the 'other land' and 'grassland' categories.

[g]The global extent of tundra is about 800 million hectares, in the present table included primarily in the 'other land' category, and that of continuously ice-covered land about 15 660 thousand hectares (table 1.3).

Table 1.7. Terrestrial habitats: plant biomass and productivity[a]

Habitat	Total plant biomass (dry weight) 10^{12} kg	Average plant biomass (dry weight) 10^3 kg/ha	Total annual net primary production (dry weight) 10^{12} kg	Average annual net primary productivity (dry weight) 10^3 kg/ha
Temperate	661	117.6	43.2	7.68
Tropical	1 154	273.2	70.7	16.74
Desert	17	7.0	2.1	0.90
Arctic, ice-free	5	6.0	1.5	1.40
Terrestrial total, ice-free	1 837	137.9	117.5	8.82

Sources and notes:

[a]This table is summarized from tables 1.5 and 1.8, the data being weighted according to the areal extents presented in table 1.6. Comparable data for oceanic habitats are provided in table 7.2. (A number of useful conversion factors for the data as presented here are provided in table 1.5, note *a.*)

Table 1.8. Major terrestrial vegetation types: plant biomass and productivity[a]

Habitat and vegetation type	Average plant biomass (dry weight) 10^3 kg/ha	Average annual net primary productivity (dry weight) 10^3 kg/ha
Temperate		
Coniferous (softwood) forest	244 (60–2 000)	9.5 (4.0–25.0)
Dicotyledonous (hardwood) forest	300 (60–600)	12.0 (6.0–25.0)
Grassland (prairie, steppe, pampa)	16 (2–50)	6.0 (2.0–15.0)
Tropical		
Dense (closed, rain) forest	450 (60–800)	22.0 (10.0–35.0)
Open (clear, seasonal) forest	350 (60–600)	16.0 (10.0–25.0)
Grassland (savanna)	40 (2–150)	9.0 (2.0–20.0)

Table 1.8 (continued)

Habitat and vegetation type	Average plant biomass (dry weight) 10^3 kg/ha	Average annual net primary productivity (dry weight) 10^3 kg/ha
Miscellaneous		
Desert	7 (0–40)	0.9 (0–2.5)
Tundra	6 (1–30)	1.4 (0.1–4.0)
Agricultural	10 (4–120)	6.5 (1.0–40.0)
Global total, ice free	**138 (0–2 000)**	**8.9 (0–40.0)**

Sources and notes:
[a]The data are derived from those of Whittaker & Likens (1975: 306). Similar data for oceanic habitats are provided in table 7.2. The ice-free global total values are taken from table 1.5. (A number of useful conversion factors for the data as presented here are provided in table 1.5, note *a*.)

Table 1.9. Distribution of the major urban centres of the world (1975 data)

Region or category[a]	Number of cities of one million or more[b]	Combined population of these cities[b] 10^6	Proportion of regional or category population[c] per cent	Regional population density exclusive of these cities[c] No./km²
Land mass				
North America	21	83.6	26.6	10.6
South America	15	42.6	19.7	9.7
Africa	10	19.0	4.9	12.6
Europe	37	80.6	16.8	39.7
Asia	47	116.9	5.3	50.5
Australia	2	5.5	40.7	1.0
Antarctica	0	–	–	0
Islands	23	70.2	16.2	50.1
of Atlantic Ocean	5	15.7	17.9	104.3
of Pacific Ocean	18	54.5	16.2	75.5
of Indian Ocean	0	–	–	16.2
of Arctic Ocean	0	–	–	0.0
Hemisphere				
Northern	135	363.6	10.0	32.3
Southern	20	54.8	12.8	7.9
Habitat				
Temperate	110	294.0	12.5	36.7
Tropical	39	107.7	6.8	35.0
Desert	6	16.7	16.4	3.2
Arctic	0	–	–	0.7
Wealth				
Rich	61	178.7	19.9	12.6
Average	38	99.0	16.5	19.7
Poor	56	140.7	5.5	48.0
Global total	**155**	**418.4**	**10.3**	**24.5[d]**

Sources and notes:

[a]The regions are described in table 1.4, note *a*. The wealth categories are described in appendix 1.4, note *c*.

[b]The numbers of cities (urban centres, metropolitan areas) and their populations are primarily from the *World Almanac and Book of Facts 1977:* 600–602 (1972 to 1975 data).

[c]Regional populations and areas are from table 1.4. The populations and areas of the wealth categories are from the *UN Demographic Yearbook 1975:* table 3 (1975 data), being the summations of the individual nations (only) appropriate to each category, as provided in appendix 1.4 (the several missing areas being taken from the *Europa Year Book 1977* and the several missing populations being taken from ACDA (1976: table 2; 1975 data)).

[d]If the continuously ice-covered land surface (table 1.3) is excluded from this calculation, the density value becomes 27.3 persons per square kilometre exclusive of the inhabitants of the 155 major urban centres.

Table 1.10. Distribution of the nations of the world (1975 data)[a]

Region or category	Total number of nations	Number founded or independent before twentieth century	Number founded or independent after World War II	Number of rich nations	Number of poor nations	Number with nil to slow population growth[b]	Number with exceedingly rapid population growth[b]
Land mass							
North America	9	8	0	2	4	0	5
South America	12	10	2	0	6	0	6
Africa	45	2	41	1	40	0	9
Europe	28	19	1	13	2	12	2
Asia	30	10	15	6	19	0	16
Australia	1	0	0	1	0	0	0
Antarctica	0	0	0	0	0	0	0
Islands	34	5	26	4	18	5	6
of Atlantic Ocean	15	4	9	2	6	5	2
of Pacific Ocean	12	1	10	2	6	0	3
of Indian Ocean	7	0	7	0	6	0	1
of Arctic Ocean	0	0	0	0	0	0	0
Hemisphere							
Northern	124	46	61	25	63	17	36
Southern	35	8	24	2	26	0	8
Habitat							
Temperate	56	34	8	19	16	14	8
Tropical	80	17	62	0	64	2	21
Desert	22	3	15	7	9	0	15
Arctic	1	0	0	1	0	1	0
Wealth							
Rich	27	14	6	27	0	10	6
Average	43	19	15	0	0	5	15
Poor	89	21	64	0	89	2	23
Global total	159	54	85	27	89	17	44

Sources and notes:

[a]The regions are described in table 1.4, note *a*. The wealth categories are described in appendix 1.4, note *c*. The data in this table are summarized from appendix 1.4. A nation that falls into more than one region is for this table counted in the one that contains the larger area.

[b]A nation is here considered to have nil to slow population growth if its population doubling time exceeds 100 years (i.e., if it has a population growth rate of less than 0.696 per cent). A nation is here considered to have an exceedingly rapid population growth rate if its population doubling time is less than 25 years (i.e., if it has a population growth rate in excess of 2.81 per cent). Population growth rates are from the *UN Demographic Yearbook 1975;* table 3 (1975 data) (the several missing populations being taken from ACDA (1976: table 2; 1975 data)).

Table 1.11. Distribution per capita of national wealth and land resources (1975 data)[a]

Region or category	GNP[b] US $	Annual cereal production[c] kilograms	Agri- cultural land[d] hectares	Grass- land[d] hectares	Forest land[d] hectares
Land mass					
North America	5 543	964	0.908	0.999	2.296
South America	1 032	278	0.471	2.066	4.259
Africa	420	167	0.530	1.821	1.582
Europe	4 040	486	0.326	0.168	0.364
Asia	669	280	0.295	0.402	0.588
Australia	5 790	1 315	3.396	33.686	10.195
Antarctica	0	0	0	0	0
Islands	1 914	178	0.137	0.189	0.575
of Atlantic Ocean	2 796	205	0.169	0.277	0.074
of Pacific Ocean	1 807	174	0.123	0.076	0.694
of Indian Ocean	283	139	0.218	1.489	0.668
of Arctic Ocean	0	0	0	0	0
Hemisphere					
Northern	1 633	345	0.361	0.484	0.752
Southern	791	267	0.455	2.747	3.140
Habitat					
Temperate	2 396	436	0.396	0.638	0.910
Tropical	343	202	0.302	0.495	1.150
Desert	1 566	285	0.739	4.650	1.246
Arctic	6 835	0	0.005	10.454	0.550
Wealth					
Rich	5 119	631	0.667	1.356	2.021
Average	1 595	379	0.459	1.088	1.558
Poor	268	222	0.247	0.439	0.541
Global total	**1 539**	**336**	**0.371**	**0.738**	**1.020**

Sources and notes:
[a]The regions are described in table 1.4, note *a*. The wealth categories are described in appendix 1.4, note *c*. The data in this table are based only on the 159 nations listed in appendix 1.4. A nation that falls into more than one region is for this table counted in the one that contains the larger area. The values are all presented on a per capita basis, the regional populations used for this calculation being from the *UN Demographic Yearbook 1975,* table 3 (1975 data), being summations of the nations (only) that fall wholly or primarily into each region (and with the several missing populations taken from ACDA (1976: table 2; 1975 data)).
[b]Gross national product (GNP) values are from ACDA (1976: table 2; 1975 data) (and with the several missing values taken from the *World Bank Atlas* 1976 (1975 data)).
[c]Annual cereal production values are from the *FAO Production Yearbook 1976:* table 9 (1975 data), being a summation of wheat, paddy rice, barley, corn (maize), rye, oats, millet, and sorghum.

*d*Agricultural, grass, and forest land areas are from the *FAO Production Yearbook 1976:* table 1 (1975 data). The present agricultural land category is FAO's 'arable' plus 'permanent crop'; the present grassland category is FAO's 'permanent pasture'; and the present forest land category is FAO's 'forest' plus 'woodland'.

Table 1.12. Distribution of the national armies of the world (1975 data)*a*

Region or category	Total number of nations*b*	Number of armies of less than 10 000*c*	Number of armies of 100 000 or more*c*	Number of armies of 500 000 or more*c*
Land mass				
North America	9	4	1	1
South America	12	2	3	0
Africa	45	25	2	0
Europe	28	6	14	2
Asia	30	2	16	6
Australia	1	0	0	0
Antarctica	0	0	0	0
Islands	34	20	6	1
of Atlantic Ocean	15	10	2	0
of Pacific Ocean	12	5	4	1
of Indian Ocean	7	5	0	0
of Arctic Ocean	0	0	0	0
Hemisphere				
Northern	124	43	38	10
Southern	35	16	4	0
Habitat				
Temperate	56	10	26	6
Tropical	80	41	12	4
Desert	22	7	4	0
Arctic	1	1	0	0
Wealth				
Rich	27	3	10	3
Average	43	16	15	2
Poor	89	40	17	5
Global total	**159**	**59**	**42**	**10**

Sources and notes:

*a*The regions are described in table 1.4, note *a*. The wealth categories are described in appendix 1.4, note *c*. A nation that falls into more than one region is for this table counted in the one that contains the larger area.

*b*The numbers of nations are summarized from appendix 1.4.

*c*The numbers of armies of various sizes are summarized from ACDA (1976: table 2: 1975 data) (with the several missing values taken primarily from the *Statesman's Year-book 1977–1978*). The term 'army' is here used broadly to include a nation's army, navy, air force, etc.

Table 1.13. Distribution of the armed forces of the world (1975 data)[a]

Region or category	Total armed forces[b] 10^3	Armed forces per nation[c] 10^3	Armed forces per 100 000 population[d]	Armed forces per 1 000 square kilometres (per 10^5 ha)[d]	Armed forces per US $ 100 million of GNP[e]
Land mass					
North America	2 350	261	745	108	134
South America	1 008	84	467	57	453
Africa	1 387	31	355	48	846
Europe	4 513	161	1 091	1 013	270
Asia	15 373	512	678	328	1 014
Australia	70	70	518	9	90
Antarctica	0	0	0	0	0
Islands	1 805	53	414	359	216
of Atlantic Ocean	525	35	635	803	227
of Pacific Ocean	1 241	103	376	334	208
of Indian Ocean	39	6	169	59	596
of Arctic Ocean	0	0	0	0	0
Hemisphere					
Northern	25 003	202	695	257	426
Southern	1 503	43	331	43	418
Habitat					
Temperate	18 746	335	828	278	345
Tropical	6 135	77	377	144	1 097
Desert	1 625	74	1 025	72	655
Arctic	0	0	0	0	0
Wealth					
Rich	9 793	363	1 091	172	213
Average	5 203	121	865	205	543
Poor	11 510	129	451	229	1 684
Global total	**26 506**	**167**	**654**	**200**	**425**

Sources and notes:
[a] The regions are described in table 1.4, note *a*. The wealth categories are described in appendix 1.4, note *c*. The data in this table are based only on the 159 nations listed in appendix 1.4. A nation that falls into more than one region is for this table counted in the one that contains the larger area.
[b] Armed-force values are summarized from ACDA (1976: table 2; 1975 data) (with the several missing values taken primarily from the *Statesman's Year-book 1977–1978*). Individual values for the five permanent members of the UN Security Council are: China, 4 300 thousand; France, 575 thousand; the United Kingdom, 345 thousand; the USA, 2 130 thousand; and the USSR, 4 600 thousand. The naval personnel included in these values are listed in table 7.3. The values in the table above can also be compared with those for military expenditures in table 8.1.
[c] The numbers of nations upon which these calculations are based are summarized from appendix 1.4.
[d] The populations and areas upon which these calculations are based are from the *UN Demographic Yearbook 1975:* table 3 (1975 data), being summations of the nations (only) that fall wholly or primarily into each region.
[e] Gross national product (GNP) values are from ACDA (1976: table 2; 1975 data) (and with the several missing values taken from the *World Bank Atlas 1976* (1975 data)).

Table 1.14. Distribution of the major wars of the twentieth century[a]

Region[b]	Number of major wars 1899–1977[c]	Occurring once every:
Land mass		
North America	0	–
South America	0	–
Africa	2	40 years
Europe	4	20 years
Asia	8	9.9 years
Australia	0	–
Antarctica	0	–
Islands	2	40 years
of Atlantic Ocean	0	–
of Pacific Ocean	2	40 years
of Indian Ocean	0	–
of Arctic Ocean	0	–
Hemisphere		
Northern	15	5.3 years
Southern	1	–
Habitat		
Temperate	8	9.9 years
Tropical	7	11 years
Desert	1	–
Arctic	0	–
World-wide	**16**	**4.9 years**

Sources and notes:
[a]A major war is here considered to be one that falls into fatality class 6 or greater (cf. appendix 1.1, note *b*).
[b]The regions are described in table 1.4, note *a*.
[c]The number of wars in each region is taken from appendix 1.1, with the Russian Revolution here assigned only to Europe and World War II only to Europe, the Northern hemisphere, and the temperate zone.

Appendix 1.1

The major wars of the twentieth century[a]

1. Philippine Insurrection of 1899 to c. 1903

(a) Description: Thwarted attempt by the Philippines to gain its independence from the USA, the latter having just acquired the Philippines by force from Spain

(b) Location: Northern hemisphere; Pacific Ocean islands; tropical habitat

(c) Type and fatality class:[b] Colonial war; 6

(d) References: Caterini (1977); Cook (1975: 11–15); Francisco (1973); Miller (1969–1970); see also the sources below

2. World War I of 1914–1918

(a) Description: A complex of several more or less distinct wars that can in simple terms be summarized as an unsuccessful war by the Central Powers—i.e., Germany, Austria–Hungary, Turkey, Bulgaria, etc.—against the Allies—i.e., France, the UK, Russia, Italy, the USA, Belgium, Portugal, Serbia, Montenegro (the latter two now part of Yugoslavia), Greece, Romania, Japan, etc.

(b) Location: Primarily Northern hemisphere; primarily Europe (but also Asia, Africa, etc.); primarily temperate habitat

(c) Type and fatality class: Interstate war; 7

3. Russian Revolution plus Civil War of 1917–1922

(a) Description: Overthrow of the Russian government by Communist insurgents (under Lenin), the latter also quelling various national independent movements (e.g., by the Ukraine) despite more or less modest interventions by France, the UK, Japan and the USA

(b) Location: Northern hemisphere; Europe and Asia; temperate habitat

(c) Type and fatality class: Civil war; 6

4. Chinese Civil War of 1927–1936

(a) Description: Attempt by Communist insurgents (in time under Mao Tse-tung) to overthrow the Chinese Nationalist (Kuomintang) government (under Chiang Kai-shek), a struggle that was postponed by the Second Sino–Japanese War

(b) Location: Northern hemisphere; Asia; temperate habitat

(c) Type and fatality class: Civil war; 6

(d) References: Ho (1959: 248–250); see also the sources below

5. Spanish Civil War of 1936–1939

(a) Description: Overthrow of the Spanish government by insurgents (under Franco), the former with help from the USSR (as well as from perhaps a dozen volunteer international brigades), and the latter with help from Italy and Germany

(b) Location: Northern hemisphere; Europe; temperate habitat

(c) Type and fatality class: Civil war; 6

6. Second Sino–Japanese War of 1937–1945

(a) Description: Japanese invasion of China, eventually repulsed in conjunction with World War II

(b) Location: Northern hemisphere; Asia; temperate habitat

(c) Type and fatality class: Interstate war; 7

(d) References: SIPRI (1977: 62 *infra*); see also the sources below

7. World War II of 1939–1945

(a) Description: A complex of several dozen more or less distinct wars, all more or less closely connected in some supportive or opposing fashion with wars of conquest by Germany and Japan. Summarized in its simplest terms as an unsuccessful war of aggrandizement by the Axis—i.e., Germany (under Hitler), Austria (annexed by Germany), Italy, Japan, Hungary, Bulgaria, Romania, Finland, etc.—against the Allies—i.e., France, the UK, Poland, the USSR, Belgium, the USA, China, Czechoslovakia, Greece, the Netherlands, Yugoslavia, Norway, etc.

(b) Location: Primarily Northern hemisphere; Europe, Asia, Africa, Pacific Ocean islands, Atlantic Ocean islands, etc.; primarily temperate and tropical, but also desert and arctic habitats

(c) Type and fatality class: Interstate war; 8.

(d) References: Liddell-Hart (1970); see also appendices 1.2 and 1.3.1 and the sources below

8. Indian Civil War of 1946–1948

(a) Description: Internal turmoil, population shifts, and rebellions following from the division of the subcontinent into India (Hindu dominated) and Pakistan (Moslem dominated) and from their independence from the UK, involving, *inter alia,* several attempts at realignment or separate independence by various of the local states

(b) Location: Northern hemisphere; Asia; tropical habitat

(c) Type and fatality class: Civil war; 6

9. Chinese Civil War of 1946–1949

(a) Description: Overthrow by Communist insurgents (under Mao Tse-tung) of the Chinese government, the latter finding refuge on Taiwan

(b) Location: Northern hemisphere; Asia; temperate habitat

(c) Type and fatality class: Civil war; 6

10. Korean War of 1950–1953

(a) Description: Invasion of the Republic of [South] Korea by the Democratic People's Republic of [North] Korea, the former assisted by the USA and 14 other nations under the auspices of the UN, and the latter by China, in an unsuccessful attempt by North Korea to reunify the two Koreas

(b) Location: Northern hemisphere; Asia; temperate habitat

(c) Type and fatality class: Interstate war; 6

(d) References: Futrell *et al.* (1961); Leckie (1962); Rees (1964); see also appendices 1.2 and 1.3.2 and the sources below

11. Algerian War of Independence of 1954–1962

(a) Description: Successful attempt by Algeria to gain its independence from France

(b) Location: Northern hemisphere; Africa; largely desert habitat

(c) Type and fatality class: Colonial war; 6

(d) References: Horne (1977); see also the sources below

12. Second Indochina War of 1961–1975

(a) Description: A complex of more or less distinct conflicts confounded by massive US involvement, summarized as follows: an unsuccessful attempt by the USA to prevent the Republic of [South] Viet Nam government from being replaced by the Revolutionary Government of South Viet Nam or, eventually, from being annexed by the Democratic Republic of [North] Viet Nam; a further unsuccessful attempt by the USA to maintain in power the former regime in Laos; also an ancillary war by the USA against Cambodia (Kampuchea), followed by an overthrow of the Cambodian government by Communist insurgents (the Khmer Rouge)

(b) Location: Northern hemisphere; Asia; tropical habitat

(c) Type and fatality class: Interstate war; 6

(d) References: SIPRI (1976); see also table 3.2, appendices 1.2 and 1.3.3, and the sources below

13. Indonesian Civil War of 1965–1966

(a) Description: Unsuccessful attempt by Communist insurgents to overthrow the Indonesian government, followed by large-scale government massacres of suspected Communists

(b) Location: Southern hemisphere; Pacific Ocean islands; tropical habitat

(c) Type and fatality class: Civil war; 6

14. Nigerian Civil War of 1967–1970

(a) Description: Unsuccessful attempt by the south-eastern region—known as Biafra—to secede from Nigeria

(b) Location: Northern hemisphere; Africa; tropical habitat

(c) Type and fatality class: Civil war; 6

(d) References: *SIPRI Yearbook 1968/69:* 381–414; see also the sources below

15. Bangladesh War of Independence of 1971

(a) Description: Successful attempt by Bangladesh, with the aid of India, to secede from Pakistan

(b) Location: Northern hemisphere; Asia; tropical habitat

(c) Type and fatality class: Civil war (also interstate war); 6

(d) References: Payne (1973); see also the sources below

16. Kampuchean Insurrections of 1975–1977

(a) Description: Unsuccessful attempts by insurgents to revolt against the newly established government, reportedly involving massive repression and massacres by government forces

(b) Location: Northern hemisphere; Asia; tropical habitat

(c) Type and fatality class: Civil war; 6

(d) References: Shawcross (1978–79); Shawcross (1979); see also the sources below

---

Sources and notes:

[a] This tabulation is meant to include all of the major wars of the twentieth century, a *major war* here considered to be one in which the total number of direct fatalities—both civil and military—falls into fatality class 6 or greater (see below). In addition to any special sources noted for the individual wars, the information presented here has been derived primarily from Dupuy & Dupuy (1977), Harris & Levey (1975), Kende (1972: 71–86), Richardson (1960: 32–43), Singer & Small (1972), Urlanis (1971), Wood (1968), Wright (1965) and Young & Calvert (1977). See also *SIPRI Yearbook 1968/69:* 359–373. A number of these wars are further described in tables 1.2 and 8.2.

[b]The wars are divided into one of three *types:* interstate, colonial, or civil (intrastate). *Fatality classes* are in accord with the concept of Richardson (1960: 4–12). In order to determine the fatality class into which a war falls here, the base-ten logarithm of the total number of direct fatalities, both civil and military, is taken and then rounded to the nearest whole number. Thus, a *class 6* war would be any for which this number of fatalities is in the neighbourhood of 10^6 (1 000 000), or, more specifically, falls between $10^{5.5}$ (316 228) and $10^{6.5}$ (3 162 277). Similarly, this number of fatalities for a *class 7* war centres around 10^7 (10 000 000), falling between $10^{6.5}$ (3 162 278) and $10^{7.5}$ (31 622 776). And for a *class 8* war it centres around 10^8 (100 000 000), falling between $10^{7.5}$ (31 622 777) and $10^{8.5}$ (316 227 766). The use of such broad logarithmic classes is a reflection of the uncertainty that must be associated with fatality information on most wars—an uncertainty, moreover, that increases exponentially as the magnitude of the war increases.

Appendix 1.2

Comparisons of World War II, the Korean War, and the Second Indochina War as they apply to the USA[a]

1. US combat fatalities. 291 557 during World War II; 33 629 during the Korean War; and 46 558 during the Second Indochina War (US Department of Defense release of 6 March 1974 and private correspondence of 14 February 1977). These figures do not include those military deaths not the result of actions by hostile forces.

2. Durations. The USA was actively in combat for 44 months during World War II (from December 1941 to August 1945); for 37 months during the Korean War (from July 1950 to August 1953); and for 103 months during the Second Indochina War (from January 1965 to July 1973).

3. US areas of action. Roughly 300 million hectares during World War II (i.e., Germany 35, Italy 30, France 55, Austria 8, Hungary 9, Greece 13, North Africa 50, Japan 37, the Philippines 30, miscellaneous Pacific Ocean islands 7, and other miscellaneous areas 26); about 22 million hectares during the Korean War (North Korea 12, and South Korea 10); and approximately 75 million hectares during the Second Indochina War (South Viet Nam 17, North Viet Nam 16, Cambodia 18, and Laos 24).

4. US munition expenditures. About 7.7×10^9 kilograms during World War II (air 3.1, ground 3.6, and sea c. 1.0) (D'Olier, 1946: 16; 1947 b: .11; Library of Congress, 1971: 9); 2.6×10^9 kilograms during the Korean War (air 0.6, ground 1.9, and sea 0.1) (Futrell *et al.*, 1961: 645; Library of Congress, 1971: 9; US Navy, private correspondence of 15 April 1974); and 14.3×10^9 kilograms during the Second Indochina War (air 7.1, ground 7.0, and sea 0.2) (US Department of Defense release of 17 August 1973 and private correspondence of 2 November 1973).

5. Combat fatalities of the forces opposed to the USA. Very roughly, 7 million during World War II; 470 thousand during the Korean War; and 800 thousand during the Second Indochina War (derived from the data of appendix 1.3).

Note:
[a]For brief descriptions of each of these wars, see appendix 1.1, wars 7, 10, and 11, respectively.

Appendix 1.3

Fatalities in World War II, the Korean War, and the Second Indochina War: an approximation[a]

Nation	Mid-war population[b] 10^3	Military fatalities[c] 10^3	Civil fatalities[c] 10^3	Total fatalities 10^3	Proportion of population killed *per cent*	Civil proportion of total fatalities *per cent*
1. WORLD WAR II						
Austria[d]	6 880	247	125	372	5.4	34
Bulgaria	6 590	20	10	30	0.5	33
Finland[e]	3 730	45	15	60	1.6	25
Germany	66 920	4 750	1 471	6 221	9.3	24
Hungary	9 070	110	290	400	4.4	72
Italy	43 680	291	440	731	1.7	60
Japan	72 540	1 500	510	2 010	2.8	25
Romania	15 990	370	200	570	3.6	35
Axis subtotal	*225 400*	*7 333*	*3 061*	*10 394*	*4.6*	*29*
Albania	1 090	20	10	30	2.8	33
Belgium	8 360	10	90	100	1.2	90
Czechoslovakia	13 670	30	390	420	3.1	93
China[f]	505 000	2 000	2 000	4 000	0.8	50
Denmark	3 920	1	4	5	0.1	80
Ethiopia	13 500	5	5	10	0.1	50
France	41 260	200	450	650	1.6	69
Greece	7 200	18	190	208	2.9	91
Netherlands	9 010	10	220	230	2.6	96
Norway	3 000	2	7	9	0.3	78
Philippines	17 260	27	2	29	0.2	7
Poland	34 360	644	5 384	6 028	17.5	89
United Kingdom	48 240	265	60	325	0.7	18
USA	135 030	292	–	292	0.2	–
USSR	185 000	10 000	10 000	20 000	10.8	50
Yugoslavia	14 990	305	1 395	1 700	11.3	82
Miscellaneous theatres[g]	10 000	50	100	150	1.5	67
Miscellaneous armies[h]	–	136	–	136	–	–
Miscellaneous groups[i]	1 000[i]	–	6 500	6 500	–[i]	–
Allied subtotal[j]	*1 051 890*	*14 015*	*26 807*	*40 822*	*3.9*	*66*
World War II total[j]	**1 277 290**	**21 348**	**29 868**	**51 216**	**4.0**	**58**
2. KOREAN WAR						
North Korea	8 300	170	330	500	6.0	66
China	516 000	300	–	300	0.1	–
Subtotal	*524 300*	*470*	*330*	*800*	*0.2*	*41*
South Korea	19 500	280	230	510	2.6	45
USA	155 230	34	–	34	0.0	–
Miscellaneous armies[j]	–	3	–	3	–	–

Nation	Mid-war population[b] 10^3	Military fatalities[c] 10^3	Civil fatalities[c] 10^3	Total fatalities 10^3	Proportion of population killed per cent	Civil proportion of total fatalities per cent
UN subtotal	*174 730*	*317*	*230*	*547*	*0.3*	*42*
Korean War total	**699 030**	**787**	**560**	**1 347**	**0.2**	**42**
3. SECOND INDOCHINA WAR						
South Viet Nam[k]	17 630	500[k]	450	950	5.4	47
North Viet Nam	19 450	500	50	550	2.8	9
Cambodia	6 650	50	150	200	3.0	75
Laos	2 890	50	50	100	3.5	50
Indochina subtotal	*46 620*	*1 100*	*700*	*1 800*	*3.9*	*39*
USA	200 690	47	–	47	0.0	–
Miscellaneous armies[l]	–	5	–	5	–	–
Subtotal	*200 690*	*52*	*–*	*52*	*0.0*	*–*
Second Indochina War total	**247 310**	**1 152**	**700**	**1 852**	**0.7**	**38**

Sources and notes:

[a]For brief descriptions of each of these wars, see appendix 1.1, wars 7, 10, and 11, respectively.

[b]Mid-war populations for World War II are from the *UN Statistical Yearbook 1948:* table 1, being an average of the mid-1937 and mid-1946 values, except for China's, which is derived from the data of Durand (1959–1960). (The global mid-war population was 2 283 million.) Mid-war populations for the Korean War are from the *UN Statistical Yearbook 1964:* table 2, the North Korean value being derived from the mid-1958 value of 9 600 thousand and the given annual growth rate of 2.2 per cent; and the South Korean value being derived from the mid-1958 value of 23 330 thousand and the given annual growth rate of 2.8 per cent. The value for China is derived from the data of Durand (1959–1960). Mid-war populations for the Second Indochina War are from SIPRI (1976: 3).

[c]*World War II* fatality data for Austria are from Maass (1975: 63); for China from Ho (1959: 250–252); for Denmark from the Museum of Denmark's Fight for Freedom 1940–1945 (private correspondence of 24 April 1978); for France from a French release of 1945 (via French Foreign Ministry private correspondence of 25 November 1975); for Germany from the Foreign Ministry of FR Germany (private correspondence of 13 November 1975); for Greece from the Greek Foreign Ministry (private correspondence of 9 January 1976); for the Italian military fatalities from the Italian Foreign Ministry (private correspondence of 16 April 1976); for Norway from the *Norwegian Statistical Yearbook 1949:* table 39; for the Philippine civil fatalities from the *Philippine Statistics Yearbook 1946:* 124–125; for Poland from a Polish People's Republic release of May 1975; for the USA from a US Department of Defense release of 6 May 1974; for the USSR from Urlanis (1971: 294); and for Yugoslavia from Donlagić *et al.* (1967: 212). For the remaining nations the data are combined from Dupuy & Dupuy (1977: 1198), Singer & Small (1972: table 4.2), Urlanis (1971: 294), and Wright (1965: appendix B).

Korean War fatality data for North Korea are based on the following information: the value for military fatalities is one-third of 520 thousand military casualties (Meid & Yingling, 1972: 532); that for civil fatalities is one-third of one million civil casualties (Rees, 1964: 461). The Chinese value is from Meid & Yingling (1972: 532). The fatality data for South Korea are from the Foreign Ministry of the Republic of [South] Korea (private correspondence of 22 December 1975); the value for military fatalities is supported by the information provided by Meid &Yingling (1972: 532), i.e., one-third of their 850 thousand military casualties. The US fatality value is from a US Department of Defense release of 6 March 1974. The miscellaneous-army fatality data are from Leckie (1962: 429) and Singer & Small (1972: 68–69).

Second Indochina War fatality data for Indochina are based on several rather uncertain sources (Dellums, 1972: 16833; Haan & Tinker, 1970; Kennedy, 1974, 1975; Library of Congress, 1971) and must therefore be looked upon as rough estimations. The US fatality data are from a US Department of Defense release of 6 March 1974, plus private correspondence of 14 February 1977. The miscellaneous-army fatality data are from Dupuy & Dupuy (1977: 1221).

It must be stressed once again that many of the fatality data for all three of the wars are only rough approximations.

*d*Austria is grouped with the Axis powers by virtue of having been annexed by Germany at the time.

*e*The Finnish fatality data for the Russo–Finnish War of 1939–1940 (totalling about 25 thousand) are not included within the present tabulation.

*f*The Chinese population and fatality data are included in the present tabulation even though they resulted from what is elsewhere considered to have been the more or less distinct Second Sino–Japanese War of 1937–1945 (cf. appendix 1.1.6).

*g*The World War II category of 'miscellaneous theatres' includes south-east Asia, Pacific Ocean islands, and others.

*h*The World War II category of 'miscellaneous armies' includes those of Australia (military fatalities 30 thousand), Brazil (1), Canada (40), India (40), New Zealand (15), and South Africa (10).

*i*The World War II category of 'miscellaneous groups' includes the 6 million Jews exterminated by Germany (perhaps 60 per cent of the European total) as well as the 500 thousand Gypsies similarly exterminated (perhaps 50 per cent of the European total). The mid-war Gypsy population of one million is (unlike that of the Jewish population) listed in the table, under the assumption that it had not been included in any of the national populations.

*j*The Korean War category of 'miscellaneous armies' includes (in descending order of numbers of fatalities) those of Turkey, the UK, Canada, France, Australia, Greece, Colombia, Ethiopia, the Netherlands, the Philippines, New Zealand, and South Africa.

*k*The table does not distinguish between the military fatalities on the side of the Republic of [South] Viet Nam (perhaps 200 thousand) from those on the side of the Provisional Revolutionary Government of South Viet Nam (perhaps 300 thousand).

The Second Indochina War category of 'miscellaneous armies' includes those of South Korea, Australia, New Zealand, the Philippines, and Thailand.

Appendix 1.4

The world's de facto *nations (as of 1977)*[a]

No. Nation	Hemisphere[b]	Land mass[b]	Habitat[b]	Wealth[c]
1. Afghanistan	Northern	Asia (land.)	Temperate (75%)	Poor
2. Albania	Northern	Europe	Temperate	Poor
3. Algeria	Northern	Africa	Desert (85%)	Average
4. Andorra	Northern	Europe (land.)	Temperate	Average
5. Angola	Southern	Africa	Tropical (90%)	Poor
6. Argentina	Southern	South America	Temperate (68%)	Average
7. Australia	Southern	Australia	Desert (55%)	Rich
8. Austria	Northern	Europe (land.)	Temperate (96%)	Rich
9. Bahamas	Northern	Island (Atl.)	Tropical	Average
10. Bahrain	Northern	Island (Ind.)	Desert	Average
11. Bangladesh	Northern	Asia	Tropical	Poor
12. Barbados	Northern	Island (Atl.)	Tropical	Average
13. Belgium	Northern	Europe	Temperate	Rich
14. Benin	Northern	Africa	Tropical	Poor
15. Bhutan	Northern	Asia (land.)	Temperate (75%)	Poor
16. Bolivia	Southern	South America (land.)	Tropical (98%)	Poor
17. Botswana	Southern	Africa (land.)	Desert (75%)	Poor
18. Brazil	Southern (92%)	South America	Tropical	Average
19. Bulgaria	Northern	Europe	Temperate	Average
20. Burma	Northern	Asia	Tropical	Poor
21. Burundi	Southern	Africa (land.)	Tropical	Poor
22. Cameroon	Northern	Africa	Tropical	Poor
23. Canada	Northern	North America	Temperate (70%)	Rich
24. Cape Verde	Northern	Island (Atl.)	Tropical	Poor
25. Central African Republic	Northern	Africa (land.)	Tropical	Poor
26. Chad	Northern	Africa (land.)	Tropical (65%)	Poor
27. Chile	Southern	South America	Temperate (77%)	Poor
28. China, People's Republic of	Northern	Asia	Temperate (67%)	Poor
29. Colombia	Northern (95%)	South America	Tropical	Poor
30. Comoros	Southern	Island (Ind.)	Tropical	Poor
31. Congo	Southern (60%)	Africa	Tropical	Poor
32. Costa Rica	Northern	North America	Tropical	Average
33. Cuba	Northern	Island (Atl.)	Tropical	Poor
34. Cyprus	Northern	Island (Atl.)	Temperate	Average
35. Czechoslovakia	Northern	Europe (land.)	Temperate	Rich
36. Denmark	Northern	Europe	Temperate	Rich
*37. Djibouti	Northern	Africa	Desert (80%)	Average
38. Dominican Republic	Northern	Island (Atl.)	Tropical	Poor
39. Ecuador	Southern (85%)	South America	Temperate (60%)	Poor
40. Egypt	Northern	Africa (94%)	Desert	Poor
41. El Salvador	Northern	North America	Tropical	Poor
42. Equatorial Guinea	Northern	Africa	Tropical	Poor

No.	Nation	Hemisphere[b]	Land mass[b]	Habitat[b]	Wealth[c]
43.	Ethiopia	Northern	Africa	Temperate (80%)	Poor
44.	Fiji	Southern	Island (Pac.)	Tropical	Average
45.	Finland	Northern	Europe	Temperate	Rich
46.	France	Northern	Europe	Temperate	Rich
47.	Gabon	Southern (70%)	Africa	Tropical	Average
48.	Gambia	Northern	Africa	Tropical	Poor
49.	German Democratic Republic	Northern	Europe	Temperate	Rich
50.	Germany, Federal Republic of	Northern	Europe	Temperate	Rich
51.	Ghana	Northern	Africa	Tropical	Poor
52.	Greece	Northern	Europe	Temperate	Average
53.	Grenada	Northern	Island (Atl.)	Tropical	Poor
54.	Guatemala	Northern	North America	Tropical	Poor
55.	Guinea	Northern	Africa	Tropical	Poor
56.	Guinea-Bissau	Northern	Africa	Tropical	Poor
57.	Guyana	Northern	South America	Tropical	Poor
58.	Haiti	Northern	Island (Atl.)	Tropical	Poor
59.	Honduras	Northern	North America	Tropical	Poor
60.	Hungary	Northern	Europe (land.)	Temperate	Average
61.	Iceland	Northern	Island (Atl.)	Arctic	Rich
62.	India	Northern	Asia	Tropical (80%)	Poor
63.	Indonesia	Southern (70%)	Island (Pac.)	Tropical	Poor
64.	Iran	Northern	Asia	Desert (60%)	Average
65.	Iraq	Northern	Asia	Desert (70%)	Average
66.	Ireland	Northern	Island (Atl.)	Temperate	Average
67.	Israel	Northern	Asia	Desert (65%)	Rich
68.	Italy	Northern	Europe	Temperate (99%)	Average
69.	Ivory Coast	Northern	Africa	Tropical	Poor
70.	Jamaica	Northern	Island (Atl.)	Tropical	Average
71.	Japan	Northern	Island (Pac.)	Temperate	Rich
72.	Jordan	Northern	Asia	Desert (65%)	Poor
73.	Kampuchea	Northern	Asia	Tropical	Poor
74.	Kenya	Northern (55%)	Africa	Tropical	Poor
75.	Korea, Democratic People's Republic of	Northern	Asia	Temperate	Poor
76.	Korea, Republic of	Northern	Asia	Temperate	Poor
77.	Kuwait	Northern	Asia	Desert	Rich
78.	Laos	Northern	Asia (land.)	Tropical	Poor
79.	Lebanon	Northern	Asia	Temperate	Average
80.	Lesotho	Southern	Africa (land.)	Temperate	Poor
81.	Liberia	Northern	Africa	Tropical	Poor
82.	Libya	Northern	Africa	Desert	Rich
83.	Liechtenstein	Northern	Europe (land.)	Temperate	Average
84.	Luxembourg	Northern	Europe (land.)	Temperate	Rich
85.	Madagascar	Southern	Island (Ind.)	Tropical	Poor
86.	Malawi	Southern	Africa (land.)	Tropical	Poor
87.	Malaysia	Northern	Island (Pac.) (60%)	Tropical	Average
88.	Maldives	Northern	Island (Ind.)	Tropical	Poor
89.	Mali	Northern	Africa (land.)	Desert (65%)	Poor
90.	Malta	Northern	Island (Atl.)	Temperate	Average
91.	Mauritania	Northern	Africa	Desert	Poor
92.	Mauritius	Southern	Island (Ind.)	Tropical	Poor
93.	Mexico	Northern	North America	Tropical (70%)	Average

No.	Nation	Hemisphere[b]	Land mass[b]	Habitat[b]	Wealth[c]
94.	Monaco	Northern	Europe	Temperate	Average
95.	Mongolia	Northern	Asia (land.)	Temperate (90%)	Poor
96.	Morocco	Northern	Africa	Temperate (65%)	Poor
97.	Mozambique	Southern	Africa	Tropical	Poor
98.	Nauru	Southern	Island (Pac.)	Tropical	Poor
99.	Nepal	Northern	Asia (land.)	Temperate (75%)	Poor
100.	Netherlands	Northern	Europe	Temperate	Rich
101.	New Zealand	Southern	Island (Pac.)	Temperate	Rich
102.	Nicaragua	Northern	North America	Tropical	Poor
103.	Niger	Northern	Africa (land.)	Desert (75%)	Poor
104.	Nigeria	Northern	Africa	Tropical	Poor
105.	Norway	Northern	Europe	Temperate (75%)	Rich
106.	Oman	Northern	Asia	Desert	Average
107.	Pakistan	Northern	Asia	Tropical (70%)	Poor
108.	Panama	Northern	North America	Tropical	Average
109.	Papua New Guinea	Southern	Island (Pac.)	Tropical	Poor
110.	Paraguay	Southern	South America (land.)	Tropical(80%)	Poor
111.	Peru	Southern	South America	Tropical (50%)	Average
112.	Philippines	Northern	Island (Pac.)	Tropical	Poor
113.	Poland	Northern	Europe	Temperate	Average
114.	Portugal	Northern	Europe	Temperate	Average
115.	Qatar	Northern	Asia	Desert	Rich
116.	Rhodesia (Zimbabwe-)	Southern	Africa (land.)	Tropical (90%)	Poor
117.	Romania	Northern	Europe	Temperate	Average
118.	Rwanda	Southern	Africa (land.)	Tropical	Poor
119.	Samoa	Southern	Island (Pac.)	Tropical	Poor
120.	San Marino	Northern	Europe (land.)	Temperate	Average
121.	São Tomé and Principe	Northern	Island (Atl.)	Tropical	Poor
122.	Saudi Arabia	Northern	Asia	Desert	Rich
123.	Senegal	Northern	Africa	Tropical (85%)	Poor
124.	Seychelles	Southern	Island (Ind.)	Tropical	Poor
125.	Sierra Leone	Northern	Africa	Tropical	Poor
126.	Singapore	Northern	Island (Pac.)	Tropical	Average
127.	Somalia	Northern (96%)	Africa	Tropical (60%)	Poor
128.	South Africa	Southern	Africa	Temperate (90%)	Average
129.	Spain	Northern	Europe	Temperate	Average
130.	Sri Lanka	Northern	Island (Ind.)	Tropical	Poor
131.	Sudan	Northern	Africa	Tropical (65%)	Poor
132.	Surinam	Northern	South America	Tropical	Average
133.	Swaziland	Southern	Africa (land.)	Temperate	Poor
134.	Sweden	Northern	Europe	Temperate	Rich
135.	Switzerland	Northern	Europe (land.)	Temperate (85%)	Rich
136.	Syria	Northern	Asia	Temperate (90%)	Poor
137.	Taiwan	Northern	Island (Pac.)	Tropical	Average
138.	Tanzania	Southern	Africa	Tropical	Poor
139.	Thailand	Northern	Asia	Tropical	Poor
140.	Togo	Northern	Africa	Tropical	Poor
141.	Tonga	Southern	Island (Pac.)	Tropical	Poor
142.	Trinidad and Tobago	Northern	Island (Atl.)	Tropical	Average
143.	Tunisia	Northern	Africa	Desert (75%)	Poor
144.	Turkey	Northern	Asia (97%)	Temperate	Average
145.	Uganda	Northern (75%)	Africa (land.)	Tropical	Poor

No. Nation	Hemisphere[b]	Land mass[b]	Habitat[b]	Wealth[c]
146. United Arab Emirates	Northern	Asia	Desert	Rich
147. United Kingdom	Northern	Island (Atl.)	Temperate	Rich
148. United States	Northern	North America (100%)	Temperate (84%)	Rich
149. Upper Volta	Northern	Africa (land.)	Tropical	Poor
150. Uruguay	Southern	South America	Temperate	Average
151. USSR	Northern	Asia (75%)	Temperate (74%)	Rich
152. Vatican City	Northern	Europe (land.)	Temperate	Poor
153. Venezuela	Northern	South America	Tropical	Average
154. Viet Nam	Northern	Asia	Tropical	Poor
155. Yemen Arab Rebublic	Northern	Asia	Desert	Poor
156. Yemen, People's Democratic Republic of	Northern	Asia	Desert	Poor
157. Yugoslavia	Northern	Europe	Temperate	Average
158. Zaïre	Southern (70%)	Africa	Tropical	Poor
159. Zambia	Southern	Africa (land.)	Tropical	Poor

Sources and notes:

[a]This catalogue of nations includes all of the 147 United Nations as of end-1977 (with Byelorussia, the Ukraine, and the USSR treated as one unit; with Taiwan treated as separate from China; with Namibia treated as separate from South Africa; with Sikkim as part of India; with East [Portuguese] Timor as part of Indonesia; and with Western [Spanish] Sahara as part of Morocco ($\frac{2}{3}$) and Mauritania ($\frac{1}{3}$)) plus 12 additional states (numbers 4, 75, 76, 83, 94, 98, 116, 120, 135, 137, 141, and 152 in the list). Selected colonies and other territories are listed in appendix 1.5.

[b]The regions (hemispheres, land masses, and habitats) are described in table 1.4, *note a*. A nation that falls into more than one region is here listed as falling into the one that includes the larger area. Each such entry is followed by a number in parentheses stating the percentage of the land area falling into that particular category. The parenthetical abbreviation 'Atl.' stands for 'Atlantic Ocean' (which here includes the Mediterranean Sea); 'Pac.' stands for 'Pacific Ocean'; 'Ind.' stands for 'Indian Ocean'; 'Arc.' stands for 'Arctic Ocean'; and 'land.' stands for 'land-locked'.

[c]The *wealth* category of each nation is based upon its gross national product (GNP) per capita. A nation is considered to be *rich* if its GNP per capita is at least twice the combined GNP per capita of all 159 nations. A nation is considered to be of *average* wealth if its GNP per capita is less than twice but more than half of the combined GNP per capita of all 159 nations. A nation is considered to be *poor* if its GNP per capita is half or less than the combined GNP per capita of all 159 nations. GNP values are from ACDA (1976: table 2; 1975 data) (with the several missing values taken from the *World Bank Atlas 1976* (1975 data)). Populations are from the *UN Demographic Yearbook 1975:* table 3 (1975 data) (with the several missing populations taken from ACDA (1976: table 2; 1975 data)). GNP is employed as an indicator of a nation's wealth since it is the only such indicator that is readily available for all of the world's nations.

   It can be noted that the present group of 27 rich nations includes 19 of the 22 developed nations (i.e., industrialized plus primary producing nations) as determined by the International Monetary Fund (IMF, 1977). The present group of 89 poor nations includes all of the 24 so-called least developed countries as identified by the UN Economic and Social Council as well as all of the 33 so-called most seriously affected countries as established by the UN General Assembly, 42 nations in all (Ceres, 1975).

Appendix 1.5

Selected possessions and other territories (as of 1977)[a]

No. Territory	Hemisphere[b]	Land mass[b]	Habitat[b]	Wealth[c]
1. Antarctica	Southern	Antarctica	Arctic	–
2. Atlantic Ocean Islands[d]	Southern	Island (Atl.)	Temperate (95%)	–
3. Belize	Northern	North America	Tropical	Poor
4. Bermuda	Northern	Island (Atl.)	Tropical	Rich
5. Brunei	Northern	Island (Pac.)	Tropical	Rich
6. Ceuta, Melilla	Northern	Africa	Temperate	Poor
7. Chagos Archipelago	Southern	Island (Ind.)	Tropical	–
8. Channel Islands, Isle of Man	Northern	Island (Atl.)	Temperate	Average
9. Faeroe Islands	Northern	Island (Atl.)	Temperate	Rich
10. Falkland Islands	Southern	Island (Atl.)	Temperate	–
11. French Guiana	Northern	South America	Tropical	Average
12. French Polynesia	Southern	Island (Pac.)	Tropical	Average
13. Gibraltar	Northern	Europe	Temperate	Average
14. Greenland	Northern	Island (Arc.)	Arctic	Average
15. Guadeloupe	Northern	Island (Atl.)	Tropical	Average
16. Hong Kong	Northern	Asia (93%)	Tropical	Average
17. Indian Ocean Islands[e]	Northern (91%)	Island (Ind.)	Tropical	–
18. Macao	Northern	Asia	Tropical	Poor
19. Martinique	Northern	Island (Atl.)	Tropical	Average
20. Namibia	Southern	Africa	Desert (90%)	Average
21. New Caledonia	Southern	Island (Pac.)	Tropical	Rich
22. New Hebrides	Southern	Island (Pac.)	Tropical	Poor
23. Pacific Ocean Islands[f, g]	Northern (66%)	Island (Pac.)	Tropical	–
24. Panama Canal Zone	Northern	North America	Tropical	Rich
25. Puerto Rico	Northern	Island (Atl.)	Tropical	Average
26. Réunion	Southern	Island (Ind.)	Tropical	Average
27. Solomon Islands[g]	Southern	Island (Pac.)	Tropical	Poor
28. Svalbard	Northern	Island (Arc.)	Arctic	–
29. West Indies[g, h]	Northern	Island (Atl.)	Tropical	–

Sources and notes:

[a]This catalogue of possessions and other territories accounts for virtually all of the land not already accounted for by the nations listed in appendix 1.4. Sikkim is not included since it is treated as part of India; and Spanish (Western) Sahara is not included since it is treated as part of Morocco (⅔) and Mauritania (⅓).

[b]The regions (hemispheres, land masses, and habitats) are described in table 1.4, note *a*. A territory that falls into more than one region is here listed as falling into the one that includes the larger area. Each such entry is followed by a number in parentheses stating the percentage of the land area falling into that particular category. The parenthetical abbreviation 'Atl.'

stands for 'Atlantic Ocean' (which here includes the Mediterranean Sea); 'Pac.' stands for 'Pacific Ocean'; 'Ind.' stands for 'Indian Ocean'; and 'Arc.' stands for 'Arctic Ocean'.

cThe wealth categories are described in appendix 1.4, note c. The numerical class limits used for the possessions in this appendix are those determined by the 159 nations.

dAtlantic Ocean islands include St Helena, Ascension, Tristan de Cunha, South Georgia, South Sandwich, and others. (The West Indies are not included here, but have a separate entry.)

eIndian Ocean islands include Christmas, Cocos (Keeling), and others.

fPacific Ocean islands include American Samoa, Canton, Cook, the Gilberts, Guam, Johnston, Midway, Niue, Norfolk, the Carolines, the Marianas, the Marshalls, Tokelau, Tuvalu (Ellice), Wake, Wallis, the Futunas, and others.

gThe Solomon Islands gained their independence in July 1978; Tuvalu in October 1978; Dominica in November 1978; St Lucia in February 1979; the Gilberts (now Kiribati) in July 1979; and St Vincent and the Grenadines in October 1979.

hThe West Indies include Antigua, the British Virgins, Caymans, Dominica, Montserrat, St Kitts, Nevis, Anguilla, St Lucia, St Vincent, Turks, Caicos, the Netherlands Antilles, St Pierre, Miquelon, the US Virgins, and others.

2. Temperate regions

The tables for this chapter appear on pages 64–66.

I. Introduction

The temperate land areas of the world—characterized by warm summers, cold winters, and precipitation sufficing to support at least grassland—occupy 38 per cent of the global land area. This land supports 36 per cent of the global biomass which, in turn, accounts for 25 per cent of the annual global biomass production. It further supports 58 per cent of the world's human population, distributed among 56 nations and about 6 colonies. The temperate land areas include most of the rich nations of the world and also most of those nations whose founding or independence predates World War II. A war likely to be environmentally disruptive occurs perhaps once every 10 years in the temperate regions of the world.

II. Environment and ecology

The temperate regions of the world, as defined here, are those lands that are located more or less between the Arctic Circle and the tropic of Cancer in the Northern hemisphere, and between the tropic of Capricorn and the Antarctic Circle in the Southern hemisphere. They are thus characterized by marked seasonal alternations in photoperiod and temperature. Summers have relatively long periods of daily illumination and are relatively warm (frost-free); winters, by contrast, have relatively short periods of daily illumination and are relatively cold (sub-freezing). For present purposes, the temperate regions are further limited to those lands that receive and retain precipitation at least sufficient to support grassland, that is, roughly 250 millimetres per year or more (appendix 2.1.1).

The temperate regions of the world extend over about 56 million square kilometres (5 600 million hectares) of the Earth's land surface, mostly—that is, 50 million square kilometres—in the Northern hemisphere (table 2.1). The largest single area is in Eurasia (33 million square kilometres) and the second largest in North America (15 million square kilometres). Europe is almost entirely temperate, North America more than two-thirds so, and Asia more than half so.

Temperate regions are divisible into a number of major habitats: forest

(1 900 million hectares), grassland (1 300 million hectares), agricultural (800 million hectares), and built-up, the last one including cities, industrial areas, transportation systems, military bases, and so forth (table 1.6). Broadly speaking, the forest habitat can be divided into coniferous (softwood) forest (roughly 1 300 million hectares) and dicotyledonous (hardwood) forest (roughly 600 million hectares). The coniferous forests are dominated by pines and spruces, whereas the dicotyledonous forests are usually characterized by a considerable diversity of species. Prominent examples include the oaks, maples, aspens, and birches. Grasslands (prairies, steppes, pampas) with relatively high precipitation support tall grasses, such as blue-stem *(Andropogon)* or switch grass *(Panicum),* whereas those with relatively low precipitation support short grasses, such as grama *(Bouteloua)* or blue grass *(Poa).* (Some areas of grassland would support forest were it not for occasionally recurring fires (Sauer, 1950; Wells, 1965).)

As to the photosynthetic productivity of temperate ecosystems, one can expect coniferous forests to have an annual net primary productivity that averages perhaps 9 500 kilograms (dry weight) per hectare (table 1.8). In the cooler boreal regions with shorter growing seasons, this value might drop to 8 000 kilograms per hectare, whereas in the more southerly regions it might be around 13 000 kilograms per hectare. Dicotyledonous forests might average 12 000 kilograms per hectare, and grassland perhaps 6 000 kilograms per hectare. The productivity of agricultural lands varies markedly, depending not only upon location but also upon how intensively they are managed. The average is perhaps 7 000 kilograms per hectare, but the value can readily vary between 4 000 and 12 000. The overall average for the world's temperate regions is of the order of 7 700 kilograms per hectare (table 1.7).

The wildlife in temperate forests is relatively sparse, consisting to a large extent of small rodents, squirrels, deer, pigs, a number of wood-peckers and other birds, and some snakes. Grasslands characteristically support large herbivores, such as bison, antelopes, and hares; and also burrowing rodents and various hawks and other birds.

As will be noted more fully in the sections to follow, the ecology of the temperate regions of the world has been extensively, often drastically, modified by man to suit his needs. Indeed, man has been a far more active agent of environmental modification in the temperate than in any other of the global habitats. Much of the land has for many centuries been given over to increasingly intensive agricultural and high-density urban and related uses, and the remainder—terrain permitting—to silvicultural and other extensive uses.

Temperate species, and the ecosystems of which they are part, have evolved through the millennia in—and adapted to—an environment not only subjected to drastic seasonal changes, but also more or less frequently to fires, hurricanes, and other drastic disturbances. Their general pattern of recovery (ecological succession) following such disturbances has been outlined in chapter 1 (section III) and is further mentioned in section IV below. The time-span involved for pre-disturbance conditions to be reattained depends, of course, on the degree of disruption and other factors. But for a temperate grassland ecosystem it is likely to be measurable in decades, and for a temperate forest ecosystem in centuries.

III. Use

Civil

About 2 400 million people currently utilize the temperate lands of the Earth to live and support themselves (table 2.1; appendix 2.1.2). The present temperate population density is 42 persons per square kilometre. If the people who are concentrated into the 110 temperate urban centres of 1 million or more are excluded from the density determination, then the value drops to 37 persons per square kilometre (table 1.9). Most by far (96 per cent) of the inhabitants of the temperate habitat live in the Northern hemisphere, the majority (56 per cent) in Asia (table 2.1). Essentially all of the European population live in this habitat, as do four-fifths of the Australian and three-quarters of the North American. The gross national product (GNP) per capita in the temperate habitat is US $2 400, as compared with a global value of US $1 500 (table 1.11).

The people of the temperate habitat are for the most part grouped into 56 nations (table 1.10). Fully 19 of these nations can be considered to be rich (this group accounting for most of the rich nations in the world), and another 21 to be of average wealth. Fourteen temperate nations have essentially stable population numbers, again a group that accounts for most of the world's nations in this category. Thirty-four (once again, most of those in this category) were founded or gained their independence before the twentieth century, and only eight have achieved this status since the close of World War II.

Some 800 million hectares of the temperate habitat has been cleared for agriculture (table 1.6), that is, 0.40 hectare per capita. Annual cereal production (a summation of all grains) is 436 kilograms per capita (table 1.11). The world's leading cereal exporter by far is the USA (80 million tonnes per year) (*FAO Trade Yearbook 1976:* table 34, 1975 data). Three of the next four nations are also temperate: Canada (15 million tonnes per year) second; France (12 million) third; and Argentina (8 million) fifth. Moreover, the USA is by far the world's leading producer (42 million tonnes per year) and exporter (17 million tonnes per year) of soya beans (*UN Statistical Yearbook 1976:* table 40, 1975 data).

The temperate regions of the world are also a major source of exploitable natural resources. Important among the renewable ones are the range lands (0.64 hectare per capita) for livestock production and the forest lands (0.91 hectare per capita) for timber production (table 1.11). The major temperate-habitat livestock nations are the USA (132 million head of cattle and 15 million sheep), the USSR (109 million; 145 million), China (64 million; 74 million), Argentina (60 million; 37 million), and New Zealand (10 million; 55 million) (*UN Statistical Yearbook 1976:* table 33, 1975 data). The major temperate-habitat timber producers are the USSR (harvesting 388 million cubic metres per year), the USA (296 million), China (194 million), Canada (121 million), and Sweden (52 million) (*FAO Forest Products Yearbook 1975:* 3–4, 1975 data). The combined timber harvest for all temperate nations is currently 1 455 million cubic metres per year, which represents 60 per cent of the global total. Of the world's current timber exporters, only four nations stand out, the top two—the USSR (18 million cubic metres per year) and the USA (17 million)—being temperate-habitat nations.

A large variety of important mineral resources exist in the temperate habitat and only a few are singled out here (data from the *UN Statistical Yearbook 1976,* 1975 data). The greatest amount of iron in the world is mined by the USSR (127 million tonnes per year, representing one-quarter of global production). Of other temperate nations, the USA (49 million tonnes per year) is third in world rank, China (33 million) is fifth, Canada (28 million) sixth, and Sweden (20 million) eighth. The six top sources for coal in the world are all temperate: the USA (568 million tonnes per year, representing one-quarter of global production), the USSR (485 million), China (470 million), Poland (172 million), the United Kingdom (129 million), and FR Germany (97 million). The USA, the USSR, and China together account for two-thirds of global coal production. The world's two leading current oil producers are both temperate nations—the USSR (574 million cubic metres per year) and the USA (483 million)—together accounting for more than one-third of global production.

Four of the five top copper producers are temperate nations (the USA, the USSR, Chile, and Canada), together accounting for more than half of global production. The four leading uranium producers are all temperate (the USA, Canada, South Africa, and France), together accounting for almost nine-tenths of global production. The two leading manganese producers are temperate (the USSR and South Africa), together accounting for more than half of global production. The three leading mercury producers are temperate (the USSR, Spain, and Italy), together accounting for half of global production. Canada is the leading nickel producer (one-third of global production). China and the USSR—the two leaders— together produce almost half of the world's output of tungsten (wolfram). The USSR and Canada—the two leaders—together account for more than half of global asbestos production. The USA and the USSR—the two leaders—together account for more than half of global phosphate production. The second and third largest producers of industrial diamonds in the world are the USSR and South Africa, together accounting for more than one-third of the global total. South Africa and the USSR lead the world in the mining of chromium, together accounting for half of global production. Moreover, South Africa is noted for its production of vanadium, antimony, and especially gold.

Military

The military activities within the temperate regions of the world are, as elsewhere, intended to serve various purposes (appendix 2.1.3). For most of the 56 included nations, their domestically maintained armed forces are meant for protection against external threats, for quelling civil wars, and occasionally for aggressive purposes. For most of the half dozen or more included colonies, the resident armed forces of the possessor nation are, again, meant for protection against external threats and also for subduing independence movements. The various armed forces of the several major powers which are deployed in foreign nations are present as part of the regional or global security postures of these powers.

Twenty-six of the 56 temperate nations maintain armies with a strength of 100 thousand or more (table 1.12). Of these, at least the following 6 nations have armies in excess of 500 thousand: China, France, Italy, South Korea, the USA, and the USSR. The average temperate-nation army has a strength of 335 thousand (table 1.13). Armies are presumably maintained in part to protect some combination of a nation's people, its land, and its wealth. The temperate nations maintain about 830 soldiers per 100 thousand inhabitants; about 280 soldiers per thousand square kilometres; and about 350 soldiers per US $100 million of gross national product.

Whereas most of the nations of the world keep their armies within their borders most of the time, several do not. Among the more important and well-established foreign military presences deployed within the temperate habitat are the US forces in Western Europe (in FR Germany, etc.), South Korea, and Japan; the British forces in Gibraltar, Malta, Cyprus, and FR Germany; and the Soviet forces in Eastern Europe (German DR, etc.) and Mongolia.

IV. Abuse

Civil

Some of the civil abuses of the temperate habitat are of very long standing and others are of more recent origin (appendix 2.1.2). For example, a substantial fraction of the temperate habitat—including its flora, fauna, and water-ways—has long been converted to agricultural or urban and related uses and otherwise drastically modified to suit human needs. Such taming of the environment continues at a relatively modest pace, especially in the form of transforming rural areas into urban or industrial ones and into the transportation networks that link them. More recently, the major abuse especially characteristic of the temperate habitat is the more or less subtle debilitation of ecosystems by domestic, agricultural, and industrial wastes. The pollution of air, water, and land by these wastes has increased in parallel with the exponential growths in population (and in the affluence of this population), in a mechanized energy-intensive agriculture heavily dependent upon chemical fertilizers and pesticides, and especially in industry in all its ramifications.

The industrialized temperate-habitat nations account not only for the major fraction of world-wide pollution, but also for the rapacious consumption of natural resources (both from within the region and from elsewhere). The exploitation of these resources is in many instances carried out with little if any regard for the basic principles of conservation, and, as a result, such exploitation degrades the environment in many of the places where it is pursued. The renewable natural resources are in many instances harvested at rates that exceed their and the soil's processes of natural renewal; and the non-renewable ones are often extracted with enormous upheaval to the local environment and to a considerable extent at the expense of future generations.

Environmental abuse in the temperate habitat is exacerbated by two factors in particular: *(a)* growth in population, and *(b)* expansion of industry. Despite the fact that virtually all of the world's nations with essentially stable populations are located in the temperate habitat (table 1.10), the overall population of this habitat nevertheless increases at the compound growth rate of 1.2 per cent—a rate that leads to a doubling time of 57 years (table 1.4). The so-called overdeveloped nations largely responsible for this environmental abuse must not only halt their population growth, but must also greatly restrain their industrial expansion, institute strict pollution controls, rigorously husband their renewable resources, and rely much more heavily for their raw materials on these renewable resources and on recycled materials.

In the long run, perhaps the most dangerous abuse of the environment associated primarily with the industrialized nations, and thus originating largely within the temperate habitat, is the enrichment of the atmosphere by carbon dioxide (Baes *et al.*, 1977; Mercer, 1978; Revelle & Munk, 1977; Siegenthaler & Oeschger, 1978). Man's use of coal, oil, and gas has increased exponentially over the past century or so and continues to do so; carbon dioxide is an unavoidable gaseous waste product of the burning of these fossil fuels (as well as of peat and wood), and during the period mentioned, atmospheric levels of this gas have increased from about 290 to 330 millilitres per cubic metre of dry air. The problem lies in the fact that atmospheric carbon dioxide presents a weaker barrier to the energy being supplied to the Earth by the Sun (largely in the form of light) than to the energy radiated away from the surface of the Earth and into outer space (largely in the form of heat). Although various complicating and as yet imperfectly understood factors are involved (including the contribution of the global biomass; cf. chapter 3), it is now widely assumed that this situation will, in the absence of concerted precautionary restraints, lead to a substantial change in the global energy balance. As a result, it is fully conceivable that in the decades to come, marked changes could occur in the global climate (Kellogg, 1978) and even perhaps in the sea-level (Mercer, 1978). Such changes would, of course, have profound social implications (Cooper, 1977–1978; Tickell, 1977).

Despite the increasing world population and the even more rapidly growing expectations of this population, it appears that a substantial curtailment in the global utilization of fossil fuels will be necessary in the years to come. It is therefore important to emphasize that restraints are called for not solely in the use of fossil fuels, but rather in man's overall utilization of energy, and thus in his standard of living. Such restraint is necessary inasmuch as nuclear energy—the only currently feasible alternative that would come even close to satisfying the present demand—merely substitutes one set of potential environmental upheavals for another.

Military

Military abuse of the temperate habitat is a continuing phenomenon, increasing in magnitude during the course of the frequent wars and diminishing in the intervals between them (appendix 2.1.3). A new major (high-fatality) war begins, on average, once in every 10 years within the temperate habitat (table 1.14), and a new minor one at least annually. Many of the major and some of the minor ones are highly disruptive of the environment. Thumb-nail sketches of a selection of 18 ecologically disruptive temperate-habitat wars are included by way of example in table 1.2.

This section gives accounts of the impact of warfare on temperate vegetation, with special emphasis on the forests of France during World Wars I and II and on agricultural crops. These accounts are followed by discussions of the impact of war on temperate wildlife and on man; then follow discussions of post-war recovery and other aspects of the inter-war periods. Since the character and magnitude of impact of the weapons and means of warfare themselves have been described elsewhere in some detail (SIPRI, 1976; 1977), they are not dealt with here.

Before the effects of war are described, however, it should be mentioned that the testing of military hardware and its subsequent use during training exercises and routine peace-time patrolling all result in environmental debilitations. Some such disruptions are of a local nature, whereas others are regional or even global in their impact. The testing of nuclear weapons is a notorious case in point (Russell *et al.*, 1966; UNSCEAR, 1972). Moreover, there have occurred a series of worrisome accidents involving nuclear weapons during routine peace-time military activities (*SIPRI Yearbook 1977:* chap. 3).

Maintaining a military posture can result in all sorts of odd environmental problems. For example, the US Navy has now for some years been planning to construct an immense extremely-low-frequency (ELF) radio transmission antenna somewhere within the conterminous USA so as to establish more reliable means of communication with its submarine fleet (McClintock *et al.*, 1971; McClintock & Scott, 1974; Wait, 1972). The antenna (originally known as Project Sanguine, but now as Project Seafarer) would, in one of its more modest versions, consist of a buried grid covering about 1.6 million hectares and drawing about 30 megawatts of power. It appears possible that the electromagnetic field generated by such an antenna could exert a subtly adverse effect on the exposed fauna (including man) within this huge area (Libber & Rozzell, 1972; Gavalas-Medici & Day-Magdaleno, 1976). One example of such an effect seems to be the disruption of the orientational ability in birds (Southern, 1975; Larkin & Sutherland, 1977).

Woody vegetation

In time of war, the vegetation is subject to severe abuse both on and off the battlefield. Whereas at least a rough estimate of damage can be made for forest trees, it is not readily feasible to attempt this for the remaining wild flora. This is an unfortunate circumstance, since an estimate restricted to such tree damage will ignore most of the taxonomic categories of extant vegetation. On the other hand, for many of the sites of interest in the present context, a forest-tree analysis will account for almost all of the vegetational biomass, indeed, for almost all of the entire biomass, both plant and animal (appendix 2.2).

The vegetation in a theatre of war can suffer either direct battle damage (i.e., that resulting from so-called hostile action) or else various forms of indirect damage. For example, Germany is said to have ruthlessly exploited the timber resource during World War II in those portions of Europe that it occupied, including France (Kernan, 1945), Poland (UN War Crimes Commission, 1948: 496), and the Netherlands (Aartsen, 1946). However, the expropriation of forest resources for military purposes need not await a time of war, nor is it a modern innovation. Albion (1962: chap. 6–7) has described in vivid detail the exploitation of North American forests by the British during the eighteenth century for naval construction (cf. also Pollitt, 1971–1972). This so-called Broad Arrow policy of the British was a major contributing factor in bringing about the US War of Independence of 1775–1783. As another example, the forests of Lebanon—including the renowned cedars (*Cedrus lebani*; Pinaceae)—were able to withstand the depredations of mankind through the millennia until World War I, when Turkey ravished them to the point of no return, primarily as fuel for its railway system (Winters, 1974: 108, 117, 132).

During time of war, moreover, a nation is likely to relax its own domestic standards of forest conservation. Such relaxation on the part of the USA during World War II was forcefully pointed out by Ward (1943), who noted a sacrifice to the war effort of the normal conservation standards (see also Steen, 1977: chap. 10). The indirect impact of war on British forests has been described for both World War I (Ridsdale, 1919*d*; Schlich, 1915) and World War II (House, 1965). The considerable indirect impact of these two wars on French forests is included in the information presented below.

Forest trees. France was for protracted periods during both World Wars I and II either the site of battle or else a nation suffering the indignities of military occupation. It is generally accepted that the forests of France were subjected to severe damage during both of these wars, indeed, in each case the worst experienced by any European nation (appendix 2.2). The forests of France covered about 11 million hectares, that is, about 20 per cent of the nation's land surface (table 2.2), a value that has remained fairly constant throughout at least the present century. These forest lands did not quite suffice to meet France's domestic timber demand.

During World War I (table 1.2.16), the battle areas and occupied zones of France are estimated to have included about 600 thousand hectares of forest, that is, about five per cent of the total forest lands (Ridsdale, 1919*b*). Of this area, some 200 thousand hectares were damaged sufficiently to require artificial reforestation. Moreover, an additional 100 thousand hectares of agricultural lands were so devastated that it was at the time considered necessary to plant them to trees as well.

The annual pre-war forest growth of France—and also its annual harvest—had been about 25 million cubic metres (with an additional 2 million cubic metres imported annually to satisfy the remaining national needs) (Graves, 1918). The allowable cut during the four years of World War I thus approximated 100 million cubic metres. This value was, however, greatly exceeded, owing largely to the war effort. In fact, during the war an estimated total of 18 million cubic metres was destroyed by military operations, and an additional 145 million cubic metres was harvested (Ridsdale, 1919*c*). This immense harvest can be broken down as follows: only 12 million cubic metres was cut by the French during these four years for civil purposes; another 22 million cubic metres was cut by or at the behest of the occupying Germans; and fully 111 million cubic metres was cut by the Allied forces for their military purposes.

With barely sufficient time to have recovered from the depredations of World War I, the forests of France became embroiled in World War II (table 1.2.18) to experience a second series of losses roughly comparable to those of the previous war. Direct military action during World War II—via bombing, shelling, burning, clearing, and so forth—was estimated to have severely damaged about 400 thousand hectares of forest, that is, about four per cent of the total forested portion of France (Kernan, 1945). Furthermore, forest fires that could be indirectly attributed to the war during the four years of German occupation accounted for severe damage to about 100 thousand hectares, that is, to another one per cent of the forest lands. Additional problems were caused by flying metal fragments ('shrapnel') embedded in standing trees, by uncleared minefields, by damage to woods, roads and bridges, and by accelerated soil erosion.

Moreover, during the occupation of France in World War II, cutting was, by German decree, increased by more than 50 per cent, thereby exceeding the annual increment by that amount. Thus, in this war, the nation's forest growing stock was again seriously depleted—in fact, by an amount similar to that in World War I. It was estimated at the end of World War II that a 20 per cent reduction in post-war cutting for a period of five years would be required to restore the pre-war status of France's forest resource. Such a restriction is, of course, an especially severe blow in view of the added demand inevitably associated with post-war reconstruction activities. It may be noted here that Frances's immediate post-war agricultural and industrial productivities were about 29 and 46 per cent, respectively, below the pre-war levels (table 2.3).

This section can be aptly concluded with the lament of a forester witnessing the impact of World War I:

Of all the injuries that are inflicted upon nature by war, forest destruction is one of the heaviest and most worthy of complaints. . . . In any case, destroyed forests . . . must be tended with total effort for many years, often decades, until you can half-way celebrate their recovery and until you have completely healed the damage and devastation. (Translated from Mammen, 1916: 45–46)

Agricultural crops

The destruction of an adversary's crops for military purposes is probably as old as war itself. As recorded in the Old Testament, Philistine crops—corn, grapes, and olives—appear to have been destroyed by Israelite opponents as long ago as the twelfth century BC (Judg. 15: 3–5). Half a millennium later, Herodotus tells us that when the Scythians retreated before the Persian army of Darius the Great around 512 BC, they withdrew, "choking up all the wells and springs as they retreated, and leaving the whole country bare of forage . . . destroying all that grew on the ground . . . the land being waste and barren . . ." (table 1.2.1). In the same era, Thucydides explains that the Spartans, in their lengthy pursuit of destroying Athens in the Peloponnesian War of 431–404 BC, repeatedly attacked the enemy just before harvest time so as to gain the added advantage of destroying the annual grain crop before it could be reaped. Such 'ravaging' and 'laying waste' of the land was chronicled by Thucydides for at least the fourth, fifth, seventh, and nineteenth years of this protracted conflict (table 1.2.2).

One can then leap ahead some 16 centuries to the incursions of Genghis Khan (table 1.2.6). In conquering Cathay (now northern China) around AD 1214, Genghis was said to wage war *à outrance* where "everything in the open country was annihilated or driven-off—crops trampled and burned, herds taken up . . ." (Lamb, 1927: 92–93). Again, several years later, in overrunning what is now Afghanistan and thereabouts, Genghis and his soldiers conquered one region after another and "trampled and burned whatever crops might be left standing so that those who escaped their swords would starve to death" (Lamb, 1927: 159). As part of his subjugation of Mesopotamia (now Iraq) to the west, Genghis deliberately set out to destroy the irrigation works of the Tigris River, upon which the indigenous civilization depended for its agriculture (Carter & Dale, 1974: 49).

In the wake of this long military tradition, the USA has since its very inception also routinely resorted to enemy food denial and destruction in all of its various conflicts. This policy was also adopted by the American colonists—for example, as early as 1629, according to a contemporary account, the Virginia colonists maintained the peace with hostile Indians "by our continuall incursions upon . . . them, by yearly cutting downe, and spoiling their corne" (Jennings, 1975: 153).

In what has been considered the most carefully planned campaign of the US War of Independence of 1775–1783, George Washington directed Major General John Sullivan to mount an elaborate 'search-and-destroy' operation against the Six Nations of Iroquois in northern New York, a primary aim of which was crop destruction (Graymont, 1972: chap. 8). The mission was accomplished in the late summer and early autumn of 1779. Among the Iroquois it has earned Washington the lasting epithet of 'Destroyer'. It is ironic that at essentially the same time as Washington was planning his mission of agricultural devastation he stated:

The more I am acquainted with agricultural affairs, the better I am pleased with them; insomuch, that I can no where find so great satisfaction as in those innocent and useful pursuits. In indulging these feelings, I am led to reflect how much more delightful to an undebauched mind is the task of making improvements on the earth, than all the vain glory which can be acquired from ravaging it. . . . (Washington, 1788: 13)

The subjugation of the Indians by the USA during the nineteenth century consistently involved the destruction of the natural resources upon which they depended for their sustenance. Regarding food or crop destruction by the US Army during the Indian wars, Robert M. Utley, Chief Historian of the US National Park Service, concludes:

. . . this was a conscious policy from beginning to end. It was not so successful in the Trans-Mississippi West . . . as in the East because most of the western tribes were nomadic or seminomadic. Nevertheless, whenever the Army succeeded in capturing a village, the food stores, along with all other contents, were invariably put to the torch. The best-known crop destruction was in the Navajo Wars of 1860–63. . . . Some of the Arizona Apache groups grew corn, which the Army burned wherever found. After the Civil War food destruction became part of the 'total war' philosophy of Generals [William Tecumseh] Sherman and [Philip Henry] Sheridan, who had practiced it so successfully in Georgia and Virginia against the Confederates. (Private correspondence of 5 September 1975)

In the Navaho Wars of 1860–1864 alluded to above, the USA in 1864 finally eliminated the Navahos as a viable enemy—indeed, as a functional society—by the systematic destruction of all their sheep and other livestock and of all their orchards and crop plantations (table 1.2.11).

In the US Civil War of 1861–1865, one of Abraham Lincoln's major strategies was to starve the Confederacy into submission (table 1.2.12). This deliberate and fairly successful Union attempt to deny sustenance to the Southern military forces and civil population alike was accomplished through blockade, interdiction of transportation (disruption of railways, etc.), tying up of manpower, and continuing destruction of crops, food stores, and farm machinery (Gates, 1965: 92–94, etc.). One of that war's most notable campaigns was Sherman's 'march to the sea' of 1864 (Liddell-Hart, 1929: chap. 20; Walters, 1973: chap. 8). During that operation, this highly successful Union general laid waste much of the land in Georgia between Atlanta and Savannah, some four million hectares in all. All crops and food supplies encountered along the way were either confiscated or destroyed so as to make, according to Sherman himself, "old and young, rich and poor, feel the hard hand of war as well as their organized armies" (Liddell-Hart, 1929: 358).

In justification of a similar operation carried out a few weeks earlier in the Shenandoah Valley of Virginia (Kellogg, 1903: chap. 11–12; Stackpole, 1961), General Philip Henry Sheridan (1888: I: 487–488) later explained:

I do not hold war to mean simply that lines of men shall engage each other in battle, and material interests ignored. This is a duel, in which one combatant seeks the other's life; war means much more, and is far worse than this. Those who rest at home in peace and plenty see but little of the horrors attending such a duel, and even grow indifferent to them as the struggle goes on, contenting themselves with encouraging all who are able-bodied to enlist in the cause, to fill up the shattered ranks as death thins them. It is another matter, however, when deprivation and suffering are brought to their own doors. Then the case appears much graver, for the loss of property weighs heavily with most of mankind; heavier often, than the sacrifices made on the field of battle. Death is popularly considered the maximum punishment in war, but it is not; reduction to poverty brings prayers for peace more surely and more quickly than does the destruction of human life, as the selfishness of man has demonstrated in more than one great conflict.

During the Second Anglo-Boer War of 1899–1902, the Boers destroyed large areas of veldt (grassland) in South Africa so as to deny the British forces a source of forage for their livestock (Wet, 1902: 181).

During both World Wars I and II, the Allies devoted considerable energy to starving their adversaries (table 1.2.16 and 18). Although blockading was in each case one of the major strategies employed to this end, more direct approaches were also employed (Mudge, 1969–1970). For example, during World War II the Allies made substantial attempts early on to destroy German grain fields via incendiary attack (Björnerstedt *et al.*, 1973: 46; SIPRI, 1975 *b*: 82). (On the other hand, it was decided not to attempt the chemical destruction of crops in the Japanese homeland, Admiral William Leahy (1950: 440) having advised the US President that "this would violate every Christian ethic I have ever heard of and all of the known laws of war".) Germany, in turn, became notorious during its occupation of the Netherlands for ruining in 1944 some 200 thousand hectares, or about 17 per cent, of that nation's productive farm land via salt-water inundation (Aartsen, 1946; Dorsman, 1947; Kolko, 1968), and again that year for its scorched earth tactics in northern Norway (as described in chapter 5, section IV).

During the Korean War of 1950–1953, the USA directed some of its most successful air attacks against North Korea's major irrigation dams (table 1.2.19). These were carried out for the expressly stated purpose of disrupting that nation's production of its staple food of rice (*Air University Quarterly Review*, 1953–1954; Futrell *et al.*, 1961: 627–628; Rees, 1964: 381–382). A second stated purpose of these attacks was to warn any future Asian enemies of their vulnerability in this respect.

The catalogue of wars in which agricultural lands were devastated, whether by intent or otherwise, could be extended almost indefinitely. The rehabilitation and rate of recovery of these lands are discussed in a subsequent section.

Wildlife

Warfare can have a variety of effects on animals, ranging from intentional to unintentional, from direct to indirect, and from favourable to unfavourable. The emphasis here is on mammalian wildlife; the effect of war on man as a species forms the subject of the next section.

Some animal fatalities can be attributed to the same agents that bring about human casualties in a theatre of war. Specifically, these might include pattern bombing of a rural area, the employment of concussion bombs, wide-area incendiary attack, or the use of chemical agents. There might also be some intentional destruction of animals by the military—for example, of birds so as to reduce the hazards of taking off and landing at airfields, or of rodents as a public health measure. There can also be incidental loss of animal life associated with military training exercises, such as practice bombing and shelling, or with the testing of weapons. The most serious impact of military activities on the fauna is often not direct, being caused rather via their effect on the faunal habitat.

The case of the European buffalo or wisent (*Bison bonasus bonasus;* Bovidae) is an especially poignant one (Browne, 1975; Curry-Lindahl, 1972: 123; Fisher *et al.,* 1969: 143–145; Ziswiler, 1967: 86–87). Already dangerously low in numbers at the start of the twentieth century, and its range having been reduced to parts of Eastern Europe, the wisent was brought close to extinction through direct and indirect adversities which befell it during World War I. The animals were avidly hunted for food by the German forces operating in the region, and their habitat was destroyed by the intensive tree-felling carried out by these forces. Post-war human endeavours barely rescued the species from oblivion, only for it to be virtually wiped out again during World War II. However, vigorous efforts since then by a group of dedicated zoologists seem to have succeeded in turning the tide once again for this animal. In fact, today more than one thousand of these wild beasts roam the 12 000-hectare Bialowieza forest reserve in eastern Poland, and they appear to be out of danger, at least for the present.

The only remaining more or less wild individuals of Père David's deer (*Elaphurus davidianus,* Cervidae) were killed off by the foreign troops in China during the Boxer Rebellion of 1898–1900, although the species survives in captivity (Curry-Lindahl, 1972: 122–123; Fisher *et al.,* 1969: 132–133). Swayne's hartebeest (*Alcelaphus buselaphus swaynei,* Bovidae) was extirpated from Somalia by the military forces of both sides during a series of uprisings against the British early in the century (Fisher *et al.,* 1969: 156, 159). A few hundred individuals survive in Ethiopia. The case of the Cyprus mouflon (*Ovis orientalis ophion,* Bovidae), also in danger of extinction for military reasons, is summarized in chapter 6 (section IV).

The large amount of traffic incidental to military activities serves well to disseminate animal (and plant) life. For example, a number of agricultural pests are said to have been introduced into Italy as a result of World War II, and were certainly permitted to spread unhindered during that time (Tirelli, 1949). The moth *Hyphantria cunea* (Arctiidae), which in its larval stage defoliates a number of horticulturally and ornamentally valuable trees, was introduced and allowed to spread widely during World War II (Elton, 1958: 60). Moreover, the micro-organisms responsible for various human diseases have in the past become widely disseminated during wartime—a matter touched upon in the next section. Indeed, it has been stressed by Elton (1958) that once a habitat has been significantly disturbed, its invasion sooner or later by foreign plant and animal species—often considered weeds or pests—is essentially inevitable.

Human preoccupation with military activities can be beneficial to certain animals because of reduced hunting pressures. For example, in Norway during World War II, various predators—including bears (*Ursus arctos,* Ursidae), foxes (*Vulpes vulpes,* Canidae), wolves (Canis lupus, Canidae), and wolverines (*Gulo gulo,* Mustelidae)—increased in numbers and in geographical extent during the German occupation because the local population was deprived of firearms (*Ukens Nytt fra Norge,* 1943). Although not relating to a temperate region, the fact may also be mentioned here that the population on Guam of the introduced sambar deer (*Rusa unicolor,* Cervidae) increased during the early 1940s owing to reduced hunting pressures during the Japanese occupation (Baker, 1946). Similar examples dealing with the marine fishery are presented in chapter 7 (section IV).

The several beneficial effects of war upon faunal populations notwithstanding, the most usual impact is, of course, an adverse one. Animal population numbers (i.e., population densities) will be reduced in part by direct fatalities, although more often largely as the result of destroyed habitat. Indeed, some species might as a result even be extirpated from the theatre of war, especially if the theatre were somehow geographically isolated—for example, if it were an island (a matter developed more fully in chapter 6, section IV). Finally, under special circumstances a species could be totally eliminated, particularly if it were already an endangered species relatively close to extinction.

Man

The impact of war on man *per se* is only a peripheral aspect of the present work. This section (together with the complementary one in the next chapter) will thus serve primarily to suggest the parameters of this interaction.

The most obvious effect of war on the human species consists in the fatalities incurred (appendix 2.3.1). Questions that arise in this context range from whether it is likely or even possible that war fatalities will lead to the extinction of *Homo sapiens* to whether they will lead to other less drastic species debilitations, or possibly even to beneficial effects. Although the many millions of human deaths that can be attributed to the countless wars of the past have not endangered the survival of the species, it is now finally within human capability to accomplish this via a large-scale 'dirty' nuclear war (SIPRI, 1977: chap. 1).

The relatively low proportion of the world's population that is killed by even a major conflict would suggest a minimal overall adverse effect on the human species. As the extreme example to date, World War II with its estimated 51 million fatalities (appendix 1.3) claimed only about two per cent of the world population of the time, that is, just twice the annual population increment of that period. In a perverse way, such mortality could even be construed to be advantageous to the extent to which it might be counteracting world-wide population growth. On the other hand, although war may have a straightforward effect on the death rate of the group involved, its effect on this group's overall populational growth rate cannot be derived from that statistic. This is the case because changes in the direction and magnitude of the birth rate during and at the end of wartime are unpredictable.

The impact of even a low level of mortality could be subtly magnified if the group killed were in some fashion a non-random sample of the species. Indeed, this is likely to occur in a number of ways. For example, the direct military battle deaths of a war largely comprise young adult males. As a second example, civilian deaths, especially when they result largely from indirect causes, include a disproportionately high number of infants, aged, and sick. Or a war might result in the severe reduction or even annihilation of some particular racial subgroup of the human species. It must be noted also that wars have always favoured outbreeding through the uprooting of endemic populations and via other populational movements. The seriousness of the effects of these and other war-related factors on the population-genetic and evolutionary processes of the human species have long been matters for study and debate. They are not further explored here (see appendix 2.3.2). Also avoided completely here is the question of whether during the course of evolution there have been selective pressures in favour of martial propensities or abilities. Finally, it can be added parenthetically that the decimation of a particular subgroup of the human species— whether "national, ethnical, racial or religious"—is a sufficiently repugnant act on the one hand and a sufficiently likely one on the other to have elicited the Genocide Convention (table 8.4.6) meant to prevent this from being repeated in the future.

The most obvious effects of warfare on humans beyond the direct killings already mentioned are the non-fatal maimings and other injuries and the multifarious diseases sustained by both soldiers and civilians. Warfare and disease have always been inseparably linked (appendix 2.3.3). Indeed, World War II appears to have been the first major war in history in which direct military casualties outnumbered the indirect medical ones for some—but by no means all—of the armies involved.

Serious as disease is for the military personnel in a theatre of war, it is almost always an even graver problem for the enmeshed civil population. Not only are the civilians of a nation accorded a lower priority status than its soldiers regarding allocations of foodstuffs, medicines, and medical personnel, but under many military conditions they may—as was previously shown—actually have their food supplies confiscated, blockaded, or destroyed by the enemy forces. Military food denial can lead to large numbers of deaths simply through starvation. For example, many thousands of Russians starved to death during the German siege of Leningrad in World War II (Pavlov, 1955; Salisbury, 1969).

Sublethal food shortages create or exacerbate numerous medical problems (Ingersoll, 1965). Not only is malnutrition known to cause lowered resistance to disease, but it also results in a number of deficiency diseases that are especially serious for growing children. Malnutrition in children leads not only to these somatic diseases, but moreover to lack of energy, increased restlessness, and various sorts of depressed levels of intellectual functioning that are in part permanent (Birch & Gussow, 1970; Blanton, 1919; Hurley, 1969; Scrimshaw & Gordon, 1968; Winick *et al.,* 1975). The last-mentioned states include diminished attention span, slower comprehension, and poorer memory. (Indeed, certain animal experiments suggest that it might even be possible that such mental impairments are subsequently passed on to the next, albeit adequately fed, generation (Zamenhof *et al.,* 1971).)

The frequencies of stillbirths, premature births, and neonatal deaths are all known to rise during wartime, owing to malnutrition and other traumas of war (Antonov, 1947; Stein *et al.,* 1972; 1975). The frequency of birth defects also rises during wartime (Eichmann & Gesenius, 1952; Stott, 1962). On the other hand, prenatal exposure to severe famine caused by war does not seem to impair subsequent mental performance—as determined at the stage of young adulthood—presumably owing to *in utero* priority of nourishment to the foetus (Stein *et al.,* 1972; 1975).

There are a number of reasons for the greatly multiplied disease problems associated with wartime conditions. In addition to the malnutrition already noted, these include the breakdown of routine sanitation and other public health services; paucity of physicians, nurses, and other medical-care personnel; shortages of drugs, dressings, and other medical supplies; and inadequate hospital facilities. In fact, hospitals and medical supplies have become routine military targets, at least for some armies. Also important are the human migrations and concourses—both military and civil—which are inevitably associated with wars. Such dislocations and crowded conditions not only bring about exposure to novel diseases for which the body is unprepared, but also facilitate their spread from individual to individual. Another major reason for increased problems of disease in war is the environmental disruption associated with military activities. Ecological upheavals of this kind frequently lead to more favourable habitat conditions for rats and a number of other important disease vectors.

The frequency of psychiatric disorders can also be expected to increase as a result of certain wartime situations, especially when there is long-drawn-out uncertainty about the future or when there is a breakdown of social structure. And there is a unique set of psychiatric and other medical problems of long duration that is associated with nuclear attack (Okada *et al.,* 1975).

In closing this section it must at least be noted that military activities influence human beings not only during wartime but also in the intervals between the wars—a subject which is touched upon in chapter 8 (section II). The most obvious and straightforward of these influences is exerted upon those engaged in military occupations. Thus, about 19 million people in the temperate habitat are continuously under arms—that is, almost one per cent of the total population of this region (table 1.13). A substantial number of civilians—somewhat greater than the number of soldiers—are also employed in military activities, several hundred thousand of these being scientists or engineers (Dolgu *et al.*, 1978: 28–29, 46). Indeed, of the order of one out of every four scientists in the temperate-habitat nations is engaged in military activities.

Recovery

Recovery of a war-disrupted temperate ecosystem occurs in due course, the speed of such recovery being dependent upon a number of factors. Important among these, beyond the type of ecosystem itself, are the severity of disruption, its areal extent, and subsequent human manipulations. The mechanism of recovery (known as ecological succession) has been described in chapter 1 (section III). Initial recovery, that is, establishment of the pioneer stage in succession, often takes only a few growing seasons (appendix 2.4). However, the time-span necessary for the full natural recovery of a severely disrupted temperate grassland ecosystem is of the order of several or more decades, and that of a forest ecosystem, several centuries.

The recovery of war-disrupted agricultural lands depends upon the severity of disruption on the one hand, and upon the degree of human effort expended in the rehabilitation process on the other. To a large extent, there is nothing esoteric about the actions that might be taken (appendix 2.4.2). Thus, craters can be filled in by hand or—if available and if the terrain will support it—with heavy mechanized equipment. Erosion can be brought under control by a variety of standard mechanical and vegetational techniques of long standing. Soil nutrients can be replenished by the establishment of leguminous cover crops and the application of fertilizers, both organic and inorganic. Old drainage patterns can be re-established, levees and dikes rebuilt, and irrigation systems restored. And orchard trees or other perennial crop plants can be replanted.

On the other hand, a variety of factors obstruct such efforts at reclamation. Chief among these can be the extensiveness of the disruption and the paucity of available human and material resources. The population can be enfeebled for a time by death, disease, and malnutrition. The residuum of unexploded munitions can present another major obstacle to agricultural (and other rural) reconstruction (Red Cross, 1973: chap. 5; SIPRI, 1978 *a*: chap. 7). Indeed, unexploded munitions can be one of the most serious legacies of a war. Many booby traps, mines and other time-delay weapons are likely to be left to remain in place after a war ends. To these must be added the expended bombs, artillery and mortar shells, rockets, and grenades that fail to detonate at the time they are used—the so-called duds. Although an undetermined fraction of these sundry unexploded munitions will never detonate, some remain dangerous for decades. World War II munitions, for example, continue to take their occasional toll (AP, 1974). Indeed, some of the dud shells and grenades that remain from the Battle of Verdun in 1914 are considered to this day to result in *danger de mort,* according to signs posted on portions of the old battlefield (*Life,* 1964). Other special forms of horrible legacies can be left by biological or nuclear attack (SIPRI, 1977).

Returning now to the question of how long agricultural recovery might take following war damage, it is important to reiterate that many variables and uncertainties are involved. These include not only the pre-war conditions and the character and level of wartime damage, but also the resources allocated to such reconstruction, both indigenous and those derived from foreign aid (to say nothing regarding the criteria of damage and recovery or of the reliability of the data employed). Nonetheless, some information from World War II experience can be provided to serve as some indication of what might be expected in this regard.

Examined here is the agricultural productivity of a group of 10 nations that were embroiled in World War II (table 2.2). It is a somewhat haphazard group, comprising all those nations for which the relevant information has been compiled by the United Nations. Examined in particular are the magnitude of war-related depression in agricultural production and the rate of post-war recovery. This group of nations had a mid-war combined population of perhaps 300 million people and a combined area of about 260 million hectares, of which roughly 89 million hectares were in agricultural use. A total of 17 million of these people (military plus civil) were killed during the war—that is, six per cent of the combined population (appendix 1.3.1).

World War II appears to have been responsible for a 38 per cent depression in agricultural production for the group of 10 nations as a whole (table 2.3). Recovery from this set-back during the post-war years was essentially linear with time, the appropriate linear least-squares regression analysis having a coefficient of determination (r^2) of 0.982. Agricultural recovery progressed at an average annual rate of 8.3 per cent. As a result, the pre-war level of agricultural production was regained after an average of 4.6 years. (By way of comparison, a composite of neutral Portugal, Sweden, and Switzerland had a post-war level of agricultural production equivalent to the pre-war level, and a linear post-war increase of only 2.8 per cent per year.)

The time-span required for recovery of agricultural production by the 10 individual nations was found to be directly proportional to the extent of the set-back ($r^2 = 0.481$; significant by 't' test at the 5 per cent level). Each additional increment of post-war depression of 9.5 per cent necessitated another year of recovery time. The time-span required for agricultural recovery appeared to be adversely influenced by—or, at any rate, correlated with—the national proportions of war-caused fatalities, the length of recovery period being directly proportional to the percentage of fatalities (r^2 = 0.413; significant at the 5 per cent level). Each additional increment of wartime fatalities of 4.4 per cent was associated with another year of recovery time. On the other hand, a nation's agricultural recovery time was found not to be correlated with either its agricultural area per capita or with its population density.

It is also of interest to compare a nation's agricultural recovery time with its industrial recovery time. The post-war depression in industrial production for the group of 10 nations under study averaged 54 per cent, and was thus rather more severe than the comparable value noted above for agricultural production (table 2.3). As with agriculture, post-war industrial recovery was essentially linear with time (r^2 = 0.993), but, in fact, proceeded twice as rapidly, averaging 17.2 per cent per year. Indeed, the pre-war level of industrial production was regained by the group after an average of only 3.2 years—and thus 1.4 years earlier than agricultural production, despite the greater initial set-back.

A final word of caution is necessary regarding the agricultural set-back and recovery data presented above. These data refer to overall agricultural production—a value determined only in part by the productivity status of the land itself, and in further part by the availability of manpower, farm implements, livestock, fuel, and so forth.

V. Conclusion

A substantial fraction of the world-wide temperate habitat has been modified drastically in the past in order to suit human needs and desires. Forest and grass lands have been cleared, swamps drained, rivers re-routed or dammed, and wildlife exterminated. Indeed, truly vast areas have been converted during the past thousand years or more to farms, cities, highways, and other human uses. Very little of the temperate habitat remains in the natural state. On the other hand, the taming process has slowed down considerably in recent decades and has even begun to reverse itself here and there. For example, the global extent of temperate forest lands—although reduced by perhaps two-thirds to three-quarters since primeval times—now appears to be essentially stable.

The major current environmental problems of the temperate habitat are an outgrowth of its developed—one should say overdeveloped—society. Both agriculture and industry have become highly mechanized and energy-intensive in a number of the world's nations, almost all of which are located within the temperate zone. These activities not only consume vast amounts of fuel and other raw materials at great environmental cost, but also produce inordinate amounts of waste products that further pollute and debilitate the environment. Carbon dioxide, perhaps the most dangerous of these pollutants in the long run, threatens to alter the global heat balance, with unpredictable consequences for man and nature.

The enormous annual military expenditures by the USA and the USSR, together with the military expenditures of the other temperate nations, contribute continuously to the environmental degradation just noted, owing, *inter alia,* to the natural resources thereby consumed and the pollution thus generated. Indeed, with all of the world's major powers located within the temperate habitat, it is not surprising that fully 90 per cent of global military expenditures are currently incurred by the temperate nations (table 8.1). The USSR and the USA together currently account for 57 per cent of them, and the top half dozen (the USSR, the USA, China, FR Germany, France, and the UK) currently account for 75 per cent (Westing, 1978 *b*). The routine abuses of the environment resulting from these expenditures are, of course, punctuated rather frequently by wars that serve to disrupt the theatres of operation still more severely.

Table 2.1. Temperate habitat: distribution and demography (1975 data)[a]

Region	Temperate area $10^3 km^2$ $(10^5 ha)$	Proportion of regional area per cent	Temperate population[b] 10^6	Proportion of regional population per cent	Temperate population density No./km²
Land mass					
North America	15 029	68.9	240.6	76.4	16.0
South America	3 277	18.4	48.1	22.3	14.7
Africa	3 027	10.2	90.0	23.0	29.7
Europe	9 705	96.6	479.3	100.0	49.4
Asia	23 051	55.5	1 316.6	59.4	57.1
Australia	1 153	15.0	10.8	80.0	9.4
Antarctica	0	0	0	0	0
Islands	983	13.5	174.3	40.2	177.2
of Atlantic Ocean	342	49.7	60.3	68.8	176.0
of Pacific Ocean	641	17.2	114.0	33.9	177.9
of Indian Ocean	0	0	0	0	0
of Arctic Ocean	0	0	0	0	0
Hemisphere					
Northern	50 290	49.6	2 270.7	62.5	45.2
Southern	5 395	12.5	89.0	20.7	15.0
World-wide	**56 225**	**37.8**	**2 359.7**	**58.1**	**42.0**

Sources and notes:
[a]The regions, which are strictly geographic, are described in table 1.4, note *a*. Sources for the areas and populations are given in table 1.4, note *b*.
[b]The population of the temperate habitat is currently increasing at the rate of 1.21 per cent per year (table 1.4), which leads to a population doubling time of 57.4 years.

Table 2.2. A group of nations involved in World War II: geographic profile

Nation	Area[a] 10^3ha (10 km²)	Mid-war popu- lation[b] 10^3	Mid-war density of popu- lation No./km²	Agri- cultural land[c] 10^3 ha	Agri- cultural land per capita ha	Grass- land[c] 10^3 ha	Forest land[c] 10^3 ha
Austria	8 385	6 880	82	1 840	0.267	2 316	3 061
Czechoslovakia	12 783	13 670	107	5 512	0.403	2 027	4 066
Finland	33 701	3 730	11	2 427	0.651	409	21 660
France	55 099	41 260	75	20 976	0.508	12 302	11 100
Germany	35 344	66 920	189	13 827	0.207	6 987	9 960
Greece	13 256	7 200	54	3 389	0.471	5 093	1 918
Italy	30 102	43 680	145	16 986	0.389	5 154	5 617
Japan	36 859	72 540	197	5 907	0.081	934	24 517
Netherlands	3 373	9 010	267	1 179	0.131	1 222	242
Poland	31 173	34 360	110	16 824	0.490	4 040	6 909
Composite	**26 008**	**29 925**	**115**	**8 887**	**0.297**	**4 048**	**8 905**

Sources and notes:
[a]Areas are taken from the *UN Statistical Yearbook 1949–50:* table 1.
[b]Populations are derived from the *UN Statistical Yearbook 1948:* table 1, being the average of the populations given for mid-1937 and mid-1946.
[c]Agricultural, grass, and forest land areas are from the *FAO Yearbook of Food and Agricultural Statistics: Production, 1949:* table 1 (the earliest year-book to provide these data). The present agricultural land category is FAO's 'arable' plus 'orchard'; the present grassland category is FAO's permanent 'meadow' plus 'pasture'; and the present forest land category is FAO's 'forest' plus 'woodland'.

Table 2.3. Impact of and recovery from World War II

Nation[a]	Pro- portion killed[b] per cent	Post-war agri- cultural production[c] per cent of pre-war	Rate of agri- cultural recovery[c] per cent per year	Post-war industrial production[d] per cent of pre-war	Rate of industrial recovery[d] per cent per year
Austria	5.4	60	5.9	0	26.5
Czechoslovakia	3.1	52	7.5	64	12.0
Finland	1.6	70	9.7	91	14.1
France	1.6	71	6.9	54	16.1
Germany, FR[e]	9.3	54	8.8	10	18.5
Greece	2.9	55	14.6	43	14.9
Italy	1.7	78	6.3	82	5.5
Japan	2.8	67	5.5	22	10.5
Netherlands	2.6	75	9.7	43	22.9
Poland	17.5	42	7.8	50	30.7
Composite[f]	**5.7**	**62**	**8.3**	**46**	**17.2**

Sources and notes:
[a]Basic geographic information on these nations is provided in table 2.2.
[b]The fatality data are taken from appendix 1.3.1.
[c]The agricultural production statistics presented here for both post-war status and recovery are calculated from the raw data on 'all commodities' provided in several of the *UN Statistical Yearbooks (UNSYB)*. The post-war production status for each nation was obtained by deriving a least-squares linear regression equation of annual status versus time for it for the period

1946–1951, and then solving for mid-1945. The rate of recovery for each nation was taken from the slope of its curve. The data for 1946 are from *UNSYB 1951:* table 12 (except for Poland's, which is from *UNSYB 1948:* table 12); the data for 1947–1949 are taken from *UNSYB 1952:* table 9; the data for 1949/50 are taken from *UNSYB 1953:* table 9; and the data for 1950/51 are taken from *UNSYB 1954:* table 10. The agricultural production data are given in comparison with an average of the years 1934–38.

*d*The industrial production statistics presented here for both post-war status and recovery are calculated from the raw data on 'general' industry provided in several of the *UN Statistical Yearbooks (UNSYB)*. The post-war production status for each nation was obtained by deriving a least-squares linear regression equation of annual status versus time for it for the period 1945–1949, and then solving for mid-1945. The rate of recovery for each nation was taken from the slope of its curve. All of the data, that is, for 1945–1949, are from *UNSYB 1949–50:* table 39 (except for Poland's 1945 value, which is from *UNSYB 1948:* table 36). The industrial production data are given in comparison with the year 1937, except for those of Germany, which are given in comparison with 1938.

*e*The data for FR Germany stem from the US and British Zones only, except for the fatality value, which refers to the whole of Germany.

*f*The 'composite' calculations are determined by regression analysis, as above, based on summations of the raw data of the 10 nations.

Appendix 2.1

Sources for the temperate habitat

1. *Environment and ecology.* Spurr & Barnes (1973) provide an excellent overview of temperate forest ecology; Likens *et al.* (1977) present an analysis of a forested watershed (catchment). For grassland ecology, see Spedding (1971) and Carpenter (1940). For a description of the temperate environment and the plants and animals it supports, see Cloudsley-Thompson (1975: chap. 6–8); for a similar treatment restricted to North America, see Shelford (1963). Temperate soils are covered by Buckman & Brady (1969) and by Lutz & Chandler (1946).

2. *Civil use and abuse.* The geography of the temperate regions of the world is well described by Heintzelman & Highsmith (1973: part 3). Temperate forest management is covered by Smith (1962) and by Davis (1966); range management by Heady (1975) and by Stoddart *et al.* (1975); and game management by Leopold (1933) and by Allen (1962). For abuse of the temperate habitat, see Ehrlich *et al.* (1977), Ehrenfeld (1972), and Dasmann (1972), among numerous others.

3. *Military use and abuse.* Martin (1973) discusses the strategy of modern defence, Perlmutter (1977) the political role of the military sector, and Hanning (1967) the civil uses of military forces. As to abuse, Glasstone & Dolan (1977) describe in detail the effects of nuclear weapons. SIPRI (1977) covers the impact of nuclear, chemical, biological, and geophysical weapons on the environment. See also appendices 2.2 and 2.3.

Appendix 2.2

Sources for the impact of World Wars I and II on forest lands

1. *World War I.* Battle damage to temperate forests during World War I has been described for several nations, but in greatest detail for France. Descriptions for France have been published by Dana (1914), Schultze (1915) (including a lengthy historical perspective), *American Forestry* (1915), Lesseux (1916), Ridsdale (1916; 1919 *b*; 1919 *c*), Buttrick (1917), Olzendam (1918), Graves (1918), Morgan (1961), Bach (1975) and others. Descriptions for Belgium have been published by Ridsdale (1916; 1919 *a*); for Italy by Brown (1919 *a*; 1919 *b*); and for Lebanon by Winters (1974: 108, 117, 132).

2. *World War II.* Battle damage to temperate forests during World War II has been described for France by Kernan (1945), Becton & Maunder (1972–1973) and Bach (1975); for the Netherlands by Aartsen (1946); for Finland by Skogen (1943); and for Poland by the UN War Crimes Commission (1948: 496). Baker (1945) gives an account of two horse-chestnuts (*Aesculus hippocastanum*; Hippocastanaceae) in London that were stimulated to flower out of season by a nearby bomb explosion, presumably in response to blast-caused defoliation. See also appendix 2.4.1.

Appendix 2.3

Sources for the impact of warfare on man

1. *Fatalities.* Fatality and other statistics have been compiled for numerous wars by Bodart (1916), Dumas & Vedel-Petersen (1923), Klingberg (1966), Prinzing (1916), Richardson (1960), Singer & Small (1972), Sorokin (1957), Urlanis (1971), Voevodsky (1970), Wright (1965), and others. See also appendix 1.3.

2. *Genetics and evolution.* The impact of war on human population genetics and evolution (including so-called eugenic and dysgenic effects) has been the subject of inquiry by Bigelow (1943), Carr-Saunders (1928–1929), Hulse (1961), Hunt (1930), Ibarrola (1964), Livingstone (1967), Nicolai (1918: chap. 3), Novicow (1911), Pearl (1940–1941) and others.

3. *Disease.* The link between war and disease has been the subject of publications by, among others, Alland (1967), Burnet & White (1972: chap. 21), Cartwright & Biddiss (1972: chap. 4), Georgievski & Gavrilov (1975), Gillett (1972: chap. 14), Lapage (1950), Major (1941), Moser (1965), McNeill (1976), Prinzing (1916), SIPRI (1975 *a*) and Zinsser (1935). To be especially recommended is chapter 8, entitled 'On the influence of epidemic diseases on political and military history, and on the relative unimportance of generals', in the work of Zinsser (1935).

4. *Culture.* The effects of war and the preparation for war on social organization, economy, cultural life, and the development of civilization in general have been studied by Mumford (1934: chap. 2), Sorokin (1942), Nef (1950), Carneiro (1970), Nelson (1971), Andreski (1971), Marwick (1974), Milward (1977) and many others. The social consequences of urban and industrial bombing are the subject of a detailed analytical study by Iklé (1958), based largely upon the strategic bombing carried out by the USA and the UK during World War II. He, in turn, leaned heavily on the US Strategic Bombing Survey of that war (D'Olier *et al.,* 1947 *a*; MacIsaac, 1976). Earlier, Brittain (1944) had provided a detailed account of the Allied saturation bombing of German cities (cf. also Bidinian, 1976; Webster & Frankland, 1961). Moreover, FitzGibbon (1957) provides a personal account of life under the World War II bombing of London. LaFarge (1946) has catalogued some of the more important art treasures of Europe that had been lost through the bombing and other destructive activities associated with World War II. Picasso's *Guernica,* which depicts the bombing of civilians during the Spanish Civil War, provides one example of the impact of war on art and the directions it takes (appendix 1.1.5; Silva & Simson, 1963: 63–64). A number of relevant bibliographies have also been compiled (Popper & Lybrand, 1960; Rayner, 1957–1958).

Appendix 2.4

Sources for the recovery of temperate biota from devastation

1. *Military devastation*. The biota to colonize several areas of London damaged by German bombing during World War II was recorded in remarkable detail by members of the London Natural History Society. Higher plants were studied by Castell (1944; 1954), Fitter & Lousley (1953), Jones (1957), Salisbury (1943 *a*; 1943 *b*), and Wrighton (1947; 1948; 1949; 1950; 1952). Higher animals were studied by Currie (1949) and Fitter and Lousley (1953). Molluscs were studied by Bensley (1951; 1954). Various kinds of insects were studied by Currie (1951), Groves (1958), Jones (1954), LeGros (1948), Owen (1949; 1951 *a*; 1951 *b*; 1954), Parmenter (1953) and Payne (1944). Unrelated to these studies, Györffy (1948–1949) studied the colonization by mosses of World War II bomb craters in Austria. See also appendix 2.2.

2. *Civil devastation*. The natural and assisted recovery of ecosystems destroyed by pit (open-cast) mining and other human disruptions has been covered by Brown *et al.* (1978), Cairns *et al.* (1977), Gemmell (1977), Heede (1976), Holdgate & Woodman (1978), Hutnik & Davis (1973), Schaller & Sutton (1978), Wright (1978), and others. A number of extensive bibliographies are available on the subject of strip-mine reclamation (Czapowskyj, 1976; Frawley, 1971; Funk, 1962; Goodman & Bray, 1975; Kieffer, 1972).

3. Tropical regions

The tables for this chapter appear on pages 100–102.

I. Introduction

The tropical land areas of the world—characterized by year-round frost-free conditions and rainfall sufficing to support at least grassland—occupy 28 per cent of the global land area. This land currently supports 63 per cent of the global biomass which, in turn, accounts for 41 per cent of the annual global biomass production. It further supports 39 per cent of the world's human population, distributed among 80 nations and about 19 colonies. The tropical land areas include most of the poor nations of the world, the majority of those with excessive population growth rates, and also most of those nations whose founding or independence post-dates World War II. Political turmoil and local wars are rather common occurrences in the tropics. A war likely to be environmentally disruptive occurs perhaps once every 11 years in the tropical regions of the world.

II. Environment and ecology

The tropical regions of the world, as defined here, are those relatively low-elevation lands that are located more or less between the tropics of Cancer and Capricorn. They are thus characterized the year round by relatively uniform warm (frost-free) temperature conditions and a relatively unchanging photoperiod. In some instances they are further characterized by a seasonal alternation of wet and dry periods, these usually coupled with seasonal alternations in the direction of the prevailing winds (known as monsoons). For present purposes, the tropical regions are further limited to those lands that receive and retain precipitation at least sufficient to support grassland, that is, roughly 250 millimetres per year or more (appendix 3.1.1).

The tropical regions of the world extend over about 42 million square kilometres (4 200 million hectares) of the Earth's land surface, almost equally divided between the Northern and Southern hemispheres (table 3.1). The two largest areas are in Africa (15 million square kilometres) and South America (13 million square kilometres). Three-quarters of South America and just over half of Africa are tropical. More than half of the combined global island area is also tropical.

Tropical regions are divisible into a number of major habitats: forest (2 100 million hectares), grassland (800 million hectares), agricultural (600 million hectares), and built-up, the last one including cities, industrial areas, transportation systems, military bases, and so forth (table 1.6). Broadly speaking, the forest habitat can be divided into dense (closed, rain) forest (1 400 million hectares) and open (clear, seasonal) forest (600 million hectares). Tropical forests are above all noted for their luxuriance of vegetation and multiplicity of species. They contain a bewildering diversity of dicotyledonous trees, lianas, epiphytes, and herbs as well as some monocotyledons, ferns, and so forth. It is not uncommon to find more than a hundred different species of trees on a single hectare, especially of dense forest. The tree species vary in height, usually forming two and occasionally three more or less distinct strata (storeys).

Many tropical forests have through the centuries supported many small nomadic groups of people practising so-called shifting slash-and-burn agriculture. In this form of land use, a forest area of several hectares is cleared of all or most of its trees, which are slashed and burned in place. The area is then farmed for several years, until the soil fertility has been exhausted, and is then abandoned. The area then reverts to forest and slowly—over perhaps one, two, or more decades—regains its nutrient capital by natural means. The area is then likely to be recleared, beginning the cycle anew. As a result, these forests are characterized by a patchwork of countless small areas in various stages of successional development.

Tropical grasslands (savannas, veldt)—which sometimes contain a scattering of shrubs or trees—usually occur in regions of relatively scanty, seasonally distributed rainfall. They are also found where the soil has been impoverished by overly intensive, shifting slash-and-burn agriculture or other form of misuse, a situation subsequently reinforced by dry-season fires or by browsing herbivores. The greatest extent of tropical grasslands is found in Africa.

As to the photosynthetic productivity of tropical ecosystems, one can expect the dense forests to have an annual net primary productivity that averages perhaps 22 000 kilograms (dry weight) per hectare (table 1.8). The open forests will average 16 000 kilograms per hectare and the grasslands perhaps 9 000 kilograms per hectare. The productivity of the agricultural lands can vary between about 4 000 and 12 000 kilograms per hectare, depending upon the intensity of management. The overall average for the world's tropical regions is of the order of 16 700 kilograms per hectare (table 1.7).

Tropical forests support an immense diversity of wildlife, especially in their upper storeys. There exist a wide variety of arboreal (climbing) mammals (e.g., monkeys), reptiles, and amphibians as well as a host of birds. As with the tropical plant species, the richness of animal species far exceeds that of any other terrestrial habitat. The tropical grasslands of Africa are famous for their herds of ungulates and other large herbivores (several dozen species of zebras, antelopes, rhinoceroses, giraffes, elephants, and so forth) and for the carnivores that live upon them (lions, several cats, hyenas, etc.). They also support burrowing rodents and other animals.

Tropical species, and the ecosystems of which they are a part, have evolved through the millennia in a relatively uniform and otherwise benign environment and are therefore less well adapted to drastic disturbance than their temperate counterparts. Their general pattern of recovery (ecological succession) following such disturbance has been outlined in chapter 1 (section III) and is further discussed in section IV below. Reattainment of pre-disturbance conditions can take decades or even centuries, depending upon the degree of disruption. Indeed, severe disruption prevents full recovery for so many centuries that the process appears to have been arrested.

The mangrove habitat is a tropical transitional zone between land and sea. In contrast with the dense upland forest type with its several thousand plant species, the mangrove type is composed of a mere several dozen. These few species have in common the ability to become established and survive in a mucky soil which is periodically inundated with salt water. The dominant mangrove vegetation usually consists of several species of small trees, mostly 3 to 15 metres high, primarily in the genera *Rhizophora* (Rhizophoraceae), *Avicennia* (Verbenaceae), and *Bruguiera* (Rhizophoraceae)—all so-called mangroves. Soil deposition often extends the coastline slowly out into the ocean. In the course of time, the soil level builds up beyond the reach of flood tide, and the so-called true mangrove type gives way to a new community known as rear (or back) mangrove. The rear mangrove type is usually dominated by *Melaleuca* (Myrtaceae) trees. Not only does the mangrove type serve to stabilize the shoreline, but this channel-dissected habitat is also of importance as the nursery or breeding ground for numerous salt-water and freshwater fish and crustaceans.

III. Use

Civil

About 1 600 million people currently utilize the tropical lands of the Earth in order to eke out a living (table 3.1.2). The present tropical population density is 38 persons per square kilometre. If the people who are concentrated into the 39 tropical urban centres of 1 million or more are excluded from the density determination, then the value drops to 35 persons per square kilometre (table 1.9). About four-fifths of the inhabitants of the tropical habitat live in the Northern hemisphere—the largest number, just over half the world total, in Asia (table 3.1). Almost two-thirds of the

African population live in this habitat, as do three-fifths of those who live on oceanic islands. The gross national product (GNP) per capita in the tropical habitat is only about US $340, as compared with a global value of US $1 500 (table 1.11).

The people of the tropical habitat are mostly grouped into 80 nations (table 1.10). None of these nations is rich; as many as 64 of them are poor, and this group accounts for most of the poor nations of the world. Only 2 tropical nations have essentially stable population numbers, whereas 21 are growing at rates that lead to a doubling time of less than 25 years. Sixty-two tropical nations (again, most of those in this category) were founded or gained their independence since the close of World War II.

Some 600 million hectares of the tropical habitat have been cleared for agriculture (table 1.6), that is, 0.30 hectare per capita. Annual cereal production (a summation of all grains) is only 202 kilograms per capita (table 1.11). There is no nation in the tropical habitat that has a significant net export of cereals, although Thailand currently exports a modest amount (3 million tonnes per year) (*FAO Trade Yearbook 1976:* table 34, 1975 data). Agricultural and horticultural (plantation) crops that are much cultivated for export by tropical nations include cane-sugar (Cuba, Brazil, India), coffee (Brazil, Colombia, the Ivory Coast), tea (India, Sri Lanka), cocoa (Ghana, Brazil, Nigeria), marijuana (Colombia), cocaine (Bolivia, Colombia), opium and heroin (Laos, Burma, Thailand), and rubber (Malaysia, 1 500 thousand tonnes per year; Indonesia, 830 thousand; Thailand, 350 thousand) (*UN Statistical Yearbook 1976:* table 45, 1975 data).

The tropical regions of the world are also a major source of exploitable natural resources. Most important among the renewable ones are the forest lands (1.5 hectares per capita) for timber production and, to a much lesser extent, the range lands (0.50 hectare per capita) for livestock production (table 1.11). India (with 180 million cows and 40 million sheep) and Brazil (92 million; 27 million) are the only tropical nations with sizeable livestock industries (*UN Statistical Yearbook 1976:* table 33, 1975 data). The major timber producers of the tropical habitat are Brazil (harvesting 164 million cubic metres per year), Indonesia (130 million), India (127 million), and Nigeria (65 million) (*FAO Forest Products Yearbook 1975:* 2–4, 1975 data). The combined timber harvest for all tropical nations is currently 944 million cubic metres per year, which represents 39 per cent of the global total. Of the world's four current timber exporters of note, the third and fourth in rank are tropical: Indonesia (15 million cubic metres per year) and Malaysia (12 million). Minor tropical exporters include the Philippines (5 million cubic metres per year) and the Ivory Coast (2 million).

A large variety of important mineral resources exist in the tropical habitat and only a few are singled out here (data from the *UN Statistical Yearbook 1976*, 1975 data). Although most of the world's iron is obtained in the temperate habitat, some is mined in the tropics, for example, in Brazil

(47 million tonnes per year) and India (26 million). Coal, also to date a temperate-habitat commodity, is mined to some extent in India (96 million tonnes per year). Oil, extracted largely in the temperate and desert habitats, is—in the tropics—produced in Venezuela (143 million cubic metres per year), Nigeria (103 million), Indonesia (75 million), and elsewhere.

Tin production is virtually a monopoly of the tropical regions of the world. Malaysia leads the world in tin production (64 thousand tonnes per year), followed by Bolivia (28 thousand), Indonesia (25 thousand), and Thailand (16 thousand). These four tropical nations together account for three-quarters of global tin production. Jamaica is the world's second largest producer of aluminium (11 million tonnes per year), followed by Guinea (8 million), and Surinam (5 million). Zaïre leads the world in the mining of industrial diamonds (2 500 kilograms per year, or 40 per cent of global production) and is also noted for cobalt production. Among the other minerals mined in the tropics are copper in Zambia, nickel in French New Caledonia, manganese in Gabon, some chromium in Rhodesia, and some uranium in Nigeria.

Military

The military activities within the tropical regions of the world, in common with those of the temperate and other regions, are intended to serve a number of purposes (appendix 3.1.3). For most of the 80 included nations, their domestically maintained armed forces are meant for protection against external threats, for quelling civil wars, and occasionally for aggressive purposes. For most of the eighteen or so included colonies, the resident armed forces of the possessor nation are again meant for protection against external threats and also for subduing independence movements. The various armed forces of the several major powers which are deployed in foreign nations are present as part of the regional global security postures of these powers.

Twelve of the 80 tropical nations maintain armies with a strength of 100 thousand or more (table 1.12). Of these, at least the following four nations have armies in excess of 500 thousand: India, Pakistan, Taiwan, and Viet Nam. The average tropical-nation army has a strength of 77 thousand (table 1.13). Armies are presumably maintained in part to protect some combination of a nation's people, its land, and its wealth. The tropical nations maintain about 380 soldiers per 100 thousand inhabitants; about 140 soldiers per thousand square kilometres; and about 1 100 soldiers per US $100 million of gross national product.

Among the more important and well-established foreign military presences deployed within the tropical habitat are the US forces in the Philippines, Taiwan, and Panama (the Canal Zone); the Soviet forces in Cuba; the Australian forces in Malaysia; and the New Zealand forces in Singapore.

IV. Abuse

Civil

The major civil abuses of the tropical habitat are for the most part explicable by its inordinate population growth (appendix 3.1.2). Only 2 of the 80 tropical nations have essentially stable population numbers, and 21 or more are growing at a rate that leads to a doubling time of less than 25 years (table 1.10). Indeed, the total population of this habitat is increasing at a compound growth rate of 2.5 per cent—a rate that leads to a doubling time of 28 years (table 1.11). The unrestrained growth of the world's tropical population—a problem with grave global ramifications—is especially lamentable because of the already profound, and generally worsening, poverty that is prevalent throughout much of this habitat. On the basis of gross national product per capita, fully 64 of the tropical nations must currently be classed as being abjectly poor, and none of them as being rich (table 1.10).

One of the environmental abuses in the tropics stemming from the ever-increasing population—currently a net increase of one million every nine days—is the clearing of new lands for agriculture. Just in order to provide every new person with the 0.3 hectare of agricultural land necessary simply to feed him by the prevailing—though inadequate—tropical standard (table 1.11) would, at present, require a conversion to farm land of 12 million hectares per year. Some of the land thus actually claimed each year is clearly submarginal for the purpose, and more than half of it is claimed at the expense of forest land. Additional net reductions in tropical forest result each year from clearing for urban and transportation purposes, from opencast (strip) mining, and from the harvesting of firewood and timber on a non-renewing basis. It should be added that much of the tropical mining, timber-cutting, and industrial plantation agriculture is done for export. The resources and energies expended on these activities contribute relatively little towards alleviating the human misery rife in the respective countries.

At first glance, tropical forests, with their biotic luxuriance, appear to stand ready to provide man with his final major terrestrial frontier: offering a supply of timber for the world market, agricultural lands to feed the growing population, and living space as well. Unfortunately, the unbelievably rich biota of the unsullied tropical forest is a most misleading indicator of either the robustness of the ecosystem or of the potential productivity of the habitat. Major disturbance results in the immediate massive loss to the area of mineral nutrients (SIPRI, 1976: 64–69). Part of this site debilitation is caused through soil erosion, especially in hilly terrain, but it is largely the result of nutrient dumping, that is, of the rapid loss of soluble nutrients from a soil that cannot hold them. The climatic and geomorphic stability of the humid tropical environment through tens of millions of years has simply not prepared the plants and animals—or, more specifically, the obligatorily interacting community they form—to cope with sudden and drastic changes on a large scale (upsets of a sort that the temperate-habitat biota have, in fact, learned in large part to live with). The result is long-term and partially irreversible damage.

Tropical lands are beset with a number of additional problems. For example, several million people practise shifting slash-and-burn agriculture in each of the major tropical regions of the world, in South America, Africa, and Asia. When the time-span of this cycle of forest clearance and regrowth is shortened from its traditional two decades or so, the site is soon degraded to the point where it can no longer support trees. Growing population numbers combined with shrinking forest availability are slowly leading to an ever-larger area of such long-term site degradation. The pressures of population are also forcing the widespread use of semi-arid tropical grazing lands beyond their carrying capacity, inevitably with results that are self-defeating in the long run. This form of site degradation, which is known as desertification (or desertization), is further mentioned in chapter 4.'

The tropical wildlife of both forest and grassland is being threatened ever more seriously (Curry-Lindahl, 1972; Fisher *et al.*, 1969; Ziswiler, 1967). The game animals of the African savannas, for example, are under severe pressure. Big game is hunted (often poached) for food, for skins, and for trophies—the food to augment an inadequate diet, and the skins and trophies for the export or tourist markets. Additionally, many of the large range-land herbivores are being destroyed or displaced in favour of livestock. Moreover, the continuous expansion of agricultural lands and built-up areas takes place at the inevitable expense of wildlife habitat—and thus inexorably of the wildlife itself. Indeed, it is the large-scale assault on wildlife habitat that is responsible for the greatest overall danger to the survival of many endangered tropical animal species.

Estimates of the total annual reduction of the tropical—and thus essentially global—forests vary, but the value appears to fall between 10 and 20 million hectares (Bolin, 1977; Brünig, 1977; Stuiver, 1978; Woodwell *et al.*, 1978; but see Broecker *et al.*, 1979). (The world's remaining—largely temperate—forests, although reduced in areal extent by perhaps two-thirds to three-quarters during the past two millennia, have changed relatively little in this regard during the past century.) A net annual loss of tropical forest biomass of 10 to 20 million hectares leads to the release of the large amounts of carbon stored in the wood and other tissues, thereby introducing between 1.2×10^{12} and 2.5×10^{12} kilograms of that element (in the form of carbon dioxide) into the atmosphere each year (table 1.7). The amount of carbon released is subject to two self-cancelling corrections. The concomitant exposure of the soil, which in the tropics accumulates relatively little organic matter (humus), would increase the release by perhaps 25 per cent. On the other hand, the utilization of the harvested biomass for lumber would result in the long-term storage of a similar fraction.

This current net annual contribution from the tropical biomass of perhaps 1.9×10^{12} kilograms of carbon into the atmosphere in the form of carbon dioxide adds substantially to the global climate problem already discussed in chapter 2. By way of comparison, the current total annual contribution of carbon to the global atmosphere from the burning of fossil fuels is of the order of 5.3×10^{12} kilograms (a value derived from the combined production data for coal, lignite, oil, and natural gas, reduced by an average of 21 per cent to allow for their non-carbon fractions; basic data from the *UN Statistical Yearbook 1976:* tables 50–53, 1975 data). The net annual loss of tropical forest must therefore be recognized as making a significant contribution to the carbon dioxide air-pollution problem discussed in chapter 2; indeed, from the figures given above, the size of this contribution works out to roughly one-quarter.

Augmentation of the carbon dioxide of the atmosphere by forest removal, as described above, by no means constitutes the only objection to this destructive practice. The dense tropical rain forest must be considered as one of the world's great biological resources. For the past 50 million years (i.e., since Tertiary times) the tropical rain forests of the world have had the opportunity to grow, develop, and evolve under relatively benign and rather constant conditions. The outcome has been an enormously complex and efficient—albeit fragile—ecosystem. Even during the past several million years, with small numbers of ancestral and primitive man upon the scene, the added perturbations have been inconsequential or perhaps even beneficial. However, the tropical rain forest is simply no match for man equipped with chain-saws, tractors, herbicides, and other tools or weapons.

Thus, to destroy tropical rain-forest communities is to degrade the site and to wipe out the irreplaceable end-product of millions of years of evolution; at the same time, it is to eliminate the surviving progenitor species from which most present-day plant and animal species—both tropical and temperate—have evolved. Such destruction will also preclude the study of many thousands of as yet undescribed plants and animals and of their ecological relationships. Finally, the destruction of tropical forest is endangering the very existence of the remaining primitive cultural groups in the Amazon basin, in equatorial Africa, and in south-east Asia, whose way of life depends upon this habitat.

Military

Military abuse of the tropical habitat is related primarily to the rather frequent wars associated with this habitat (appendix 2.2.3). A new major (high-fatality) war begins, on average, once in every 11 years within the tropical habitat (table 1.14), and a new minor one at least annually. Many of the major wars and some of the minor ones are highly disruptive of the environment. Thumb-nail sketches of a selection of seven ecologically disruptive tropical-habitat wars are included by way of example in table 1.2 (nos. 15, 21–26).

This section describes the impact of warfare on tropical vegetation and the way in which this might affect the people dependent upon it. Special emphasis is placed on the forests and agricultural crops of South Viet Nam during the Second Indochina War (table 1.2.22). The effects on tropical animals and man *per se* are noted in brief, again largely with reference to the Second Indochina War. The section concludes with some comments on recovery. For a description of the impact of warfare on the biota of tropical islands, see chapter 6 (section IV).

Woody vegetation

The Second Indochina War was the first in modern history in which environmental disruption was a substantial intentional component of the strategy of one of the belligerent powers. In an attempt to subdue a largely guerrilla opponent, the USA pioneered a variety of hostile techniques causing widespread environmental disruption which were aimed at denying its enemy concealment, freedom of movement, and local sources of food and other supplies. Of these techniques, the three ecologically most disruptive were: *(a)* the massive and sustained expenditure of high-explosive munitions (c. 14 million tonnes of bombs, shells, and the like); *(b)* the profligate dissemination of chemical anti-plant agents (c. 55 thousand tonnes of herbicides); and *(c)* the large-scale employment of heavy land-clearing tractors (c. 200 of the so-called Rome ploughs). The strictly ecological impact of these techniques has been described elsewhere (SIPRI, 1976). Emphasized below is the impact they had on the human ecology of the region.

Although no portion of Indochina seems to have been exempt from military punishment, it was the 17 million hectares of largely rural South Viet Nam that bore the brunt of the attack and suffered the worst mutilation (table 3.2). Indeed, South Viet Nam was subjected to 71 per cent of the total high-explosive munitions used and to virtually all of the herbicidal attacks and Rome-plough land-clearing. US hostilities directed against the rest of Indochina—mounted largely from the air—were in large measure ancillary to those directed against South Viet Nam. The remaining 29 per cent of the munitions were distributed as follows: Laos, 16 per cent; North Viet Nam, 8 per cent; and Cambodia, 5 per cent.

Forest trees. About 5.9 million hectares, or 58 per cent, of the woody vegetation of South Viet Nam is considered to be commercial forest, suitable for the production and exploitation of merchantable timber. This combined area largely consists of dense (closed) upland forest (the layman's 'jungle') and, to a lesser extent, of open (clear) upland forest. These forest categories are exemplified by the stands that once made up the so-called War Zones C and D and the Iron Triangle within Military Region III—that is, a large region lying mainly to the north of and surrounding Saigon (Ho Chi Minh

City) (SIPRI, 1976: map 1.2). These forests support some 200 commercial species, a dozen or more of which are of exceedingly high quality and suitable for the world market. Chief among these so-called luxury woods are three rosewood species (*Dalbergia bariensis, D. cochinchinensis,* and *Pterocarpus pedatus;* all Leguminosae), an ebony (*Diospyros mun;* Ebenaceae), and a false mahogany (*Melanorrhoea laccifera;* Anacardiaceae).

The dense forest type is the most extensive vegetational type in South Viet Nam as well as being the most important from the standpoint of forestry. It is also the type that can provide a guerrilla force with the greatest degree of protection and manoeuvrability; and, indeed, the indigenous forces controlled virtually all of these forests throughout the war. Thus, the US offensive against Indochina was largely directed towards destroying these forests and the armed forces sheltering in them.

The damage to the forests of South Viet Nam caused by bombs and shells is best presented under two heads: (*a*) complete obliteration, and (*b*) severe damage. The first category comprises the forest land that was converted to craters by high-explosive munitions. On the assumption that in South Viet Nam a forested area was twice as likely to constitute a target for a bomb or a shell than an unforested one, it can be calculated from available data (SIPRI, 1976: table 2.5; these data being reduced by 5 per cent to account for crater overlap) that such crater-obliterated forest areas add up to about 104 thousand hectares. The second category comprises the forest land that was subjected to damage caused by flying metal fragments (shrapnel). If one takes the zone subjected to such abuse at an intensity sufficient to be lethal to 50 per cent or more of the exposed personnel (SIPRI, 1976: 22–23; these data being reduced by 25 per cent to account for overlap), the area in question works out at about 4.9 million hectares. Many of the trees in this area were injured by shrapnel, which in turn leads to fungal entry and to decay, inevitably followed by a significant proportion of tree mortality. The worst damaged trees are unusable for lumber; those that can be used entail extra work, lost time, and added expense. Sawmill operators have laboriously to chop away the metal fragments embedded in the logs—any that they miss result in snapped saw-blades, Moreover, those trees that are not harvested soon after being punctured by shrapnel drop in value because of the fungal rot, which spreads up and down from the wounds. On average, the main timber species in South Viet Nam lose about 50 per cent of their value in two to three years after sustaining a puncture wound.

A profusion of craters in the forests makes logging a much more difficult operation than it normally is. In regions of South Viet Nam that were heavily bombed (e.g., Military Region III), logs must now be frequently cut shorter than desired so as to provide the added manoeuvrability required during the skidding operation.

The damage caused by chemical anti-plant agents to the forests of South Viet Nam is also best presented under two heads: *(a)* virtually complete obliteration, and *(b)* partial damage. The first category comprises the forest land that was sprayed four or more times if an upland area, but only once if a lowland mangrove area (mangrove being an oddly sensitive forest type). This category of virtual obliteration covers about 202 thousand hectares, 51 thousand being upland and the remaining 151 thousand mangrove. The second category comprises upland forests that were sprayed one to three times. This area has been calculated to cover some 1.3 million hectares. The first of these categories is estimated to have experienced between 85 and 100 per cent tree mortality, whereas the second experienced between 10 and 50 per cent.

For a more precise estimate to be made of the timber losses resulting from the herbicide operations in South Viet Nam during the war, it is necessary—in the absence of any suitable forest survey or inventory—to make a number of assumptions. Firstly, the analysis is here restricted to the dense forest type of South Viet Nam on the assumption that this will account for most of the herbicidal timber losses sustained. Secondly, 90 cubic metres per hectare is used as the average standing merchantable timber crop for this type. This value is adopted primarily on the basis of a survey made by Rollet (1962) of the equivalent type just across the border in Cambodia, east of the Mekong River. There it had been determined by conventional methods that the 600 thousand hectares of dense forest in the region had a merchantable stock—that is, of Luxury, I, II, and III class woods with a diameter at breast height[1] (DBH) of 60 centimetres or more (strictly, 57.5 centimetres or more)—averaging 89 cubic metres per hectare. Lowering the utilization standard to the 40 centimetre DBH class increased this stock to 130 cubic metres per hectare. Moreover, the South Vietnamese Forest Service was at that time also using the value of 90 cubic metres per hectare (Tân, 1971). Thirdly, 0.5 cubic metre per hectare per year is employed as the average value for annual net merchantable increment. Hiep (1969: 13) had reported 0.6 cubic metre for the five northern provinces of South Viet Nam (Military Region I), and Rollet (1962) 0.3 cubic metre for eastern Cambodia.

It now becomes possible to calculate at least a rough approximation for the amount of timber directly destroyed by the herbicides in the 1.11 million hectares of dense forest that was sprayed one or more times (SIPRI, 1976: table 3.6). It can be estimated on the basis of data provided by SIPRI (1976: table 3.4) that 731 thousand hectares of this total were sprayed once, 248 thousand twice, 88 thousand three times, 31 thousand four times, and the remaining 12 thousand five or more times. Next it can be estimated that one spraying resulted in a merchantable timber loss of 10 per cent, two in a loss of 25 per cent, three in a loss of 50 per cent, four in a loss of 85 per cent, and five or more in a loss of essentially 100 per cent. On the basis of these figures, one finds that the direct timber loss approximated 19.6 million

---

[1]Breast height is the height of 130 centimetres above ground level at which the diameters of standing trees are usually measured.

cubic metres, giving an average of 17.6 cubic metres per hectare. It can be seen, moreover, that at the compound growth rate assumed here, it will take the 1.11 million hectares of sprayed forest a period of about 40 years without logging to recoup this level of loss.

The direct timber loss of 19.6 million cubic metres calculated above is subject to two adjustments, which, however, tend to cancel each other out. Firstly, this figure for the loss should be reduced by the amount of herbicide-killed timber that was salvaged before it rotted *in situ*. This amount appears to have been about 10 per cent of the total kill (Westing, 1971), that is, about 2.0 million cubic metres. Secondly, on the other hand, the figure for the loss must be increased by the amount resulting from the loss of young growing stock (the loss of so-called ingrowth) during the 40-year period of recovery. In fact, this latter category of loss was considered by Lang *et al.* (1974: chap. 4: 86) to be among the most damaging results of the spraying. This loss of ingrowth can be estimated to have been about 2.6 million cubic metres (on the basis of the difference between the annual growth of timber that would have been cut during the 40-year period if the forest had not been sprayed, and the amount that was killed by the spraying).

Thus, the above two adjustments having been made, the herbicide-caused timber loss in the dense upland forest type of South Viet Nam can be considered to have been approximately 20.2 million cubic metres. This is, of course, a conservative estimate of the total loss. The sprayings of the dense forest type made up only 76 per cent of the total spraying of woody vegetation (SIPRI, 1976: table 3.6). Therefore, some modest additional losses of merchantable timber must have been incurred in conjunction with the remaining sprayings of woody vegetation, and still further losses in conjunction with the crop sprayings. Moreover, the estimated recovery period of 40 years is based upon a straightforward compound growth formula and does not take into account the situation where areas were taken over semi-permanently by monocotyledonous weeds. Such an occurrence was, in fact, likely in the 131 thousand hectares of dense forest sprayed three or more times, and highly likely in the 43 thousand hectare portion of this area sprayed four or more times. Finally, it should be pointed out that although the timber loss might be considered inflated in the sense that it is partially based on currently inaccessible timber reserves, this over-estimation is more than counterbalanced by the destruction wreaked in Military Region III, with its high proportion of prime timber lands. For example, the most extensively and repeatedly hit areas—War Zones C and D and the Iron Triangle—had been the best, the most accessible, and the closest to markets of any commercial timber lands in South Viet Nam.

The damage caused to the forests of South Viet Nam by Rome ploughs need only be presented in one category—that of essentially complete obliteration. This category comprises some 325 thousand hectares (SIPRI, 1976: 47).

Combining the several separate estimates of damage given above by simple addition would inflate the extent of damage, since some of the areas were subjected to more than one category of insult. The summations are therefore reduced by 10 per cent to allow for such overlap. Thus, complete or essentially complete devastation applies to an estimated 568 thousand hectares, representing 5 per cent of the forest lands of South Viet Nam (or 3 per cent of this entire region). The partially (severely) damaged forest lands were estimated to come to at least an additional 5.6 million hectares, representing 54 per cent of the forest lands of South Viet Nam (or 32 per cent of this entire region). These values do not, of course, take into account a variety of additional abuses to the land—both hostile and non-hostile—that resulted from the massive decade-long US military presence in Indochina.

It is further possible to make a crude approximation of the merchantable timber losses in South Viet Nam that resulted from the three forms of attack discussed above. If one assumes that the commercial forest represents 58 per cent of the total forest, that the commercial forest averages 90 cubic metres per hectare, that the portions designated above as obliterated (or essentially so) in fact sustained a loss of 95 per cent, and that those designated as partially (severely) damaged sustained only a 20 per cent loss, then the war damage examined here amounted to a merchantable timber loss exceeding 75 million cubic metres—that is, to about 15 per cent of the standing merchantable timber crop of South Viet Nam. For comparison, it may be pointed out that domestic timber consumption in South Viet Nam during the 1960s was about 1.5 million cubic metres per year (Westing, 1971).

Before leaving the timber resources, brief mention may be made of the so-called secondary forest products, some of which are of great local importance. Thus, considerable quantities of wood intended for use as fuel—either directly or by conversion to charcoal—were destroyed by the herbicide sprayings. This occurred not only in the dense and other upland forest types, but also in the coastal mangrove type. Indeed, the mangrove forests, which sustained fully 10 per cent of the total spraying of woody vegetation (SIPRI, 1976: table 3.6), have traditionally been a major source of charcoal. Other secondary forest products must also have been adversely affected—for example, tannin from the bark of various of the mangrove species in the Delta region (Military Region IV) and cinnamon from the bark of *Cinnamonum* (Lauraceae) trees in Quang Ngai and Quang Tin provinces (Military Region I).

Rubber plantations. The rubber trees (*Hevea brasiliensis*; Euphorbiaceae) of Indochina were introduced into the region about half a century ago, and rubber plantations today cover approximately 185 thousand hectares (Union of Rubber Planters, 1969; Prud'homme, 1969). Rubber production rapidly assumed enormous economic importance both in South Viet Nam and in Cambodia. Up-to-date methods of culture and exploitation, together with highly favourable climatic and soil conditions and the absence of major pests, made this region the most highly productive on a unit-area basis of any in the world. Rubber once led all exports from both countries, accounting for about 60 per cent of the value of total South Vietnamese exports and about 35 per cent of Cambodian.

The South Vietnamese rubber plantations cover approximately 135 thousand hectares, 90 per cent of this area lying in Military Region III. The Cambodian plantations are about 50 thousand hectares in extent, 95 per cent of this area lying in Kompong Cham province, in the so-called Fish Hook region (SIPRI, 1976: map 1.2). It is most unfortunate that these two regions were the scenes of extraordinarily intense military activity. The damage to the rubber industry was drastic in both countries and it is virtually impossible to apportion this damage among the various means used to inflict it—principally bombing and shelling, herbicidal attack, and Rome ploughing (McIndoe, 1969; Westing, 1972 a).

In South Viet Nam, a number of war-related problems—including the destruction of rubber trees and disruption of processing facilities—resulted in a sharp decline in rubber production. By early 1967, more than 20 thousand hectares of rubber plantations had suffered herbicidal damage of varying extent, either via direct spray or via drift (Polinière, 1967). By the end of 1968, 30 per cent of the rubber plantations of South Viet Nam had reportedly been destroyed from all war causes (Union of Rubber Planters, 1969) and 60 per cent of the national rubber output wiped out (McIndoe, 1969: 6). Subsequently, the situation deteriorated even further.

In Cambodia, some 30 per cent of the rubber trees suffered damage via direct spray or drift during one brief period in the spring of 1969 (Westing, 1972 a). Approximately two-thirds of the affected trees were thereby permanently damaged to some extent and a small fraction (perhaps 5 per cent of the total population of rubber trees in Cambodia) died. The military action in Cambodia during and after 1970 caused enormous additional damage to the plantations and disrupted the major processing facilities, thereby virtually wiping out rubber production in that country (Whitaker *et al.*, 1973: 268–269).

Bombing and shelling damage a rubber plantation far more severely than is immediately obvious. According to the local manager of a major French corporation, the fungal rot that enters the war wounds of rubber trees weakens them sufficiently so that about 80 per cent of such trees are simply blown over by the wind within a year or two (R. Piechaud, CEXO, Saigon, private communication, 19 August 1971).

A herbicidal attack renders rubber trees leafless within a few weeks. However, the extent of lasting herbicide damage varies with age and variety. (clone, *sensu stricto*) (Westing, 1972 a). Seedlings and young graftlings of all varieties are highly sensitive, and most die as a result of dose levels even substantially less than the military ones (Hutchison, 1958). Older (producing) trees respond less uniformly. Thus, of the three major varieties utilized in South Viet Nam and Cambodia, mature 'PB.86' trees seem ultimately to recover essentially undamaged from military attack with hormonal herbicides. On the other hand, mature 'GT.1' trees suffer branch dieback of two to three metres or more, and occasionally they die; moreover, their latex production drops more sharply than is explicable on the basis of their reduction in crown size. 'PR.107' is intermediate in sensitivity between 'PB.86' and 'GT.1'. Among some of the other, less used varieties, 'TR.1600', 'BD.5', and 'TJR.1' stand out as being highly sensitive to attack by the hormonal herbicides used as chemical anti-plant agents.

Agricultural crops

As elsewhere, agricultural crops have often been the object of attack in tropical regions. Thus, in crushing resistance during the Philippine Insurrection of 1899 to c. 1903, the USA systematically destroyed villages, storehouses, crops, and draught animals throughout entire provinces (table 1.2.15). Indeed, these campaigns were at that time compared favourably by US officers with those carried out by the Union forces during the US Civil War of 1861–1865 (cf. chapter 2, section IV). In their desultory decade-long attempt to suppress an insurgency in Malaya during the 1950s, the British carried out chemical attacks—both by air and from the ground—on crops, which were presumably grown by or for the insurgents (Clutterbuck, 1966; Henderson, 1955; Henniker, 1955: 180–181; Kutger, 1960–1961). The best recent example of tropical crop destruction is, however, provided by the Second Indochina War.

In its pursuit of the Second Indochina War, the USA carried out a routine military policy of systematic, large-scale, and indiscriminate crop destruction (Hay, 1974: 92–93; Westing, 1972 b). Intentional crop destruction in that war began as early as 1961 and continued relentlessly at least until mid-1971. Indeed, chemical crop destruction from the air of presumably enemy crops made up the greatest proportion of the largely unheralded though major US resource-denial programme. The US Chief of Staff in South Viet Nam directed that all US forces in South Viet Nam wage 'economic warfare' of this sort as a major component of their combat operations against the 'Viet Cong' enemy (Rosson, 1966). Rice, salt, and medicines not under US control were singled out for destruction in these orders. The stated aims of the programme were, among others, "to deny food (rice, cereals, and broad leaf crops) to VC [Viet Cong] and VC sympathizers, to direct VC manpower to crop production and to weaken VC strength . . . ".

Although much of the US 'economic warfare' was carried out from the air, a significant amount was also waged by ground forces. A US Army major has explained: "In many ways, the struggle for [Quang Nam province's] rice production reflected the whole effort to control the people and resources in I Military Region . . . '' (Rowe, 1971: 39). In another description, a US Marine colonel was able to report that the innovations in rice destruction techniques introduced under his command not only added a new level of efficiency to these operations, but were also "enjoyed" by all hands (Beck, 1970). A former US Army commander found that these ground operations—referred to in his outfit as 'environmental adjustment' or else as 'coconut raids'—were simple enough to accomplish. He explained that they were merely a matter of destroying the coconut (*Cocos nucifera*; Palmae) and mango (*Mangifera indica*; Anacardiaceae) groves, along with the other fruit orchards, the paddy dikes, and then the village structures themselves (Herbert & Wooten, 1973: 339–340).

Initial US military appraisals of the crop destruction programme must have been favourable, since in early 1964 the Chairman of the Joint Chiefs of Staff recommended to the Secretary of Defense that US armed forces intensify the use of herbicides for crop destruction (Defense, 1968: IV.C.1: 37–38; Gravel *et al.,* 1971–1972: vol. 3: 44–45).

The USA has not released any comprehensive information on the amounts of food that were intentionally destroyed by its forces during the course of the Second Indochina War. That portion alone which was destroyed by the aerial application of chemical anti-plant agents intended for crops (SIPRI, 1976: table 3.3) can be estimated—in terms of milled rice—to have been of the order of 306 million kilograms (table 3.3). This amount, in turn, represented the equivalent of more than 1.6 million entire diets.

The only official figures with which these calculations of intentional food destruction can be compared are some data that refer to just one year of the US crop destruction activities. The scientific advisory group to the Commander-in-Chief of all US forces in the Pacific theatre estimated that the USA had destroyed 108.9 million kilograms of food during 1967 in its intentional aerial herbicide crop destruction programme (Warren *et al.,* 1967). Of this total, 75.0 million kilograms was classified as rice (which would reduce to 45.0 million kilograms in milling) and the remaining 33.9 million kilograms was classified as dicotyledonous (broad-leafed) food crops. The total food destruction of 81.9 million kilograms calculated here for 1967 (table 3.3) accordingly compares rather well with this official figure.

The same scientific advisory group reported, moreover, that an additional 12.7 million kilograms of rice was intentionally destroyed during 1967 via ground operations (Warren *et al.,* 1967). All told, the group estimated that about 80 per cent of all crops grown in enemy-controlled territory in South Viet Nam that year had been destroyed. It concluded that crop destruction operations were an integral, essential, and effective part of the total US war effort in Indochina.

Looked at superficially, the destruction of 1.6 million entire annual diets through the intentional aerial spraying of 400 thousand hectares of agricultural lands over a period of a decade is not an overwhelming amount.

In terms of the 17.6 million inhabitants of South Viet Nam at the time this amount represents just under one per cent of the total number of annual diets presumably consumed during that period. Alternatively, in terms of the three million hectares of agricultural lands in South Viet Nam, this amount represents just over one per cent of the total number of hectares presumably tilled during that period. However, since most of this food destruction was carried out in the Central Highlands (especially in Military Regions I and II) (Lang *et al.,* 1974: map 8), one cannot meaningfully average out this deprivation over all of South Viet Nam.

The Central Highlands, the population of which then consisted largely of primitive hill tribesmen (Montagnards), are a traditionally food-poor region. As already mentioned, official estimates placed the level of food destruction in areas not under physical US control at about 80 per cent during 1967, including therefore essentially all of the Central Highlands. There is no doubt that similar levels of food destruction were accomplished during 1968 and 1969 as well. Moreover, on the basis of the official 1967 information, one can readily calculate the average of so-called enemy food destruction for the entire decade of spraying as having been 30 per cent per year. The following fragmentary information on two provinces in the Central Highlands of South Viet Nam further supports the conclusion that the USA was able to accomplish a high level of food destruction in this hapless region.

Quang Ngai—a particularly war-torn province in Military Region I—had a total area of 698.1 thousand hectares, an estimated 1969 population of 761 thousand (of which perhaps 15 per cent lived in Quang Ngai City), and agricultural lands that covered about 87.2 thousand hectares (Engineer Agency, 1968: 87–89; Development & Resources Corp., 1969: 51). Fifteen aerial crop-destruction missions were approved for Quang Ngai province for the year 1970, covering a total of some 73.7 thousand hectares (Lt. Tyson, US Army, Office of the US Province Senior Advisor, private communication, 22 August 1970). Thus, approximately 85 per cent of the agricultural lands had at least been scheduled for aerial destruction during 1970, presumably representing virtually all the crop lands in the province not under physical US control at that time. Moreover, the 73.7 thousand hectares scheduled for aerial chemical destruction that year did not include what was additionally scheduled for destruction by other aerial and ground operations.

Kontum—a province in Military Region II—had a total area of 911.2 thousand hectares and an estimated 1969 population of only 109 thousand (Engineer Agency, 1968: 87–89). According to a bomb-damage assessment officer stationed in that province throughout 1968, it was his continuing assignment to seek out by aerial reconnaissance all lands under cultivation throughout the province (with the exception of the tiny proportion under US control) and then oversee their destruction, usually by bombing (J. O. Pelton, US Army, private communication, 28 March 1972).

The main avowed purpose of the USA crop-destruction programme was to deny food to the enemy soldier. The guerrilla force in question—the 'Viet Cong'—had a strength estimated at about 600 thousand (Adams, 1975), that is, approximately three per cent of the South Vietnamese population of that time. However, since this force controlled at least four-fifths of the rural economy of South Viet Nam, it is plain that enormous amounts of food had to be destroyed by the USA for the enemy even to begin to experience any significant hardship. In one study commissioned by the US Department of Defense, it was concluded that for one tonne of rice denied to the 'Viet Cong' about 550 civilians would have to be deprived of their food (Russo, 1967). At an average daily per capita food consumption of 511 grams (table 3.3, note c), this is the equivalent of just over 110 civil deprivations for every military deprivation. This and a companion study (Betts & Denton, 1967) both concluded that the crop destruction programme resulted in drastic local food shortages among the civilian population—that is, in actual starvation among the Montagnards. By contrast, with respect to the military forces primarily against which the programme was ostensibly directed, the results were concluded to be "insignificant at best".

The two above-mentioned studies (Betts & Denton, 1967; Russo, 1967) were subsequently corroborated in their essential details by a third study, the latter having been jointly carried out by the US Department of Defense and the US Department of State (Herbicide Policy Review Committee, 1968). With respect to the crop destruction programme, this official investigation concluded: ". . . the available evidence indicates that the civilian population in VC [Viet Cong] controlled areas bears the brunt of food denial activities" (p. 17); and further concluded: ". . . it does seem highly unlikely that destroying crops to the extent that more than 99 per cent (or 95, or perhaps even 90 per cent) are civilian grown is appropriate" (p. 21). In other words, of the estimated 1.6 million entire annual diets which the USA intentionally destroyed by the aerial application of chemicals over the years during which this programme continued, somewhere between 1.5 million and 1.6 million are known to have been intended for civilian consumption (cf. Army, 1956:18).

The discussion has so far dealt with the intentional crop destruction brought about by the aerial application of chemical anti-plant agents and by other means. To this intentional crop destruction must be added the incidental crop destruction—large in amount—which was a side-effect of the widespread forest spray missions. Such secondary food destruction seems to be impossible to quantify, although it is known to have been extensive (Carrier, 1974; Fall, 1965–1966; Murphy *et al.*, 1974: chap. 5; Thomas, 1974; Westing, 1972 *a*; White, 1965). On the basis of local studies, Thomas (1974: 58) goes so far as to say that more unintentional than intentional crop destruction occurred in South Viet Nam. One example of incidental crop destruction is given below merely to indicate the actual scope of this casual food devastation.

About 70 thousand hectares of Kompong Cham province in the so-called Fish Hook region of eastern Cambodia were subjected to attack by chemical anti-plant agents by the USA during the spring of 1969 (Westing, 1972 a). Although rural and largely wooded, the sprayed area nevertheless supported some 309 thousand semi-destitute inhabitants, dependent essentially for their entire food supply on subsistence farming. The spraying wiped out virtually all their local garden and field crops already planted for that year. Equally or even more detrimental to the well-being of the local population, tens of thousands of privately owned papaya (*Carica papaya*; Caricaceae), jack (*Artocarpus heterophyllus*; Moraceae), mango (*Mangifera indica*; Anacardiaceae), and other fruit trees lost their fruits. Moreover, a high proportion of these trees were killed outright. For example, it was estimated that perhaps 45 thousand of the locally important jackfruit trees had succumbed to the 'poison from the sky'.

Reverting to the overall US crop-destruction programme, one of its results—if not one of its aims as well—was the displacement of large numbers of indigenous rural civilians into areas under physical control by the USA. However, large numbers of the affected population chose not to abandon their ancestral lands in spite of the deprivation and hazards that such a decision entailed. It is not unreasonable to assume that within this group the effects of food deprivation were most acutely felt by infants, the aged, expectant mothers and their unborn children, nursing mothers, and the sick.

Not inventoried or quantified by the USA was the extent to which its Rome-plough clearing operations in South Viet Nam destroyed agricultural lands—often including extensive systems of paddy dikes—and even entire rural residential areas and farming hamlets. By way of example, Peterson (1971) gave a brief description of the destruction by Rome ploughs of the 560 hectares of once fertile paddies of Duc Hue in west-central Hau Ngai province (in Military Region III). Peterson reported that the soil was left "bare, gray and lifeless". When this observer inquired about the destruction of homes in the area, a land-clearing platoon sergeant explained: "How do I decide about houses? Well, if it don't have anybody in it we knock them down." Elsewhere, a captain of engineers (after detailing the techniques he had pioneered in Sa Dec and Vinh Long provinces in the Delta region [Military Region IV] for land-clearing in wet paddy areas) at least provided his colleagues with the admonition, "One point worthy of special thought is that the Vietnamese hold land particularly dear, and the clearing of [it] destroys part of their livelihood" (Draper, 1971: 258).

In practice, however, not much seemed to be immune from destruction by the Rome ploughs. Indeed, military spokesmen did not seem to be reticent about reporting such destruction in the open literature. Thus, Draper (1971) reported not only the destruction of agricultural fields, but also the discovery and subsequent destruction of a 10-bed hospital. Massey

(1970) reported the destruction of X-ray equipment, surgical equipment, blood plasma, antibiotics, and other medicinal supplies. An inventory of three years of US Rome-plough devastation in the five northern provinces of South Viet Nam (Military Region I), between 1969 and 1971, included the razing of hundreds of hamlets, the obliteration of thousands of graves, and the levelling of many thousands of hectares of rice fields and orchards (Agence Presse Gouvernement Provisoire, 1972: 14). It may be noted here in passing that US Rome-plough operating procedures in South Viet Nam occasionally seemed to call for a grotesque extension of the topiary art. At least four huge designs—one a divisional emblem extending over almost 400 hectares—were carved into the vegetational cover and soil surface of that region by exuberant army engineers (Kiernan, 1967; *Life,* 1971; *Times,* 1970).

Certainly the most notorious and well-documented case of obliteration by tractors of an entire village and its fields is that of Ben Suc. Ben Suc had been a farming community of 3 800 inhabitants in west-central Binh Duong province (in Military Region III). The wiping out of this village was the opening phase of Operation Cedar Falls—a massive search-and-destroy operation through the Iron Triangle which began in January 1967 (Rogers, 1974).

The destruction of Ben Suc rated only two sentences in the published description of Operation Cedar Falls by the colonel of engineers who commanded the tractor operations involved (Kiernan, 1967). A somewhat more detailed and probing description has been provided by Mirsky (1967), and Schell (1967) has prepared an eloquent book-length analysis. One can turn to Shipler (1973) for a brief account of the still pitiful condition of the displaced survivors of Ben Suc more than six years after the day of infamy.

The US approach at Ben Suc is reminiscent of the total destruction of ancient Carthage at the close of the Third Punic War (149–146 BC) at the hands of the Romans, who dealt similarly—but not quite as efficiently—with this city (table 1.2.3). To quote Scullard (1961: 307):

The final agony of Carthage was at hand. . . . For six days and nights the Romans fought . . . amid the houses which they burned and destroyed one after another. . . . For ten more days the fires of Carthage burned; the ruins were razed; a plough was drawn over the site; salt was thrown in the furrows; a solemn curse was pronounced against its future re-birth; Carthage had been destroyed.

Wildlife

As previously suggested, the most profound impact of military activities on the fauna is usually an indirect one, via their impact on the faunal habitat. Thus, any of various operations that decimate the vegetative cover also decimate concomitantly the sources of food and shelter of the associated animal life. This obligate relationship between an animal and its milieu is a fundamental tenet of wildlife biology (Leopold, 1933; Allen, 1962). The connection becomes even more evident in tropical than in temperate forests because an especially high proportion of the tropical fauna are restricted to the tree-tops (Allee & Schmidt, 1951: 511–514; Richards, 1970; Ripley *et al.*, 1964). As Audy (1948) so aptly conceived of it, forest destruction in the tropics converts a rich three-dimensional habitat to a depauperate two-dimensional one.

Severe site disturbance leads more or less rapidly to the establishment of a new vegetational community, one that is likely to be drastically different from the original one. Not only will the new plant and animal communities contain species that are new to the area (and frequently undesirable in human terms), but they will as well comprise substantially fewer species. For example, Audy (1948) in Malaysia was able to link high population levels of the scrub typhus vector mites (*Leptotrombidium*; Trombiculidae) to habitat disturbance. Also in Malaysia, Harrison (1968) has observed that the destruction of indigenous tropical rain forest resulted in the virtual elimination of the native mammalian fauna, previously introduced rats then being the most prominent residual species.

It should come as no surprise that the destruction of wildlife habitat was one of the pervasive concomitants of battle damage during the Second Indochina War. Nowhere was this more obvious than in the mangrove estuaries that were laid waste (SIPRI, 1976: 38–40). The normally rich avian fauna populating the mangroves was decimated. The aquatic fauna—both vertebrate and invertebrate, both freshwater and marine—that depends upon this habitat for at least part of its life cycle suffered as well. There are also persuasive indications that the widespread military destruction of the mangrove habitat in South Viet Nam led to increased numbers of the malaria vector mosquito *Anopheles* (Culicidae). The increase in mosquitoes seemed to be partly attributable to the many millions of water-filled bomb craters, which provide breeding grounds containing a relatively limited range of mosquito predators (Westing & Pfeiffer, 1972). Rodent population levels also increased dramatically in some of the herbicide-decimated areas of South Viet Nam (Desowitz *et al.*, 1974).

Threatened or endangered species are scattered throughout the world (Curry-Lindahl, 1972; Fisher *et al.*, 1969; Greenway, 1967; Ziswiler, 1967). Ngan (1968), for example, listed five animal species as being on the verge of extirpation, at any rate from South Viet Nam: a tapir (*Tapirus indicus*; Tapiridae), a bear (*Ursus tibetanus*; Ursidae), a gibbon (*Hylobates pileatus*; Pongidae), a pheasant (*Lophura imperialis*; Phasianidae), and the kouprey (*Bos sauveli*; Bovidae). In fact, some Indochinese zoologists fear that the Second Indochina War may have dealt the *coup de grâce* to the already highly endangered kouprey species (cf. also Curry-Lindahl, 1972: 149–150; Fisher *et al.*, 1969: 142–143; Fitter, 1973–1974: 447; Nowak 1976: 16–17). Another animal should also be mentioned here, the well-being of which—if not its existence—has been threatened by that war. The large freshwater tarpon *Megalops cyprinoides* (Megalopidae) seems to have been at least locally extirpated from the Mekong Delta region of South Viet Nam (Le Van Dang, South Viet Nam Inland Fisheries Service, private communication, 7 August 1970).

Some of the larger wildlife escape direct battle injury by their ability to flee from areas of military commotion. For example, in the relatively peaceful eastern Cambodia of 1969, the population of muntjacs (*Muntiacus muntjak*; Cervidae) and other species of deer; of wild cattle, such as gaurs (*Bos gaurus*; Bovidae), bantengs (*B. banteng*), and some koupreys (*B. sauveli*); of elephants (*Elephas maximus*; Elephantidae); of a number of monkey species (Cercopithecidae); and of wild pigs (*Sus* spp.; Suidae) had all increased shortly before that time to relatively high levels—refugees from the fighting in neighbouring South Viet Nam (Westing, 1972 *a*: 197). However, for many animals such escape is not possible even if they are mobile: the undisturbed areas of potential refuge are already likely to be populated to their maximum carrying capacity, or else the animals may instinctively be incapable of deserting their home territory.

Scavengers—both large and small—benefit from the aftermath of battle. Indeed, there exist macabre reports to the effect that tigers (*Panthera tigris*; Felidae) in South Viet Nam were thriving during the Second Indochina War on the widely scattered bodies of dead and wounded soldiers (Orians & Pfeiffer, 1970: 553; Nowak, 1976: 18).

Some experience with livestock gained after herbicidal attacks during the Second Indochina War may be mentioned here inasmuch as it is likely to be similarly applicable to wildlife (Hickey, 1974: 15–16; Orians & Pfeiffer, 1970; Westing, 1972 *a*: 196–197). The livestock in sprayed villages were commonly reported to fall ill for a period of several days soon after the attack. The larger domestic animals, such as water buffaloes (*Bubalus bubalus*; Bovidae), zebus (*Bos indicus*; Bovidae), and mature pigs (*Sus scrofa*; Suidae), became only mildly ill and recovered. On the other hand, the smaller animals, such as chickens (*Gallus gallus*; Phasianidae), ducks (*Anas*; Anatidae), and young pigs, suffered more severely, and in some cases even died. The domestic mammals were described as being afflicted with digestive disorders, anorexia (loss of appetite), and in some cases with fasciculation (muscular twitching). The poultry were said to have become partially paralysed for a time. Wild birds became similarly disabled and could be captured with ease.

Whereas damage to vegetation is expected to be the natural outcome of herbicidal attack, a number of explanations can be offered for the reported damage to livestock. Among these are exposure to high agent doses (especially from the rather frequent emergency dumpings of entire loads) and to toxic impurities in the agents, most notably dioxin (2,3,7,8-tetrachlorodibenzo-*p*-dioxin) (*SIPRI Yearbook 1977*: chap. 4; Westing, 1978 *a*). Moreover, some damage could have resulted from unexpected varietal sensitivities or from increased susceptibilities caused by unfavourable nutritional or health conditions. It should also be noted that when plants are exposed to sublethal doses of phenoxy herbicides of the type employed as chemical anti-plant agents, some species are stimulated to produce nitrate levels that are sufficiently high to be toxic to livestock feeding on them (Stahler & Whitehead, 1950; Swanson & Shaw, 1954; Whitehead *et al.*, 1956).

Whereas much of the wildlife disruption during the Second Indochina War was of a secondary nature, in other parts of the world wildlife disruption has been caused more directly. For example, in Africa, the northern white (square-lipped) rhinoceros (*Ceratotherium simum cottoni*: Rhinocerotidae) has been placed under great pressure owing partly to encroachment by a growing population, but mostly to ruthless shooting for its horns, thought in some parts of the world to have aphrodisiac properties (Curry-Lindahl, 1971–1972; Fisher *et al.*, 1969: 117–119; Fitter, 1973–1974: 445). This huge placid beast was once distributed in Africa north of the equator, but by the early 1960s had apparently been reduced to four populations—three quite small-sized ones, in south-western Sudan, north-western Uganda, and the Central African Republic respectively; and only one relatively large one of about 1 200 or so individuals in the Garamba National Park in north-eastern Zaïre.

Rebels holding sway over south-western Sudan during the late 1950s and early 1960s either carried out or permitted the slaughter of the rhinoceroses in this region, the local population dwindling from about 350 to fewer than 25. Similarly, in Zaïre, during the latter part of the Congo Civil War of 1960–1964 (table 8.2.5), rebel forces took control of the Garamba National Park, and during their tenure the animals were pitilessly massacred, the number shrinking during this brief period from just over 1 200 to fewer than 30. By the early 1970s there appeared to be fewer than 200 northern white rhinoceroses in existence, and the race (although not the species as a whole) is in danger of imminent extinction.

Man

As previously noted, the impact of war on man *per se* is largely beyond the scope of the present work (appendix 2.3). The human consequences of the Second Indochina War summarized below are presented only to indicate the possible dimensions of this impact in a tropical habitat.

The social effects of bombing and shelling stem from at least the following categories of destruction: *(a)* loss of human life, injury, disease, and displacement; *(b)* devastation of urban and industrial areas and of the associated artefacts; and *(c)* disruption of rural areas—both the agricultural and the more natural ones—and of natural resources (raw materials). Indeed, the impact of the high-explosive munitions on the once largely rural peoples of Indochina has been profound by any conceivable measure. The high population densities in parts of Indochina—102 persons per square kilometre in South Viet Nam at the time—made it simply impossible for 14 million tonnes of munitions not to take their toll. By the end of its overt participation in the war, the USA had expended 306 kilograms of munitions per inhabitant of all Indochina, and far higher amounts per capita in selected regions (table 3.2). Although pertinent statistics are very hard to come by, the resulting casualties and the numbers displaced are known to have added up to many millions. Throughout Indochina, the war resulted in perhaps 1.8 million fatalities (table 1.3.3) as well as in 3.8 million serious injuries; it also created some 17 million refugees. Thus, 1 person in 26 having been killed, 1 person in 12 having been seriously injured, and more than 1 person in 3 having been displaced (i.e., made a refugee), the social upheaval was truly phenomenal. This impact has been well described by Kennedy (1974: 99–103 *passim*).

Regarding South Viet Nam, Kennedy reported:

The dislocations caused by the war have shattered the social fabric of [South] Vietnamese life. The full extent of the war's impact upon the land and people of [South] Vietnam is extensive and difficult to record. Along with the toll in lives and lost limbs, there has been an accompanying toll in the strength and functioning of societal institutions. Once a predominantly rural society, today over 65% of South Vietnam's population is in urbanized areas. South Vietnam is now an agricultural deficit area. A massive social welfare problem has emerged in the needed care of 880 000 orphans or half orphans, 650 000 war widows, and some 181 000 disabled amputees, paraplegics, blind and deaf.

For North Viet Nam, Kennedy stated: ". . . massive damage did occur throughout the country to medical facilities, schools, housing, churches, cultural centers, etc. At least 1 000 000 persons became homeless and civilian casualties numbered in the thousands" (cf. also Westing, 1973).

For Cambodia, Kennedy reported:

Half its population have become refugees. . . . War damage has been extensive. Once a rice-rich nation, Cambodia depends now [January 1974] for three-fourths of its rice from the United States. Nearly 50% of the hospital facilities have been destroyed; over 40% of the roads are out; some 35% of all bridges are down; communications and transportation are severely disrupted; and its meagre industrial capacity shattered.

For Laos, Kennedy noted:

Urgently needed . . . is physical rehabilitation of war victims. As a result of the bombing and war, there is probably a higher percentage [of] handicapped or lame people among the population of Laos than among the people of South Vietnam and, perhaps, even of Cambodia. The children of Laos were especially hard hit. Uncounted thousands are handicapped or lame. The problem of orphans is swept under the rug. . . . Malaria and other diseases are rampant all over the country.

Moreover, it is clear that, apart from the direct injuries sustained, numerous medical problems were attributable to the massive US bombing and shelling. Thus, with respect to malaria—just mentioned above—the additional breeding opportunities for the vector mosquito *Anopheles*

(Culicidae) provided by the millions of water-filled craters were assumed by local physicians to have contributed to the significant regional increase in the incidence of this disease (Lewis, 1970; Westing & Pfeiffer, 1972). To take another serious disease, the alarming regional increase in plague reported by the World Health Organization could also be substantially attributed to the habitat disruption brought about by the bombing and shelling (WHO, 1973; 1976).

Throughout rural Indochina the bombing destroyed hospitals and other public health facilities, and interrupted public health practices (Melman, 1968: chap. 16; Westing, 1970; WHO, 1976). Moreover, the food-producing capacity of many Indochinese was severely reduced. This led to higher levels of malnutrition and thus to lowered disease resistance. Among other things, the massive population displacements caused by the bombing and shelling brought the refugees in contact with novel strains of viruses such as those causing haemorrhagic fever, against which they had no immunity. Rickets was reported by Vietnamese physicians among children forced by the US bombing to spend prolonged periods living underground (Lewis, 1970). During the war, Indochina experienced major epidemics of malaria, plague, cholera, haemorrhagic fever, leprosy, tuberculosis, and syphilis (Neel, 1973: chap. 13; WHO, 1968; 1976). Malaria was also the major cause of medical disablement of military personnel during the Second Indochina War and was responsible for more duty-time lost than any other factor, enemy action included (Canfield, 1972; Dirks, 1974; Neel, 1973). This situation is all the more striking in the light of the massive and sustained US vector control programme and the prophylactic medication constantly imposed upon all US personnel in that theatre of war. Plague increased and spread throughout the war years despite intensive attempts at vector control and the most massive plague vaccination programme in history (Marshall *et al.*, 1967; Velimirovic, 1974; WHO, 1973). Finally, the frequency of psychiatric disorders rose during the Second Indochina War—for example, the rise of schizophrenia in South Viet Nam (Markham, 1975). Besides, Vietnamese subjected to herbicidal attack during that war were found, as a result, to have been suffering from long-term psychological damage (Murphy *et al.*, 1974: chap. 8).

Unexploded munitions. Both anti-vehicle and anti-personnel mines (the former primarily blast weapons, and the latter primarily fragmentation weapons) were used widely during the Second Indochina War. Moreover, time-delay and other anti-personnel weapons were dispensed by the millions from US aircraft, particularly in Laos, Cambodia, and North Viet Nam. The wide and grotesque variety of this class of weapons developed by the USA for use against the Indochinese have by now been described a number of times (Council on Economic Priorities, 1970; Kanegis *et al.*, 1970; Krepon, 1973–1974; Prokosch, 1972; 1976; SIPRI, 1979: chap. 7), but the actual numbers expended have not been made public.

On the other hand, a rough estimate is possible of the magnitude of the problem of dud munitions in Indochina. Approximately 20 million bombs of various sizes and an additional 230 million artillery and naval shells were expended by the USA during the Second Indochina War (table 3.4). Expenditures by the other side amounted to less than 0.3 per cent of those by the USA. Using conservative estimates of 2 per cent for the bomb dud rate and 1 per cent for the shell dud rate, it can be seen that there might now be more than 400 thousand unexploded bombs and over 2 million unexploded shells buried just beneath the surface of Indochina. Moreover, despite their importance, no attempt is made here to estimate the numbers of dud mortar shells, rockets, and grenades that really should be added to the present compilation.

In human terms, the problem of unexploded munitions in Indochina is a truly grave one, and promises to remain so for decades to come. For example, Morrow (1972), reporting from Laos, wrote: "One or two country people are brought to Luang Prabang hospital almost every day with the wounds of bombs that did not go off when they were supposed to. . . . It is easy to understand the villagers' complaints that they can no longer tend some of their bananas, plant hill rice, nor let their children out to play freely." Hickey (1973: 56), reporting on South Viet Nam, wrote:

. . . there is a serious problem from things like mine fields, unexploded bombs, unexploded artillery rounds all over the place. There are places in the highlands where Montagnards will not even go into the forest to hunt because of bombs lying around. Lots of people come into provincial hospitals with wounds from stepping on old mines or who somehow detonated unexploded rounds. It is a problem all over the rural areas.

In a visit to Quang Tri province in South Viet Nam, Luce (1974) found that injuries from previously unexploded munitions constituted the most serious medical problem in the province, ahead of even malaria or tuberculosis. Another visitor to this province learned that some 300 people and 1 thousand water buffaloes (*Bubalus bubalus*; Bovidae) had been killed there by previously unexploded munitions during the year before (Fonda, 1974). In Vinh Giang village (in the Vinh Linh district of Quang Tri province just north of the former Demarcation Line), with a population of 5 thousand, there were 10 explosion casualties—none fatal—during the first half of 1973 (Ngo Duc Cam, Village Chairman, private communication, 9 August 1973). In Quang Binh province in North Viet Nam, with a population of 450 thousand, there were during this same time about 40 human casualties and more than 10 times that number of livestock casualties (Dinh Van Ich, Vice-President, Province Administrative Committee, private communication, 10 August 1973). Indeed, there are large portions of Indochina where there seems to be no peasant family that cannot recount a personal tragedy—whether of death or maiming—caused by previously unexploded munitions (Westing, 1975).

Recovery

The rates of ecological and social recovery from the devastation and trauma of war are, of course, dependent upon a large number of intrinsic and extrinsic variables, which means that only some general remarks can be made. Whereas the general principles of recovery of disrupted ecosystems were summarized in chapter 1 (section III), the following comments refer to the peculiarities of the tropical habitat, and deal with the natural and agricultural ecosystems.

Where the vegetational cover is destroyed on tropical upland sites, the land soon becomes fully occupied by vegetation, often within months. The pioneer vegetation on such greatly disrupted sites is likely to be a relatively pure stand of grassy vegetation, sometimes woody but more often herbaceous. In South Viet Nam and elsewhere in Indochina, the woody grasses (Gramineae) likely to colonize these disturbed areas are frutescent (shrubby) bamboos, such as *Bambusa, Thyrsostachys,* and *Oxytenanthera* (Drew, 1974), whereas the most likely herbaceous grass is the pantropically notorious *Imperata cylindrica* (for information on *Imperata,* see Hubbard *et al.,* 1944). Severe disturbance may also invite invasion by herbaceous non-grasses, or forbs, such as *Eupatorium* (Compositae), especially, for example, in North Viet Nam.

The tenure of these weedy species, known for their ability to survive on severely impoverished sites, may be quite lengthy. The stands of bamboo (known as 'brakes') may readily dominate the site they have occupied for half a century or longer. Dicotyledonous forest trees are presented a possible opportunity to regain a foothold—that is, to take over as the next successional stage—only once every several or more decades, at the time of general flowering and culm (stem) death. Moreover, the tenure of the bamboo pioneer stage is prolonged by an occasional fire (Drew, 1974). The occupancy of a site by these bamboo brakes can be so protracted that this pioneer stage of succession could at the same time be referred to as a pseudo-climax stage.

The *Imperata* grass may also become a semi-permanent feature of the tropical landscape, in particular if its competition is weakened by an occasional fire. Vast tracts of seemingly permanent tropical savanna are maintained in just this fashion (Budowski, 1956; Holmes, 1951; Wharton, 1966; 1968). Experience gained in Sumatra, Indonesia, suggests that if fires do not occur on the site, forest can usually crowd out the *Imperata* within 10 to 15 years or so (Nye & Greenland, 1960: chap. 7). On the other hand, according to the work done by Holmes (1951) in Ceylon (Sri Lanka), if the tenure of this grass is extended for long periods, it will then be able to maintain itself even in the absence of fires. However, he found that the stage could be set for natural reinvasion by native trees if a plantation of the exotic *Eucalyptus robusta* (Myrtaceae) were first established (Holmes, 1951: 52–54). Although no other biological means of controlling *Imperata* seems

97

to be available at present (Rao *et al.*, 1971: 112–113), it is possible to resort to a number of mechanical and chemical means (Laurie, 1974; Soerjani, 1970).

The successional progress towards the tropical steady-state climax community has not been studied nearly as much as its temperate counterpart (Richards, 1952: chap. 17; SIPRI, 1976: 76–80; Whitmore, 1975: chap. 18). It may, in fact, be as slow in the tropics as it is in the temperate zones (Opler *et al.*, 1977). For example, Meijer (1970) investigated a forest in North Borneo (Sabah) some 40 years after logging and found it to be still remarkably different from the neighbouring uncut forest (cf. also Meijer, 1973). Taylor (1957) found the same to be the case for a site in northern New Guinea which had been drastically disturbed some 83 years before his observations. In the disturbed site only 110 different tree species were present (of which 56 were climax species) as opposed to considerably more than 500 in the equivalent undisturbed forest nearby. Moreover, Chevalier (1948: 110) found that a forest in north-central Cambodia known to have been developing on cleared land which had been abandoned to nature some 500 to 600 years previously, although closely resembling nearby primeval forest, still exhibited noticeable differences.

A rather different picture emerges when one examines the tropical coastal mangrove habitat. When this association is destroyed—as was extensively done by herbicides during the Second Indochina War (SIPRI, 1976: 38–40)—the site does not readily become recolonized. Lack of adequate seed source, destruction of available propagules by crabs (Brachyura), and other more obscure factors combine to turn such mangrove sites into a muddy wasteland for the indefinite future. It has been calculated that substantial initial recovery may be expected to take more than a century (Odum *et al.*, 1974: 289).

Recovery following war damage to tropical agriculture can be a slow and laborious process. Once a rice paddy or other farm land has been bombed or shelled, the peasants are reluctant to reclaim it even after the war has moved to a different location or has ended. The task of filling in the craters is an arduous one, an average of 67 cubic metres of soil being required to fill a typical '500 pound' (241 kilogram) bomb crater (SIPRI, 1976: 23). A US intelligence report suggests that it takes up to about 500 man-hours of hard labour to fill in such a crater (*Times*, 1972). Moreover, the shards of metal are dangerous to the water buffaloes (*Bubalus bubalus*; Bovidae) or other livestock used as draught animals, since the resulting foot injuries are liable to become infected. There also exists the continuing threat, previously described, of unexploded munitions. Disrupted ,irrigation systems must be rebuilt; and bomb-destroyed sea-walls necessitate not only reconstruction, but also a lengthy process of soil reclamation. Finally, sundry social, political, and other factors have been suggested as placing additional impediments in the way of post-war recovery (Lumsden, 1972; 1975).

V. Conclusion

The tropical habitat is beset by a number of grave ecological problems, the origins of which can be traced to the already serious and rapidly growing regional over-population, to the political, economic, and educational immaturity of the many newly independent tropical nations and the related legacy of colonial exploitation, or to a combination of these two groups of factors. The renewable natural resources of the tropics are being widely utilized beyond their capacity to regenerate. Forests are being cut without regard to renewal, savannas are being overgrazed and thereby turned to desert, and agricultural lands are being farmed too intensively for the soil to maintain its fertility. Agricultural and urban expansion is occurring at the expense of lands that should best be maintained as forest or savanna. The short-term gains from these practices shrink to insignificance in the light of the long-term disasters they portend—regional disasters with global ramifications.

The rather frequent wars that occur in the tropics are not only an outgrowth of the unstable human ecosystem represented by the tropical habitat of today, but they also serve to hasten the process of environmental deterioration. Among the ecological lessons that have been learned from one major recent tropical conflict—the Second Indochina War—are: *(a)* that the vegetation can be severely damaged or even destroyed with relative ease over extensive areas—and, of course, with it the ecosystem for which it provides the basis; *(b)* that natural, agricultural, and industrial-crop plant communities are all likewise vulnerable; and *(c)* that the ecological impact of such actions is likely to be of long duration.

Long ago, John Stuart Mill (1871: Book 1, chap. 5, p. 7) was able to explain that countries had the capacity for recovering rapidly from the ravages of war because their land and its permanent improvements remained undestroyed. It is clear from recent tropical warfare that Mill would not have had the same grounds for optimism today.

Table 3.1. Tropical habitat: distribution and demography (1975 data)[a]

Region	Tropical area $10^3\,km^2$ $(10^5\,ha)$	Proportion of regional area per cent	Tropical population[b] 10^6	Proportion of regional population per cent	Tropical population density No./km²
Land mass					
North America	1 904	8.7	70.8	22.5	37.2
South America	13 190	74.1	166.4	77.1	12.6
Africa	15 494	52.2	256.0	65.5	16.5
Europe	0	0	0	0	0
Asia	5 410	13.0	831.2	37.5	153.6
Australia	2 306	30.0	2.0	15.0	0.9
Antarctica	0	0	0	0	0
Islands	3 935	54.2	259.3	59.7	65.9
of Atlantic Ocean	244	35.4	27.1	30.9	111.1
of Pacific Ocean	3 031	82.5	208.8	64.7	68.9
of Indian Ocean	661	99.9	23.4	98.9	35.4
of Arctic Ocean	0	0	0	0	0
Hemisphere					
Northern	20 734	20.5	1 247.9	34.3	60.2
Southern	21 505	45.3	337.8	78.7	15.7
World-wide	**42 239**	**28.4**	**1 585.7**	**39.0**	**37.5**

Sources and notes:
[a] The regions, which are strictly geographic, are described in table 1.4, note *a*. Sources for the areas and populations are given in table 1.4, note *b*.
[b] The population of the tropical habitat is currently increasing at the rate of 2.49 per cent per year (table 1.4), which leads to a population doubling time of 28.2 years.

Table 3.2. Hostile actions by the USA during the Second Indochina War: regional intensities[a]

Region[b]	On an area basis *(per hectare)*			On a population basis *(per capita)*		
	Munitions fired kg	Herbicides sprayed[c] litres	Land cleared m²	Munitions fired kg	Herbicides sprayed[c] litres	Land cleared m²
South Viet Nam	587	4.2	190	577	4.1	180
Military Region I	1 166	4.4	250	1 066	4.0	230
Military Region II	268	2.0	60	669	4.9	160
Military Region III	1 431	12.7	660	890	7.9	410
without Saigon				1 833	16.3	850
Military Region IV	134	1.7	10	77	1.0	0
North Viet Nam	67	?	0	57	?	0
Cambodia	42	?	0	113	?	0
Laos	94	?	0	773	?	0
Indochina	**189**	**1.0**	**40**	**306**	**1.6**	**70**

Sources and notes:
[a] Adapted from SIPRI (1976: table 1.4), the added Rome-plough land-clearing data being hitherto unpublished estimates.

[b] The regions are depicted by SIPRI (1976: maps 1.1 and 1.2).
[c] To convert any of the given herbicide volume data to average kilograms of active ingredients, multiply by 0.7569.

Table 3.3. Herbicidal crop destruction from the air by the USA during the Second Indochina War

Year	Crop lands sprayed[a] 10^3 ha $(10$ km²$)$	Food destroyed (dry weight)[b] 10^6 kg	Entire annual diets denied[c] 10^3
1961	?	?	?
1962	0.3	0.27	1.5
1963	1.4	1.20	6.4
1964	5.4	4.50	24.1
1965	12.7	10.63	56.9
1966	48.3	40.55	217.2
1967	97.5	81.92	438.8
1968	96.9	81.37	435.9
1969	86.8	72.89	390.5
1970	14.4	12.14	65.0
1971	0.2	0.16	0.9
1972	0	0	0
1973	0	0	0
Total	**363.8**	**305.62**	**1 637.3**

Sources and notes:
[a] The crop lands aerially sprayed each year are based on the total volume of herbicides expended each year (SIPRI, 1976: table 3.2), the standard application rate of 28.062 litres per hectare (SIPRI, 1976: table 3.1), and the overall proportion of crop-destruction missions carried out, that is, 14.1 per cent (SIPRI, 1976: table 3.3).
[b] The amount of food destroyed is based entirely upon the production levels of upland rice (*Oryza sativa*; Gramineae) in South Vietnamese shifting slash-and-burn, or *rai,* agriculture. An average annual yield of such upland rice is reported to be 1 400 kilograms per hectare, which—with a weight loss of 40 per cent in the conversion to milled rice—becomes 840 kilograms (Lafont, 1967).
[c] The number of entire annual diets denied is based upon South Vietnamese *rai* agriculture being able to sustain an average of 4.5 Montagnards per hectare per year, which represents 511 grams per capita per day of milled rice or its equivalent (Lafont, 1967).

Table 3.4. Numbers of unexploded bombs and shells remaining from the Second Indochina War: an estimate

Region[a]	Bombs dropped[b] 10^3	Bomb duds[c] 10^3	Shells fired[b] 10^3	Shell duds[c] 10^3
South Viet Nam	10 036	201	222 061	2 221
Military Region I	3 234	65	71 548	715
Military Region II	2 037	41	45 076	451
Military Region III	4 262	85	94 307	943
Military Region IV	503	10	11 130	111
North Viet Nam	2 746	55	2 581	26
Cambodia	1 916	38	4 526	45
Laos	6 686	134	0	0
Indochina	**21 384**	**428**	**229 168**	**2 292**

Sources and notes:

[a] The regions are depicted by SIPRI (1976: maps 1.1 and 1.2).

[b] Basic munition tonnage data are from SIPRI (1976: table 2.2, the values for each region being reduced as in 1976: table 2.5). Basic munition information is from SIPRI (1976: table 2.4), the following somewhat arbitrary expenditure proportions by weight replacing the rankings. For the bombs: '500 pound', 60 per cent; '750 pound', 30 per cent; and '2 000 pound', 10 per cent. For the artillery shells: 105 millimetre, 60 per cent; 155 millimetre, 25 per cent; 8 inch, 10 per cent; and 175 millimetre, 5 per cent. For the naval shells (in the light of Korean War data): 5 inch, 40 per cent; 16 inch, 40 per cent; and 8 inch, 20 per cent (1 pound = 0.454 kilogram; 1 inch = 25.4 millimetres).

[c] A dud rate factor of two per cent is used for bombs and of one per cent for shells (US Department of Defense, private correspondence, 8 October 1971; cf. also Kennedy, 1974: 23; Mahon, 1972: 198).

Appendix 3.1

Sources for the tropical habitat

1. *Environment and ecology.* For a description of the tropical environment and the plants and animals it supports, see Cloudsley-Thompson (1975: chap. 3 and 4) and Richards (1970); for tropical Asia in particular, see Ripley *et al.* (1964). The classical study of tropical forest ecology was made by Richards (1952), and there is a more recent work on the subject by Walter (1971); for the Far East in particular, see the excellent study by Whitmore (1975). The mangrove habitat has been described by Chapman (1976), Davis (1939–1940), Macnae (1968), and others. Tropical soils are covered by Mohr *et al.* (1972) and Nye & Greenland (1960). Strahler (1975: chap. 15) provides a summary of tropical climate.

2. *Civil use and abuse.* The geography of the tropical regions of the world has been well described by Heintzelman & Highsmith (1973: part 2). For treatments of tropical conservation in general, see Talbot & Talbot (1968) and Bouillenne (1962). The use and abuse of tropical forests are covered by Brünig (1977), Donaldson *et al.* 1978, Gómez-Pompa *et al.* (1972), Lamb (1977), Leslie (1977–1978), Richards (1971; 1973), and others. Tropical game management is reviewed by Vos (1977–1978). The use and abuse of tropical agricultural lands are covered by Croat (1972), Fernando & Thomas (1977–1978), Janzen (1973), Sanchez & Buol (1975), and others.

3. *Military use and abuse.* Benoit (1977–1978) and Daalder (1962) outline the role of the military sector in the development of the poor—and thus, in effect, mostly tropical—nations, suggesting a number of beneficial results. Tropical military training and combat are the subjects of articles by Cross (1971) and Lance (1965). SIPRI (1976) analyses the ecological consequences of warfare in the tropics (cf. also Neilands *et al.*, 1972). The social impact of warfare in the tropics has been especially well presented by Branfman (1972), Chaliand (1968), Gerassi (1968), Lewallen (1971), Luce & Sommer (1969), and Schell (1968). Four recent reports—by Casella (1978*a*), Kennedy (1976), Umbricht *et al.* (1976), and Umbricht *et al.* (1978)—provide excellent summaries of the aftermath of the Second Indochina War, placing special emphasis on the social and economic consequences.

4. Desert regions

The tables for this chapter appear on page 112.

I. Introduction

The desert areas of the world—characterized by great aridity and an annual frost-free season—occupy 18 per cent of the global land area. This land supports only one per cent of the global biomass which, in turn, accounts for one per cent of the annual global biomass production. It further supports 2.5 per cent of the world's human population, distributed among 22 nations and one colony. Among the desert nations are found several of the richest nations of the world, owing to their oil deposits. The majority of the desert nations were founded or gained their independence since World War II. Although among the most environmentally hostile on Earth, some of the desert regions of the world are of major economic or military significance owing to their mineral resources, locations, or quirks of history. Local wars have been occurring with some frequency among desert nations. A war likely to be environmentally disruptive occurs perhaps once every 40 years in the desert regions of the world.

II. Environment and ecology

The desert regions of the world, as defined here, are those arid lands that are located more or less between the Arctic and the Antarctic Circles. For present purposes, the desert regions are restricted to those lands that receive and retain precipitation inadequate to support grassland—that is, roughly 250 millimetres per year or less. They are dry because of some combination of the following factors: *(a)* great paucity of annual precipitation; *(b)* long periods (sometimes years) without any precipitation; and *(c)* evaporation or run-off that removes the precipitation about as rapidly as it arrives (appendix 4.1.1). The arctic regions—both polar and alpine—can be continuously dry because the water present remains frozen; they are thus, in a sense, also deserts (e.g., all of Antarctica), but are considered in chapter 5.

The desert regions of the world extend over about 27 million square kilometres (2 700 million hectares) of the Earth's land surface, three-quarters of this lying in the Northern hemisphere (table 4.1). More than half of Australia, more than one-third of Africa, and more than one-fifth of Asia are covered by desert. On the other hand, both Europe and most oceanic islands are without desert regions. The three largest individual deserts in the world are the Sahara of North Africa (nine million square kilometres), the central Australian desert (four million square kilometres), and the desert occupying the Arabian peninsula (four million square kilometres).

The central and overriding environmental feature of the desert habitat is its dearth of water. Deserts are characterized by little, infrequent, and erratic precipitation, cloudless skies, and low humidity (often around five per cent relative humidity, unless near a coast), and thus high evaporation. The rare and brief torrential rains that occur in some desert regions run off or sink rapidly. Some deserts, such as the Sahara or the Kalahari of southern Africa, are hot all the year round. Others, such as the Gobi of north-central China or the Great Basin Desert of western USA, are seasonally hot and cold. High daytime temperatures in the desert—which in some deserts can readily reach 40°C to 50°C in the shade—often alternate with rather cool (near freezing) night-time temperatures. Deserts are also often windy, especially in daytime and especially in the summer; dust storms or sandstorms are thus a recurring phenomenon.

The desert regions of the world, as defined in this work, contain (on the basis of national reports to FAO) modest amounts of forest, presumably scrubby woodland (200 million hectares); some grassland, much of it actually desert or semi-desert used as extensive range land (900 million hectares); and a small amount of agricultural land (100 million hectares), some portion of which is irrigated. These desert regions also include, of course, built-up environments, comprising cities, transportation systems, military bases, and so forth (table 1.6). The global extent of the desert vegetation type *sensu stricto* is of the order of 1 800 million hectares. Plant and animal life does flourish locally in desert regions where water is supplied. Such oases are produced naturally by springs and exotic streams (i.e., those originating outside the region), of which some—the so-called *arroyos* or *wadis*—are intermittent. Conversely, there are desert regions which are totally barren. In the Sahara, for example, roughly 15 per cent of the overall area comes under the oasis category, 70 per cent is very sparsely vegetated, and the remaining 15 per cent is without vegetation. Desert fauna are mostly small, burrowing, and nocturnal. It cannot be over-emphasized that all the desert biota—plant and animal—depend upon the spatial and temporal distribution of water on the one hand, and upon the efficiency with which they capture and retain that water on the other. Many have evolved unique means for coping with aridity.

As for the overall photosynthetic productivity of desert ecosystems, one can expect them to have an annual net primary productivity ranging up to perhaps 2 500 kilograms (dry weight) per hectare (table 1.8), but averaging about 900 kilograms per hectare (table 1.7).

III. Use

Civil

The desert regions of the world have, in many respects, been of only limited human interest in the past (appendix 4.1.2). Only about 100 million people currently utilize the desert lands of the Earth to live and support themselves (table 4.1). The present desert population density is only about four persons per square kilometre. If the people who are concentrated into the six desert urban centres of one million or more are excluded from the density determination, then the value drops as low as three persons per square kilometre (table 1.9). Virtually all (98 per cent) of the inhabitants of the desert habitat live in the Northern Hemisphere, almost equally divided between Asia and Africa (table 4.1). Almost one-eighth of the African population live in this habitat. The gross national product (GNP) per capita in the desert habitat is about US $1 600, similar to the overall global value (table 1.11).

Human occupancy of a site depends, of course, upon a local supply of water. Thus the people living in desert regions are for the most part restricted to oases—both natural and artificial—and to the banks of exotic streams, such as the Nile, Tigris, Euphrates, or Indus. For example, more than 90 per cent of the population of Egypt live in the Nile Valley. The world's true desert inhabitants probably total fewer than one million. Nomadic desert dwellers have never been numerous and their numbers are dwindling. Among the nomadic desert groups—some proportion of whom are still carrying on traditional (and in some instances rather primitive) methods of gathering, hunting, herding, and (especially in North Africa) trading—are the Tuaregs and Tibus of the Sahara, the San (bushmen) of the Kalahari Desert, the Bedouins of the Arabian Desert, the aborigines of the Australian desert, and the Papagos of the Sonoran (Arizona) Desert. Many more small groups pursue more nearly sedentary lives along the margins of the world's desert regions, being primarily dependent for their livelihood upon the raising of livestock (cattle, sheep, goats, etc.).

The people of the desert habitat are for the most part grouped into 22 nations (table 1.10). Seven of these nations are rich, 6 are of average wealth, and 9 are poor. No desert nation can boast a stable population size; indeed, fully 15 are growing at rates leading to a doubling time of less than 25 years. Only 3 were founded or gained their independence before the twentieth century, and 15 did so since the close of World War II.

Only about 100 million hectares of the land of the desert nations has been cleared (and often irrigated) for agriculture (table 1.6), that is, 0.74 hectare per capita. Annual cereal production (a summation of all grains) is 285 kilograms per capita (table 1.11). Australia is the only desert nation that is a net exporter of cereals (11 million tonnes per year) (*FAO Trade Yearbook 1976:* table 34, 1975 data).

The desert regions of the world are a major source of exploitable natural resources, although, of course, primarily of the non-renewable sort. The woodlands (1.25 hectares per capita) are for the most part of little commercial value for timber production, although some of the range lands (4.65 hectares per capita) can be utilized on an extensive basis for livestock production (table 1.11). The major desert-habitat livestock nations are Australia (33 million head of cattle and 152 million sheep, the latter figure being the highest of any nation) and Iran (7 million; 35 million) (*UN Statistical Yearbook 1976:* table 33, 1975 data). The limited desert wildlife population appears also to be amenable to management as a renewable resource (Child, 1970–1971). The timber harvest for all desert nations combined is currently 31 million cubic metres per year, which represents one per cent of the global total (derived from the *FAO Forest Products Yearbook 1975:* 3–4, 1975 data).

Desert nations are noteworthy for their oil and other mineral deposits, only a few of these minerals being singled out here (data from the *UN Statistical Yearbook 1976,* 1975 data). Large amounts of iron are mined by Australia (61 million tonnes per year, second only to the USSR and representing 12 per cent of global production). Australia leads the world in aluminium production (22 million tonnes per year) and also mines a relatively modest amount of coal (62 million tonnes per year) as well as some manganese, nickel, zinc, and other metals. Morocco (together with its recently annexed portion of the former Spanish Sahara) is noted for its phosphate mines (16 million tonnes per year, ranking third in the world and representing 14 per cent of global production). Gem diamonds are mined in the Kalahari Desert of Namibia (330 kilograms per year, ranking third in the world and representing 14 per cent of global production). Some nitrates are mined in the Atacama Desert of Chile.

The major mineral wealth of the desert is, of course, in the form of oil (and associated gas) deposits. The eastern Arabian Desert alone overlies more than one-third of all currently known oil reserves of the Earth. The major current producers of oil among the desert nations include Saudi Arabia (412 million cubic metres per year, representing 13 per cent of global production), Iran (313 million, 10 per cent), Iraq (130 million, 4 per cent), Kuwait (123 million, 4 per cent), the United Arab Emirates (94 million, 4 per cent), Libya (84 million, 3 per cent), and Algeria (53 million, 2 per cent). These nations, together with a number of other minor desert producers, currently account for over 40 per cent of global oil production.

Military

The military activities within the desert regions of the world, in common with those of the temperate and tropical regions, are intended to serve a number of purposes. For most of the 22 included nations, their domestically maintained armed forces are meant, among other things, for protection against external threats, for quelling civil wars, and occasionally for aggressive purposes (appendix 4.1.3).

Four (Egypt, Iran, Iraq, Israel) of the 22 desert nations maintain armies with a strength of 100 thousand or more, none going as high as 500 thousand (table 1.12). The average desert-nation army has a strength of 74 thousand (table 1.13). The desert nations maintain about 1 030 soldiers per 100 thousand inhabitants; about 70 soldiers per thousand square kilometres; and about 650 soldiers per US $100 million of gross national product.

The newly oil-rich desert nations are currently militarizing at an exceedingly rapid pace. Thus during the 1970s, the combined military expenditures of the seven leading desert oil-producing nations noted above (Saudi Arabia, Iran, Iraq, Kuwait, the United Arab Emirates, Libya, and Algeria) have been increasing at an annually compounded growth rate of 35.2 per cent; during this period their gross national products have been compounding at 11.3 per cent (calculated from the figures of ACDA (1976: table 2, 1970–1975 constant currency data)). By way of contrast, during this same period, total world military expenditures have been compounding at only 1.89 per cent, and the total world GNP at 3.90 per cent.

IV. Abuse

Civil

The population of the desert regions of the world is expanding at an incredible rate, leading to numbers far beyond the carrying capacity of the habitat. Nine of the 22 desert nations are exceedingly poor, none has an essentially stable population, and 15 are growing at a rate that leads to a doubling time of less than 25 years (table 1.10). Indeed, the overall population of this habitat is currently increasing at the compound growth rate of 2.7 per cent, a rate that leads to a doubling time of only 26 years (table 1.11). Given this situation, it is not surprising to find that the desert habitat is today under severe strain (appendix 4.1.2).

Over-use by livestock appears to be by far the greatest civil abuse of the desert at present. When too many cattle, sheep, or goats are permitted to forage for graze or browse in the arid desert habitat or in the semi-arid border habitat, the already naturally sparse vegetation is destroyed by a combination of over-grazing/browsing, trampling, and soil compaction. A second major form of abuse is the utilization of wood and other vegetal matter for fuel at a rate more rapid than its ability to regenerate. These two assaults upon nature are occurring in the Sahara region and elsewhere, with the result that various deserts of the world are not only becoming increasingly barren, but are growing in size as well, that is, beyond the limits determined by the climate (appendix 4.1.2). The habitat disruption and pollution associated with the extraction of oil and other minerals lead to further environmental debilitation of desert ecosystems.

The crux of the matter on a technical level is simply that the numbers of livestock are too great for the carrying capacity of the lands concerned. The long- and well-known principles of range management—more specifically, the treatment of forage vegetation as a renewable resource and the fundamental concept of carrying capacity—are being ignored. Thus, livestock must be—but are not—adjusted downward during the years of low rainfall. The fact must also be recognized that goats are more destructive of the habitat than sheep on a per head basis, and that sheep in turn are more so than cattle. The resulting problem of so-called desertification (or desertization) is, however, proving to be an exceedingly refractory one because of its large social component (rampant population growth, long-standing traditions, etc.). No solution is currently in sight for most of the problem areas.

Relatively large areas of desert in the south-western USA and elsewhere are irrigated, permitting them to be settled, farmed, and otherwise intensively used. Although such action is not generally regarded as an abuse of the desert habitat, the ecosystems formerly occupying these areas were obliterated in the process of being tamed.

Military

Peace-time

The principal military abuse of the desert during peace-time has been its employment as a nuclear-weapon test site (appendix 4.1.3). Beginning with man's first nuclear detonation in the Sonoran Desert near Alamogordo, New Mexico, USA (33°N 106°W) in July 1945, about 595 nuclear devices have been exploded in at least five of the major deserts of the world, more than 130 of these as above-ground detonations (table 4.2).

The ecological impact of above-ground nuclear explosions in a desert habitat has been investigated at the US Nevada test site in the Mohave (Great Basin) Desert (Allred *et al.*, 1965; Schultz, 1966). Of particular interest here are the studies dealing with the vegetational damage and recovery at Yucca Flat, Nevada (37°N 116°W) (Rickard & Shields, 1963; Shields & Rickard, 1961; Shields & Wells, 1962; 1963; Shields *et al.*, 1963). The magnitudes of the detonations studied were not given, but according to the data of Glasstone (1964: 671–681 *b*), most of them must have been in the neighbourhood of 10 'kilotons', although one could have been as large as 74 'kilotons'.

Initially, each of the detonations studied had totally cleaned all life from an area that ranged in size between 73 and 204 hectares. Moreover, depending upon local site conditions—and presumably also on the type of device, its energy yield, and height of burst—the original zone of complete or severe vegetational damage per detonation was roughly 400 to 1375 hectares in extent. No evidence could be found of initial vegetational damage at any explosion site beyond an area of approximately 3255 hectares.

The denuded central areas were invaded by pioneer species over a period of three to four years, and the adjacent zones of severe damage also began their slow process of ecological recovery. So far as could be recognized, the subsequent pattern of succession was of the sort and rate to be expected in this desert region following any severe disturbance of the habitat—a process spanning scores of decades.

Combat

Desert regions have served as theatres of war on numerous occasions. Prominent recent examples include the North African campaign of World War II (table 1.2.18), the Algerian War of Independence (table 1.2.20), the Arab–Israeli Wars of 1948–1949, 1956, 1967, and 1973 (DeVore, 1976; *SIPRI Yearbook 1974:* chap. 2; table 8.2.6), the Indo–Pakistani War of 1965 (O'Ballance, 1966), and the Western Sahara Revolt of 1976– (table 8.2.11). It should be noted here, moreover, that the Soviet armed forces are said to be well equipped and trained for desert warfare, partly motivated perhaps by the desert terrain in the region of the Soviet–Chinese border (Turbiville, 1974).

The major effects of desert battle are the destruction of vegetation and disruption of the soil surface. These are brought about by the mechanical disturbance associated with tank and other vehicular traffic, with bombing and shelling, and so on. As a case in point, during 1939–1945, Oliver (1945–1946) recorded in detail the increased number and severity of dust-storms occurring at a location about half-way between El Alamein and Alexandria in Egypt as a result of military and related activities in the area, including, *inter alia,* the Battle of El Alamein of October–November 1942. These activities had severely disrupted large surface areas and destroyed much of the vegetation, primarily the shrub *Thymelaea hirsuta* (Thymelaeaceae). The disturbed areas gave rise to dust-storms with only half the wind velocity usually needed, thereby increasing their annual frequency by an order of magnitude. The problem persisted for the several years that it took for the re-establishment of a soil-stabilizing vegetative cover. It might be added that the presence of extensive minefields contributed to the rapidity of recovery of the vegetation by denying human access to large areas. In fact, where (for other military reasons) routine civil access for grazing and other purposes has been greatly limited in the Negev

Desert in Israel, this has resulted in substantial habitat improvement (Otterman, 1974; Otterman *et al.*, 1975).

At least some effects of desert battle can persist for long periods. To this day, some of the vegetation on portions of the Negev Desert that had been the scene of battle during World War I exhibits a curious spatial distribution (I. Perath, Israel Geological Survey, private correspondence of 16 July 1971; D. Shimshi, Gilat [Israel] Agricultural Experiment Station, private correspondence of 7 May 1974). It turns out that the unique circular pattern of distribution of the sparse vegetation found there for some reason outlines the locations of the half-century-old shell craters.

V. *Conclusion*

At least 36, or one-quarter, of the world's nations contain substantial areas of desert within their borders. Indeed, the subarctic desert areas of the world represent one-fifth of the Earth's land surface. On the other hand, the number of people actually living in the desert is minimal, probably less than 0.025 per cent of the world population; of course, far greater numbers inhabit the associated oases. Numerous wars have been fought in these desert regions from biblical times to the present, and more can be expected to occur in the future. Oil, with its immense strategic significance and vast abundance in certain desert regions, may well be the precipitating factor for some of these wars (SIPRI, 1974 *b*).

The desert is only sparsely populated with plants and animals, many unique to this habitat, and both the biomass and the productivity of desert ecosystems are exceedingly modest. Moreover, this living community is easy to disrupt and its recovery is slow. Large areas of the world's desert and semi-desert ecosystems are currently becoming degraded owing to agricultural (livestock) over-utilization and other forms of cultural mismanagement. The plight of the people caught in this situation is a terrible one. Damage to the desert brought about by military activities in war and peace thus exacerbates this already socially disastrous process of desertification. World-wide adoption of the Partial Test Ban Treaty (table 8.4.9) would at least put an end to above-ground explosions, a major peace-time military abuse of the desert.

Table 4.1. Desert habitat: distribution and demography (1975 data)[a]

Region	Desert area 10^3 km^2 $(10^5$ ha)	Proportion of regional area per cent	Desert popula- tion[b] 10^6	Proportion of regional population per cent	Desert population density No./km^2
Land mass					
North America	1 331	6.1	3.3	1.1	2.5
South America	1 238	7.0	1.3	0.6	1.0
Africa	11 133	37.5	45.1	11.5	4.1
Europe	0	0	0	0	0
Asia	8 758	21.1	51.2	2.3	5.8
Australia	4 228	55.0	0.7	5.0	0.2
Antarctica	0	0	0	0	0
Islands	1	0.0	0.3	0.1	411.6
of Atlantic Ocean	0	0	0	0	0
of Pacific Ocean	0	0	0	0	0
of Indian Ocean	1	0.1	0.3	2.6	411.6
of Arctic Ocean	0	0	0	0	0
Hemisphere					
Northern	19 783	19.5	99.4	2.7	5.0
Southern	6 905	14.6	2.4	0.6	0.3
World-wide	**26 688**	**17.9**	**101.8**	**2.5**	**3.8**

Sources and notes:
[a]The regions, which are strictly geographic, are described in table 1.4, note *a*. Sources for the areas and populations are given in table 1.4, note *b*.
[b]The population of the desert habitat is currently increasing at the rate of 2.70 per cent per year (table 1.4), which leads to a population doubling time of 26.0 years.

Table 4.2. Above-ground nuclear test explosions in the desert habitat[a]

Desert[b]	Location	Nation	Years	Number
North American	37°N 116°W, etc.	USA	1945–1962	102
Gobi	c. 41°N 89°E	China	1964–1977	19
Sahara	27°N 0° and 24°N 5°E	France	1960–1961	4
Australian	30°S 131°E	United Kingdom	1956–1957	7
Total		4	1945–1977	132

Sources and notes:
[a]The data for 1945–1962 are summarized from Glasstone (1964: 671–681*b*); those for 1963–1971 from Zander & Araskog (1973: 35–53); those for 1972–1974 from *SIPRI Yearbook 1975:* 506–509; those for 1975–1976 from *SIPRI Yearbook 1977:* 400–402; and those for 1977 from SIPRI files.
[b]The nuclear explosion in the Thar (Rajputana) Desert (27°N 72°E) by India in 1974 was underground.

Appendix 4.1

Sources for the desert habitat

1. *Environment and ecology.* McGinnies *et al.* (1968) have compiled a comprehensive review of what is known of the desert habitat—both physical and biological—together with extensive bibliographies. For brief descriptions and maps of the various deserts of the world, see McGinnies *et al.* (1968: xxi–xxviii, 6–17). Peel (1960) has summarized the geomorphology of the Sahara, and Holm (1960) that of the Arabian Desert. For a description of the desert environment and the plants and animals it supports, see Cloudsley-Thompson & Chadwick (1964) and Cloudsley-Thompson (1975: chap. 5).

2. *Civil use and abuse.* Excellent sources of cultural and other information on the desert have been compiled by Hills (1966), by Stamp (1961), and, on a more popular level, by Leopold (1961). The geography of the tropical deserts of the world is described by Heintzelman & Highsmith (1973: chap. 8). Cultural mismanagement and desertification (desertization) as well as approaches to reclamation have been covered by Cloudsley-Thompson (1971–1972; 1974; 1977 *a;* 1977 *b*), Curry-Lindahl (1974: 119–121), Eckholm (1975 *a*), Eckholm & Brown (1978), Ghabbour (1971–1972), Hare (1977), Hassanyar (1977), Rapp *et al.* (1976), Wright (1978), and others.

3. *Military use and abuse.* Desert operations have been described by Turbiville (1974), and military engineering in the desert by Cohen (1973).

5. Arctic regions

The table for this chapter appears on page 126.

I. Introduction

The arctic land areas of the world—characterized above all by cold conditions—occupy 16 per cent of the global land area (two-thirds of which is continuously covered by snow and ice). The seasonally unfrozen portion supports 0.3 per cent of the global biomass, which, in turn, accounts for almost one per cent of the annual global biomass production. It further supports 0.4 per cent of the world's human population, distributed among one nation and three colonies, apart from a few high-elevation areas. Despite their inhospitable nature, the arctic regions of the world are becoming ever more important in both economic and military terms. The resultant increasingly heavy, though to a large extent transient, use of these regions by man is to a great extent incompatible with their ecological fragility. Few wars have in the past been fought in the arctic regions of the world.

II. Environment and ecology

The arctic regions of the world, as defined here, are those lands that are located more or less north of the Arctic Circle or south of the Antarctic Circle (the two polar regions), and at high elevations (the various alpine regions). The polar arctic regions are characterized by low temperatures, windy conditions, scanty precipitation, and a unique photoperiod; the alpine arctic regions share the temperature and wind conditions and additionally have a low-density atmosphere. In the Northern hemisphere, the mean July temperature decreases as one travels northward by roughly 0.58°C per degree of north latitude (or 5.3°C per 1 000 kilometres) (derived from the *Times,* 1977: plate 5). In the case of mountains, air temperature drops more or less uniformly with increasing altitude (in fact, up to the tropopause) at a rate that averages 6.4°C per kilometre (Strahler, 1975: 105). In other words, a northward move of one degree of latitude leads to a decrease in average summer air temperature comparable to a rise in altitude of about 91 metres (i.e., a northward shift of 1 000 kilometres is in this respect equivalent to a rise in altitude of about 820 metres). In the arctic regions the average air temperature of the warmest month usually falls below 10°C and the soil is characterized by spatially continuous permafrost. For present purposes, the arctic regions are further limited to those lands that are too cold (or too cold and windy) to sustain tree growth of upright stature, that is, to those lands lying beyond the so-called timber-line (appendix 5.1.1).

The arctic regions of the world extend over about 24 million square kilometres (2 400 million hectares) of the Earth's land surface, somewhat more than half of this area lying in the Southern hemisphere (table 5.1). Antarctica (13 million square kilometres) falls entirely within this category, as does one-third of the combined global oceanic island area. The areas of North America and Asia are each more than one-tenth arctic. The alpine arctic regions (which account for nearly two million square kilometres of the total) are found especially in the Himalayas and to a lesser extent in the Andean, Rocky, and Scandinavian mountains, in the Alps, and elsewhere.

Arctic regions are divisible into two major habitats: *(a)* seasonally snow- and ice-covered land (800 million hectares), and *(b)* continuously snow- and ice-covered land (1 600 million hectares). The former category, found primarily in the Northern hemisphere, supports a tundra ecosystem. It is distributed throughout the world approximately as follows (in millions of hectares): Alaska, USA (50), Canada (300), Greenland (30), Iceland (10), Norway (10), the USSR (300), and mountains (100). Some fraction of the tundra category (perhaps 10 million hectares) can loosely be referred to as grassland (pasture-land) since it is utilized as range land (table 1.6). The latter category of continuously snow- and ice-covered lands could be extended for many purposes to include the adjoining area of continuously ice-covered ocean, amounting to roughly 800 million hectares—700 in the Northern hemisphere and 100 in the Southern (table 1.3).

With respect to arctic temperatures, in the warmer equatorial polar zone of summer thaw that supports tundra, the average air temperature of the warmest month varies between approximately 10°C and 0°C. In the colder poleward polar zone of perpetual ice and snow, the average temperature of the warmest month varies between approximately 0°C and − 30°C. Even in the warmer of the two zones, the average monthly temperature remains very cool, rising above 0°C for only one to three (rarely four) months out of the year. Winds—with their desiccating action and so-called wind chill effect—occur commonly, and blizzards are frequent, especially in winter-time. Winters are long and harsh, tempera- tures occasionally dropping to − 70°C and even lower. Temperature inversions occur rather frequently.

The photo-régime of the polar regions is characterized in summer by lengthy to continuous periods of daily illumination; and in winter by brief to non-existent illumination. More precisely, in shifting from the Arctic Circle to the North Pole—or from the Antarctic Circle to the South Pole—the portion of the year with 24 hours of daily illumination is found to vary from one day (at the summer solstice) to about half a year (from vernal to autumnal equinoxes). The Sun is always low, however, and thus supplies less total warmth to the Earth's surface than might be expected on the basis of the long photoperiod.

The meagre precipitation of the polar arctic regions is rather evenly distributed throughout the 12 months, accordingly occurring most often in the form of snow. In the warmer equatorward polar zone, it is likely to total between 200 and 300 millimetres; and in the colder poleward zone, between 100 and 200 millimetres. Some of the coastal zones are often quite humid during the brief summer period, with a concomitant reduction in the usually highly evaporative conditions.

In the arctic regions, the soil and subsoil are permanently frozen down to bedrock. In the tundra zone, however, the surface layer of this permafrost thaws for a few months each year. This horizon—referred to as the active layer—averages somewhat less than two metres in depth (range, approximately zero to four metres). The active layer is often fully water-saturated, owing in large measure to the impervious frozen base upon which it rests. The soil is peaty (i.e., rich in organic matter) since micro-organismal decomposition is retarded by the low temperatures and somewhat anaerobic conditions that are prevalent.

Tundra ecosystems are dominated by a relatively limited flora of low-growing habit that forms a more or less continuous mat. Most of the genera and many of the species have a circumpolar distribution. The growing season is short, cool, and variable. Most of the plants depend to a sub-stantial extent upon asexual means for their reproduction; they exhibit a number of appropriate morphological adaptations as well. Several hundred species of lichen—including *Cladonia,* the well-known reindeer 'moss'—often constitute the most prominent component of the arctic flora. It also includes many mosses and liverworts, various sedges and grasses, and a number of dwarf, prostrate tree species, including examples of birch *(Betula),* spruce *(Picea)*, and, most importantly, willow *(Salix).*

The lichens and other plants provide food for a number of herbivores, including the small vole-like lemming *(Lemmus)*—well known for its periodic population explosions—snow-shoe hares *(Lepus)*, and the grouse-like ptarmigan *(Lagopus)*. There are also a number of large herbivores, the best known among them being *Rangifer*—the caribou of North America and the reindeer of Eurasia—the domesticated form of which is so important to the traditional culture of the Lapps (Samer). Carnivores that utilize the herbivores include wolves *(Canis)*, foxes *(Vulpes)*, and owls *(Nyctea)*. Numerous species of insects, including flies and mosquitoes (the 'curse of the arctic'), also flourish in the tundra ecosystems. Moreover, various wide-ranging migratory birds—such as plovers *(Pluvialis)* and terns *(Sterna)*—and many other birds make use of the tundra as their breeding grounds. All in all, however, arctic ecosystems comprise substantially fewer species than do temperate or tropical ones.

The loose mat of tundra vegetation—perhaps 10 to 20 centimetres thick—provides not only a habitat for small animals, but also an insulating layer for the soil underneath and the life it supports. The mat absorbs much of the solar energy that reaches it (perhaps 80 per cent of it) and reflects the rest. Some of the absorbed energy is subsequently lost to the atmosphere as the plants transpire (this being an evaporative, cooling process) and some is transferred to the soil underneath; a minute fraction is captured in photosynthesis. It is the integrity of the mat that largely determines the depth to which the soil thaws each summer (i.e., the depth of the active layer), and thereby the amount available to the dynamic living and non-living processes of the ecosystem.

As for the photosynthetic productivity of arctic ecosystems, one can expect tundra to have an annual net primary productivity that ranges between 100 and 4 000 kilograms (dry weight) per hectare (table 1.8), but that averages about 1 400 kilograms per hectare (table 1.7). Moreover, nutrient (biogeochemical) cycling is relatively sluggish in a tundra ecosystem, owing largely to the reduced rates of micro-organismal decomposition of biotic detritus. Food-chains are short. Violent oscillations in animal population densities are common. Successional recovery by biotic communities is characteristically so slow in its progress as to seem fully arrested. In short, the rigours of the local climate—inhospitable in summer and grim in winter—are largely responsible for the precarious foothold that living things have barely been able to establish here.

III. Use

Civil

The arctic regions of the world have been of only limited human interest in the past (appendix 5.1.2). The northern Arctic is only sparsely populated, the southern Arctic (Antarctica) has no permanent inhabitants, and few people live at high mountain elevations. All told, about 18 million people currently utilize the arctic lands of the Earth in order to live and to support themselves (table 5.1). The present arctic population density is less than one person per square kilometre, or about twice that value if the permanently iced-covered land is excluded from the calculation. The great majority of the few inhabitants of the arctic habitat live in northern Asia (in the USSR) and others live in Alaska (USA), northern Canada, Greenland, Iceland (the only arctic nation), and northern Norway (table 5.1).

The Eskimos (Inuit) and Aleuts of northern North America and the Lapps (Samer), Samoyeds (Nentsi), Tungus (Evenki), and other small groups of northern Eurasia still leading traditional lives today probably represent of the order of one per cent of the total arctic population. The traditional cultures of these semi-nomadic indigenous peoples of the circumpolar far north have been based on hunting, fishing, and (in Eurasia) herding. The encroachment by modern man into these regions is irrevocably changing the cultural patterns—a process that each year affects a greater proportion of the original inhabitants.

The ever-growing interest of modern society in the arctic regions of the world is motivated primarily by two factors: *(a)* natural resources, and *(b)* military importance, the latter being partly linked with the former. The collecting of weather data and other scientific data for civil and military purposes has supplied additional motives.

The northern Arctic is noted for its hitherto largely untapped deposits of fossil fuels (including both coal and oil) and metals (nickel, copper, gold, lead, uranium, platinum, tungsten, etc.). Coal has long been mined on Svalbard (over 800 thousand tonnes per year), and the oil resources of northern Alaska as well as the non-ferrous metals of northern Siberia are currently under especially intensive development. The southern Arctic (Antarctica) also has some mineral deposits of potential value, but these are commercially inaccessible and will presumably remain so for some time to come. Another potential resource of Antarctica is fresh water (Weeks & Campbell, 1973). The feasibility of tugging Antarctic icebergs northward to water-deficient areas is currently under study by a number of nations.

The airspace above the northern Arctic is heavily utilized for commercial air transportation inasmuch as polar great-circle routes offer the shortest distances between many major North American and Eurasian cities.

Military

The strategic significance of the northern Arctic today hinges upon its location between the world's two great powers, the USA and the USSR. Polar great-circle routes provide the shortest distances of travel for military aircraft or ballistic missiles between these two nations. Moreover, the Arctic Ocean provides navigable submarine routes all the year round between their northerly coastlines. The one arctic nation, Iceland, maintains essentially no armed forces of its own. Antarctica has essentially no military presence (appendix 5.1.3).

The North American Arctic has been put to military use by the USA and its continental allies so as to provide an early-warning system for aerial attack by the USSR over the top of the world. Included in this defence system is a series of manned radar installations across Alaska, Canada, Greenland, and Iceland known as the Distant Early Warning or DEW Line (Carlson, 1962: chap. 20). The DEW Line runs eastward from the vicinity of Barrow, Alaska (latitude 71°N) for about 5 900 kilometres to that of Keflavik, Iceland (latitude 64°N). Roughly speaking, it follows the 70°N parallel of latitude across Canada, and the Arctic Circle across Greenland. The USA additionally maintains a number of major military bases of various kinds in the Arctic. Those of strategic significance include the ones near Thule, Greenland (latitude 77°N) and Keflavik. The USSR operates one of the largest military complexes in the world in the Murmansk area (latitude 69°N), including the world's largest naval base (Synhorst, 1973). It also maintains a major nuclear-weapon test site on Novaya Zemlya (latitude 75°N), discussed more fully below.

The arctic regions of the world are in part within the territorial limits (or claimed limits) of various nations and are in part inhabited by their nationals. Valuable natural resources are being exploited in numerous arctic locations. Alaskan oil is a specific case in point (Simpson, 1976). Moreover, some arctic areas are considered to be potential avenues of approach in possible wars of the future between certain nations. These factors have together provided the justification for establishing a number of far northern military defence facilities of local rather than strategic significance.

IV. Abuse

Civil

Any disturbance of the tundra ecosystem is most likely to result in ecological damage of long duration (appendix 5.1.2). Disruption of the vegetational mat leads to substantial changes in the depth of the active layer of the soil (i.e., in the behaviour of the permafrost) and concomitant local disturbances in both the energy (heat) balance and the hydrology. Under certain conditions it can initiate serious local soil erosion. Even the simple scars in the vegetational mat left by a vehicle doing nothing more than driving over such terrain in summer can remain visible for decades (Rickard & Brown, 1974). The construction of heavy-duty all-weather roads across tundra terrain creates wide bands of major habitat disturbance. Indeed, all but the lowest of human population densities and the mildest of utilization pressures result in major overall environmental degradation of the warmer equatorward terrestrial arctic zones.

The recovery of oil in arctic regions and the associated employment of overland pipelines result not only in construction and transportation abuses of the kinds alluded to above, but also in occasional—and inevitable—oil-spills. Oil-spills constitute a major ecological menace in the arctic habitat. Such accidents can introduce enormous quantities of this toxic contaminant into an ecosystem. The introduced oil evaporates and decomposes to insignificance far more slowly at the low temperatures characteristic of the arctic regions than it does under similar circumstances in more temperate climates. The affected ecosystem is thus not only burdened for a much longer time with the poisonous intrusion itself, but it subsequently recovers far more slowly.

To provide an example, a small (20-centimetre) pipeline with a throughput of 158 cubic metres per hour extends for about one thousand kilometres between Haines and Fairbanks, Alaska, USA (latitudes 59°N to 65°N) (Murrmann & Reed, 1972: 6–10). At least 28 oil-spills, some of them of substantial size—although unspecified—were associated with the immediate post-installation period. Then, during the first 15 years of routine operation, at least 12 accidental ruptures were recorded that resulted in spills ranging in volume from 10 to 760 cubic metres. The plant life directly exposed to these oil-spills was thereby killed, and no natural replacement of the vegetation occurred during the period of observation of up to 15 years. (Destroyed arctic lichens might not regenerate for half a century.) The pipeline in question crosses 107 major streams; where the spilled oil ran into these, fish kills resulted. Fish subsequently taken from the contaminated streams tasted of oil for periods of four to five years.

Pipelines, railway tracks, and major highways provide obstructions or at least substantial impediments to the migrations and other movements of the larger arctic mammals, including caribou or reindeer *(Rangifer)* (Klein, 1971; 1971–1972), a situation quite deleterious to their well-being.

The adverse effects of air pollution that are normally associated with human occupancy are exacerbated in arctic regions for a number of reasons. Not only are per capita heating requirements greater in the Arctic, but temperature inversions that serve to impede the dissipation of the generated contaminants are more common. Moreover, the dominant lichen vegetation—and thus the first link in a number of important arctic food-chains—is far more sensitive to damage from fossil-fuel pollution than the higher plants that commonly fulfil this ecological role in more temperate regions (Ferry *et al.*, 1973).

Disposal of waste—solid or liquid—is most difficult to carry out properly in arctic regions because of the exceedingly slow micro-organismal decomposition in low-temperature environments. Some discarded wastes maintain their integrity indefinitely.

Finally, many fragile high-altitude ecosystems are being severely debilitated throughout the world as a result of the upward extension of agricultural lands; and others, as a result of increasingly heavy utilization of mountains by tourists.

Military

Much of the military abuse of arctic regions is qualitatively similar to that inflicted by the civil sector of society, especially so in times of peace (appendix 5.1.3). The establishment and maintenance of radar stations, airfields, naval bases, and other military installations as well as the carrying out of military manoeuvres all involve the construction of diverse facilities and lines of communication, with the inevitable attendant habitat disruption previously described. Moreover, the military personnel associated with these activities generate air-, soil-, and water-pollution and also contribute to the pressures on the local wildlife. Most of these quite straightforward military abuses of the arctic environment have been well summarized by Murrmann & Reed (1972).

Two special categories of military abuse are radioactive pollution and the very concentrated level of damage that is likely to occur when an arctic region becomes a theatre of war. These are singled out for special discussion below, the former primarily with reference to incidental contamination and the latter in the form of two case histories (the one being a case of unintentional damage and the other intentional). However, not discussed at this point are the extraordinary levels of local damage that would result from massive local oil-spills (as when a supertanker might be destroyed by hostile action) or from the local employment of nuclear weapons or other weapons of mass destruction.

Contamination by radioactive isotopes

The existing radioactive contamination of arctic regions is almost entirely of military origin. Some fraction of this has been the result of readily identifiable incidents, but most has arrived as stratospheric fall-out usually originating from distant subarctic nuclear-weapon testing. Specific incidents of radioactive contamination of the arctic include the accidental introduction into Baffin Bay of an estimated 390 grams (25 curies) of plutonium-239 (^{239}Pu) when a US aircraft carrying four nuclear bombs crashed 11 kilometres west of Thule, Greenland (latitude 77°N) in January 1968 (Aarkrog, 1971; UNSCEAR, 1972: 54). Further direct radioactive contamination of the arctic has occurred as a result of local testing. During 1957–1962 the USSR detonated at least 77 nuclear devices in the atmosphere at its Novaya Zemlya test site (latitude 75°N); and, further, at least one underwater device during October 1961 in the Barents Sea south of Novaya Zemlya (latitude c. 70°N) (Glasstone, 1964: 680–681 b); three underground tests carried out by the USA during 1965–1971 on Amchitka, Aleutian Islands (latitude 51°N) may also be mentioned (Duke, 1971; Zander & Araskog, 1973). One of the unfortunate side-effects of this series of tests has been the set-back in the efforts to save the Aleutian Canada goose (*Branta canadensis leucopareia,* Anatidae) from extinction, a matter dealt with more fully in chapter 6 (section IV).

Radioactive fall-out on to arctic tundra is retained for a relatively long time by the lichen flora, which forms such an important component of the diet of caribou or reindeer *(Rangifer)*, especially in winter. Strontium-90 (^{90}Sr) and caesium-137 (^{137}Cs) are among the radioactive nuclides that are thus transferred to these animals, which in turn constitute part of the diet of the indigenous humans—especially Eskimos and Lapps leading traditional lives (Hanson, 1967; Palmer *et al.*, 1965; Svensson & Lidén, 1965; UNSCEAR, 1972: 52–53). The result of this short and pernicious food-chain has been that many of the native peoples of far northern North America and Eurasia have been subjected to body burdens of these biologically dangerous nuclides far in excess of any other populations in the world, exclusive of the residents of Hiroshima and Nagasaki of August 1945. Any future atmospheric testing or wartime use of nuclear weapons will, of course, exacerbate the dilemma of these bystanders.

Aleutian Islands in World War II

Various arctic regions have served as theatres of war and have thereby been subjected to substantial habitat disruption; this is especially true of the tundra regions (appendix 5.1.3). During World War II, for example, the USA established a number of military facilities at Dutch Harbor (latitude 54°N) and elsewhere on the Aleutian Islands. (The Aleutians support a tundra ecosystem despite their relatively southerly geographic location.) During 1942 Japan invaded and occupied a number of these islands, which were then regained by the USA during the following year (Garfield, 1969; Morton, 1963). Attu and Kiska Islands were subjected to heavy bombardment in the process. The Battle of Attu (latitude 53°N) in May 1943 was especially fierce—some 3 000 lives being lost—and exceedingly destructive of the habitat.

Almost three decades had elapsed when Sekora (1973: 61) summed up the impact of World War II in the following words:

The physical marks of this chapter in Aleutian history are, like all the others, there for all to see. Unlike the others, however, these marks need not be carefully sought out in kitchen middens or communal dwelling sites 150 or more years old. Aircraft runways, piers, roads, telephone and power distribution systems, temporary buildings, and damaged ships of both Japanese and U.S. origin are to be seen throughout the length of the Chain. On Attu and Kiska the marks of combat are implanted for at least the duration of this geological age. Abandoned military buildings are still much in evidence on over 20 islands.

The small population of native Aleuts—then of the order of 1 000 in number—suffered severely as a result of World War II. Many were killed; the remainder were deported for the duration of the war, either by the USA or, from Attu, by Japan (Teal, 1955: 154–155). When the survivors returned in 1945, they found their houses and belongings destroyed or gone, and post-war rehabilitation was a tedious process of many years' duration (Sekora, 1973: 65).

Northern Norway in World War II

The arctic portion of Norway was also embroiled in World War II (Johnson, 1948: chap. 14; Petrow, 1974: chap. 18; Ziemke, 1959). The Germans invaded and fortified northern Norway, occupying the area during 1940–1945. In 1944 they became fearful of a major Soviet attack from the Kola Peninsula to the east. In order to consolidate their position, in October of that year the Germans withdrew westward from the border by about 400 kilometres and established a defensive line at the Lyngen Fjord (c. 50 kilometres east of Tromsø, the capital of Troms County). As an impediment to the expected Soviet advance, the Germans decided to evacuate the resident local population and to remove or destroy almost everything of potential use to their enemy. The zone in question between the Lyngen Fjord and the border amounted to about 5.8 million hectares, comprising all of Finnmark County (4.9 million hectares) and the north-eastern third of Troms County (0.9 million hectares). This zone had an estimated 1944 population of 75 000 (60 000 in Finnmark and 15 000 in the north-eastern third of Troms), of whom roughly 10 per cent were semi-nomadic Lapps (Samer) (Lund, 1947).

As it turned out, the USSR mounted no major offensive on this front. After taking the border town of Kirkenes (latitude 70°N) in mid-October 1944—a bitter battle that left the town 90 per cent destroyed—the Soviets penetrated eastward for only about 100 kilometres, that is, as far as the Tana River. The Germans, for their part, from October 1944 to the end of the year and on into the following one, depopulated and laid waste substantial portions of the zone of abandonment. They evacuated about 43 000 of the local residents, and perhaps as many as 7 000 departed of their own accord. Left behind, therefore, in this zone east of Lyngen Fjord were 25 000 or more people: the 4 000 inhabitants of Kirkenes; the 15 000 inhabitants of Vadsø (the capital of Finnmark), Vardø, and the rest of the Varanger Peninsula; plus another 1 000 or more residents who evaded the evacuation or were overlooked. Moreover, some 8 000 semi-nomadic Lapps were exempt from the German evacuation order and many may have remained. It should be noted that both Vadsø (latitude 70°N) and Vardø (latitude 70°N) were about two-thirds destroyed by bombing during this period.

The area of German destruction at least nominally extended over the western four-fifths of Finnmark County (3.9 million hectares; latitudes 69°N to 71°N) and the north-eastern third of Troms County (0.9 million hectares; latitudes 69°N to 70°N). However, at least 90 per cent of the populations of Finnmark and Troms lived within 10 kilometres of the sea, and about 50 per cent lived in villages of 100 people or more (some 14 000 being concentrated in Hammarfest, Vardø, Vadsø, and Kirkenes alone). On the one hand, this concentration of human occupancy permitted a high level—perhaps 80 per cent—of destructive efficiency with respect to permanent structures. On the other hand, it localized the areal ur geographic extent of the damage somewhat. Accordingly, as a rough approximation, it may be suggested that the actual area of complete devastation amounted in total to perhaps one-quarter of the nominal area of devastation, that is, to perhaps 1.2 million hectares (1.0 million in Finnmark and 0.2 million in Troms).

Most of the permanent structures within the area of devastation were destroyed, including all of the homes, barns, schools, hospitals, municipal buildings together with all their records, power stations, poles for overhead power-transmission lines plus the wires they carried, snow fences and other fences, pipelines, bridges, piers, quays, and lighthouses; however, many of the churches in the area were spared. Most of the private property was either removed or destroyed, including virtually all of the vehicles, boats, livestock (except for reindeer), and food and feed stores (primarily potatoes and hay). As an indication of the magnitude of livestock loss, the following 1939 census data are provided for the 6 100 farms existing throughout Finnmark County (the figures probably being close to those applying to the zone of devastation in western Finnmark and north-eastern Troms): 1 200 horses, 9 400 cows, 40 300 sheep, 7 300 goats, and 400 pigs. Moreover, only about half of the estimated 95 000 reindeer in the abandoned zone were said to have survived this period. Finally, the zone evacuated by the Germans had been heavily mined, and this mining was only partially mapped. By the end of 1945, the Norwegians had removed some 80 000 mines—an estimated 10 per cent of the total that had been emplaced.

A vigorous domestic and foreign economic recovery effort (the 'North Norway Plan') was begun soon after the war ended. This turned out to be a slow and expensive process, although ultimately successful in some respects (Bourneuf, 1958; Lund, 1947; Teal, 1953–1954). Homes and basic services were restored over a period of several years; an industrial base for the area has now been established, linked largely to the extraction and refining of various metals (Fullerton & Williams, 1975: chap. 29; Vorren, 1960). Agriculture has also slowly expanded since the war; the area is again more or less agriculturally self-sufficient. Fishing remains an important aspect of the regional economy. Fifteen years after the end of the war, Finnmark's reindeer herd stood at about 90 000. The extent of wartime damage to the rural lands of northern Norway and their degree of recovery do not appear to have been studied.

V. Conclusion

It is clear that the arctic regions of the world—occupying some five per cent of the total global surface—support some of the most labile and slowly developing or recovering ecosystems on Earth. The harsh environment that underlies this ecological fragility and slowness of natural repair of tundra ecosystems has fortunately also discouraged the intensive occupancy and utilization characteristic of the Earth's non-arctic regions. Thus, although the arctic land regions comprise 16 per cent of the global land surface, they support only 0.4 per cent of the world population. On the other hand, their mineral wealth and military significance do attract a certain level of attention to these areas. This attention continues to grow in step with society's ever-growing demands for natural resources and concerns with defence, and with its technological ability to overcome the environmental impediments in its way.

Two of the three demilitarized zones on Earth set up by multilateral agreement are located in arctic regions (Skagestad, 1975): *(a)* the Svalbard (Spitsbergen) archipelago, having an aggregate land area of some 62 thousand square kilometres lying between latitudes 74°N and 81°N (more than 90 per cent of this surface being permanently covered with snow and ice); and *(b)* the Antarctic continent, covering some 13 million square kilometres of land south of latitude 60°S (virtually 100 per cent of which being permanently covered with snow and ice).

As a result of the Spitsbergen Treaty (table 8.4.3), 39 or more nations have agreed never to use this far northern island group for warlike purposes; the treaty further charges Norway with the task of preventing any nation from doing so (Article IX) (cf. also Orvin, 1951–1953; Teal, 1950–1951). As a result of the Antarctic Treaty (table 8.4.8), 19 or more nations have agreed to refrain from any activities of a warlike nature on the Antarctic land mass and associated ice shelves (Article I), and each appears to have further agreed to impose the same limitation upon all other states as well (Article X) (cf. also Goldblat, 1973; *SIPRI Yearbook 1973:* chap. 14). It is to be hoped that these two treaties will not only be purged of their exclusionary clauses, but will also be extended to encompass the rest of the arctic regions of the world.

Table 5.1. Arctic habitat: distribution and demography (1975 data)[a]

Region	Arctic area $10^3 km^2$ $(10^5 ha)$	Proportion of regional area per cent	Arctic population [b] 10^6	Proportion of regional population per cent	Arctic population density No./km^2
Land mass					
North America	3 555	16.3	0.1	0.0	0.0
South America	102	0.6	0	0	0
Africa	0	0	0	0	0
Europe	344	3.4	0.2	0.0	0.6
Asia	4 317	10.4	17.1	0.8	4.0
Australia	0	0	0	0	0
Antarctica	13 000	100	0	0	0
Islands	2 341	32.2	0.3	0.1	0.1
of Atlantic Ocean	103	14.9	0.2	0.2	2.1
of Pacific Ocean	0	0	0	0	0
of Indian Ocean	0	0	0	0	0
of Arctic Ocean	2 238	100	0.1	100	0.0
Hemisphere					
Northern	10 556[c]	10.4	17.7	0.5	1.7
Southern	13 102	27.6	0	0	0
World-wide	**23 658**[c]	**15.9**	**17.7**	**0.4**	**0.7**[d]

Sources and notes:
[a] The regions, which are strictly geographic, are described in table 1.4, note *a*. Sources for the areas and populations are given in table 1.4, note *b*. Both polar and alpine arctic areas are included in the present table.
[b] The population of the arctic habitat is currently increasing at the rate of 0.46 per cent per year (table 1.4), which leads to a population doubling time of 151 years.
[c] The Northern hemisphere and world-wide totals include 8 million square kilometres of tundra (Whittaker & Likens, 1975: 306).
[d] If the continuously ice-covered land surface (table 1.3) is excluded from this calculation, the density value becomes 2.2 persons per square kilometre.

Appendix 5.1

Sources for the arctic habitat

1. *Environment and ecology.* Asimov (1975) provides a lucid overview of the arctic regions of the world. For descriptions of the arctic environment and the plants and animals that it supports, see Dunbar (1968), Irving (1972), and Cloudsley-Thompson (1975: chap. 9). For the structure and function of tundra ecosystems, see Rosswall & Heal (1975). Strahler (1975: chap. 17) provides a summary of arctic climate. Mountain ecology has been covered by Cloudsley-Thompson (1975: chap. 10) and, at a more popular level, by Milne & Milne (1962) and Brooks (1967). Lemons & Wood (1967) have prepared a summary of the physical environment at high elevations.

2. *Civil use and abuse.* The geography of the arctic regions is well described by Heintzelman & Highsmith (1973: chap. 18). The civil importance and uses of the northern Arctic have been comprehensively compiled by Kimble & Good (1955). For information on the North American (primarily Canadian) Arctic, see Blakesley & Thompson (1971–1972) and Lloyd (1969–1970); for the Norwegian Arctic, see Vorren (1960). For information on the southern Arctic (Antarctica), see Mitchell (1977). For a discussion of the implications of arctic exploitation, see Sollie (1974). Abuse and recovery of disturbed arctic tundra ecosystems are discussed by Bliss & Wein (1972), VanCleve (1977), and West (1976). Abuse of mountain environments is reviewed by Eckholm (1975 b).

3. *Military use and abuse.* The military importance and uses of the northern Arctic have been described by Baumann (1962), Carlson (1962), Descheneau (1977), Huitfeldt (1974), Lindsey (1976–1977), and Vincendon (1965). Information laying emphasis on specific regions is available for the USSR (Araldsen, 1967; Griswold, 1972; Synhorst, 1973), Alaska, USA (Pearson, 1961), Finland (Rissanen, 1977), and Scandinavia (Army, 1975; Roush, 1975). Erfurth (1951), Garfield (1969), and Ziemke (1959) have analysed combat conditions in the far north during World War II. King (1977) discusses cold-weather combat in brief. Murrmann & Reed (1972) have prepared a good review of the environmental abuses associated with military facilities in cold regions.

6. Islands

The tables for this chapter appear on pages 140–142.

I. Introduction

The oceanic islands of the world number in the untold thousands. Together they account for only 5 per cent of the global land area; yet they support 11 per cent of the world's human population, distributed among 34 nations and about 20 major colonies. A majority of the island nations of the world have a tropical climate, many are poor, and most were founded or gained their independence since World War II. A goodly number of islands are attractive to man for varying combinations of their location, climate, the retreat they offer, the natural or cultural resources they contain, their intrinsic beauty, the unique biota they support, and the tax or duty haven they provide. As a result, islands have been important throughout history in both civil and military affairs, and promise to remain so. Indeed, a number of environmentally disruptive wars have already occurred on oceanic islands so far during this century.

II. Environment and ecology

Oceanic islands have in common a physical habitat that is undeniably finite, in fact, often severely circumscribed. The inevitable consequences of this limitation become especially pronounced on small and isolated islands. It is, in fact, those oceanic islands that can be thought of as being relatively small, relatively isolated, and relatively undisturbed that are of particular concern from an environmental standpoint (appendix 6.1.1).

The oceanic islands of the world together constitute somewhat more than 7 million square kilometres (700 million hectares) of the Earth's land surface, almost two-thirds of this lying in the Northern hemisphere (table 6.1). Half of the combined global island area is located in the Pacific Ocean, and another third in the Arctic Ocean. As to habitat, more than half of the combined island area is tropical, and one-third arctic.

It is, of course, difficult to make many meaningful generalizations that would be applicable to the many thousands of oceanic islands in the world. One need only reflect upon the ramifications of the following parameters in order to recognize the complexities involved in categorizing islands; *(a)* their size, ranging from tiny to virtually continental; *(b)* their degree of isolation, especially their distance from some mainland; *(c)* their origin and age, that is, whether they rose from the sea or separated off from the mainland, and the length of time that has elapsed since their birth; *(d)* their geomorphology and topography, especially whether they are 'high' (either of continental or of volcanic origin) or 'low' (of coral origin); *(e)* their climate, especially their rainfall status (ranging from arid to pluvial) and their temperature régime (ranging from arctic to tropical); *(f)* their state of human habitation, that is, whether they are uninhabited or inhabited and, if the latter, whether by primitive or modern peoples, and by how many; and *(g)* their past use or exploitation, and thus their present degree of disturbance.

A relatively small and remote island forms an ecological microcosm that can be of considerable scientific interest, both by virtue of its intrinsic merits and by virtue of the fact that it can be compared with other islands and mainlands. The total number of species of plants and animals on such an island is limited in comparison with a mainland site of equal size. In fact, the total number of species present bears a roughly log/log linear relationship to island area. Moreover, a relatively high proportion of insular species of plants and animals is endemic, such species having evolved through time from a relatively limited number of relicts or immigrants. The number of immigrants bears an inverse log relationship to distance from a mainland source. Interspecific competition is usually less severe on an island than on a mainland, with the result that bizarre and ill-adapted forms have a higher likelihood of survival than on the mainland—barring alien intrusions, of course.

From these traits it becomes apparent why island biotas have played such an enormously important role in the development of theoretical biology—especially in the fields of ecology, population genetics, and evolution. It was on islands that the concept of evolution became evident, during the nineteenth century, both to Darwin (1859) and to Wallace (1880). The somewhat simplified and exaggerated conditions obtaining on islands have, since that time, continued to allow the elucidation of the principles of biogeography, of ecological succession, and of competition and other internal ecosystematic relationships.

Finally, it must be pointed out that the several traits that make island ecosystems so interesting also, unfortunately, make them highly vulnerable to damage—some of it irreversible—a matter that is further discussed below.

III. Use

Civil

One of the major uses of islands is, of course, as a place of human habitation (appendix 6.1.2). More than 400 million people currently live and support themselves on the oceanic islands of the world (table 6.1). The present island population density is 60 persons per square kilometre, as compared with the continental density figure of 26. If the people who are concentrated into the 23 insular urban centres of one million or more are excluded from the density determination, then the figure drops to 50 persons per square kilometre (table 1.9). The effect of this relatively high insular population density is alleviated to some extent by the ocean, which provides food and also helps to impart an impression of added space. More than two-thirds of the global island population live in the Northern hemisphere, and the great majority (almost four-fifths) live on Pacific Ocean islands (table 6.1). About 60 per cent of the island inhabitants of the world live under tropical conditions, and most of the remainder under temperate conditions. The gross national product (GNP) per capita of the island habitat is US $1 900, as compared with a global value of US $1 500 (table 1.11).

Thirty-four island nations exist in the world today– 15 in the Atlantic Ocean (including 2 in the Mediterranean Sea), 13 in the Pacific Ocean, 6 in the Indian Ocean, and none in the Arctic Ocean (table 1.10). Whereas only 4 of the island nations can be considered to be rich, fully 18 of them are poor. Five island nations have essentially stable population numbers, although, on the other hand, 6 are growing at rates that lead to a doubling time of less than 25 years. As many as 26 were founded or gained their independence since the close of World War II. In addition to the 34 island nations, there exist a large number of island colonies of greater or lesser importance (appendix 1.5).

Some 50 million hectares of the island habitat have been cleared for agriculture (table 1.6), that is, only 0.14 hectare per capita. Annual cereal production (a summation of all grains) is as low as 178 kilograms per capita (table 1.11). Agricultural and horticultural (plantation) crops that are much cultivated for export on islands include cane-sugar (Cuba, Mauritius), tea (Sri Lanka), rubber (Malaysia, 1 500 thousand tonnes per year; Indonesia, 830 thousand; these nations respectively ranking first and second in world production (*UN Statistical Yearbook 1976*: table 45, 1975 data)), pineapples (Hawaii), and coconut oil and kernels (copra) (Malaysia, Indonesia).

Islands are the source of a wide range of exploitable natural resources. Among the renewable ones are the range lands (0.19 hectare per capita) for livestock production, and the forest lands (0.58 hectare per capita) for timber production (table 1.11). The most important insular livestock nation is New Zealand (10 million head of cattle and 55 million sheep) (*UN Statistical Yearbook 1976*: table 33, 1975 data). The major island timber producers are Indonesia (harvesting 130 million cubic metres per year), Japan (37 million), the Philippines (30 million), and Malaysia (27 million) (*FAO Forest Products Yearbook 1975*: 3–4, 1975 data). The combined timber harvest for all island nations is currently 263 million cubic metres per year, which represents 11 per cent of the global total. The currently leading island timber exporters (ranking respectively fourth and fifth among the world's nations) are Malaysia (12 million cubic metres per year) and the Philippines (5 million).

A large variety of important minerals are also mined on islands, and only a few of these minerals are singled out here (data from the *UN Statistical Yearbook 1976*, 1975 data). There appears to be little iron found on islands, only modest amounts being extracted in the United Kingdom (one million tonnes per year), the Philippines, Japan, and elsewhere. Moreover, World War II scrap-iron is still being gathered and exported from various small Pacific islands. The United Kingdom is the only major coal-producing island (129 million tonnes per year, ranking fifth in the world). Some coal is also extracted in Japan (19 million tonnes per year), Svalbard (0.8 million), New Zealand (0.5 million), and in other islands. The leading oil-producing islands are Indonesia (75 million cubic metres per year) and Bahrain (3 million).

Large amounts of aluminium are mined in Jamaica (11 million tonnes per year, 11 per cent of global production, ranking second in the world). Malaysia leads the world in tin production (64 thousand tonnes per year) and Indonesia (25 million tonnes) ranks third, the two together accounting for half of current global production. New Caledonia produces large amounts of nickel (133 thousand tonnes per year, one-fifth of global production, ranking second only to Canada). Additional insular mineral extractions—of greater importance to the islands in question than to the global economy—include copper (Bougainville, Cyprus), phosphates (Tinian, Nauru), sulphur (Iwo Jima), and asphalt (Trinidad).

Some islands are especially noteworthy for their scientific value—for example, Galápagos (Thornton, 1971), Aldabra (Stoddart, 1967; Stoddart & Wright, 1967), Krakatoa (Furneaux, 1964), and Surtsey (Fridriksson, 1975).

Finally, one of the fastest growing civil uses of islands is for tourism. Among the currently very popular islands for this purpose are the Virgins, the Bahamas, the Canaries, the Hawaiian islands, Fiji, Guam, Tahiti, Saipan, Rhodes and Crete.

Military

The military activities on the oceanic islands of the world are, as elsewhere, intended to serve a number of purposes (appendix 6.1.3). For most of the 34 island nations, their domestically maintained armed forces are meant for protection against external threats, for quelling civil wars, and occasionally for aggressive purposes. For most of the 20 or so major island possessions and some of the numerous minor ones, the resident armed forces of the possessor nation are meant, again, for protection against external threats and also for subduing independence movements. The various armed forces of the several major powers which are deployed in foreign island nations are present as part of the major powers' regional or global security postures.

Six of the 34 island nations (Cuba, Indonesia, Japan, the Philippines, Taiwan, and the United Kingdom) maintain armies having a strength of 100 thousand or more; in the case of one of them—Taiwan—this figure exceeds 500 thousand (table 1.12). The average island-nation army has a strength of 53 thousand (table 1.13). The island nations maintain about 410 soldiers per 100 thousand inhabitants; about 360 soldiers per thousand square kilo-metres; and about 220 soldiers per US $100 million of gross national product.

Scores of strategically located islands throughout the world ocean have situated upon them army garrisons, naval bases (for surface ships or sub-marines), air bases, missile and satellite tracking stations, or military com-munications or electronic intelligence-gathering facilities that belong to the USA or other major powers (table 6.2). The employment of islands as weapon-testing and training sites—yet another military use of islands—is covered in the section below dealing with the military abuse of islands.

IV. Abuse

Civil

Islands are subject to abuse both by the permanent human population and by the large numbers of transients (appendix 6.1.2). The indigenous island population density already stands at a high level—60 persons per square kilometre, as opposed to the world-wide figure of 27 (table 1.4)—and it is rapidly rising. Only 5 of the 34 island nations have essentially stable popula-tions, and 6 are growing at a rate that leads to a doubling time of less than 25 years (table 1.10). The overall population of the island habitat is currently increasing at the compound growth rate of 1.8 per cent—a rate that leads to a doubling time of 40 years (table 1.11).

The indigenous carrying capacity of the island habitat is being stretched far beyond its limits, and trade can make up the deficit in only a limited number of cases. Only 4 of the island nations can be considered rich on the basis of their gross national product per capita, and 18 or more must be classed as terribly poor (table 1.10). In an increasing number of cases this dilemma is being redressed by tourism. Indeed, modern means of trans-portation, together with the leisure and prosperity enjoyed by a growing number of inhabitants of the rich nations, have made many hitherto relatively unspoiled islands into major tourist attractions—almost inevitably, however, with ecologically highly damaging results.

The damage caused by human activities to islands—especially small isolated islands—hinges largely upon their limited number of ecological niches and their severely circumscribed carrying capacity on the one hand, and upon their numerically limited and specialized biota on the other. Insular damage is made likely for a number of reasons, among them being ignorance and indifference on the part of human beings. Thus, a level or intensity of disruption that would give little cause for concern on a mainland (where the intuitive norms of society about such matters are developed) can be disastrous on an island. Moreover, the exploitation of an island's resources is often carried out by non-residents, who would tend not to have too keen an interest in the long-term welfare of the island.

One of the classic island abuses has been the introduction of exotic plants or animals. Some of these alien species have been introduced intentionally—for example, goats (*Capra*, Bovidae)—and others unintentionally—for example, rats (*Rattus*, Muridae). Some indigenous insular plants cannot withstand the grazing or browsing of introduced herbivores, and those having shallow root systems cannot withstand their trampling. These abuses can, in turn, result in the extirpation of these plants and sometimes also in severe soil erosion. Indigenous insular animal species often fall ready prey to introduced carnivores—again, with the possibility of local extirpation or, in the case of endemic species, of extinction. Moreover, the introduced species are often relatively free of enemies in their new habitat. The outcome—particularly of the faunal introductions, which have been made on so many islands—has frequently been to displace a portion of the indigenous island biota and thus to wreak utter havoc among the island ecosystems. For example, although less than 10 per cent of the 8 600 or so extant bird species of the world are confined to islands, 90 per cent (85 out of 94) of the bird extinctions since the year 1600 have occurred within this group (Fisher *et al.*, 1969: 17; Gosnell, 1976). In this regard, Chapple (1971-1972) has suggested on the basis of a successful trial that military units should combine training exercises with the extermination of insular pests, such as feral goats. It should also be noted here that although plant introductions can lead to severe damage to island ecosystems (Stoddart, 1968 *a*: 30-32), there is evidence to suggest that such aliens are most likely to remain established as pests in conjunction with continued habitat intervention by human beings (Egler, 1942: Harris, 1962).

It becomes clear that the uses to which man puts islands—whether as a place to live in or to visit, or as a source of natural resources—inevitably lead to substantial alterations in both their habitat and their biota. These alterations can—and some will say must—be interpreted as being ecologically undesirable. Thus the question of where to draw the dividing line between man's *use* of islands and his *abuse* of them is at best a difficult matter. However, it must be recognized that, owing to the relative ecological vulnerability of islands, any level or intensity of use is likely to be more damaging on an island than on a mainland. As the number of relatively undisturbed islands diminishes, the need for conserving the remainder grows more acute.

Military

Countless islands have been, and continue to be, coveted by foreign powers for their resources, their strategic locations, or for a variety of other reasons. As a result, islands have been conquered and occupied time and again, and otherwise militarily abused (appendix 6.1.3). By way of example, the small (10-thousand hectare) Micronesian island of Tinian (15°N 146°E) has sustained a long series of major ecological and social disturbances (Caulfield *et al.*, 1974). Spanish military forces occupied the Marianas, including Tinian, in the seventeenth century. When the native Chamorros became too unruly, they were all simply deported to Guam, where they were forced to remain for the next 150 years or more. Germany took control of Tinian in 1898 and enticed back a group of Chamorros, primarily to provide labour for their copra plantations. Japan began its rule of Tinian in 1914. The German copra plantations were destroyed and replaced by sugar plantations. In July 1944, 9 000 defending Japanese troops were defeated by the USA in a fierce battle that devastated the island. The USA then established important naval and air facilities on the island and maintained them for the rest of the war. It was from Tinian that the two nuclear attacks on Japan were launched. Today, the 750 inhabitants are awaiting a decision by the USA as to whether their island will once again be transformed into a giant military complex.

The discussions to follow dwell upon the use of islands as military bases, as sites for weapon-testing or for military training exercises, and as theatres of war.

Aldabra island as a military base

The ecologically disruptive nature of island development for military purposes became a major issue in 1967, when scientists and conservationists discovered that the USA and the UK planned to establish a major military air base and communications facility on Aldabra (10°S 46°E) in the western Indian Ocean (Peterson, 1968; Walsh, 1967). Aldabra is a slightly lifted atoll, consisting of several small islands having a combined area of almost 16 thousand hectares; it lies some 640 kilometres off the African coast and about 420 kilometres north of Madagascar. The atoll is quite inhospitable for human beings, and the one small settlement of less than 100 fishermen that had been living on one of the islets abandoned it several years ago.

Aldabra is one of the very few relatively undisturbed islands of its kind still remaining anywhere in the world, and the last such refuge in the Indian

Ocean (Stoddart, 1967; Stoddart & Wright, 1967). For example, Aldabra serves as one of the major breeding grounds of the majestic frigate birds *(Fregata minor* and *F. ariel)* of the Indian Ocean. It appears likely that these birds would have been extirpated in conjunction with the establishment of the air base, since their presence is incompatible with the safe landing and take-off of jet aircraft. A sad situation of this kind materialized, in fact, in connection with the maintenance of the US air base on Midway (28°N 177°W) in the Pacific Ocean. There it was considered essential to kill off a substantial fraction of the insular breeding population of the Laysan albatross *(Diomedea immutabilis),* the existence of the species being jeopardized in the process (Fisher, 1966).

Aldabra is also the home of the white-throated rail *(Dryolimnas cuvieri)*—the last surviving of three species of flightless rails once found on Indian Ocean islands. This island, in fact, supports dozens of endemic species of birds and insects; moreover, of the 173 recorded species of higher plants on Aldabra, some 10 per cent are unique to the island. Finally, Aldabra is the home of the last remaining colony of the once widespread giant land tortoise *Testudo gigantea* (whose only close relative, *T. elephatopus,* leads an endangered existence on Galápagos).

Establishment of the military base would have entailed not only an influx of people, but also the construction of buildings, airstrips, an artificial harbour, and a road system including causeways and bridges connecting the islets. This activity plus the subsequent utilization of the base would have resulted in massive habitat disturbance and irreversible species decimation. As it happened, an international campaign opposing this ecologically disastrous project finally resulted in its official abandonment in 1971.

The case of Aldabra illustrates what must be expected to occur—at any rate to some extent—in the development of any small and remote island for military purposes. Moreover, once an island is given over to military purposes, it becomes a candidate for utter devastation during time of war.

Weapon-testing and practice firing

Weapon-testing and training exercises result in some of the major military abuses of islands. Some islands have been employed as test grounds for conventional high-explosive munitions, others for testing biological warfare agents, and yet others for testing nuclear weapons.

In connection with the testing of conventional munitions and of training exercises employing them, one may give the example of the Puerto Rican island of Culebra (18°N 65°W), used for many years by the US Navy as a bombing and shelling range (*Armed Forces Journal International,* 1975; Prina, 1974; Swann, 1971). Other US test and practice-firing sites of this kind have been located on the Hawaiian islands of Manana (21°N

158°W) (Elepaio, 1942) and Kahoolawe (20°N 157°W) (Courson, 1972; LeBarron & Walker, 1971). The habitat of such islands is severely disrupted; and their rehabilitation, when attempted, becomes extraordinarily difficult, owing in no small part to the copious presence of dangerous unexploded munitions.

As regards the testing of biological warfare agents, the United Kingdom used the Scottish island of Gruinard (58°N 5°W) during 1941–1942 for testing the military potential of *Bacillus anthracis* (Bacillaceae), the causative agent of anthrax (Clarke, 1968: 16, 60). The island was reported to be still dangerously contaminated in 1966. Elsewhere, the USA is reported to have carried out preliminary research on the dissemination of biological warfare agents on a number of Pacific islands (Boffey, 1969).

Islands have been among the locations favoured for nuclear explosions, having provided sites for one-fourth of all such detonations to date. Indeed, nuclear devices have been exploded on (or immediately above or adjacent to) at least 11 islands in three oceans on some 265 occasions during the past three decades (table 6.3).

Some of the damage from nuclear explosions results in local geomorphological modifications of an essentially permanent nature. For example, surface bursts on Bikini and Enewetak (Eniwetok) atolls have blasted out huge craters, now water-filled. The thermonuclear device tested at Enewetak on 31 October 1952 literally obliterated the 14-hectare island of Elugelab (11° 40′N 162° 12′E) on which it was detonated—the island no longer exists (Hines, 1962: 139–140). On some islands, the much larger concentric zone perijacent to the crater in which the plants and animals have been eradicated becomes—depending upon local terrain and soil conditions—subject to soil erosion, from which even minimal recovery could take centuries. In the further zone where damage is mostly confined to the plants and animals (the soil being more or less left undisturbed), invasion by pioneer species usually occurs quite soon—a process that initiates ecological (successional) recovery.

Ecological recovery from nuclear decimation has been studied in the Marshall Islands, especially at Bikini and Enewetak atolls (Berrill, 1966; Hines, 1962; Williams, 1967). Vegetational recovery seems to take its normal—here relatively rapid—successional course (Fosberg, 1959 *a*; 1959 *b*; Palumbo, 1962). In a study of radionuclides, with particular reference to the indigenous crabs, Held (1960) noted that population levels soon returned to normal on Enewetak following the termination of nuclear testing. Moreover, two years after testing ceased, strontium-90 (^{90}Sr), caesium-137 (^{137}Cs), and cerium-144 (^{144}Ce) seemed to have established themselves permanently in the biogeochemical cycling involving these crustaceans. Jackson (1969) attributed the extirpation of the Polynesian rat (*Rattus exulans*, Muridae) from Enewetak to the nuclear testing there.

Nuclear testing at Amchitka Island has placed the Aleutian Canada goose (*Branta canadensis leucopareia,* Anatidae) in danger of extinction.

This was once an abundant bird in the Aleutians, large breeding colonies existing on a number of islands; at present there remains only one small nesting colony of several hundred individuals on Buldir Island (Bureau of Sport Fisheries & Wildlife, 1973: 109–110). With some difficulty, the US Fish & Wildlife Service had been successful in re-establishing a second nesting colony on Amchitka, only to have the subsequent activities connected with nuclear testing ruin these last-ditch efforts (R. D. Jones, Jr, US Fish & Wildlife Service, private correspondence of 14 July 1977).

Nuclear testing on islands has also provided the opportunity for examining the medical impact of nuclear contamination. A large fission/fusion device was detonated at Bikini on 1 March 1954 that accidentally exposed more than 100 persons who had unfortunately been within 185 kilometres of the detonation (23 on a fishing vessel and 89 on Rongelap atoll) to roughly 0.2 kiloröntgen of nuclear radiation from early fall-out (Conard *et al.*, 1975; Glasstone & Dolan, 1977: 436–439; Lapp, 1958). Several deaths as well as a substantial number of tumours—some of them malignant—are attributable to this exposure, including a particularly high frequency of thyroid tumours among those who were *in utero* or youngsters at that time. The number of these cases continues to rise.

The use of Pacific islands as nuclear test sites has had a tragic social impact on the forcibly displaced islanders—a matter that has been pursued to some extent by Baines (1970–1971) and Tate & Hull (1964). US testing ended at Bikini and Enewetak in 1958. The USA has recently recognized that neither Bikini nor Enewetak is as yet habitable, owing to the continued radioactive contamination of the drinking-water, soil, and vegetation, despite enormous US clean-up efforts (Pincus, 1978*a*; 1978*b*; 1978*c*). In fact, it has been tentatively concluded that these islands may not be safe for habitation for thousands of years.

Combat

Many islands throughout the world have been the scene of combat on one or more occasions. For example, several islands in the Mediterranean Sea have had prominent battles fought upon them many times during the past few thousand years—among them Cyprus, Rhodes, Malta, and Khios (Dupuy & Dupuy, 1977). Much of the combat in the Pacific theatre of operations during World War II occurred on islands. As a result, more than a dozen Pacific Ocean islands were subjected to heavy bombardment and intense combat, with concomitant high loss of life and severe habitat disruption, as well as social and ecological upheaval (table 6.4).

In describing the battle impact of World War II on Midway Atoll (28°N 177°W), Fisher & Baldwin (1946) provided an informative summary of this drastic form of military impact on the specialized biota of islands. For example, they showed the various ways in which thousands upon thousands of adult birds or hatching eggs were destroyed by the war. A more subtle factor contributing to population reduction was shown to be the disruption of behavioural patterns normally associated with mating activities. However, the major lesson provided by Fisher & Baldwin is that the most serious impact of conventional military activities on fauna occurs via upheaval of the faunal habitat. Thus, they found that the population levels of the many bird species that they investigated were reduced more or less in direct proportion to the loss of available space and vegetation. The observations made by Baker (1946) on Iwo Jima, Peleliu, Kwajalein, Saipan and other Micronesian islands, as well as those made by Donaghho (1950) on Guadalcanal and Tulagi, confirm this finding for both bird and other animal populations.

It was the sad duty of Fisher & Baldwin (1946) to confirm the war-caused extinction of one already endangered bird species—the Laysan rail (*Porzanula palmeri*, Rallidae) (cf. also Greenway, 1967: 231)—and the probable extinction of another—the Laysan finch (*Telespiza cantans*, Fringillidae). Their observations regarding these two birds provide useful case histories. The main factor in the extermination of the Laysan rail—a flightless and ground-nesting shore bird—was the inadvertent introduction of rats (*Rattus*, Muridae) which during 1943 and 1944 rapidly multiplied to overrun the Midway Island group. A second factor, considered to have been almost as important, was the widespread removal ('clean-up') of the brushy shore vegetation, largely consisting of the shrub *Scaevola frutescens* (Goodeniaceae), the major refuge for this bird. The cause of what appeared to be the extinction of the Laysan finch—a shrub-nesting species—is somewhat more obscure, although here again rat infestation plus major vegetational disturbance were tentatively concluded by Fisher & Baldwin to be the reasons.

A number of additional insular bird extinctions or near extinctions can be catalogued here. Thus, the large flightless Wake Island rail (*Rallus wakensis*, Rallidae), endemic to that island, was brought to extinction during World War II by a combination of bombing, rat depredations, and human (Japanese) appetites (Fisher & Baldwin, 1946; Greenway, 1967: 216; Peterson, 1942–1943). The Marianas mallard (*Anas oustaleti*, Anatidae) was extirpated from Guam by military activities during World War II and appears to be in danger of complete extinction (Baker, 1946; Greenway, 1967: 169). The Marianas megapode (*Megapodius lapérouse lapérouse*, Megapodiidae), once native to a number of Pacific islands, is a seriously endangered species, brought closer to extinction by military construction activities during World War II (Greenway, 1967: 185). Finally, the brown booby (*Sula leucogaster plotus*, Sulidae) was exceedingly common on Midway before World War II, but was extirpated from the island, largely because its nesting areas were requisitioned for military purposes (Fisher & Baldwin, 1946). However, unlike some of the mono-insular endemics previously described, this colonial bird still appears to be quite plentiful on a number of other Pacific islands.

To turn now to an island in a different sea, the Cyprus mouflon (*Ovis orientalis ophion,* Bovidae) provides an example of an endangered insular mammal (Fisher *et al.,* 1969: 168–169; Cyprus Department of Forests, Nicosia, private communication of 26 March 1976). It was once a prominent component of the island fauna; today, the hundred or so surviving wild individuals are restricted to the 60-thousand hectare Paphos forest reserve in western Cyprus. This mouflon and its rugged mountainous forest habitat have both been under rigorous protection since 1938, when the once plentiful numbers of the animal had dwindled to an alarming 15 or so. It is, therefore, most unfortunate that during the summer of 1974 invading Turkish forces brought their war to the Paphos forest. They killed some of the animals directly via bombing and incendiary attack, but—more importantly—destroyed more than one-third of the forest through these activities. The current status of the Cyprus mouflon is assumed to be precarious, the unsettled political and social situation hampering vigorous efforts at amelioration.

Before concluding this section, it must at least be pointed out that when modern warfare engulfs an island, it is certain to be disruptive to any local indigenous human population. Although the various indigenous Pacific island cultures had been exposed to 'civilization' in many ways before World War II, that conflict nevertheless resulted in enormous social upheaval (appendix 6.1.3).

V. Conclusion

The abuse of islands is becoming an increasingly important cause for concern. Various of the factors responsible for island abuse—both civil and military—are becoming ever more pronounced, frequent, or likely. Island categories can no longer be considered safe by virtue of numbers nor can individual islands be considered immune by virtue of remoteness.

Substantial disruption of any island is unfortunate at least to the extent that its ecology differs from that of others. In fact, most small isolated islands are not only ecologically unique in many respects, but also ecologically fragile. Once such an island is substantially disrupted and a fraction of its endemic plant and animal species driven to extinction, its ecosystem has been irreversibly harmed.

The few small remote islands of the world that have somehow escaped the heavy hand of man are clearly in urgent need of protection. Accordingly, international agreements should be reached with the aim of preventing these relatively pristine microcosms from being abused by human beings. No military or other use—no matter how seemingly benign—should be permitted on them if it might be likely to incur the wrath of some belligerent power in time of war (see, for example, table 8.4, treaties 3 and 4). Seen solely from the angle of island welfare, it may be considered 'fortunate' that—as missiles and their delivery and guidance systems continue to improve, and as increasing reliance is placed on nuclear-powered naval vessels—island bases are losing some of their former significance.

To recapitulate, when the ecology of an island is disrupted, the damage is, at any rate, partly irremediable.

Table 6.1. Island habitat: distribution and demography (1975 data)[a]

Region	Island area $10^3 km^2$ $(10^5 ha)$	Proportion of regional land area per cent	Island population[b] 10^6	Proportion of regional population per cent	Island population density No./km²
Ocean					
Atlantic	689	100	87.6	100	127.0
Pacific	3 672	100	322.8	100	87.9
Indian	661	100	23.6	100	35.8
Arctic	2 238	100	0.1	100	0.0
Hemisphere					
Northern	4 485	4.4	305.9	8.4	68.2
Southern	2 774	5.8	128.2	29.9	46.2
Habitat					
Temperate	983	1.7	174.3	7.4	177.2
Tropical	3 935	9.3	259.3	16.4	65.9
Desert	1	0.0	0.3	0.3	411.6
Arctic	2 341	9.9	0.3	1.5	0.1
World-wide	**7 259**	**4.9**	**434.1**	**10.7**	**59.8**[c]

Sources and notes:
[a] The regions, which are strictly geographic, are described in table 1.4, note *a*. Islands of the Mediterranean Sea are included with those of the Atlantic Ocean. Sources for the areas and populations are given in table 1.4, note *b*.
[b] The population of the island habitat is currently increasing at the rate of 1.77 per cent per year (table 1.4), which leads to a population doubling time of 39.5 years.
[c] The comparable continental population density is, by contrast, 25.6 persons per square kilometre.

Table 6.2. Insular military facilities: a selection [a]

Island and group	Location	Ocean	Military presence
Adak, etc. (Aleutains)	52°N 177°W, etc.	Pacific	USA
Ascension	8°S 14°W	Atlantic	USA
Bahrain	26°N 41°E	Indian	USA
Corsica	42°N 9°E	Atlantic (Med.) [b]	France
Crete	36°N 24°E	Atlantic (Med.)	NATO, USA
Cuba (West Indies)	20°N 75°W, etc.	Atlantic	USA, USSR
Cyprus	35°N 33°E	Atlantic (Med.)	UK, Greece, Turkey
Diego Garcia (Chagos)	7°S 72°E	Indian	USA, UK
East Falkland (Falklands)	52°S 58°W	Pacific	UK
Great Britain	52°N 0°, etc.	Atlantic	USA
Greenland	78°N 69°W	Arctic	USA
Guam (Marianas)	14°N 145°E	Pacific	USA
Hao (Tuamotu Arch.)	18°S 141°W	Pacific	France
Honshu, etc. (Japan)	35°N 139°E, etc.	Pacific	USA
Iceland	64°N 23°W	Atlantic	USA
Jan Meyen	71°N 8°W	Arctic	Norway
Johnston	17°N 170°W	Pacific	USA
Kwajalein (Marshalls)	9°N 168°E	Pacific	USA
Luzon, etc. (Philippines)	15°N 120°E, etc.	Pacific	USA
Maddalena (Sardinia)	41°N 9°E	Atlantic (Med.)	USA
Mahé (Seychelles)	5°S 56°E	Indian	USA
Malta	36°N 15°E	Atlantic (Med.)	UK, NATO
Midway (Hawaiian Is.)	28°N 177°W	Pacific	USA
New Caledonia	22°S 166°E	Pacific	France
Oahu, etc. (Hawaiian Is.)	21°N 158°W, etc.	Pacific	USA
Okinawa (Ryukyu Is.)	26°N 128°E, etc.	Pacific	USA
Puerto Rico (West Indies)	18°N 66°W	Atlantic	USA
Réunion (Mascarenes)	21°S 56°E	Indian	France
Sicily	37°N 15°E	Atlantic (Med.)	USA
Singapore (East Indies)	1°N 104°E	Pacific	New Zealand
Tahiti (Societies)	18°S 149°W	Pacific	France
Taiwan	25°N 122°E, etc.	Pacific	USA
Terceira, etc. (Azores)	39°N 27°W, etc.	Atlantic	USA
Tsushima	34°N 129°E	Pacific	USA
Wake	19°N 167°E	Pacific	USA

Sources and notes:
[a] The data are from Cottrell & Moore (1977); Grimmett (1977); *SIPRI Yearbook 1972:* chap. 7; and SIPRI files. See also appendix 6.1.3. It must be emphasized that this tabulation is only a sampling, representing only a small fraction of the oceanic islands of the world that are used at least in part for military purposes. For example, at least 11 islands have been subjected to nuclear explosions (table 6.3). Also, at least 14 of the 34 island nations maintain domestic armies having a strength of 10 thousand or more (table 1.12).
[b] The parenthetical abbreviation 'Med.' stands for 'Mediterranean Sea'.

Table 6.3. Nuclear explosions associated with islands[a]

Island and group	Location		Ocean	Nation	Year(s)	No.
Amchitka (Aleutians)	51°N	179°E	Pacific	USA	1965–1971	3
Bikini (Marshalls)	11°N	165°E	Pacific	USA	1946–1958	23
Christmas (Line Is.)	2°N	157°W	Pacific	UK, USA	1957–1962	34
Enewetak[b] (Marshalls)	11°N	162°E	Pacific	USA	1948–1958	35
Fangataufa (Tuamotu Arch.)	22°S	139°W	Pacific	France	1975	2
Honshu (Japan)	34°N	132°E	Pacific	USA	1945	1
Johnston	17°N	170°W	Pacific	USA	1958–1962	12
Kyushu (Japan)	33°N	130°E	Pacific	USA	1945	1
Monte Bello	20°S	115°E	Indian	UK	1952–1956	3
Mururoa (Tuamotu Arch.)	22°S	139°W	Pacific	France	1966–1977	51
Novaya Zemlya	75°N	55°E	Arctic	USSR	1957–1977	100
Total			3	4	**1945–1977**	**265**

Sources and notes:
[a] The data for 1945–1962 are summarized from Glasstone (1964: 671–681 *b*); those for 1963–1971 from Zander & Araskog (1973: 35–53); those for 1972–1974 from *SIPRI Yearbook 1975*: 506–509; those for 1975–1976 from *SIPRI Yearbook 1977*: 400–402; and those for 1977 from SIPRI files.
[b] Enewetak is the former Eniwetok.

Table 6.4. Major Pacific island battles of World War II[a]

Island and group	Location		Date
Attu (Aleutians)	53°N	173°E	May 1943
Enewetak[b] (Marshalls)	11°N	162°E	February 1944
Guadalcanal (Solomons)	10°S	160°E	August 1942–February 1943
Guam (Marianas)	14°N	145°E	July–August 1944
Iwo Jima (Volcano Is.)	25°N	141°E	February–March 1945
Kwajalein (Marshalls)	9°N	168°E	January–February 1944
Okinawa (Ryukyu Is.)	26°N	128°E	April–June 1945
Peleliu (Palaus; Carolines)	7°N	134°E	September–October 1944
Saipan (Marianas)	15°N	146°E	June–August 1944
Tarawa (Gilberts)	2°N	173°E	November 1943
Tinian (Marianas)	15°N	146°E	July 1944
Tulagi (Solomons)	9°S	160°E	August 1942
Wake	19°N	167°E	December 1941

Sources and notes:
[a] The listed battles have been described by Dupuy & Dupuy (1977: 1123–1198) and/or Liddell-Hart (1970). See also Garfield (1969: 208–258) for the Battle of Attu; Tregaskis (1943) for the Battle of Guadalcanal; Leckie (1967) for the Battle of Iwo Jima; Sherrod (1944) for the Battle of Tarawa; and Donovan (1967: 32–59) for a brief overview. Bahrenburg (1971) has described about two dozen World War II Pacific battle sites as they appeared in 1970, including the following of those listed above: Guadalcanal, Guam, Iwo Jima, Okinawa, Peleliu, Saipan, Tarawa, Tinian, and Wake.
[b] Enewetak is the former Eniwetok.

Appendix 6.1

Sources for the island habitat

1. *Environment and ecology.* The two volumes of Carlquist (1965; 1974) provide an excellent introduction to island biology; Hubbell (1968) presents a fine brief treatment of the subject. The work by MacArthur & Wilson (1967) is a classic study of island biogeography. Snow (1970) has prepared very useful summaries on the islands of the eastern Indian Ocean; for Aldabra, see Stoddart (1967); and for Diego Garcia, see Stoddart & Taylor (1971).

2. *Civil use and abuse.* Henderson *et al.* (1971) and Oliver (1961) provide very useful overviews of the islands of the Pacific Ocean. Many of the islands of the western Pacific have been well covered by Brookfield & Hart (1971) and Coates (1970). Of the works that deal with the ecologically rational use and development of islands, those by Barrau *et al.* (1973), Dasmann *et al.* (1973: 134–137), Fosberg (1963), and McEachern & Towle (1974) are to be recommended; another by Carlozzi (1972) deals with the Caribbean islands in particular. Maude & Doran (1966) provide an excellent history of Tarawa; Spoehr (1954) presents the history and anthropology of Saipan; and Newcombe *et al.* (1978) have prepared a brilliant analysis of Hong Kong as a human ecosystem. Man's detrimental—sometimes catastrophic—effects on islands have been especially well presented by Stoddart (1968 *a*; 1968 *b*) and by Fosberg (1972). See also Gosnell (1976) and Summerhays (1973).

3. *Military use and abuse.* For pertinent information on some of the militarily important islands of the world, see Cottrell & Moorer (1977). Similarly, for the Pacific Ocean, see Cameron (1975–1976), Hobbs (1945), Mihaly (1972–1973; 1973–1974), Murray (1975), and Pincus (1975). Similarly, for the Indian Ocean, see Boxhall (1966), Fuller (1977), Prina (1974), Siegel (1977), *SIPRI Yearbook 1975;* chap. 5, and Unna (1974). For several Mediterranean islands, see Grimmett (1977); for Crete, see Richardson (1977); for Svalbard, see Teal (1950-1951); for Tinian, see Caulfield *et al.* (1974); and for the Falklands, see Tremayne (1977–1978). With specific reference to a number of South Pacific islands, Coulter (1946) summarized some of the economic and more subtle social consequences of World War II as they manifested themselves right at the end of that war. Some years later, Spoehr (1954) dealt with similar questions in his study of Saipan, as also did Oliver (1961: chap. 20–21) for various Pacific islands. Some of the social and economic long-term consequences of World War II can be gleaned from the more recent account of Bahrenburg (1971).

7. The ocean

The tables for this chapter appear on pages 170–177.

I. Introduction

The world ocean covers 71 per cent of the global surface. Although the ocean supports only 0.3 per cent of the global biomass, this biomass accounts for fully 32 per cent of the annual biomass production. Eighty-one per cent of the world's nations have direct access to the ocean, although only about 32 per cent of all nations maintain navies of any significance. The vast extent, enormous volume, remarkable buoyancy, low level of friction, partial opacity, and extensive resources of the ocean all combine to make it an ever more important theatre of both commercial and military operations. The most recent major naval battles occurred during World War II.

II. Environment and ecology

The world ocean is an immense continuous body of salt water, which—although interspersed with land masses of various sizes—covers most of the surface of the Earth. Its waters support a vast array of living things; by various means it also exerts a crucial influence on the terrestrial biota of the world (appendix 7.1.1).

The world ocean extends over about 361 million square kilometres (36 100 million hectares) of the global surface, somewhat more than half of this area lying in the Southern hemisphere (table 7.1). It has a total volume of perhaps 1.4×10^{18} cubic metres, distributed among several major basins. The largest by far is the Pacific, having a surface area of 181 million square kilometres and a volume of 0.8×10^{18} cubic metres. The surface area of the ocean within the temperate zone is roughly 187 million square kilometres, that within the tropical zone about 153 million square kilometres, and that within the arctic zone about 21 million square kilometres—of which about 8 million square kilometres is continuously ice-covered. However, the world ocean not continuously ice-covered is perhaps more usefully divided into the following major habitats: *(a)* open ocean (32 400 million hectares); *(b)* continental shelves (2 700 million hectares); *(c)* estuaries (140 million hectares); *(d)* algal beds plus reefs (60 million hectares); and *(e)* upwelling zones (40 million hectares).

The gently sloping continental shelves of the world have an average width of about 78 kilometres (range, zero to 1 500 kilometres) and a depth that varies from zero at the shoreline to an average of 130 metres (range, 20 to 550 metres) at the outer edge. They then slope down rather more abruptly (average slope 7 per cent) to form the ocean basins. Much of the floor of these basins is rather flat and horizontal—the so-called abyssal plain—and is often between 4 000 and 5 000 metres below the surface. The abyssal plains are, however, broken up both by submarine ridges (some of which are tall enough to be islands) and by deep ocean trenches.

In the arctic zones the vast bulk of the water—some 99.9 per cent of it—is, of course, in the liquid state, remaining at a temperature that hovers about $-1°C$. In the warmer equatorward regions it is covered by a layer of ice for more than half the year, and in the colder poleward regions for the entire year. The ice cover (which forms at $-2°C$) varies in thickness between zero and more than four metres, the average being almost two metres. However, even in the permanently frozen zone, the ice cover—especially the pack-ice covering the Arctic Ocean—routinely develops cracks and gaps, and slowly shifts about.

Wind action, the Earth's rotation (Coriolis forces), density differences caused by temperature and salinity differences, and tidal action brought about by the gravitational pull of the Moon and the Sun combine to produce not only surface waves, but also a complex system of great ocean currents within and between the various ocean basins. One to several major currents are likely to be found in any vertical ocean profile, each having a more or less characteristic direction and velocity. Their velocities vary with location and season, but are of the order of 10 kilometres per day for surface currents and, apparently, perhaps half that for subsurface currents. Water can be forced downward at the convergence of two surface currents. Conversely, a deep current can be forced upward by a land mass, this latter phenomenon being referred to as an upwelling. The ceaseless ocean tides and currents serve to keep the ocean water of the world more or less well mixed and uniform.

Ocean water has an overall salt concentration averaging 36 kilograms per cubic metre (range, 34–38 kg/m³). Numerous inorganic and organic compounds can be found in solution in ocean water; they together provide at least trace levels of all or most of the elements. However, the bulk of such material is accounted for by a rather limited number of chemical species. Indeed, perhaps 99.9 per cent of the solid constituents in solution consist of the following four cations and four anions (in kg/m³): sodium, Na^+ (11.0); magnesium, Mg^{++} (1.3); calcium, Ca^{++} (0.4); potassium, K^+ (0.4); chloride, Cl^- (19.7); sulphate, SO_4^{--} (2.8); bicarbonate, HCO_3^- (0.1); and bromide, Br^- (0.1). Of the essential major mineral nutrient elements (calcium, potassium, magnesium, nitrogen, phosphorus, sulphur, and iron), the following are generally, however, in very low available (ionized) supply (in mg/m³): nitrogen (c. 250 to 500), phosphorus (c. 50 to 100), and iron (c. 10 to 25). Of the various gases dissolved in ocean water, the three major ones are (in g/m^3): carbon dioxide, CO_2 (in equilibrium with the HCO_3^- ion) (c. 100); nitrogen, N_2 (inert) (c. 15); and oxygen, O_2 (c. 6 in the top 20 to 150 metres, but c. 3 overall). The acidity (hydrogen ion concentration) is quite well buffered at about pH 8.2.

The overall average temperature of the world ocean is about 4°C. The surface waters have an average temperature of about 17°C, ranging between about $-2°C$ (the freezing-point) and perhaps 27°C. Ocean water has an average density of 1 025 kilograms per cubic metre. The hydrostatic pressure in the ocean increases with depth at the rate of about 10 kilopascals per metre (0.1 atmosphere per metre). In non-turbulent ocean water having a minimum of suspended particles, more than 50 per cent of the sunlight has been absorbed at a depth of 5 metres, and more than 99 per cent at 100 metres. In coastal waters these depths must usually be reduced by perhaps one-half to two-thirds.

The world-wide hydrological cycle plays an indispensable role in the global ecosystem or biosphere, its series of pathways serving to link all the ecosystems on Earth. The ocean is the great reservoir for this cycle, representing over 97 per cent of the Earth's total supply of water and more than 99 per cent of its supply of liquid water. The ocean supplies some 40×10^{12} cubic metres per year of water to the land via evaporation and subsequent precipitation. An essentially equal amount is returned to the ocean annually via stream and underground flow (the combined run-off carrying roughly 6 kilograms per cubic metre of dissolved substances). Although the land and the ocean receive approximately proportionate shares of world-wide precipitation in terms of their surface areas, the land supplies only about half of its proportionate share of evaporative replenishment to the atmosphere, the ocean making up this deficit. One can thus see that the ocean is intimately involved not only in the global water balance, but also in global mineral nutrient cycling and in global climate.

The ocean provides suitable niches for an amazing diversity of living things—plant and animal, large and small, sessile and mobile. Taxonomic diversity is substantially greater in the ocean than on land. Although some life can be found in almost any area of the ocean and at any depth, most of the marine biomass is to be found within its shallow regions of one kind or another (table 7.2).

Marine food-chains begin, of course, with autotrophic green plants as the producers. These are restricted to the photic (euphotic) zone—the stratum of ocean where sufficient sunlight for photosynthesis can penetrate. The depth of the photic zone ranges from zero at the shoreline to a maximum that averages between 30 and 100 metres or more. Relatively few kinds of green plants exist in the ocean that are attached to the bottom (the so-called benthic forms). This is understandable since only about 6 million square kilometres (less than 2 per cent) of the ocean floor is reached by sufficient sunlight for photosynthesis to take place. Rather, most of the green plants of the ocean are passively floating diatoms, dinoflagellates, and other microscopic algae, collectively referred to as phytoplankton.

Some ocean habitats, such as coral reefs and algal beds, are exceedingly productive. Certain close-inshore areas supplied with nutrients from terrestrial run-off (littoral zones, such as mangrove swamps or other estuaries) are also highly productive, as are regions of upwelling, where sunken nutrients are brought up from the lower reaches of the ocean. The open ocean, by contrast, is minimally productive. As for the actual photo-synthetic productivity of these marine ecosystems, one can expect coral reefs or algal beds to have an annual net primary productivity averaging perhaps 25 000 kilograms (dry weight) per hectare, and estuaries an average value of 15 000 kilograms per hectare (table 7.2). Upwelling zones will average about 5 000 kilograms per hectare, and the zones overlying the continental shelves about 3 600 kilograms per hectare. However, inasmuch as the value for the open ocean is only about 1 250 kilograms per hectare, that for the world ocean as a whole is only of the order of 1 500 kilograms per hectare.

The energy captured by the autotrophic organisms is in turn utilized by the multiplicity of heterotrophic marine organisms, either directly or indirectly. Such consumers include tiny floating fauna (the zooplankton) as well as large-sized swimmers (the nekton) and sessile bottom dwellers (the benthic forms). Some of the primary consumers (herbivores) feed directly on the living producer organisms; others feed on their sheddings and remains, since such detritus sinks out of the photic zone, through the aphotic zone, and to the bottom. The zooplankton comprises the most important group of herbivores, including, among others, the microscopic copepod crustaceans and the somewhat larger euphausid crustaceans known as krill. The secondary consumers (or carnivores) in turn feed upon the krill and other primary, as well as other secondary, consumers. The more prominent carnivores include the numerous sorts of cartilagenous and bony fishes, various decapod crustaceans (e.g., crabs, shrimps, lobsters), several cephalopod molluscs (e.g., squids, octopuses), some kinds of reptiles (e.g., turtles), several groups of mammals (e.g., whales, seals), and a host of birds. Some of these larger marine fauna spend a greater or lesser fraction of their time on land, often during the breeding season. Another important category of consumers consists of the saprophytic bacteria that reside largely in the bottom sediments, serving a decomposing function similar to that of the soil bacteria on land. The major food-chains in the ocean usually have three or four (occasionally two or five) consumer links beyond the initial producer link and prior to the final decomposer link. It must be noted here as well that mangrove swamps and other estuaries are important not only for their high productivity, but also because at least three-quarters of all species of marine fishes require these inshore habitats during at least one critical stage in their life cycle.

Moreover, they also form a crucial habitat for numerous sorts of birds for at least some part of the year.

III. Use

Civil

Human beings use the ocean in an enormous and increasingly vital number of ways. In considering the wide range of marine resources, it is useful to distinguish between the non-extractive and the extractive ones, the latter category in turn being divisible into non-living and living (appendix 7.1.2).

Firstly, the ocean serves as a separator or buffer—of varying importance—among nations. In fact, of the 159 nations, 34 are entirely surrounded by the sea, 95 abut the ocean in part, and only 30 are land-locked (appendix 1.4). Secondly, and of the greatest importance, the ocean is used for transportation, both coastal and intercontinental. Some 23 100 large merchant ships plus an additional 42 800 small ones currently ply the seas (appendix 7.2.1). Of the large ones, 5 or more are nuclear-powered and at least 32 can carry over 400 thousand cubic metres of oil. Among the further non-extractive uses that man makes of the ocean are for the laying of submarine communication cables and oil pipelines, for the dumping of wastes, and for the reclamation of land (e.g., some 40 per cent of the surface area of the Netherlands consists of polder lands). Man also uses the ocean for a variety of scientific, recreational, and aesthetic purposes.

The non-living extractive resources of the ocean are assuming an ever-greater share of the world economy. This has resulted from a combination of factors, among them being the inequable distribution of minerals *vis-à-vis* national territories, the ever-rising world demand for minerals, and the increasing range of exotic products manufactured by industry (both civil and military) that make growing inroads on the periodic chart of elements.

Important ocean extractives include sodium chloride (30 per cent of global production), bromine (70 per cent), magnesium (60 per cent), thorium (30 per cent), and pearls (almost 100 per cent). By far the most important mineral claimed today from the ocean (more precisely, from under it) is oil. The several thousand producing wells in the continental shelves of the world account for about 20 per cent of current world production (and the associated natural gas for perhaps 10 per cent of world production).

The living ocean resources of commercial importance include both flora and fauna. The marine fishery—which includes true fish (finfish), crustaceans and molluscs (shellfish), and marine mammals, such as whales and seals—is an indispensable source of food and other products. The annual world fish catch (exclusive of marine mammals) seems to have levelled off, temporarily at any rate, at about 66 million tonnes fresh weight (*UN Statistical Yearbook 1976:* table 46, average of 1970–1975 data, with seaweed, such as kelp, subtracted out). This corresponds to a dry weight of about 22 million tonnes and to a usable protein content of about 10 million tonnes. Thus, the marine fishery currently provides the world's human population with about 17 per cent of its annual animal protein intake (or about 5 per cent of its annual total protein intake). In Japan, fish protein represents about 50 per cent of the animal protein intake, in the USSR about 20 per cent, and in the USA about 3 per cent. Between 80 and 90 per cent of the commercial fish catch of the world occurs above the continental shelves. Incidentally, it is of interest to note here that a jurisdictional dispute over fishing rights in such waters has led to at least one international clash (table 8.2.9).

There are perhaps 100 commercial species of marine fish, but only 4 or so are currently of real importance. Herring (*Clupea,* Clupeidae), cod (*Gadus,* Gadidae), mackerel (*Scomber,* Scombridae), and anchovy (*Engraulis,* Engraulidae) (the last converted largely to meal) together represent well over half by weight of the annual take. Of course, some estuarine fish-farming—primarily involving shellfish of one kind or another—is also carried out. Such mariculture will presumably become more important in the future.

The annual recorded whale catch has been declining during the 1970s by about seven per cent per year. The recorded catch for the 1974–1975 season was 29 thousand, all having been taken in Antarctic waters and more than two-thirds being sperm whales (*UN Statistical Yearbook 1976:* table 47). The major whaling nation was the USSR (14 thousand), followed by Japan (9 thousand), South Africa (2 thousand), Peru (1 thousand), Australia (1 thousand), and a number of others.

Antarctic waters are exceedingly rich in krill *(Euphausia),* and these five-centimetre-long crustaceans could be harvested on a large scale for processing into edible protein. This is already being done on a small scale by the USSR, Japan, Poland, and several other nations. According to some estimates, the annual krill catch could safely be expanded to provide a self-renewing harvest at least equal in amount to the present annual world-wide fish catch (and thus roughly equivalent to five per cent of today's annual human consumption of plant and animal protein) (appendix 7.1.2).

As regards marine plants (seaweed), virtually three million tonnes fresh weight of giant kelp (*Macrocystis,* Laminariaceae) and other large algae were harvested in 1975 throughout the world for fertilizer, food, feed, and various chemical constituents (Ceres, 1976; extrapolation of 1972–1974 data). The harvest of these plants has been increasing in recent years by about nine per cent per year.

Military

The military use of the ocean is rapidly growing both in importance and in complexity (appendix 7.1.3). Such use can be either defensive or offensive; it can take place either in territorial waters or on the high seas, either on the sea surface or below it. Military use of the ocean is generally made by nations in support of their direct terrestrial interests, although the proportion of such use in support of direct ocean interest is increasing.

The navies of the world together maintain about 1 130 large ships plus an additional 1 330 small ones (appendix 7.2.2). Of the large ships, more than 260 are nuclear-powered. There are some 51 navies in the world; those of the USA and the USSR together dwarf all the rest (table 7.3). The relative military importance that the USA attaches to its navy is indicated by the fact that 25 per cent of the total number of personnel in its armed forces are naval (table 1.13, note *b;* table 7.3, note *b*), and that 33 per cent of its total military budget is directly devoted to the navy (Rumsfeld, 1977: A1).

The tasks of a navy continue to be the protection of a nation's shores, the safeguarding of its merchant fleet on the high seas, and the intimidation of other—especially smaller—nations ('naval presence' or 'showing the flag'). For example, the US Navy has carried out this function of intimidation on more than 170 occasions since the end of World War II (Blechman & Kaplan, 1977–1978: 81–82). Another naval task that has taken on a new dimension of importance is the establishment and subsequent protection of a nation's interests in the extractive resources—both living and non-living—of the ocean, described previously. Other standard naval missions include the protection of a nation's military troop and supply carriers and the denial of the use of the ocean to an enemy (including blockading). The primary targets of a navy continue to be the military (naval) and civil (merchant) ships and coastal facilities of enemy nations.

Superimposed upon all these traditional naval functions have been two strategic tasks of vast significance. The first of these is strategic deterrence (or attack). This role has been made possible over the past 15 years or so by the as yet essentially invulnerable missile-armed nuclear-powered submarines, having a nuclear second-strike capability (Garwin, 1972; Scoville, 1972) and now acquiring a first-strike capability (*SIPRI Yearbook 1979:* chap. 7). The second of these tasks is the counter-ability, that is, strategic anti-submarine warfare (ASW) (SIPRI, 1974c), which is becoming a serious threat to missile submarines (*SIPRI Yearbook 1979:* chap. 8). Most by far of the extensive oceanographic research and much of the marine biological research in the world are carried out (either directly or via financial support) by the several major navies of the world. The fruits of these efforts—while they have great civil value—are, of course, meant to enhance naval capabilities, largely with reference to anti-submarine warfare (Behrens, 1971–1972; Shulenherger, 1977).

IV. Abuse

Civil

The ocean continues to be abused in ever-increasing ways and to an ever-increasing extent, despite its obvious importance to man and despite an enormous literature of concern (appendix 7.1.2). Port facilities are frequently developed at the expense of estuaries and similar habitats—so important to marine ecology. Virtually no estuary is left undisturbed—some are dredged, others are filled, and all of them are befouled with a continuing stream of the noxious refuse of society. Indeed, the ocean has always been either the direct or the ultimate sump, sewer, and cesspit for most of the wastes produced by man. These wastes are energetic or material, soluble or insoluble, lighter than or heavier than water, non-radioactive or radioactive, and degradable or non-degradable.

Marine pollution reaches the ocean in various ways: *(a)* by the discharge of sewage, industrial wastes, and agricultural wastes (pesticides, fertilizers, food-processing residues) into the ocean, either directly or via streams; *(b)* by the fall-out or wash-out of volatile compounds and particulate matter from the atmosphere; *(c)* by the disruption associated with the extraction of sea-bed minerals; and *(d)* by the accidental release or intentional dumping of noxious material or cargoes from ships, and by the sinking or scuttling of ships. Wastes that are too complicated to dispose of on land—either because of the bulk or the hazard involved—are routinely dumped into the ocean.

The marine pollutant of greatest current concern appears to be oil, not only because of the large quantities that are regularly introduced into the ocean, but also because of the increasing risk of even greater levels of such contamination being caused by offshore facilities and tankers (this is dealt with more fully in a subsequent section). Oil-spills in arctic waters can be especially dangerous (Campbell & Martin, 1973; Ramseier, 1974; cf. also Kukla & Kukla, 1974). Not only will there be the expected local decimation of biota, but an oil-spill on the pack-ice will decrease its albedo and may thereby cause it to melt. It is considered that if the spill were of sufficient magnitude, the occurrence might adversely alter the global climate.

Ocean wastes exert their adverse influence by covering littoral (near-shore) and other benthic (sea-bed) habitats, by their direct toxicity, by stimulating the overgrowth of bacteria (which in turn use up the dissolved oxygen necessary for the survival of marine fauna), and in other ways. Fortunately, however, the ocean is immense, continuous, interlaced with currents, and the home of a wide array of micro-organisms. Thus, considering the ocean as a whole, the continuing influx of pollutants into this vast and complex system has so far been rendered more or less innocuous by dilution and decomposition (both abiotic and biotic). On the other hand, local areas subjected to especially high levels of continuing discharge or partially cut off from the rest of the ocean—for example, the New York City bight and the Baltic Sea—have not fared so well (Gross, 1971). Moreover, the deep-sea habitat is particularly slow to recover from contamination (Jannasch *et al.*, 1971) or other disturbance (Grassle, 1977). Thus, with the world gross national product increasing annually—and with it, the production of pollutants—there is little room for complacency about the future health of the world ocean.

Finally, one of the most tragic civil abuses of the world ocean is the extraction of fish beyond the capacity of that great natural resource for self-renewal. This flagrant abuse of natural providence provides an excellent example of the now classical concept of Hardin (1968) of the 'tragedy of the commons'. Individual nations find it in their own best interests knowingly to overfish on the high seas in the knowledge that the fish they fail to land may well be taken by other nations. Such a strategy, while profitable in the short term, is of course self-defeating in the long term. Cod (*Gadus,* Gadidae) and herring (*Clupea,* Clupeidae) are among the finfish that have been harvested excessively, with the result that their stocks have become seriously depleted; the flagrantly excessive harvesting of whales, seals, and marine turtles and their eggs, and the incidental killing of dolphins in association with tuna fishing provide even more striking examples (Curry-Lindahl, 1972: chap. 10). It may be mentioned here in passing that a good many whales appear to have been killed during World War II, having been mistaken for submarines (R. Revelle, Harvard University, private communication of 21 November 1976). The extirpation of a species of marine animal from a region can lead to spectacular perturbations within the residual biotic community (Estes & Palmisano, 1974). What is even more serious is that such an occurrence might be a step towards the extinction of the species.

Military

A number of military abuses of the ocean are comparable to the civil abuses discussed above and even merge in them, whereas others are more readily separable from the civil ones (appendix 7.1.3). An overview of the military abuses is provided in the present section; the following specific kinds are discussed in subsequent sections: underwater explosions; contamination with radioactive isotopes, chemical warfare agents, and oil; coastal (littoral) disruption; and the cutting of canals.

To begin with, some portion of the pollutants continually introduced into the ocean via stream flow and atmospheric fall-out have their origin in munition factories and other military facilities and activities. Since about six per cent of the combined gross national products of the world is devoted to military activities (table 8.1), one can make a first rough approximation that this same fraction of the routine inflow of ocean pollution is of military origin. Regarding the abuse of the ocean attributable specifically to its military use by ships, it can be seen from the figures presented in section III above that 3.0 per cent of the world's small ocean-going ships and 4.7 per cent of its large ones are naval (cf. also appendix 7.2).

It might be suggested that the military fraction of the overall ocean pollution is somewhat less than the above percentages indicate. This could be the case since environmental standards might, on average, be somewhat more stringently established and more rigidly enforced at military than at civil installations. This, in fact, appears to be the case in the USA (Defense, 1976; Groff, 1977; Holt, 1973). A more substantial objection to attributing a fraction of ocean pollution to the global military sector of the economy comparable to its share of the world gross national product is that military reduction would probably lead to almost equivalent civil increases, thus leading to little net environmental gain (cf. chapter 8, section III).

The twentieth century has up to now witnessed, in addition to minor naval engagements, the following four truly major naval engagements (Warner *et al.*, 1975): *(a)* the Battle of Tsushima in the Sea of Japan (c. 34°N 129°E) in May 1905; *(b)* the Battle of Jutland in the North Sea (c. 57°N 5°E) in May 1916; *(c)* the Battle of Midway in the central Pacific Ocean (c. 29°N 177°W) in June 1942; and *(d)* the Battle of Leyte Gulf in the western Pacific Ocean (c. 11°N 125°E) in October 1944. Such naval battles can result in severe local environmental disruption through underwater explosions, through the discharge of various pollutants when ships (and aircraft) are sunk, and in other ways.

The sinking of naval and merchant ships that could release so-called dangerous forces is of particular ecological concern. Nuclear-powered ships and large oil-tankers are discussed in subsequent sections. Also of potential concern are the increasingly common bulk carriers capable of carrying huge cargoes that are hazardous, owing to their toxicity or to their explosive nature. Liquefied natural gas (LNG) tankers are an example of the latter category (Coast Guard, 1976; Drake & Reid, 1977; Fay, 1972; Fay & MacKenzie, 1972). The 35 LNG tankers currently in operation have an average capacity of 46 thousand cubic metres; moreover, the 41 now under construction have an average capacity of 124 thousand cubic metres.

In addition to containing some trace constituents, natural gas might consist of approximately 85 per cent methane, 10 per cent ethane, and 5 per cent propane (*Merck Index,* 1976: 6258). The density of a mixture of such composition may be calculated as being 0.846 kilogram per cubic metre in the gaseous state, or 439 kilograms per cubic metre in the liquid state. The average energy yield of natural gas is 38.3 megajoules per cubic metre in the gaseous state, or 19.9 gigajoules per cubic metre in the liquid state (calculated from the *UN Statistical Yearbook 1976:* table 53). Thus, if the entire cargo of a 46 thousand cubic metre LNG tanker could be caused to explode through hostile action, it might conceivably release a blast wave having an energy approaching 915 terajoules. This theoretical maximum value is roughly comparable to the blast wave generated by a 437 'kiloton' atomic bomb (appendix 7.3). Fortunately, according to Drake & Reid (1977), such an explosion is a highly unlikely event, barring sophisticated sabotage.

Whereas the specific military activities singled out for discussion here and below are all more or less detrimental to marine life, it should be pointed out that there can be some beneficial corollaries as well. Thus, the denial of large areas of ocean to commercial exploitation for extended periods owing to wartime activities permits the build-up of fish populations. For example, fish catches on the Atlantic continental shelf of Europe were remarkably greater—threefold or more, depending upon the species—immediately after World War II than before it (Clark, 1947; Jensen, 1948; Wimpenny, 1953: 75–88). Both numbers and sizes increased substantially during the war years for important commercial fish varieties, such as haddock (*Melanogrammus aeglefinus,* Gadidae), plaice (*Pleuronectes platessa,* Pleuronectidae), ling (*Molva molva,* Gadidae), and hake (*Merluccius merluccius,* Merlucciidae). The Newfoundland seal fishery—based primarily on the harp-seal (*Pagophilus groenlandicus,* Phocidae) and to a much lesser extent on the hooded seal (*Cystophora cristata,* Phocidae)—was similarly improved as a result of World War II (Colman, 1949).

Fishing can also be substantially hampered during a post-war period owing to the residuum of military artefacts. The sea-mines, sea-mine anchors, and sunken ships remaining from World War II continue to this day to prevent access to large fishing areas in Swedish waters (B. Anderberg, Swedish Army, private communication, 10 February 1977). Similarly, large quantities of unwanted barbed wire were simply dumped off the Pacific coast of Canada after World War II that today still create a local hazard to fish-nets (R. O. Brinkhurst, Canada Institute of Ocean Sciences, private correspondence, 25 January 1977).

The question has been raised whether sonar waves for anti-submarine warfare or for other purposes might have an adverse effect—if any at all—on marine life. There appears to be no convincing evidence to substantiate such a possibility (Moulton & Backus, 1955).

Finally, a rather specialized military abuse of the ocean may be mentioned in this section—that of employing marine mammals for military purposes (Irvine, 1970; Lubow, 1977: chap. 7; Wood, 1973). Although very little is known about some aspects of such naval operations, it has been suggested that the US Navy is training dolphins (Dolphinidae) and sea-lions (Otariidae) for various missions, among them the suicidal one of delivering warheads (Wallace, 1973).

Underwater explosions

Underwater explosions associated with military activities can occur *(a)* in conjunction with undersea warfare and other hostile actions; *(b)* during military training exercises; *(c)* when sea-mines are set off by unintentional or other civil actions; and *(d)* when unwanted explosive munitions are disposed of at sea. Adverse effects on marine life can stem from the shock (blast) wave generated and from the toxic or radioactive properties of the chemicals released.

The size of the lethal zone of an underwater explosion depends upon numerous factors, such as: *(a)* the type of explosive; *(b)* the magnitude of the explosion; *(c)* the dimensions of the body of water, that is, its surface area and its depth; *(d)* the nature of the bottom; *(e)* the depth at which the charge is set off; and *(f)* the organisms in question.

The explosive is either of the conventional or of the nuclear type (see, for example, Wilcke, 1971; Glasstone, 1964). If the latter, it is either an atomic bomb or a hydrogen bomb (see appendix 7.3). If the former, it can be one of quite a number of explosive formulations. The two most commonly employed basic ingredients in conventional munitions are 2,4,6-trinitrotoluene (TNT) and hexahydro-1,3,5-trinitro-*s*-triazine (also referred to as cyclonite or RDX or hexogen). Nitramine (also known as tetryl) is perhaps the most frequently used detonator. One commonly employed bomb-filler is a 4 : 1 mixture of TNT and powdered aluminium (this formulation being known as tritonal). Another is a 9 : 6 : 4 : 1 mixture of cyclonite, TNT, powdered aluminium, and ammonium picrate (the ammonium salt of 2,4,6-trinitrophenol) (the code-name for this formulation being H6). A common cannon shell-filler is a 3 : 2 mixture of cyclonite and TNT. The explosive filler in some depth-charges is a 8 : 1 mixture of ammonium picrate and powdered aluminium. If the magnitude of the shock (blast) wave is taken to be 1, then that of cyclonite is 1.2, and that of ammonium picrate plus powdered aluminium is 1.5. The various formulations used in conventional munitions probably all fall within the range 1–1.5.

The over-pressure of the shock wave of an underwater explosion travels outwards in all directions and can therefore be expected (under ideal conditions) to diminish as an inverse function of the cube of the distance travelled. Thus, if the over-pressure at a radius of 1 metre is taken to be 100 per cent, then it will diminish by 90 per cent at a radius of 2.15 metres, by 99 per cent at 4.64 metres, and by 99.9 per cent at 10 metres. The over-pressure at a radius of 100 metres will be one-millionth of that at 1 metre. It also follows from this relationship that in order to double the blast over-pressure at any given distance from an explosion, one must increase the size of the charge by a factor of 8 (i.e., by a factor of 2^3); to triple it, by a factor of 27 (i.e., 3^3); and so on. It should also be noted here that shock waves which reach the sea-bed reflect back to a greater or lesser extent, depending on the nature of the floor. Shock waves that reach the surface also reflect back or—if of sufficient magnitude—break through to the atmosphere. Finally, the over-pressure wave is followed by a rarefaction or negative pressure wave, which can also contribute to any damage done.

The amount of over-pressure required to kill a marine organism—and hence also the size of lethal zone from any given charge—varies considerably from one type of organism to another. Broadly speaking, the marine organisms of interest here can be divided into *(a)* the true fish, *(b)* the crustaceans, *(c)* the molluscs, and *(d)* the warm-blooded vertebrates (mammals and birds). (In the marine fishery, the true fish are referred to as 'finfish', and the crustaceans and molluscs together as 'shellfish'.)

The great majority of the true marine fishes fall into one of two groups—the cartilagenous fish (e.g., sharks, rays, skates) or the ray-finned bony fish. The latter group accounts for perhaps 95 per cent of all the true fish and for all the commercially important ones. Among other things, these ray-finned bony fish are characterized by a large thin-walled sac in the body cavity known as the swimming- or air-bladder. This organ regulates the state of buoyancy of the animal and also has other functions.

The air-bladder is found to be readily ruptured by an underwater explosion. For example, Aplin (1947) studied representatives of nine genera of Pacific Ocean fish off the coast of California, five having air-bladders and four being without. Under similar blast conditions (c. 16 metres from a c. 7-kilogram charge of dynamite), all four of the genera without air-bladders survived unhurt, whereas four out of the five having air-bladders were killed. According to US Department of Defense data, marine animals possessing air-bladders are, on average, 64 times as vulnerable to blast damage as those without air-bladders (Council of Environmental Quality, 1970: 15).

Of the crustaceans that have been studied, shrimp and lobsters appear to be considerably more resistant to blast damage than air-bladder fish, but crabs only somewhat more so. Gowanloch & McDougall (1946) observed in the Gulf of Mexico that blast over-pressures which killed air-bladder fish left shrimp uninjured. (Their data suggested that the shrimp were at least 43 times as resistant as the air-bladder fish.) Aplin (1947)—in conjunction with the work noted above—made equivalent and confirmatory observations on lobsters. Trials made by the Chesapeake Biological Laboratory (1948) in Atlantic coastal waters suggest (on the basis of distance for attaining 50 per cent mortality from a 14-kilogram charge of TNT) that crabs are about 11 times as resistant as air-bladder fish.

As regards the molluscs for which there is information, Aplin (1947) observed that a benthic (bottom-dwelling) gastropod—the abalone (*Haliotis,* Haliotidae)—appeared to be almost as sensitive as the air-bladder fish that he had studied. Studies made by the Chesapeake Biological Laboratory (1948) suggest that oysters are perhaps 12 times as resistant as air-bladder fish. The studies carried out by Gowanloch & McDougall (1946) suggest an even greater relative resistance.

Observations on marine mammals and birds are very scanty. Fitch & Young (1948) noted off the coast of California that sea-lions (*Zalophus,* Otariidae) were killed by blast over-pressures that seemed not to damage grey whales (*Rhachianectes,* Eschrichtidae). These same authors noted that cormorants (*Phalacrocorax,* Phalacrocoracidae) appeared to be especially sensitive, since they were invariably killed when diving in the general area of an underwater explosion. Pelicans (*Pelecanus,* Pelecanidae) would be similarly killed if they were dipping their heads below the surface at the same time of such an explosion.

As previously stated, the actual dimensions of the lethal zone of an underwater explosion are determined by the magnitude of the charge, together with several other factors. The explosion of a typical depth-charge could be expected to be lethal to most marine animals within a radius of 77 metres and thus (assuming a sufficient size of surrounding water) within an area of 1.9 hectares and a volume of 1.9 million cubic metres; for fish possessing air-bladders, these values would have to be multiplied by 4, 16, and 64, respectively (table 7.4).

In addition to the depth-charge just described, underwater military explosions are likely to be associated with the use of torpedoes, sea-mines, and bombs (both conventional and nuclear), as well as with the disposal of unwanted munitions (table 7.4). The disposal of obsolete or otherwise surplus munitions can result in huge underwater explosions. For example, on at least 11 occasions during 1965–1970 the USA loaded unwanted explosive munitions aboard ships that were subsequently scuttled beyond the continental shelf (in both the Atlantic and the Pacific Oceans) and their cargoes blown up at depths between 300 and 1 200 metres (Council on Environmental Quality, 1970: 7). The actual amounts of explosive involved were reported for eight of these events: they ranged from 370 thousand to 1.95 million kilograms, the average being 920 thousand kilograms. A charge of 920 thousand kilograms has a radius lethal to most marine animals of about 1 600 metres, and thus a lethal area of 820 hectares and a lethal volume of 18×10^9 cubic metres; for data pertaining to air-bladder fish, these figures must, as above, be multiplied by 4, 16, and 64 respectively. Only the nuclear explosives provide more impressive figures than these (table 7.4).

The number of underwater explosions that might occur, and their frequency in space and time, depend on the military situation. It does appear clear, however, that the combined lethal zone of a number of underwater explosions is close to a simple function of the number of non-overlapping explosion zones. This is the case because sessile forms cannot vacate a danger area, and because neither fish (Alpin, 1947; Coker & Hollis, 1950; Fitch & Young, 1948) nor whales (Fitch & Young, 1948) are frightened out of an area by explosions. In fact, certain carnivorous fish are known to be attracted to such an area by the casualties present (Fitch & Young, 1948).

The actual number of fish and other marine animals killed by an underwater explosion depends, of course, entirely upon the number present within the lethal zone. This density depends, in turn, upon location, depth, season, and so on. However, as already mentioned, it does not significantly depend upon even the immediate past local explosion history. The data of Coker & Hollis (1950) provide an example of the sort of variation that can occur. These authors observed a series of 21 explosions at intervals between May and August of one year, set off at a particular site in an Atlantic Ocean bay on the Maryland coast. These were charges of 'HBX' (a mixture of TNT, cyclonite, and powdered aluminium) weighing an average of 324 kilograms and detonated at an average depth of 22 metres in water about 48 metres deep. The numbers of fish killed and surfacing per charge fluctuated markedly, ranging from a low of zero to a high of 8 035 (average, 1 555); or, in terms of fresh weight, from zero to 2 497 kilograms (average, 407 kilograms). A small number of dead fish (or those about to die) do not float to the surface, including especially those not possessing air-bladders. On the basis of three underwater post-explosion surveys, Fitch & Young (1948: 66) determined that 7.8 per cent of the total kill sinks to the bottom.

The toxic properties of the chemical constituents of underwater munitions, as well as the damaging radioactivity additionally associated with nuclear munitions (see next section), provide further possible sources of stress to marine biota. These substances include not only the explosive fillers as modified by the detonation, but also the substances themselves following partial or non-detonation, the various breakdown products (via alkaline hydrolysis, etc.), and the substances making up the munition casings and mechanisms. The danger to marine life from the introduced chemicals hinges upon a number of factors, such as: *(a)* the intrinsic toxicity of the substances and their ability to gain entry into the organism; *(b)* their solubility and density; *(c)* the rapidity of their breakdown to harmless substances; and *(d)* the amount of water movement, and thus the rate at which the substances are diluted.

TNT may be taken as the first example of a chemical contaminant of munition origin (Dacre & Rosenblatt, 1974: 94–166; Hoffsommer & Rosen, 1973; *Merck Index,* 1976: 9397; Won *et al.,* 1976). This material is sparingly soluble in sea-water (94 g/m³) and is heavier than it (1 654 kg/m³ as opposed to 1 025 kg/m³); it thus mostly sinks to the bottom and slowly dissolves. Moreover, it is highly stable in sea-water with its pH of 8.2 (there being no measurable decomposition for at least 108 days). TNT is known to kill or inhibit the growth of a number of freshwater micro-organisms and to be lethal to several species of freshwater fish at concentrations of less than 5 grams per cubic metre. Moreover, it is acutely toxic to various mammals at less than 200 milligrams per kilogram of body weight.

Cyclonite—another of the important military explosives—is a dangerous mammalian nerve poison, sometimes used commercially as a rat (*Rattus,* Muridae) killer (Hoffsommer & Rosen, 1973; *Merck Index,* 1976: 2741). Its solubility in sea-water is 56 grams per cubic metre and its weight is 1 820 kilograms per cubic metre. The half-life in sea-water of cyclonite can be calculated to be about 630 days.

Nitramine, a favoured detonator, provides a third example (Hoffsommer

& Rosen, 1973; *Merck Index,* 1976: 6389). Its solubility in sea-water is 26 grams per cubic metre and its weight is 1 570 kilograms per cubic metre. The half-life in sea-water of nitramine can be calculated to be about 33 days. The major decay product is picric acid (2,4,6-trinitrophenol), which is highly soluble (13 kg/m³). Both nitramine and picric acid are considered to be highly toxic. The lethal concentration to the Pacific coral-reef damsel-fish (*Dascyllus,* Pomacentridae) (i.e., the 96-hour LC_{50}) of ammonium picrate is about 95 grams per cubic metre (Jameson, 1975).

The sinking or scuttling of munition-laden ships can provide a large source of explosive contamination. During 1964–1967 the USA scuttled at least 4 ships (different to the 11 previously mentioned) loaded with surplus explosive munitions, but not subsequently blown up (Council on Environmental Quality, 1970: 7). To give another example, during World War II a Japanese freighter carrying a cargo of c. 45 thousand kilograms of depth-charges sank in about 34 metres of water in the Truk lagoon, Eastern Carolines (Jameson, 1975). The casings began to deteriorate about three decades later, and the leaking explosive (ammonium picrate plus powdered aluminium) was considered a threat to the fish in the lagoon. It was decided to blow up the cargo as a means of getting rid of the toxic chemical, but the detonation was incomplete and some subsequent local fish mortality could be directly attributed to the toxic releases.

Contamination with radioactive isotopes

Radioactive contamination of the ocean associated with military activities occurs as a result of (*a*) nuclear weapon manufacture, (*b*) nuclear weapon testing and training exercises, (*c*) the hostile use of nuclear weapons, (*d*) routine emissions from nuclear-powered naval vessels, (*e*) the accidental or intentional destruction of nuclear-powered ships and military satellites, and (*f*) accidental introductions of various kinds. Indeed, almost all of the present global burden of radioactive pollution is of military origin.

Atomic bombs produce about 56.7 grams of mixed fission products per 'kiloton' of yield, and hydrogen bombs about 28.4 kilograms per 'megaton' of yield (appendix 7.3). There have been only two instances to date of the hostile use of nuclear weapons, namely, the detonation by the USA during World War II of atomic bombs over the cities of Hiroshima and Nagasaki in August 1945. These two bombs—14.6 and 23.0 'kilotons' in size, respectively—produced a total of about 2.13 kilograms of miscellaneous fission products (disintegrating, after 100 days, at the rate of about 1.32 megacuries), some small fraction of which found its way into the ocean. The World War II experience is barely suggestive of what a nuclear war of the future might entail (see, for example, SIPRI, 1977: chap. 1; Vellodi *et al.,* 1968).

Of the various sources of radioactive pollution, nuclear weapon testing has, up to now, been by far the worst offender. During the three decades that have elapsed since the first experimental device was set off at Alamogordo, New Mexico, in July 1945, the USA, the USSR and several other nations have detonated almost 1 000 additional 'small' (<1 'megaton') nuclear bombs as well as over 100 immense (>1 'megaton') hydrogen bombs (table 7.5, note *a*). Of the total number of nuclear detonations during 1945–1977, 6 were conducted below the surface of the ocean, 35 on the ocean surface, and some 374 in the atmosphere (table 7.5).

The 6 underwater detonations to date had a combined yield of about 2.1 'megatons' and thus produced about 56.5 kilograms of mixed fission products (table 7.5), virtually all of which contaminated the ocean. The 35 water-surface detonations to date had a combined yield of 63.6 'megatons' and thus produced about 1 710 kilograms of mixed fission products. It is convenient to divide these many fission products into two categories—the fast-decaying or short-lived ones (the half-lives of which are measurable in seconds or days), and the slow-decaying or long-lived ones (the half-lives of which are measurable in years). Perhaps 50 per cent (855 kilograms) of the short-lived component of these fission products entered the ocean from the water-surface detonations. Of that minute but important fraction of long-lived isotopes, on the other hand, an estimated 90 per cent (i.e., originating from about 1 540 kilograms of original fission products) eventually entered the ocean.

The 374 other atmospheric detonations—both air bursts and land-surface bursts—had a combined yield estimated at about 230 'megatons' and thus produced about 6 190 kilograms of mixed fission products. It may be assumed that virtually none of the short-lived component entered the ocean. Of the long-lived component, it may be estimated that 80 per cent originating from the air bursts and 40 per cent originating from the land-surface bursts reached the ocean. Of the total of 6 190 kilograms, about 3 900 kilograms (63 per cent) had been derived from air bursts and the remaining 2 290 kilograms (37 per cent) from land-surface bursts. Accordingly, from these data it can be calculated that the long-lived isotopes originating from 4 030 kilograms (65 per cent) of the originally produced mixed fission products eventually entered the ocean.

To summarize, of the estimated 415 nuclear detonations that occurred either in or on the ocean or in the atmosphere during 1945–1977, about 912 kilograms of short-lived fission products entered the ocean (disintegrating, after 100 days, at the rate of about 565 megacuries). Added to this must be the long-lived fission-product component from about 5 630 kilograms of initially produced fission products.

Let us now turn to the contribution of nuclear-powered ships to the radioactive contamination of the ocean. There are in operation today about 258 large nuclear-powered submarines plus an additional 7 or so surface naval vessels with such propulsion (table 7.6). Five or more nuclear-powered merchant ships are afloat as well. The routine annual releases from a nuclear-powered ship have been estimated to disintegrate at an average rate of 250 microcuries (Comar *et al.,* 1972: 18), which, assuming 100 days of 'cooling', represents 403 nanograms of mixed fission products per year. Accordingly, the 266 naval ships might in this way contribute about 107 micrograms of mixed fission products (disintegrating, after 100 days, at the rate of about 65 millicuries) to the ocean each year.

Of far greater significance is the potential for massive radioactive releases that might be associated with an accidental sinking (see below). Even more serious would be the intentional destruction during wartime of enemy nuclear-powered ships, both military and civil. Under the latter (wartime) conditions it would be less likely that an intact reactor would be retrieved and more likely that it would be ruptured in the first place.

A nuclear-powered submarine might have a 56-megawatt (thermal) reactor, and a nuclear-powered cruiser one of 224 (appendix 7.4). Their reactors would thus be producing about 35.9 and 144 grams, respectively, of mixed fission products during each day of operation. The short-lived component of this conglomerate decays almost as fast as it is being produced (the equilibrium value, soon reached, being between 108 and 109 per cent of daily production). The long-lived component, on the other hand, builds up in almost direct proportion to the number of days of operation. Under peace-time conditions a nuclear submarine might be on patrol for 60 days out of every 180 days (*SIPRI Yearbook 1975*: 64). Under wartime conditions it might well be in continuous operation for many months at a stretch.

Thus, if a nuclear-powered submarine were destroyed, it would at essentially any time release about 38.1 grams of mixed fission products (disintegrating, after 100 days, at the rate of 23.6 kilocuries). These fission products, consisting primarily of short-lived isotopes, are equivalent in amount to the release of a 0.67-'kiloton' atomic bomb. The long-lived component, on the other hand, would be derived from an additional 1.08 kilograms of original fission products for every 30 days at sea. As a result, after 32 days of operation they would build up to the equivalent of what a 20-'kiloton' atomic bomb would release.

The manufacture of nuclear weapons and of the fuel for nuclear-powered naval vessels results in some modest amount of routine radioactive air- and stream-pollution that eventually finds its way into the ocean. A somewhat greater amount of such contamination has resulted—in the past at any rate—from the ocean dumping of radioactive wastes arising from these operations. For example, during 1949–1960 the USA dumped relatively large quantities of both liquid and solid radioactive wastes—primarily of military origin—into the ocean (Council on Environmental Quality, 1970: 6–7; Dyer *et al.,* 1975). At the time of disposal (divided between the Atlantic and Pacific Oceans), these were reported to be disintegrating at the rate of 93.7 kilocuries, which, assuming 100 days of 'cooling', is the equivalent of 151 grams of original fission products. The USA has virtually ended such dumping, having only added an amount disintegrating at 1.0 kilocurie (1.6 grams) during 1961–1970. The United Kingdom is said similarly to have disposed of radioactive materials disintegrating at some 40 kilocuries (65 grams) in the Atlantic Ocean during 1951–1966 (Turner, 1975).

Accidents involving nuclear weapons and other military items containing radioactive isotopes can also lead to ocean contamination. The hydrogen bomb that dropped into the Mediterranean Sea off Palomares on the south-east coast of Spain in January 1966 was a well-publicized event. The bomb was eventually retrieved, but there have been a number of similar losses with less benign outcomes (*SIPRI Yearbook 1977*: 52–85). For example, plutonium-239 sufficient to disintegrate at an estimated 25 curies (390 grams) was introduced into the Atlantic Ocean 11 kilometres off the coast of Thule, Greenland, in January 1968 as the result of an accident involving four nuclear bombs (Aarkrog, 1971; UNSCEAR, 1972: 54). Marine organisms over a considerable area became contaminated with this material.

At least eight military satellites equipped with nuclear generators (six US and two Soviet) are known to have failed to achieve orbit (Lyons, 1978). Two or more of these have accidentally contaminated the ocean with their radioactive contents (Hardy *et al.*, 1973; UNSCEAR, 1972: 54). In the one known instance, in April 1964, the satellite burned up at an altitude of about 50 kilometres and thereby injected almost one kilogram of plutonium-238 (c. 17 kilocuries) into the stratosphere, roughly three-quarters of which has by now entered the ocean. In the other known instance, in April 1970, the satellite re-entered the atmosphere and simply fell into the Pacific Ocean and was lost.

Regarding nuclear-powered ships, the USA has now lost at least two such submarines: the *Thresher* in the western Atlantic in April 1963 and the *Scorpion* also in the Atlantic, off the Azores, in May 1968. The USSR may have lost as many as four nuclear submarines during 1968–1971: two in the Atlantic Ocean, one in the Mediterranean Sea, and one in the Pacific Ocean (*SIPRI Yearbook 1977*: 74).

Apart from the cataclysmic immediate nearby effects of a nuclear explosion, the ecological impact of radioactive contamination from such and other sources depends, of course, upon their magnitude and areal extent (see, for example, Goldberg, 1976: 79–95; Nier *et al.*, 1975: 102–161; Small, 1963; UNSCEAR, 1972; Vellodi *et al.*, 1968). On the basis of observations on the effects of the bomb trials at the Bikini and Enewetak test sites in the western Pacific, it appears that the overall structure and dynamics of the marine communities recover in due course (Hines, 1962). Moreover, regarding the ocean as a whole, one would expect to observe little if any overall impact from the level of radioactive contaminants introduced so far. As previously suggested, all the nuclear testing to date has introduced an estimated total of 912 kilograms of fission products into the ocean. One tentative means of evaluating the significance of this introduction is to compare it with the natural level of radioactivity present in the ocean. Thus, as a crude approximation, one can compare the disintegration activity from these fission products (which represents most of the activity of military origin) with that originating from potassium-40 (which represents most of the activity of natural origin). Potassium-40 has a half-life of 1.28×10^9 years, and one kilogram thus disintegrates at the rate of 7.27 millicuries (via β^- emission). The potassium in nature includes 118 milligrams per kilogram of potassium-40, and potassium is present in the ocean at 390 grams per cubic metre. Thus, since the ocean contains 1.37×10^{18} cubic metres of water, the total continuing disintegration activity emanating from the potassium-40 can be estimated to come to 458 gigacuries. The continuing activity from the natural potassium-40 is thus about 800 times that of the 100-day activity from the 912 kilograms of fission products (i.e., 565 megacuries) and about 8000 times that of the one-year activity (i.e., 55.7 megacuries).

On the other hand, an examination of the overall radioactivity of the above kind overlooks the possibility of adverse biological effects arising from the long-lived isotopes produced by such tests. A number of these isotopes are of particular concern because they mimic certain of the elements essential to life and are taken up by plants and animals for that reason, and others because they are taken up anyway. Having once gained entry into living organisms, they travel up food-chains (some of which culminate in man) and also continue to cycle within the marine ecosystems, eventually being dispersed (diluted) and decaying to insignificance. Among those of particular concern are strontium-90 and caesium-137, because they mimic calcium and potassium, respectively (table 7.7). Carbon-14 is of concern because it mimics carbon-12 in carbon dioxide, and hydrogen-3 because it mimics hydrogen-1 in water (H_2O). The problem in the latter case is mitigated somewhat, however, by the natural abundance of the isotope mimicked (table 7.7). Plutonium-239 and americium-241 are of concern because of their radioactive and chemical toxicities, and because they are taken up by marine organisms—both plant and animal—attaining levels that can be 1000 to 10000 or even more times higher than in the ambient water. Moreover, 16 years after the cessation of testing, these two elements were found to be ensconced in the biogeochemical cycles at Bikini and Enewetak (Schell & Watters, 1975). The amounts of these isotopes arising from nuclear bombs—both atomic and hydrogen (table 7.8)—and from destroyed nuclear-powered submarine (or cruiser) reactors (table 7.9) are formidable.

Contamination with chemical warfare agents

Chemical warfare agents have been introduced into the ocean both accidentally and intentionally, although in the latter case not for hostile purposes.

Intentional introductions have been made on a large scale for the purpose of disposing of obsolete or otherwise surplus chemical munitions. For example, large amounts of surplus German World War II munitions of all kinds were dumped during 1945–1948 into the southern Baltic east of the island of Bornholm. Among these was an unknown fraction containing the lethal dermal (blister) agent mustard gas (HD; bis [2-chloroethyl] sulphide). In a recent 4½-year period, Danish fishermen netted at least 16 of these mustard gas bombs, some of which contaminated their catches and eventually resulted in human illness (Garner, 1973).

Obsolete British chemical munitions were dumped into the Atlantic Ocean off the coasts of Scotland and Ireland at various times during 1945–1956. These contained either mustard gas, as in the case above, or else the lethal lung (choking) agent phosgene (carbonyl chloride). Some of the mustard gas bombs were washed ashore along the Welsh coast during 1976 (*Marine Pollution Bulletin*, 1976).

Obsolete US chemical munitions containing the lethal nerve (anticholinesterase) agent sarin (GB; isopropyl methylphosphonofluoridate) have been disposed of in the ocean at one or more sites on at least several occasions. In three known cases (in 1967, 1968 and 1970) these were embedded in concrete within steel vaults and placed aboard ships that were subsequently scuttled several hundred kilometres out to sea at depths of several thousand metres. For example, the 1970 disposal site, code-named CHASE-X, was located 400 kilometres east of Florida at a depth of almost 5 000 metres (Ferer, 1975). The ship scuttled in 1970 contained 61 thousand kilograms of sarin (2.5 per cent of total cargo weight). On the basis of the 1970 data, one can estimate that the ship scuttled in 1967 contained 204 thousand kilograms of sarin, and the one scuttled in 1968 contained 176 thousand kilograms (based on total cargo weights from the Council on Environmental Quality, 1970: 6–7). The USA also dumped a small quantity of the lethal nerve agent VX (*S*-[2-diisopropylaminoethyl] *O*-ethyl methyl phosphonothiolate) as part of these operations (Ferer, 1975), and perhaps some mustard gas as well (Poor, 1969).

Turning now to ·accidental releases of chemical agents, the most spectacular and tragic incident occurred during World War II in the Adriatic Sea along the coast of Italy (Infield, 1971; Saunders, 1967). One evening in December 1943 the Germans carried out a major bombing attack against the Allied ships in the harbour of Bari. Of the two dozen ships destroyed, one was a US freighter carrying a cargo of about 100 thousand kilograms of mustard-gas bombs. As a result, much of the mustard gas was released into the water and some of it dissolved in the floating oil. More than 1 000 people were killed by the raid; of these deaths, more than 100 were determined to have been specifically caused by mustard-gas poisoning, and many more to have been due to various indirectly associated reasons, such as disablement followed by drowning.

The likelihood of ecological damage resulting from the release into the ocean of chemical warfare agents depends on the various factors previously noted in conjunction with the release of explosive chemicals. Sarin, for example, is completely miscible with water, a medium in which it breaks down rapidly (Adams, 1972; Army & Air Force, 1967: 15–16; Epstein, 1970; *Merck Index,* 1976: 8127). Its half-life in sea-water is of the order of 1 hour and its decomposition products (isopropyl alcohol, etc.) are relatively harmless. Sarin is exceedingly toxic to both mammals and insects, and thus, perhaps, also to many additional kinds of vertebrates and arthropods. One could accordingly expect considerable mortality for a brief time in the immediate area of release.

Mustard gas is an oily liquid that solidifies at 14°C (Army & Air Force, 1967: 21–22; *Merck Index,* 1967: 6142). It is very sparingly soluble in water and it sinks to the bottom since it is heavier than water (liquid weight, 1 274 kg/m³; solid weight, 1 338 kg/m³). Its rate of hydrolysis is "very slow" and its intermediate breakdown products (2,2'-thiodiethanol, etc.) are also somewhat toxic. In mammals, at least, mustard gas is a 'cellular' poison (LD_{50} in laboratory rodents, c. 6 milligrams per kilogram of body weight). It would seem that mustard gas lying on the sea-bed will provide a continuing local source of poison for some time.

Contamination with oil

The ocean can be contaminated with oil as the result of military activities in at least two ways: *(a)* oil-tankers can be sunk by hostile actions; and *(b)* offshore oil facilities can similarly be destroyed.

Of all the large merchant ships currently afloat, about 5 350 (or 23 per cent) are oil-tankers (and of the small ones, an additional—though relatively unimportant—1 670) (appendix 7.2.1). These 5 350 tankers have cargo capacities that range from about 2 thousand to 653 thousand cubic metres, the average being 70.8 thousand cubic metres. At least 32 of the oil-tankers currently in use have capacities in excess of 400 thousand cubic metres; 7 of these vessels have capacities over 500 thousand cubic metres. These tankers together transport about 1.5×19^9 cubic metres of oil per year—that is, roughly half of annual world production, which stands at about 3.1×10^9 cubic metres (*UN Statistical Yearbook 1976:* table 52, 1975 data).

In time of war, enemy oil-tankers could become prime naval targets of opportunity, owing to the crucial importance of oil to the functioning of most kinds of sustained military effort. During World War II, for example, 674 large US merchant ships were sunk by hostile actions, 152 of these vessels being oil-tankers (Stephens, 1973: 42–44). The combined 'gross registered tonnage' of these 152 sunk tankers was 1 235 097. They thus had a total oil-carrying capacity of perhaps 2.73 million cubic metres (average, 18 thousand cubic metres) (appendix 7.2.1). The data of Revelle *et al.* (1971: 303–304) suggest that tanker losses sustained by the USA during World War

II represented one-quarter of the total wartime losses; and half can be assumed to have been loaded when sunk. Therefore, an estimated number of 300 tankers released an estimated quantity of 5.5 million cubic metres of oil into the ocean during World War II—that is, approximately 1.5 million cubic metres per year for a period of about 3½ years. The far larger tankers in service today (and the even larger ones envisaged for the future) would enormously exacerbate any problems associated with this aspect of naval warfare in the years to come.

Turning now to offshore oil production, several thousand wells drilled into the continental shelves of the world currently produce about 600 million cubic metres per year—that is, almost 20 per cent of annual world production; and more such wells are in the offing. Although offshore oil facilities have not yet been subjected to military attack, their vulnerability in this regard is obvious, as has been pointed out on a number of occasions (Judd, 1975; Marriott, 1974–1975 a; Wall, 1976–1977). Despite their vulnerability, however, their target value would in many instances be over-shadowed by that of refineries and terminal areas, which are fed by a multiplicity of offshore and other facilities. If an offshore oil-production facility were, in fact, to be destroyed in war, it would probably release relatively little oil into the ocean. This is the case owing to the variety of shut-off devices that are now routinely built into such systems so as to protect against calamities of natural (or human) origin—something that cannot be done for an oil-tanker.

To put the magnitude of possible military introductions of oil into the ocean into some sort of perspective, it is useful to note that an estimated quantity of 700 thousand cubic metres of oil per year enters the ocean from natural sources (Wilson *et al.*, 1974). Moreover, current anthropogenic additions from civil activities have been estimated to be about 4 million to 6 million cubic metres per year (Goldberg, 1976: 122) (i.e., about 0.16 per cent of production). Moreover, about 95 per cent of the annual anthropogenic introductions are routine and more or less deliberate, and thus only about 5 per cent are accidental (sinkings, and so forth). The worst offshore accidents to date have been the Ekofisk blow-out in the North Sea between Scotland and Denmark in April 1977, which released about 24 thousand cubic metres of oil into the ocean and the Ixtoc I blow-out in the southern Gulf of Mexico in June, which released more than 250 thousand cubic metres. The two worst tanker accidents have been the break-up of the *Torrey Canyon* off the south-west coast of England in March 1967, releasing about 120 thousand cubic metres of oil (Bellamy *et al.*, 1967; O'Sullivan & Richardson, 1967); and that of the *Amoco Cadiz* off the north-west coast of France in March 1978, releasing 260 thousand cubic metres.

An extensive literature has accumulated on the fate and ecological impact of oil that is introduced into the ocean (see, for example, Boesch *et al.*, 1974; Carthy & Arthur, 1968; Evans & Rice, 1974; Goldberg, 1976: 117–136; Ruivo, 1971: 15–21). In brief, of the oil that is introduced into the ocean, the volatile fraction—perhaps 25 per cent of it—evaporates within several days (although this takes rather longer under arctic conditions). Photo- and bacterial-degradation and decomposition account for a further 60 per cent or so within several months. The remaining 15 per cent forms into small, more or less dense clumps of asphaltic substance (1 to 100 millimetres in diameter) having a longer life-span (Horn *et al.*, 1970; Wong *et al.*, 1974). Some of these so-called tar balls float on the surface, some are washed ashore, and some sink to the bottom.

A massive oil-spill of the sort that might result from the sinking of an enemy oil-tanker could have a dramatic local ecological impact, particularly if it occurred along the coast or in some other biotically rich area, and all the more so if the area were partially isolated from the main body of the ocean (Blumer *et al.*, 1971; Blumer & Sass, 1972). One of the most immediately obvious effects of such a spill is on the marine avifauna. For example, following the 12 thousand cubic metre Santa Barbara blow-out of January–February 1969, some 9 thousand to 15 thousand birds—of the order of five per cent of the entire local sea-bird population at risk at that time—were killed (Foster & Holmes, 1977). One might estimate that the zone of contamination posing a threat to birds could be of the order of 10 hectares per thousand cubic metres of oil-spill. Bird mortality is attributable in part to the direct toxicity of ingested oil (Miller *et al.*, 1978), but primarily to feather fouling.

It appears that the fish present in a spill zone experience no serious level of mortality. There is, however, some modest level of mortality usually observable among the benthic (sea-bed) molluscs and crustaceans. Moreover, commercial finfish and shellfish present in the area become 'tainted' and unusable—a condition that persists for perhaps as long as six months to one year. Various of the intertidal lower flora and fauna are killed by a coating of oil, partly via poisoning and partly via oxygen deprivation. Substantial ecological recovery of a locally oil-disrupted area takes several years, perhaps as many as six.

The foregoing suggests that the ecological impact of oil-spills of military origin could have serious local consequences of several years' duration. Regarding the ocean as a whole, however, such incidents need not be a cause for major concern. This is concluded on the basis of the current levels of continuing civil anthropogenic introductions, which—though at least an order of magnitude greater than those of natural or potential military origin—have as yet resulted in no demonstrable impact on the overall marine ecology. There is one potential problem, however, that requires special mention. It has been suggested with sufficient authority to provide cause for concern that a major oil-spill in the Arctic Ocean could conceivably initiate a chain of events leading to extensive ice-melting of long duration (Campbell & Martin, 1973; Ramseier, 1974). Such an occurrence would in turn modify global albedo, perhaps sufficiently to modify the global climate substantially.

Coastal (littoral) disruption

As previously stated, near-shore ocean habitats are especially important from an ecological standpoint. Such littoral habitats are also the marine ecosystems most often disrupted by human activity. Military activities routinely contribute to such littoral disruption through the development and use of naval bases and other port facilities and in a number of other ways, several of which are mentioned below.

To begin with, military landing operations disrupt the near-shore benthic (sea-bed) fauna. For example, Tolmer (1947) has described the severe local damage that occurred to the littoral (coastal) fauna as a result of the heavy landing traffic along the coast of Normandy on D-Day in June 1944, and that is still in evidence many years later.

The mangrove habitat in South Viet Nam suffered especially heavy damage during the Second Indochina War (SIPRI, 1976: 38–40). An estimated 124 thousand hectares of true mangrove (41 per cent of that entire subtype) plus another 27 thousand hectares of rear (back) mangrove (13 per cent of that subtype) were subjected to military herbicide spraying. The result was virtual annihilation of the vegetation and severe coastal erosion. Sylva & Michel (1974) were able to note significant decreases in the number and variety of planktonic and benthic forms (diatoms, copepods, etc.) as well as in fish eggs; and Davis (1974) described reductions in molluscan populations, including a drastic one in the clam *Polymesoda coaxans* (Corbiculiidae). Moreover, declines in the offshore fishery, involving both finfish and shellfish, have been attributed to the disruption of these breeding and nursery grounds (Brouillard, 1970: 21; Loftas, 1970; Sylva & Michel, 1974: 113–117). It is expected that substantial habitat recovery will take a century or more (Odum *et al.*, 1974: 289).

Finally, it must be noted here that under special conditions underwater nuclear explosions might generate a tsunami (tidal wave) (Clarke, 1962) that could, in turn, bring about substantial damage to a coastal habitat.

Cutting of canals

A number of major interoceanic straits have been dug in the past, the two most notable being the Suez and Panama Canals. The construction of the latter, at any rate, was motivated in large measure by military considerations—namely, to facilitate the movement of US naval ships between the Atlantic and Pacific Oceans (Cameron, 1972: 106; McCullough, 1977). The continuing US interest in this canal is similarly motivated—an interest that could even lead to its rebuilding or replacement (McDonald, 1975; Ryan, 1977; Speller, 1972). Another link of considerable strategic importance is the canal system between the White and Baltic Seas, which adds greatly to the flexibility of the Soviet fleet. The ecological impact of linking more or less isolated bodies of sea-water is a source of some concern (Briggs, 1969; Rubinoff, 1968; 1970–1971; Topp, 1969) and is therefore discussed here in brief.

The breaching of the Isthmus of Suez in 1869 re-established a ready sea-level connection between the Mediterranean and Red Seas that had not existed since the late Miocene epoch, perhaps 12 million years ago. During the century or so following the opening of the canal, some two dozen species of fish are known to have emigrated from the Red Sea to the Mediterranean, although none appears to have done so in the opposite direction (Topp, 1969). Moreover, some of the immigrants seem to be supplanting indigenous species. This pattern of events has been attributed largely to a pauperate fish fauna in the Mediterranean.

The breaching of the Isthmus of Panama in 1914 re-established a near-equatorial connection between the Atlantic and Pacific Oceans that had not existed since the mid-Pliocene epoch, perhaps four million years ago. During the half-century or so following the opening of this canal, only one species of fish is known to have managed to emigrate successfully from the Atlantic to the Pacific, and none has apparently done so in the reverse direction (Rubinoff & Rubinoff, 1968). The low level of immigration can be attributed to the barrier to such movement provided by the locks and especially to that provided by the lengthy included stretch of inhospitable fresh water (viz., Lake Gatun). Whether or not the differing habitat conditions between the oceans have additionally contributed to the existing state of affairs will not become evident until such time as a sea-level canal is dug. It is, however, an established tenet of plant and animal geography that unsatisfied habitat requirements are the only certain preventive to range extensions.

Small marine invertebrates are known to be transported through the Panama Canal either attached to ship hulls (the so-called fouling organisms) or in sea-water being used as ballast (Menzies, 1968), and some of these animals might survive such passage (Rubinoff, 1970–1971). On the other hand, such ocean life is constantly carried from ocean to ocean anyway by the endless number of ships plying the high seas.

One can conclude that the construction of sea-level canals creating links between previously isolated seas and oceans could lead to at least some successful invasions into newly available habitats. Such colonization may, in turn, cause perturbations in the established biotic communities, perhaps even leading to species replacement and local extirpations. The possibility of interspecific hybridizations has also been suggested, particularly if the isthmus being breached is of relatively recent geological origin and the isolation of some of the species of common origin has not been sufficiently firmly established.

V. Conclusion

The world ocean is an inextricable and indispensable component of the global system of nature—the world ecosystem. It is, moreover, an essential and increasingly important source of both living and non-living natural resources for man. Superimposed upon these attributes, the ocean is also the immediate or ultimate sump for most of the wastes produced by man—wastes that continue to grow in both quantity and complexity.

Despite the immensity and ecological resilience of the world ocean, there is growing concern that it is being abused at a level approaching the point where natural self-renewal will not be able to match the various anthropogenic insults, particularly overfishing and the excessive introduction of wastes.

Of the order of six per cent of all human activity is devoted to military matters, and it is here concluded, as a first approximation, that this proportion also represents the fraction of ocean pollution attributable to the military sector. There appears to be no aspect of ocean abuse unique to military activities. However, the present radioactive contamination of the ocean is largely of military origin and could, moreover, increase to catastrophic dimensions in time of war.

It is becoming increasingly urgent for man to curtail his abuses of the ocean, and the military ones would be among the most suitable candidates for such action. The Partial Test Ban Treaty (table 8.4.9) and the Sea-Bed Treaty (table 8.4.13) are small steps in the right direction; and the attempts at establishing the Indian Ocean as a zone of peace, if successful, would constitute another such step (cf., for example, *SIPRI Yearbook 1974:* 388–394; *SIPRI Yearbook 1975:* 436–438).

Table 7.1. Ocean regions and habitats

Region	Area[a] $10^3 km^2$ (10^5 ha)	Proportion of world ocean area per cent	Average depth[b] metres	Volume[c] $10^{15} m^3$
Basin[d]				
Atlantic	82 000	22.7	3 700	300
Pacific	181 000	50.1	4 300	780
Indian	73 000	20.2	3 400	250
Arctic	14 000	3.9	1 400	20
Miscellaneous	11 254	3.1	1 800	20
Hemisphere				
Northern	153 662	42.5	—	—
Southern	207 592	57.5	—	—

Region	Area[a] 10^3 km² (10^5 ha)	Proportion of world ocean area per cent	Average depth[b] metres	Volume[c] 10^{15} m³
Habitat[e]				
Open ocean	323 512	89.6	4 200	1 365
Continental shelf[f]	27 000	7.5	65	2
Estuarine	1 400	0.4	2	0.003
Algal bed plus reef	600	0.2	4	0.002
Upwelling zone	400	0.1	50	0.02
Continuously ice-covered	8 342	2.3	500	3
Global total	**361 254**	**100**	**3 800**	**1 370**

Sources and notes:

[a] The basin areas are combined from Sverdrup *et al.* (1942: chap. 2) and Harris & Levey (1975). The hemispheric, continuously ice-covered, and total areas are taken from table 1.3. The habitat areas are taken from Whittaker & Likens (1975: 306), the open-ocean area representing the remainder.

[b] The basin depths are combined from Sverdrup *et al.* (1942: chap. 2) and Harris & Levey (1975). The habitat depths are estimates based on several sources. The open-ocean depth is calculated from the area and volume.

[c] The volumes are calculated from the areas and depths, with the exception of the open-ocean volume, which represents the remainder.

[d] An Antarctic (Southern) Ocean is sometimes recognized, but it does not possess a basin. This very stormy and more or less nebulous ocean is bounded on the north by the Atlantic Convergence, the zone in which cold north-flowing ocean waters encounter and sink beneath the warmer, less dense Atlantic, Indian, and Pacific waters to the north. It is a meandering band about 40 to 50 kilometres wide encircling the Earth at an average latitude of perhaps 50°S. This band coincides more or less well with a January air-temperature isotherm of 10°C. The Antarctic Ocean, thus defined, has an area of about 45 million square kilometres, which would represent about 13 per cent of the surface area of the world ocean.

[e] The approximate surface-area distribution of the ocean into arctic, temperate, and tropical zones can be calculated from data provided by Sverdrup *et al.* (1942: 13): about 21 200 million square kilometres (5.9 per cent) of the ocean surface is found beyond the Arctic and Antarctic Circles; about 187 500 million square kilometres (51.9 per cent) lies between the Arctic Circle and the tropic of Cancer and between the tropic of Capricorn and the Antarctic Circle; and about 152 600 million square kilometres (42.2 per cent) lies between the tropics of Cancer and Capricorn.

[f] The continental-shelf habitat does not here include that portions of the continental shelves that are continuously ice-covered (perhaps 5 million square kilometres).

Table 7.2. Ocean habitats: plant biomass and productivity[a]

Habitat	Total plant biomass (dry weight) 10^{12} kg	Average plant biomass (dry weight) 10^3 kg/ha	Total annual net primary production (dry weight) 10^{12} kg	Average annual net primary productivity (dry weight) 10^3 kg/ha
Open ocean	0.97	0.030	40.44	1.25
Continental shelf	0.27	0.100	9.72	3.60
Estuarine	1.40	10.000	2.10	15.00
Algal bed plus reef	1.20	20.000	1.50	25.00
Upwelling zone	0.01	0.200	0.20	5.00
Ocean total, ice-free	**3.85**	**0.109**	**53.96**	**1.53**

Sources and notes:
[a]Average plant biomass and average plant productivity values are derived from those of Whittaker & Likens (1975: 306). Total plant biomass and total annual production values are calculated from the average values, using the not continuously ice-covered areas presented in table 7.1. Comparable data for terrestrial habitats are provided in table 1.7. (A number of useful conversion factors for the data as presented here are provided in table 1.5, note *a*.)

Table 7.3. Navies of the world (1975 data)

Nation	Large surface ships[a]	Large submarines[a]	Total number of large ships	Naval personnel[b] *10³*
China	20	3	**23**	230
France	38	5	**43**	69
United Kingdom	47	13	**60**	76
USA	181	106	**287**	536
USSR	195	186	**381**	500
46 others	340	0	**340**	850
Total	**821**	**313**	**1 134**	**2 261**

Sources and notes:
[a]Numbers of large surface ships are from the 51 navies of the world listed in *Jane's Fighting Ships 1976–1977:* 804, being a summation of battleships, aircraft carriers, cruisers, destroyers, and half the frigates. Numbers of submarines are from the same source, being a summation of ballistic missile, cruise-missile, and fleet submarines. For an explanation of ship sizes, see appendix 7.2.2. For a listing of nuclear-powered ships, see table 7.6. For additional naval inventories, see *SIPRI Yearbook 1975:* 255–307; *SIPRI Yearbook 1976:* 212, 228–231; *SIPRI Yearbook 1979:* 329–388; and also SIPRI (1974 *c:* 102–109).
[b]Numbers of naval personnel are from the *IISS Military Balance 1975–1976:* table 3 (1975 data), being a summation of the 45 listed navies corresponding to those above; estimates (totalling 36 thousand) have been supplied for the six missing nations. The naval-personnel values in this table can be compared with the comparable total armed-forces values in table 1.13, note *b*.

Table 7.4. Lethal blast zones resulting from underwater explosions

Munition and explosive content[a]	Lethal radius[b] *metres*	Lethal area[c] *hectares*	Lethal volume[c] *m³*
Depth-charge or rocket (100 kg)			
Most fauna	77.1	1.87	1.92×10^6
Most fishes	309.	29.9	123. $\times 10^6$
Torpedo or moored sea-mine (250 kg)			
Most fauna	105.	3.44	4.81×10^6
Most fishes	419.	55.1	308. $\times 10^6$
Sea-bed mine (750 kg)			
Most fauna	151.	7.16	14.4 $\times 10^6$
Most fishes	604.	115.	923. $\times 10^6$
Munition disposal (10⁶ kg)			
Most fauna	1 660.	868.	19.2 $\times 10^9$
Most fishes	6 650.	13 900.	1.23×10^{12}

Munition and explosive content[a]	Lethal radius[b] metres	Lethal area[c] hectares	Lethal volume[c] m³
20 kT atomic bomb ('9.07×10⁶' kg)			
Most fauna	3 470.	3 780.	175. ×10⁹
Most fishes	13 900.	60 400.	11.2 ×10¹²
1 MT hydrogen bomb ('494×10⁶' kg)			
Most fauna	13 100.	54.300.	9.51×10¹²
Most fishes	52 600.	868 000.	609. ×10¹²
10 MT hydrogen bomb ('4.94×10⁹' kg)			
Most fauna	28 300.	252 000.	95.1 ×10¹²
Most fishes	113 000.	4.03×10⁶	6.09×10¹⁵

Sources and notes:

[a]*Munitions and explosive contents.* The average or likely quantity of explosive to be found in depth-charges, rockets, torpedoes, moored (floating) sea-mines, and sea-bed sea-mines is taken from Wilcke (1971); see also SIPRI (1974 *c*: 85–95). Depth-charges up to 10 times as large have been used. Torpedoes usually fall within the range of 200 to 300 kilograms (*Jane's Fighting Ships 1977–78:* 789). Moored (floating) sea-mines can weigh as much as 350 kilograms (Marriott, 1974–1975 *b*). Sea-bed sea-mines can weigh between 500 and 1 000 kilograms. A likely quantity of munition disposal is estimated from the examples given by the Council on Environmental Quality (1970: 6–7). The equivalent quantity for the 20-kiloton (kT) atomic bomb is 50 per cent of its yield, and for the 1 and 10 megaton (MT) hydrogen bombs it is 54.5 per cent of their yields, as estimates of the proportion of total energy expended in the blast wave (appendix 7.3). The modest differences in energy yield between 2,4,6-trinitrotoluene (TNT) and other military explosives are not taken into consideration here.

[b]*Radii and lethal over-pressures.* Radii are derived via cube-root scaling from US Department of Defense values for a charge weighing 907 thousand kilograms, reported to be lethal to most marine organisms for a radius of 1 610 metres; and to fish possessing air-bladders (swimming-bladders), that is, to about 95 per cent of all fish, for a radius of 6 440 metres (Council on Environmental Quality, 1970: 15). Based on graphed data of recorded underwater over-pressures from TNT by the Chesapeake Biological Laboratory (1948: 15), the lethal over-pressure necessary to kill most marine organisms is about 2 000 kilopascals, and that for air-bladder fish about 750 kilopascals. See also Gaspin (1975), Hubbs & Rechnitzer (1952), and Lavergne (1970).

[c]*Areas and volumes.* The area and volume figures presented are arithmetic calculations of a circle and sphere, respectively. Water dimensions of sufficient magnitude are assumed. A sea-bed explosion, for example, would reduce a given lethal volume by roughly half (in fact, somewhat less than half because of reflection).

Table 7.5. Oceanic and atmospheric nuclear explosions[a]

Year	Underwater[b] USA	USSR	Total	Water-surface[c] USA	UK	Total	Other atmospheric[d] USA	USSR	France	UK	China	Total	Total
1945							3					3	3
1946	1		1									1	2
1947													0
1948							3					3	3
1949								1				1	1
1950													0
1951				15	2							17	17
1952	1		1	10								10	11

173

Year	Underwater[b] USA	USSR	Total	Water-surface[c] USA	UK	Total	Other atmospheric[d] USA	USSR	France	UK	China	Total	Total
1953							11	2		2		15	15
1954				4		4	2	1				3	7
1955	1		1				13	4				17	18
1956				6		6	8	7		6		21	27
1957							27	13		7		47	47
1958	2		2	24		24	33	25		5		63	89
1959													0
1960									3			3	3
1961		1	1					30	1			31	32
1962	1		1				40	39				79	80
1963													0
1964											1	1	1
1965											1	1	1
1966									5		3	8	8
1967									3		2	5	5
1968									5		1	6	6
1969											1	1	1
1970									8		1	9	9
1971									5		1	6	6
1972									3		2	5	5
1973									5		1	6	6
1974									7		1	8	8
1975													0
1976											3	3	3
1977											1	1	1
Total	**5**	**1**	**6**	**34**	**1**	**35**	**166**	**124**	**45**	**20**	**19**	**374**	**415**
Yield (MT)			2.1			63.6						230	296

Sources and notes:
[a]The data for 1945–1962 are summarized from Glasstone (1964: 671–681 *b*); those for 1963–1971 from Zander & Araskog (1973: 35–53); those for 1972–1974 from *SIPRI Yearbook 1975*: 506–509; those for 1975–1976 from *SIPRI Yearbook 1977*: 400–402; and those for 1977 from SIPRI files. It is possible that up to several of the reported detonations during 1945–1962 are misplaced as to year. Moreover, a number of the detonations during this period have gone unreported (perhaps in the neighbourhood of 30). All of the detonations listed in the table were intended for military purposes—two for hostile purposes and the remainder for weapon-testing and related activities. (Some half dozen of the many underground tests are claimed to have been intended for civil purposes.)

The overall total number of nuclear detonations during 1945–1977 has been estimated by SIPRI (1978 *b*: 228) to be 1 117, divided among the nations as follows: the USA, 626; the USSR, 371; France, 70; the United Kingdom, 27; China, 22; and India, 1. Most of the 702 detonations not accounted for in the table were underground. Of the estimate of 1 117 nuclear detonations during 1945–1977, about 1 013 have been atomic (fission) bombs and thus only about 104 (or 9 per cent) have been hydrogen (fission/fusion) bombs. On the other hand, the hydrogen bomb explosions represent about 95 per cent of the combined yield of the 1 117 detonations (this actually being the percentage that can be calculated from the atmospheric detonations that occurred during 1945–1958 and 1964–1973, on the basis of the data of Glasstone (1964: 483–484) and SIPRI (1974 *a*: 33–37)). A fission-product estimate for this mix of bombs is thus 26.9 grams per 'kiloton' of yield (i.e., 47.5 per cent of 56.7; cf. appendix 7.3).
[b]*Underwater detonations*. The five US underwater detonations were all carried out in the Pacific Ocean—three in the western Pacific (one near Bikini and two near Enewetak) and two in the eastern Pacific. The depth of four of these ranged from 27 to 610 metres (average, 209 metres). Three had yields of 30 'kilotons' or less each. At least three of them vented to the

atmosphere. The Soviet detonation occurred in the Barents Sea (near Novaya Zemlya) and had a yield of less than 20 'kilotons'. An estimate for the total yield of the six underwater detonations is 2.1 'megatons'.

c Water-surface detonations. The 34 US water-surface detonations were all carried out in the western Pacific (19 near Bikini and 15 near Enewetak). The British detonation was carried out in the Indian Ocean (near north-western Australia). The 35 water-surface detonations had a total yield of 63.6 'megatons' (Glasstone, 1964: 483–484).

d Other atmospheric detonations. The 373 detonations in this category include those that occurred in the air (63 per cent by yield); on the land surface (37 per cent by yield); and underground, but sufficiently close to the surface to have vented (0.02 per cent by yield). For the locations of most (and the yield estimates of some), see the sources cited in note *a* above. The 201 detonations in this category that occurred during 1945–1958 had a combined yield of 110.2 'megatons' (based on Glasstone, 1964: 483–484). Based on the average yield of all past US atmospheric tests, the 40 remaining detonations had a total yield of 27.4 'megatons'. Based on the average yield of all past Soviet atmospheric tests, the 69 remaining Soviet detonations had a total yield of 62.5 'megatons'. Based on an extrapolation through 1977 from the data of SIPRI (1974 *a:* 33–34), the total French yield comes to 10.6 'megatons'. Based on a similar extrapolation from the data of SIPRI (1974 *a:* 37), the total Chinese yield comes to 18.1 'megatons'. The sum is thus 228.8, which rounds to 230 'megatons'. (The range was substantially less than 1 'kiloton' to 58 'megatons'.)

Table 7.6. Nuclear-powered ships of the world (1975 data)

Nation	Civil (merchant)[a] Surface	Military (naval)[b] Surface	Submarine	Total
China	0	0	(1?)	(1?)
France	0	0	4	4
FR Germany	1	0	0	1
Japan	1	0	0	1
United Kingdom	0	0	13	13
USA	1	7	106	114
USSR[c]	2	0	135	137
Total	**5**	**7**	**258**	**270**

Sources and notes:
[a] Numbers of civil ships are summarized from the *World Almanac and Book of Facts 1977*: 147.
[b] Numbers of military ships are summarized from *Jane's Fighting Ships 1976–77*.
[c] Press reports indicate that the USSR launched two additional nuclear surface ships early in 1978—its first surface warship and its third ice-breaker.

Table 7.7. Characteristics of selected fission products

Isotope	Half-life[a] years	Disintegration rate[b] kCi/kg	Type of decay[a]	Mimic of	Mimic present at g/m³
Strontium-90 (^{90}Sr)	28.1	147.	β^-	Calcium (^{40}Ca)	410
Caesium-137 (^{137}Cs)	30.23	89.8	β^-, γ	Potassium (^{39}K)	390
Plutonium-239 (^{239}Pu)	24 400.	0.0638	α		
Americium-241 (^{241}Am)	458.	3.37	α, γ		
Hydrogen-3 (^{3}H)	12.26	10 100.	β^-	Hydrogen (^{1}H)	114 000
Carbon-14 (^{14}C)	5 730.	4.64	β^-	Carbon (^{12}C)	c. 60

Sources and notes:

[a]The half-lives and types of decay are taken from the *Handbook of Chemistry and Physics 1974–1975:* Section B, pp. 248 ff.

[b]Disintegration rates are calculated on the basis of the individual mass numbers and half-lives.

[c]Sea-water concentrations of calcium and potassium are derived from the *Handbook of Chemistry and Physics 1974–1975:* Section F, p. 190, based on a sea-water density of 1 025 kilograms per cubic metre. The concentration of hydrogen-1 is based upon the water (H_2O) molecule. The concentration of carbon-12 is composed of c. 29 grams per cubic metre of inorganic solids in solution plus c. 2 grams per cubic metre of organic solids in solution plus c. 27 grams per cubic metre from the carbon dioxide (CO_2) in solution.

Table 7.8. Quantities and decay rates of selected nuclear-bomb fission products

1. *Atomic (fission) bombs*[a]

Isotope[c]	Quantity remaining after 1 hour[d] g/kT[b]	Activity remaining after				
		1 hour[e] Ci/kT[b]	100 days	1 year	10 years	25 years
^{90}Sr	0.680	100.	99.3	97.6	78.1	54.0
^{137}Cs	1.78	160.	159.	156.	127.	90.2
^{239}Pu	31.3	2.00	2.00	2.00	2.00	2.00
^{241}Am	0.237	0.800	1.10	1.89	2.98	2.93
^{14}C	9.49	44.0	44.0	44.0	43.9	43.9
^{3}H	>0	>0	>0	>0	>0	>0

2. *Hydrogen (fission/fusion) bombs*[a]

Isotope[c]	Quantity remaining after 1 hour[d] kg/MT	Activity remaining after				
		1 hour[e] kCi/MT	100 days	1 year	10 years	25 years
^{90}Sr	0.340	50.0	49.7	48.8	39.1	27.0
^{137}Cs	0.890	80.0	79.5	78.2	63.6	45.1
^{239}Pu	15.7	1.00	1.00	1.00	1.00	1.00
^{241}Am	0.119	0.400	0.548	0.944	1.49	1.47
^{14}C	4.74	22.0	22.0	22.0	22.0	21.9
^{3}H	0.0874	885.	871.	836.	503.	215.

Sources and notes:

[a]For information on nuclear bombs, see appendix 7.3.

[b]To convert the data in table 7.8.1 to values in terms of the amounts of combined fission products generated—that is, to grams (or curies) of isotope per kilogram of combined fission product generated (as determined after one hour)—divide the given values by 0.0567.

[c]For basic characteristics of the selected fission products, see table 7.7.

[d]The one-hour weight values are calculated from the one-hour disintegration values, on the basis of the disintegration rates provided in table 7.7.

[e]One-hour disintegration values: The value for strontium-90 is taken from Glasstone (1964: 484). The values for caesium-137 (UNSCEAR, 1972: 52), plutonium-239 (UNSCEAR, 1972: 54), americium-241, and carbon-14 (UNSCEAR, 1972: 104) are factors of the value for strontium-90. The value for hydrogen-3 (tritium) is calculated from the data of UNSCEAR (1972: 57), for which see appendix 7.3. The subsequent disintegration values are calculated from the individual half-lives provided in table 7.7, with the exception of americium-241, the values of which are derived from the data of Netzén *et al.* (1976: 36, 39). The unexpected amounts of americium-241 result from neutron capture by plutonium-239.

Table 7.9. Quantities and decay rates of selected submarine-reactor fission products after one month at sea [a]

Isotope [b]	Quantity remaining after 1 hour [c] g/submarine	Activity remaining after				
		1 hour [d] curies/submarine	100 days	1 year	10 years	25 years
^{90}Sr	17.3	2 540.	2 520.	2 480.	1 980.	1 370.
^{137}Cs	40.3	3 620.	3 590.	3 530.	2 880.	2 040.
^{239}Pu	181.	11.5	11.5	11.5	11.5	11.5
^{241}Am	1.44	4.84	6.64	11.4	18.1	17.7
^{14}C	0.003 31	0.015 4	0.015 4	0.015 4	0.015 4	0.015 3
^{3}H	0.002 67	27.0	26.6	25.5	15.3	6.6

Sources and notes:

[a] For information on submarine reactors, see appendix 7.4. For additional months of operation, the values presented in the table can be multiplied by the additional number of months. To make the values in the table applicable to a nuclear-powered cruiser, multiply by 4.

[b] For basic characteristics of the selected fission products, see table 7.7.

[c] One-hour weight values are calculated from the one-hour disintegration values, on the basis of the disintegration rates provided in table 7.7.

[d] The disintegration values are calculated from the 30-day disintegration values of Netzén *et al.* (1976: 36–37), on the basis of the half-lives provided in table 7.7, with the exception of americium-241, the values of which are derived from the data of Netzén *et al.* (1976: 36, 39). The unexpected amounts of americium-241 result fron neutron capture by plutonium-239.

Appendix 7.1

Sources for the ocean habitat

1. *Environment and ecology.* The classic description of the ocean has been prepared by Sverdrup *et al.* (1942). For a useful recent summary, see Anikouchine & Sternberg (1973). Carson (1961) offers a magnificent introduction to the ocean. Succinct treatises on marine ecology have been prepared by Steele (1974) and Odum (1971: chap. 12–13).

2. *Civil use and abuse.* Ocean resources and their use have been described by Charlier & Vigneaux (1974), Loftas (1976), Lucey (1972), and Ray (1970–1971). Franssen (1973–1974) has dwelt upon oil and gas. Fish production has been covered by Ackefors (1977), Cushing (1975), Gulland (1977), Ryther (1969), and Tont & Delistraty (1977). Bondar & Bobey (1974), Eddie (1977), Everson (1977), Grantham (1977), and Kryuchkova *et al.* (1971) have singled out krill as a potential resource. Ceres (1976) has summarized the seaweed (primarily kelp) resource. Ocean pollution has been admirably reviewed by Goldberg (1976) and Ruivo (1971). Boesch *et al.* (1974) provide a good review of oil-spills (cf. also Gundlach, 1977). Curry-Lindahl (1972: chap. 10) has reviewed the status of marine animals in danger of extinction (cf. also Fisher *et al.,* 1969).

3. *Military use and abuse.* National security interests in the ocean have been analysed by Hoffmann (1971), Klare (1975–1976), and, in part, by Blechman & Kaplan (1977–1978); a bibliography to somewhat earlier literature has been compiled by Eller (1956–1957). Araldsén (1967), Østreng (1977), and Synhorst (1973) focus upon the strategic importance of the Arctic Ocean. For the Indian Ocean, see *SIPRI Yearbook 1975*: chap. 5. The security of offshore resources is covered by Judd (1975), Marriott (1974–1975 a), and Wall (1976–1977). SIPRI (1974 c) has analysed anti-submarine warfare capabilities (see also *SIPRI Yearbook 1979:* 427–452). Sea warfare during the past century has been summarized by Warner *et al.* (1975). Seymour *et al.* (1971) provide a synoptic coverage of radioactive contamination of the ocean (cf. also Preston *et al.,* 1971–1972; Small, 1963). For legal problems dealing with military aspects of the ocean, see Burke *et al.* (1969), SIPRI (1972 a), Goldblat (1975 a), and *SIPRI Yearbook 1975:* chap. 16.

Appendix 7.2

Ship numbers and sizes

1. *Civil (merchant) ships.* The numbers of merchant ships used in the text refer to 30 June 1976 and are taken from *Lloyd's Register of Shipping* via the Shipbuilders Council of America (Washington), the Institut für Seeverkehrswirtschaft (Bremen), and the *World Almanac and Book of Facts 1977:* 146–147. For merchant ships, the designation *small* here refers to ships having a 'gross registered tonnage' of between 100 and 1000; and the designation *large* to those of 1000 or more. The 'gross registered ton' is a measure of volume where one 'ton' represents 2.832 cubic metres of permanently enclosed space. Merchant ships are additionally measured in terms of their 'deadweight tonnage', which is a measure of weight where one 'ton' represents 1016 kilograms of cargo-carrying capacity. Using a conversion factor that is based on summations of all the world's large merchant ships with the exception of oil-tankers, the approximate 'deadweight tonnage' of a ship (other than an oil-tanker) is obtained by multiplying its 'gross registered tonnage' by 1.51. For an oil-tanker, the equivalent factor comes to 1.86. Moreover, the average weight of oil can be taken to be 855.4 kilograms per cubic metre (calculated from the *UN Statistical Yearbook 1976:* table 52).

2. *Military (naval) ships.* The numbers of naval ships presumably refer to late 1975, being taken from *Jane's Fighting Ships 1976–1977:* 804–805. For naval ships, the designation *small* here refers to corvettes, the smaller frigates, and patrol submarines; and the designation *large* to battleships, aircraft carriers, cruisers, destroyers, the larger frigates, ballistic-missile submarines, cruise-missile submarines, and fleet submarines. Naval ships are measured in terms of 'standard displacement tonnage', a measure of weight where one 'ton' represents 1016 kilograms of total ship weight. There is no ready means of interconversion between 'standard displacement tonnage' and 'gross registered tonnage'. The approximation used here (based on data provided in the British *Admiralty Manual of Navigation 1964:* Vol. 1, pp. 61–63) is to multiply 'gross registered tonnage' by 2.21 in order to arrive at 'standard displacement tonnage'. The designations 'small' and 'large' as used in the text are on this basis comparable for merchant and naval ships.

Appendix 7.3

Nuclear bomb characteristics

Nuclear bombs are rated according to their total energy yield in terms of the weight of 2,4,6-trinitrotoluene (TNT) that would produce an equivalent energy yield. The energy yield of so-called standard TNT is taken to be 4.615 megajoules per kilogram (Kinney, 1962: 2). The total energy yield of a nuclear bomb is thus 4.187×10^{12} joules per 'kiloton' (kT) or 4.187×10^{15} joules per 'megaton' (MT). (The 'ton' referred to here weighs 907.2 kilograms.)

Two basic categories of nuclear bomb exist: (*a*) the atomic bomb, which relies on the complete fission of 58.8 grams of uranium-235 (^{235}U) and/or plutonium-239 (^{239}Pu) per 'kiloton' of yield; and (*b*) the hydrogen bomb, which relies on fission to trigger the fusion of hydrogen isotopes (largely ^2H with ^2H and ^2H with ^3H). For purposes of approximation, the yield of the hydrogen bomb is here considered to be derived half from fission and half from fusion. A bomb relying on the fission of uranium-235 is about 5 per cent efficient and thus contains about 1.18 kilograms of uranium-235 per 'kiloton' of fission yield; one relying on plutonium-239 is about 15 per cent efficient and thus contains about 392 grams of plutonium-239 per 'kiloton' of fission yield (Vellodi *et al.*, 1968: 54–55). Atomic bombs are usually in the 'kiloton' range, whereas hydrogen bombs are usually in the 'megaton' range but can also be in the 'kiloton' range. In the case of an atomic bomb, about 50 per cent of the energy yield is released in the form of a blast (shock) wave, about 35 per cent as thermal radiation, and the remaining 15 per cent as nuclear radiation. For a regular hydrogen bomb, the comparable values are about 54.5 per cent, 38 per cent, and 7.5 per cent, respectively. (In the low-yield, enhanced-radiation hydrogen bombs currently under development, the blast and thermal fractions are reduced in favour of the nuclear fraction (Westing, 1978 *c*).)

The fission reaction of a nuclear bomb produces about 290×10^{21} fission fragments per 'kiloton' of fission yield (UNSCEAR, 1972: 57) weighing about 56.7 grams (Glasstone, 1964: 417), these two values, it is assumed, referring to the situation one hour after the detonation. On the basis of Avogadro's number (602×10^{21} particles per mole), the fission products per 'kiloton' of fission bomb after one hour thus represent the equivalent of 482 millimoles of a conglomerate of radioactive isotopes having an average mass number of 118. This mixture (the result of both fission and neutron activation) contains some 200 isotopes of about three dozen elements.

The fusion reaction of a hydrogen bomb results in an excess of between 100×10^{21} and 1×10^{24} atoms of hydrogen-3, or tritium (^3H), per 'kiloton' of fusion yield (UNSCEAR, 1972: 57). Using the geometric mean of these two extremes, that is, 316×10^{21}, and dividing this value by Avogadro's number as well as by the mass number (i.e., 3), one arrives at 175 milligrams of hydrogen-3 per 'kiloton' of fusion yield.

To recapitulate, a one 'kiloton' atomic (fission) bomb produces about 56.7 grams of mixed fission products (i.e., as determined one hour after detonation). A one 'megaton' hydrogen bomb (½ fission, ½ fusion) produces about 28.35 kilograms of mixed fission products plus about 87.4 grams of hydrogen-3.

The numerous fission products of a nuclear bomb decay at greatly varying rates. One hour after the detonation of an atomic (fission) bomb, disintegration is said to be proceeding at 400 megacuries for each 'kiloton' of fission yield (Shapiro, 1974), that is, at 7 055 megacuries for each kilogram of mixed fission products. The hydrogen-3 disseminated by a fusion reaction (with its half-life of 12.26 years) has, for each kilogram, a decay rate of 10.12 megacuries. Thus, one hour after the detonation of a hydrogen bomb (½ fission, ½ fusion), there would be 200 000 megacuries for each 'megaton' of total yield among the mixed fission products plus an additional 885 kilocuries or so in the hydrogen-3 present.

Most of the fission products are extremely short-lived. Their combined decay rate during the initial half-year approximates a log/log linear curve having a slope of -1.2; thereafter, the overall decay rate becomes even more rapid, following a new log/log linear curve of slope -2.3 (Glasstone, 1964: 420). In other words, 50 per cent of the fission products present one hour after the detonation have disappeared about 1.78 hours after detonation, 90 per cent about 6.81 hours after detonation, 99 per cent about 46.4 hours after detonation, and 99.9 per cent about 316 hours (13.2 days) after detonation. About 42.6 parts per million (p.p.m.) remain after half a year and about 8.66 parts per million after one year. One hundred days after detonation is sometimes used as a reference point. If what remains at 100 days (i.e., 87.85 parts per million of the one-hour value) is taken as 100 per cent, then 48.5 per cent remains one-half year after detonation and 9.86 per cent remains one year after detonation.

These decay parameters can also be expressed more directly in relation to the nuclear bombs themselves. In a fission bomb, the 400 megacuries that occur for each 'kiloton' of yield one hour after detonation have decayed to 35.1 kilocuries after 100 days, and to 3.46 kilocuries after one year. (Thus, at 100 days there occur 620 kilocuries for each kilogram of fission products that was present after one hour.) In a hydrogen bomb, the 200 000 megacuries that occur for each 'megaton' of total yield at one hour after detonation have decayed to 17.6 megacuries after 100 days, and to 1.73 megacuries after one year. The hydrogen-3 of the latter bomb, disintegrating at 885 kilocuries after one hour for each 'megaton' of total yield, has decayed to 871 kilocuries after 100 days, and to 836 kilocuries after one year. For both categories of bomb, a small but biologically important group of fission products is rather long-lived (i.e., having half-lives measurable in years), including strontium-90 (^{90}Sr) and caesium-137 (^{137}Cs) (cf. table 7.8).

Appendix 7.4

Reactor characteristics of nuclear-powered naval vessels

The nuclear reactor of a naval vessel (submarine or surface) is taken to be a pressurized light-water cooled and moderated reactor—as is the case where such information has been provided by *Jane's Fighting Ships 1976–77*. Sizes have been estimated as follows: A number of nuclear-powered submarines are recorded in *Jane's Fighting Ships 1976–77* as having shaft horsepowers of 15 000; and a number of such cruisers are rated at 60 000 shaft horsepower. One horsepower is the equivalent of 746 watts. The efficiency of conversion of heat to electricity is taken to be one-fifth, on the basis of that of the USNS *Savannah* (Seymour *et al.*, 1971: 29). Such a nuclear submarine would thus have a reactor of about 56 megawatts (thermal), and a nuclear cruiser one of about 224.

A pressurized light-water reactor can be expected to use up about 513 milligrams of uranium-235 (^{235}U) per megawatt (thermal) per day of operation. This value is based on an average of six recent civil reactors of this sort to have become operational in the USA (all those during 1975–1976), being the arithmetic mean of US reactor numbers 312, 315, 317, 334, 336, and 344 (IAEA, 1976).

For each kilogram of uranium-235 used up in a nuclear reactor (these data being based on a boiling light-water reactor), about 1.25 kilograms of a large variety of fission products is produced (Netzén *et al.*, 1976: 36), that is, about 641 milligrams per megawatt (thermal) per day. For a 56 megawatt (thermal) submarine that has operated for 30 days, the total amount thus comes to 1.08 kilograms, and for a 224 megawatt (thermal) cruiser to 4.31 kilograms.

As was the case with the fission products of an atomic bomb (cf. appendix 7.3), the overall decay rate of this conglomerate is exceedingly rapid, for the first half-year again following a log/log linear course having a slope of − 1.2, and then decaying even more rapidly. During operation, however, these products are also constantly being added to. The net effect of these two opposing trends is that within a week the cumulative amount is 105 per cent of the daily production, within two weeks it is 106 per cent, within a month 107 per cent, and within two months 108 per cent. The equilibrium value, reached after half a year or so, is almost 109 per cent.

As soon as the reactor ceases to operate, the short-lived fission products (those having half-lives measurable in seconds or days) diminish at a precipitous rate. On the other hand, the small fraction of long-lived fission products formed (those having half-lives measurable in years) build up almost arithmetically during the months of operation, and then—when operation ceases—disappear only slowly (cf. table 7.9).

8. The global ecology

The tables for this chapter appear on pages 194–202.

I. Introduction

In previous chapters the several major global habitats—both terrestrial and oceanic—have been examined in the light of their use and abuse by man. It was noted that the human race shares the Earth with other living things, but that man's use of the Earth is increasingly occurring to the detriment of the entire global biota—man himself included. It was suggested that the abuses to which the Earth's several habitats are being subjected are to a substantial extent unavoidable, inasmuch as the world population exceeds a global carrying capacity that would permit all to enjoy an adequate standard of living. Moreover, this already inauspicious situation is being continuously exacerbated in a number of important ways: (*a*) by an ever-increasing world population; (*b*) by utilization of the global soil, forest, range, and fishery resources more rapidly than their rates of natural renewal; (*c*) by discharge of wastes into the environment (atmosphere, land, fresh waters, and ocean) more rapidly than their rates of natural dissipation; and (*d*) by non-essential environmental debilitations—namely, those that result from military and other frivolous human activities.

This final chapter begins with an examination of the role of natural resources (raw materials) *vis-à-vis* military activities. It goes on to explore the relationship between man and nature, as well as the question of imposing legal restraints on environmental disruption caused by warfare and by other military activities. It then sounds a warning note about the potentially bright military future of various recently developed conventional weapons and techniques that lead to environmental debilitation. It concludes with a plea to mankind to come to its senses while there is still the opportunity to do so with respect to two of the greatest threats to its decent survival—massive over-population and nuclear holocaust.

II. Natural resources

Raw materials

War is a voracious consumer of natural resources, both renewable and non-renewable. Even during peace-time, however, the maintenance of a military

183

posture consumes large quantities of raw materials (Huisken, 1975). These military uses serve to divert raw materials not only from the civil sector of society to the military sector, but also in part from the poor nations to the rich. Additionally, such uses serve partially to divert the raw materials from future utilization (i.e., from reserves) to present utilization. These several tendencies would all seem to include a substantial component of wasteful or otherwise undesirable aspects when viewed in humanistic terms (appendix 8.1).

The extraction or exploitation of raw materials and their manufacture into military paraphernalia each add to the air- and water-pollution of the world. About six per cent of the combined gross national products of the world's nations is devoted to military expenditures (table 8.1). In one sense, therefore, roughly six per cent of the world's environmental pollution could be attributed to the military sector of the global economy. On the other hand, were these expenditures not being devoted to military affairs, they presumably would in large measure be shifted, directly or indirectly, to the civil sector of the economy. As a case in point, it has been calculated that about 3.5 per cent of the annual global consumption of a group of 10 major metals—aluminium, chromium, copper, iron, lead, manganese, molybdenum, nickel, tin, and zinc—is devoted to US military purposes (Chacko *et al.*, 1972: 48). A complete US military moratorium might therefore be expected to reduce the annual global expenditures of these non-renewable resources by that amount. However, it was further calculated that the US civil economy would as a result of such a cessation expand to consume about 2.6 per cent more of the global consumption, thus effecting a net overall saving of only about 0.9 per cent.

The total military expenditures of the world are distributed among 135 or more nations (Westing, 1978 c). However, the 27 rich nations account for 75 per cent of the current total (table 8.1). Moreover, there are only 6 nations that contribute at least 2 per cent each to that total, and only 2 nations that really dominate the scene. Thus, during the decade 1966–1975, the world's military expenditures were distributed as follows: the USA, 31 per cent; the USSR, 31 per cent; China, 9 per cent; FR Germany, 4 per cent; France, 3 per cent; the United Kingdom, 3 per cent; and the remaining 153 nations together, 20 per cent (calculated from ACDA, 1976: table 2). The combined world military expenditures remained essentially constant on a per capita basis during the decade mentioned; they even declined—at the compound growth rate of − 2.67 per cent per year—in relation to summations of the world's gross national products (calculated from ACDA, 1976: table 1). Nevertheless, in absolute terms, total world military expenditures continued to increase during the decade in question at the compound growth rate of 1.68 per cent per year—a value leading to a doubling time of 42 years. In 1975 this total amounted to some US $371 thousand million, virtually all of it (97 per cent) accounted for by nations of the Northern hemisphere, and most of it (90 per cent) by temperate-habitat nations (table 8.1).

Global deficiencies of raw materials coupled with their uneven distribution throughout the world can lead to unlikely—and thus unstable—alliances, to national rivalries, and, of course, to war (appendix 8.1). By way of example, a dozen recent wars in which natural resources constituted an important factor are listed in table 8.2. Deficiencies of raw materials become intolerable partly because of the immense amounts of *matériel* and munitions required to equip and maintain an army in the field, and the exacting and often exotic raw-material requirements of today's technologically sophisticated weaponry. Indeed, throughout history, wars have been fought in order to gain control over one natural resource or another.

One of the simplest though most fundamental of all environmental resources is the land itself, a commodity that in effect keeps shrinking as the world population keeps rising. A felt need for greater living-space has often been used as one of the justifications for going to war. The need for added *lebensraum* was one of the major reasons given by Germany for pursuing World War II (Kruszewski, 1940; table 8.2.3). Over-population was also at the root of the El Salvador–Honduran War of 1969 (table 8.2.8). On the other hand, Bremer *et al.* (1973–1974) could not establish high population density as a significant cause of war in Europe during the past 150 years.

The Lorraine region just south of Luxembourg, one of the rare iron-rich regions of Europe, provides a fine example of the military significance of raw materials (Cheney, 1967; Leith, 1931: 145). A part of France since 1766, Lorraine was ceded to Germany as one outcome of the Franco-Prussian War of 1870–1871. It reverted to France as a result of World War I, but was reacquired by Germany early in World War II, only to be reannexed by France at the end of that war, this status having been maintained since then.

Oil is another of the unequally distributed mineral resources of enormous potential military significance (Christman & Clark, 1978; Meyerhoff, 1976; SIPRI, 1974 *b*: chap. 5). Oil can pose an especially difficult problem for those nations that must depend completely or largely upon foreign supplies. For example, Germany—which virtually has no oil deposits of its own—was greatly hampered in its military efforts towards the end of World War II by a shortage of oil (SIPRI, 1974 *b*: 142–145). The USA—now about 65 per cent self-sufficient in oil—has routinely been using about 7 per cent of its total annual consumption for military purposes (table 8.3). It is interesting (and somewhat surprising) to note, moreover, that despite the magnitude of the overall US military effort in the Second Indochina War, its war-related consumption of oil was substantially less than other military or civil uses.

The USA is self-sufficient for military purposes in a substantial number of minerals of importance, but by no means in all of them (Kirby & Prokopovitsh, 1976; Schwab, 1976: chap. 5). Cheney (1967) develops the plausible argument that the foreign policy of the USA is governed to a far greater extent by its mineral insufficiencies than by any political philosophy. As one of a number of examples, Cheney suggests that US relations with South Africa are tempered largely by its need for chromium, a metal in which the USA is only nine per cent self-sufficient. Morris (1974) suggests that the newly blossoming friendship between the USA and Burundi finds its basis in the recently discovered deposits of nickel in the latter country, the USA being only 27 per cent self-sufficient in this metal.

It thus appears quite safe to surmise that in the future—as has been the case in the past—some wars will stem from the unequal distribution of natural resources in the world. The frequency of such wars will decrease to the extent that lengthy wars of attrition, with their voracious appetite for raw materials, will give way to more quickly consummated conflicts (Huisken, 1975). Conversely, they will increase to the extent that local and overall shortages of the world's natural resources will be intensified by increases in population, in civil expectations regarding living standards, and in pollution-related losses. Leider (1973: 881) predicted:

Within the next decade what has been called 'the environment' holds promise of emerging as the most troublesome of all international irritants. Complex enough in a physical sense, the issue grows even more intricate on the political plane through its powerful association with health and survival. National interests that may hitherto have been difficult to define shed their turbidity under an onslaught of new and immediate concerns—the depletion of vital resources, the threats to life support systems, and the question of continued growth. In this charged atmosphere, options become limited. The policies flowing from them tend to channel nations in directions that make strife, conflict and collisions all but unavoidable.

Man

The human species is in a sense also a natural resource—one that is influenced by military activities during war and peace. The mortality, maimings, and other effects associated with warfare have been touched upon previously (chapter 2, section IV; chapter 3, section IV; cf. also appendix 2.3). Some interwar influences—both positive and negative—on this human resource are noted below.

It is widely taken for granted that military expenditures provide for national security and that they facilitate the pursuit of a nation's foreign policy. A critical analysis of these possibly illusory assumptions and of their alleged benefits is, however, far beyond the scope of this work (cf., for example, Myrdal, 1976).

Shifts in employment patterns brought about by military expenditures constitute another interwar influence on the human resource. The armies of the world provide jobs for some small segment of the global population. About 0.65 per cent of the global population is at any one time found to be in uniform (table 1.13). Boulding (1962: 339) ventures to suggest that the armed forces of the world form a self-justifying social system of their own, almost independent of the nations that support them. Moreover, military research and development (SIPRI, 1972*b*) and the production of arms also provide employment for some tiny fraction of the labour force that might otherwise be unemployable. All in all, however, a number of pragmatic analyses have shown that the total employment generated by a nation's military expenditures is substantially less, dollar for dollar, than that generated by its civil expenditures (ACDA, 1972; Banerjee *et al.*, 1975; Dolgu *et al.*, 1978; Myrdal *et al.*, 1972; *SIPRI Yearbook 1978:* chap. 10; Väyrynen, 1978). In the last analysis, military expenditures by a nation channel raw materials (and the tax funds that purchase them) into swords rather than ploughshares, and into bombs and missiles rather than hospitals and schools.

Finally, it must be noted that preparation for war appears to have had an important influence on social or cultural evolution in its diverse ramifications, especially in the areas of industrial technology and political organization (appendix 2.3.4).

III. Man and nature

The Earth serves as a self-sustaining life-support system for man in concert with his fellow creatures, both higher and lower. Such life support is accomplished through an intricate system of interactions among its many living and non-living components. Today, however, this long-established harmony of nature is being undermined and subverted as a result of man's ever-increasing numbers and ever more disruptive activities (appendix 8.2).

Man represents the dominant animal species on Earth not only as a result of his intellectual and tool-making abilities, but also owing to his sheer bulk. The human biomass currently stands at about 50×10^9 kilograms, representing 4 per cent of the terrestrial animal biomass (table 1.5). Moreover, man's several species of domestic livestock—having a combined biomass of perhaps 200×10^9 kilograms—represent another 15 per cent of the total terrestrial animal biomass. Any increase in either of these two sets of biomass values displaces (i.e., occurs at the expense of) an equal or greater amount of wildlife biomass—an outright loss to wild nature. The current doubling time for the world's human biomass is only 39 years (table 1.4); and that for the global bovine biomass is 43 years (calculated from the *UN Statistical Yearbook 1976:* table 33, 1961–1975 data).

One yardstick of the environmental disruption that has been brought about by human society is the increased rate of plant and animal extinctions. The extinction of existing species and the evolution of new species of biota are, of course, natural phenomena that have always occurred and that continue to occur. For example, the natural turnover rate for avian species—of which approximately 8 600 exist—appears to be of the order of one every 230 years (0.43 per century); and that for mammalian species—of which approximately 4 200 exist—appears to be of the order of one every 140 years (0.70 per century) (Fisher *et al.*, 1969: 11–13). On the other hand, during the three centuries odd between the year 1600 and the mid-1960s, an estimated 94 species of birds (26 per century) and 36 species of mammals (10 per century) have suffered extinction—most, therefore, at the hand of man. What is worse, the rate is accelerating, and today an estimated 200 or so species of birds and 100 or so of mammals are known to be threatened with extinction (Curry-Lindahl, 1972; Fisher *et al.*, 1969; Greenway, 1967; Ziswiler, 1967). Although comparable information on other kinds of animals and plants is essentially lacking, at least as many have met, and will continue to meet, a similar fate.

The reasons for the many anthropogenic plant and animal extinctions of recent times are, of course, varied. Man has hunted some species to extinction for food or for other commodity, or has exterminated them because they were considered pests. Other species have disappeared because of alien species introduced intentionally or unintentionally by man. A few extinctions can be traced to environmental pollutants. In the great majority of cases, however, the reason can be reduced to competition between man and the other species for space (often on islands), which man needs to live and to grow his food and industrial crops.

Once man has tamed a region to suit his needs and desires, the habitat simply cannot any longer provide suitable food and cover (shelter) for the indigenous wild species. To put it quite simply, every three years the human population increases by another 220 million (table 1.4) at the expense of one species of wild bird or mammal plus one or two additional species of some other kind of animal or plant.

Various reasons have been put forward to justify or support the necessity for protecting wildlife and for conserving nature generally (appendix 8.2.1). Prominent among these reasons are the economic advantages to be gained from wild plants and animals or their habitat. Emphasis is also laid on the cultural importance of the biota and their milieu—including their aesthetic and recreational values and their contribution to the development and maintenance of a healthy human psyche—as well as on their importance to the advancement of science. A number of ecological arguments are also advanced, among them the necessity for at least certain species to maintain a local balance of nature (i.e., ecosystem stability); and also the idea that in the process of conserving wildlife (especially in preventing an extinction) one is protecting man's environment as well.

Perhaps the most cogent reason for conserving nature is that man, despite his awesome might, does not possess the concomitant right to destroy wantonly the living things with which he shares the Earth. Nature must be accorded a certain level of immunity from human depredations. Man must not consider the land and what it supports wholly in terms of property or real estate. Rather, he should think of himself as a temporary custodian of the land, entrusted to him for passing on unimpaired to future generations. In the words of Stone (1972: 498–499):

The time may be on hand when these sentiments, and the early stirrings of the law, can be coalesced into a radical new theory or myth—felt as well as intellectualized—of man's relationships to the rest of nature. . . . What is needed is a myth that can fit our growing body of knowledge of geophysics, biology and the cosmos. In this vein, I do not think it too remote that we may come to regard the Earth, as some have suggested, as one organism, of which Mankind is a functional part—the mind, perhaps: different from the rest of nature, but different as a man's brain is from his lungs.

IV. Legal restraints on environmental disruption

A number of instruments of international law exist or have been proposed that have relevance to environmental disruption by military activities (appendix 8.3). It seems appropriate to begin a discussion of these with the Charter of the United Nations inasmuch as it has the force of treaty law for its 147 member nations (appendix 1.4, note *a*). This Charter establishes that "All Members shall settle their international disputes by peaceful means . . .[and] . . . shall refrain in their international relations from the threat or use of force . . ." (UN, 1945: Article 2; but cf. Article 51). Adherence to the spirit of that covenant would, among other things, obviate the necessity of further proscriptions against military actions of an anti-environmental nature.

Various treaties focus on the prohibition of the use of specific classes of weapons which, intentionally or unintentionally, can be caused to do harm to the environment. For example, chemical warfare agents—both anti-personnel and anti-plant—can result in enormous environmental harm (SIPRI, 1976; 1977). Relevant here, therefore, are the Hague Declaration of 1899 (table 8.4.1) and the Geneva Protocol of 1925 (table 8.4.5), both of which forbid to the ratifying nations the use of poisonous gases as weapons of war; and the Hague Convention of 1907 (table 8.4.2), which similarly forbids the use of poison. The employment of biological weapons is forbidden both by the Geneva Protocol of 1925 and by the Biological Weapon Convention of 1972 (table 8.4.14), the latter prohibiting possession as well. There exists as well a hotchpotch of partial controls of nuclear weapons and their delivery systems (table 8.4: treaties 7–12; SIPRI, 1978). Others are the basis for interminable international negotiations. A straightforward proscription of nuclear weapons—with their extraordinarily high potential for environmental destruction (SIPRI, 1977: chap. 1; Westing, 1978 c)—would be a most welcome addition to the category of treaty that prohibits specific weapons.

Another relevant class of treaties are meant to protect specified regions on Earth or beyond it. Protection is thereby provided not only for the ecosystems involved, with their living and non-living components, but also perhaps for some crucial link in the greater cycles of nature that serve to maintain our world-wide ecosystem. Thus, treaties have been concluded in which the ratifying nations have agreed to demilitarize the Svalbard archipelago (table 8.4.3), the Åland islands (table 8.4.4), Antarctica (table 8.4.8), and the Moon and other celestial bodies (table 8.4.10). Other treaties have barred nuclear weapons from Latin America (table 8.4.11), from being emplaced on the ocean floor (table 8.4.13), and from being placed in orbit round the Earth (table 8.4.10). Specified natural (and cultural) areas of outstanding universal value are meant to be protected by the World Heritage Convention (table 8.4.15). Various localized or otherwise limited treaties on conservation and arms control have also been concluded, usually between neighbouring nations (UNEP, 1977–1978; SIPRI, 1978).

A small number of treaties provide for the protection of certain classes of biota. The most prominent of these is the Genocide Convention (table 8.4.6), which is meant to protect racial and other subgroups of man. Another that is relevant to military depredations is the Convention for the Protection of Birds (table 8.4.7), meant to protect birds in the wild state; this treaty deserves to be adopted far more widely than it has been up to the present.

Some treaties are meant to prevent or regulate the discharge of dangerous waste materials into the environment. The radioactive contamination by nuclear test explosions of the atmosphere, outer space, and the ocean is forbidden to those nations ratifying the Partial Test Ban Treaty (table 8.4.9). Nuclear explosions and the disposal of radioactive wastes are prohibited in Antarctica (table 8.4.8). The harmful contamination of outer space and of celestial bodies is also prohibited (table 8.4.10). Moreover, several treaties exist that are meant to control the discharge of harmful substances into the ocean (UNEP, 1977–1978).

An incident from World War II and its post-war sequel provide an example of yet another approach to environmental protection from military depredations. The plundering of Polish forests by Germany during that war was classed as a war crime by the UN War Crimes Commission (1948: 496) at Nuremberg (Case Number 7150), on the basis that it violated the Hague Convention (IV) of 1907, which prohibits pillaging in occupied territory (table 8.4.2).

Some very recent treaties are meant to provide a wider range of protection to the environment in time of war than any in force today. Geneva Protocol I of 1977 (table 8.4.17) would prohibit means of interstate warfare which are intended to or may be expected to cause widespread, long-term, and severe damage to the natural environment, particularly where such damage would prejudice the health or survival of the population. This treaty would also prohibit attacks against agricultural lands and water supplies indispensable to the survival of the civil population. Attacks against dams, dikes, and nuclear electrical generating stations would also be prohibited lest 'dangerous forces' be released that might threaten the civil population. Indiscriminate (area) bombing would be prohibited as well. Geneva Protocol II of 1977 (table 8.4.18)—applicable to civil (intrastate) wars—would similarly prohibit attacks on agricultural lands, water supplies, and works or installations containing dangerous forces.

It is perhaps, to some extent, already possible to manipulate certain forces of nature for hostile purposes—a class of capabilities that will presumably be developed more fully in the future (SIPRI, 1977: chap. 3). The Environmental Modification Convention (table 8.4.16) addresses itself to this possibility, albeit in a rather circumscribed fashion. This treaty would prohibit the ratifying nations from deliberately manipulating for hostile purposes the natural processes of outer space or of the Earth (including the biota, lithosphere, hydrosphere, or atmosphere of the latter) in such a way as to have a widespread, long-lasting, or severe effect as the means of damage to any other party to the treaty. It is unfortunate that this treaty specifies the level of damage prohibited. It should simply have proscribed outright any environmental manipulations for hostile purposes.

It is a truism that warfare is detrimental to the environment. However, military disruption of the environment in warfare is pernicious because it spills over both the spatial and temporal boundaries of the attack, because of its partially unpredictable ramifications, and because its impact assails combatants and non-combatants alike. Military disruption of the environment is, however, exceedingly difficult to limit or control by means of legal instruments. This is the case largely because, whether intended—overtly or covertly—or not, most hostile and many non-hostile military actions result in at least some level of environmental disturbance, and because of the subsequent difficulties in establishing the extent of disruption.

It can be argued, therefore, that the most urgent—and also the most straightforward—arms control measures required at this juncture from an ecological or environmental standpoint are the absolute prohibition of nuclear weapons and the complete demilitarization and conversion to protected status of ecologically important regions. Regions are ecologically important (*a*) if they contribute substantially to the global balance of nature, (*b*) if the ecosystems they contain are intrinsically fragile, (*c*) if they support unique habitats, (*d*) if they provide the habitat for species in danger of extinction, or (*e*) perhaps for other reasons. In addition to these two approaches, any military weapon or technique that has the effect of devastating a wide area should be proscribed as a threat to the regional ecology (Westing, 1974).

V. Conclusion

The situation in which man finds himself today is a grave one. He is utilizing all the world's major renewable natural resources—agricultural soils, forest trees, range grasses, and ocean fishes—at rates exceeding their natural capacities for renewal. He is consuming fossil fuels and other minerals at ever-increasing rates, thereby bringing these non-renewable resources closer and closer to the point of exhaustion. He is introducing pollutants into the environment at levels increasingly above the point at which they can dissipate and decompose to insignificance—among them radioactive isotopes from weapon-testing and carbon dioxide from the burning of fossil fuels. Facing an inevitable shortage of fossil fuels and the present lack of safe workable alternate-energy systems, he is turning increasingly to nuclear fuels, which are unavoidably linked with the spread of nuclear-weapon competence and with other intractable problems. He is becoming poorer by the day; that is to say, despite continued advances in science and technology, the world-wide average standard of living—already unconscionably low—continues to decline; and his ability to cope with over-population and the other root causes of his many-sided predicament is not improving.

In view of his bleak situation, it is a tragedy that man continues to consider it necessary to devote a substantial portion of his resources to military preparations and to war. The frequent wars that man engages in not only divert his energies from constructive civil pursuits, but also disrupt the theatres of operation. Military weapons and technologies are becoming increasingly disruptive of the environment. Even setting aside nuclear and other weapons of mass destruction (SIPRI, 1977), the Second Indochina War has amply demonstrated that nominally conventional means of attack can devastate the local ecology (SIPRI, 1976). During that war, for example, the USA inflicted enormous environmental damage through continued rural area-bombing and forest removal, both chemical and mechanical. In analysing the role of massive rural bombing in counter-insurgency warfare, the chief historian of the US Strategic Air Command explained that guerrillas are no longer to be fought with rifles; rather, they are to be located and then bombed to oblivion (Kipp, 1967–1968). Fortunately, the military utility of massive interdiction (use-denial) bombing carried out over wide rural areas for protracted periods has become a matter of relatively open debate in military circles. In fact, an analysis of this technique led a US Army officer to conclude: "Massive strategic interdiction fosters the illusion that it will force the enemy to one's desires. It envisions eliminating the evil at its source with all the remote impunity of a surgeon severing a cancerous tumor. It was not a new idea [in Indochina] nor . . . a successful one" (VanderEls, 1970: 90; cf. also Biles, 1972).

The tactical importance of forests has been recognized throughout the sweep of military history, and the Second Indochina War was certainly no exception (appendix 8.1). Military evaluations of the use of chemical anti-plant agents as a means of forest destruction have been sufficiently favourable to suggest their future applicability in a diversity of potential operational theatres (Engineers, 1972; Howard, 1972). For example, they are said to have potential military applicability to Cuba, Ethiopia, the two Koreas, Venezuela, Western Europe (Engineers, 1972: Vol. 3), and Central Europe (Lyons *et al.*, 1971). It should be added that the technology of chemical anti-plant warfare is widely available and is presumably within the reach of many armed forces of the world. On the other hand, there appears to exist a rather widespread revulsion against the use of chemical anti-personnel warfare agents—a feeling which encompasses the herbicides used to a greater or lesser extent in war.

Mechanical means of forest removal through the use of large land-clearing tractors (the so-called Rome ploughs) has been repeatedly lauded by military analysts of the Second Indochina War as an aid to counter-insurgency actions. The chief US Army engineer in that war stated: "The new land-clearing machinery is an exciting development [which] is changing the face of this jungle-covered country, and eventually may change the face of the war being fought there" (Ploger, 1968: 72). There is no difficulty in finding support for his conclusion. The commander of the first land-clearing battalion formed by the USA concluded: "The B-52 bomber is the battle-ax of this war, and our plow is the scalpel. . . . Land clearing in South Vietnam may turn out to be the war's No. 1 [tactical development]" (*Engineering News-Record,* 1970). A survey of several hundred US Army officers with combat experience in the Second Indochina War revealed that Rome ploughs were considered superior for clearing operations to herbicides, napalm, high-explosive bombs, or felling and burning (Engineers, 1972; cf. also Howard, 1972). Post-war military evaluations have also been sprinkled with superlatives (Hay, 1974: 87–89; Kerver, 1974; Ploger, 1974: 95–104; Rogers, 1974: 61–66). Moreover, as with herbicidal attack, mechanized land-clearing would appear to be within the technological and financial capabilities of many of the armies of the world.

It would thus seem—at least from the military perspective—that various environmentally disruptive conventional weapons and techniques that have recently been developed and utilized have a potentially bright military future. Environmentally devastating nuclear weapons also stand ready, of course, for instant use by the several major powers. Any necessary restraints would therefore have to find their basis in ecological, moral, or ethical considerations (as discussed in section III of this chapter), these presumably being expressed in the form of legal sanctions of an international character (as discussed in section IV). Failing this, it may be hoped at least that consideration for the natural ecology of the different world habitats (some of which are indeed fragile) and for the Earth as a whole will deter armed forces from pursuing their more blatant anti-ecological strategies and tactics. The present situation is such that it seems as if the continued integrity of the global ecology will have to depend for some time upon unilateral restraints of this kind.

Ecological considerations have not played a dominant role in man's past conduct, whether civil or military. Where such considerations did, in fact, obtrude upon his decision-making processes, man simply took for granted a position of dominance for himself in the natural global hierarchy (appendix 8.2.2). The validity of this supremacy has, however, never been put to the proper test. To date, even the most severe anthropogenic perturbations of the global ecosystem have in fact been modest and transitory. However, man has finally attained the stage where he can do much more than this. It is possible that the world's first true 'ecodisaster' will result from rampant over-population and its corollaries. However, it is equally possible that man, with his nuclear and other modern military capabilities, will one day perpetrate some rash hostile environmental manipulation which will at one and the same time demonstrate his mastery over nature and put a lasting end to war on Earth—leaving perhaps a handful of survivors to reap the grim harvest of a global Carthaginian peace. It remains to be seen whether or not man will come to his senses in time.

Table 8.1. Distribution of military expenditures (1975 data)[a]

Region or category	Military expenditures[b]					
	$US \$ \times 10^6$	Per nation[c] $US \$ \times 10^6$	Per soldier[d] $US \$$	Per capita[e] $US \$$	Per km^2 [e] $US \$$	Proportion of GNP[f] per cent
Land mass						
North America	94 826	10 536	40 351	300.59	4 348	5.42
South America	5 197	433	5 156	24.09	293	2.33
Africa	6 004	133	4 329	15.37	208	3.66
Europe	64 768	2 313	14 351	156.60	14 540	3.88
Asia	178 461	5 949	11 609	78.69	3 802	11.77
Australia	2 480	2 480	35 429	183.61	323	3.17
Antarctica	0	0	0	0	0	0
Islands	19 591	576	10 854	44.95	3 901	2.35
of Atlantic Ocean	10 796	720	20 564	130.54	16 514	4.67
of Pacific Ocean	8 729	727	7 034	26.45	2 353	1.46
of Indian Ocean	66	9	1 692	2.85	100	1.01
of Arctic Ocean	0	0	0	0	0	0
Hemisphere						
Northern	360 938	2 911	14 436	100.32	3 715	6.14
Southern	10 389	297	6 912	22.85	294	2.89
Habitat						
Temperate	333 731	5 959	17 803	147.37	4 950	6.15
Tropical	16 360	205	2 667	10.04	384	2.93
Desert	21 236	965	13 068	133.95	946	8.55
Arctic	0	0	0	0	0	0

Region or category	Military expenditures[b]					
	Per nation[c] US $\times 10^6$	Per soldier[d] US \$$\times 10^6$	Per soldier[d] US \$	Per capita[e] US \$	Per km^2 [e] US \$	Proportion of GNP[f] per cent
Wealth						
Rich	280 320	10 382	28 625	312.43	4 931	6.10
Average	43 024	1 001	8 269	71.56	1 692	4.49
Poor	47 983	539	4 169	18.79	955	7.02
Global total	371 327	2 335	14 009	91.63	2 802	5.96

Sources and notes:

[a]The regions are described in table 1.4, note *a*. The wealth categories are described in appendix 1.4, note *c*. The data in this table are based only on the 159 nations listed in appendix 1.4. A nation that falls into more than one region is for this table counted in the one that contains the larger area. See also Westing (1978 *b*).

[b]Military expenditures are summarized from ACDA (1976: table 2; 1975 data), the several missing values having been taken primarily from *SIPRI Yearbook 1977*: appendix 7A (1975 data).

[c]The numbers of nations upon which these calculations are based are summarized from appendix 1.4.

[d]The numbers of soldiers (i.e., total armed forces) upon which these calculations are based are taken from table 1.13.

[e]The populations and areas upon which these calculations are based are from the *UN Demographic Yearbook 1975*: table 3 (1975 data), being summations of the nations (only) that fall wholly or primarily into each region.

[f]The gross national product (GNP) values upon which these calculations are based are from ACDA (1976: table 2; 1975 data), the several missing values having been taken from the *World Bank Atlas 1976* (1975 data).

Table 8.2. Wars and skirmishes involving natural resources: a selection from the twentieth century[a]

1. World War I of 1914–1918

(a) *Description:* A complex of several more or less distinct wars that can in simple terms be summarized as an unsuccessful war by the Central Powers—i.e., Germany, Austria-Hungary, Turkey, Bulgaria, etc.—against the Allies—i.e., France, the UK, Russia, Italy, the USA, Belgium, Portugal, Serbia, Montenegro (the last two now part of Yugoslavia), Greece, Romania, Japan, etc.

(b) *Location:* Primarily Northern hemisphere; primarily Europe (but also Asia, Africa, etc.); primarily temperate habitat

(c) *Type and fatality class:* Interstate war; 7

(d) *Natural resource aspect:* Among the causes of World War I were territorial rivalries (e.g., over the iron-rich Lorraine region, now part of France) and conflicts over colonies or spheres of influence in resource-rich Africa, eastern Asia, Pacific Ocean islands, etc.

2. Chaco War of 1932–1935

(a) *Description:* Successful war by Paraguay against Bolivia, primarily in order to annex the Gran Chaco wilderness area

(b) *Location:* Southern hemisphere: South America; tropical habitat

(c) *Type and fatality class:*[b] Interstate war; 5

(d) *Natural resource aspect:* The Gran Chaco was thought (incorrectly) to contain oil

3. World War II of 1939–1945

(a) Description: A complex of several dozen more or less distinct wars, all more or less closely connected in some supportive or opposing fashion with wars of conquest by Germany and Japan; summarized in its simplest terms as an unsuccessful war of aggrandizement by the Axis—i.e., Germany (under Hitler), Austria (annexed by Germany), Italy, Japan, Hungary, Bulgaria, Romania, Finland, etc.—against the Allies—i.e., France, the UK, Poland, the USSR, Belgium, the USA, China, Czechoslovakia, Greece, the Netherlands, Yugoslavia, Norway, etc.

(b) Location: Primarily Northern hemisphere; Europe, Asia, Africa, Pacific Ocean islands, Atlantic Ocean islands, etc; primarily temperate and tropical habitats, but also desert and arctic

(c) Type and fatality class: Interstate war; 8

(d) Natural resource aspect: A need for added living space *(Lebensraum)* was one of the justifications given by Germany (1937 population density, 190 persons per square kilometre) for pursuing the war; Japan's expansionist tendencies were motivated in large part by its paucity of indigenous natural resources; Germany annexed the iron-rich Lorraine region of north-eastern France and the agriculturally flourishing and iron-rich Ukraine region of the USSR (only to lose them again at the end of the war); Germany made large-scale use of slave labour imported from Poland, the USSR, France, etc.; Germany pillaged the Polish timber resource; in 1944 the USSR annexed from Finland the nickel-rich Petsamo (now Pechenga) territory on the Barents Sea

(e) References: Boldt & Queneau (1967: 70); Kruszewski (1940); UN War Crimes Commission (1948: 496); see also the sources below

4. Algerian War of Independence of 1954–1962

(a) Description: Successful attempt by Algeria to gain its independence from France

(b) Location: Northern hemisphere; Africa; largely desert habitat

(c) Type and fatality class: Colonial war; 6

(d) Natural resource aspect: France was reluctant to lose Algeria partly because of its rich oil deposits

(e) References: Horne (1977: 241–242); see also the sources below

5. Congo Civil War of 1960–1964

(a) Description: Internal turmoil following independence that evolved into an unsuccessful attempt by Katanga (now Shaba) province to secede from the newly independent Republic of the Congo (now Zaïre), the latter being helped by UN forces

(b) Location: Southern hemisphere; Africa; tropical habitat

(c) Type and fatality class: Civil war; 5

(d) Natural resource aspect: The secession was in large part fomented by Belgian and other foreign interests so as to protect their investments in copper and other minerals (Katanga having rich deposits of copper, uranium, chromium, cobalt, tin, iron, gold, etc.)

6. Third Arab–Israeli War of 1967

(a) Description: Conquest by Israel of portions of Egypt (Sinai Peninsula), Jordan (Old Jerusalem), and Syria (Golan Heights), including also the closing by Israel of the Suez Canal and the opening of the port of Aqaba (thereby restoring access for itself to the Indian Ocean)

(b) Location: Northern hemisphere; Asia; desert habitat

(c) Type and fatality class: Interstate war; 4

(d) Natural resource aspect: The oil deposits of the Sinai Peninsula constitute one of the attractions of this region to Israel; the deposits are apparently sufficient to supply one-tenth of Israel's current needs

(e) References: SIPRI Yearbook 1968/69: 414–428; see also the sources below

7. Nigerian Civil War of 1967–1970

(a) Description: Unsuccessful attempt by the south-eastern region—which proclaimed itself the independent Republic of Biafra—to secede from Nigeria

(b) Location: Northern hemisphere; Africa; tropical habitat

(c) Type and fatality class: Civil war; 6

(d) Natural resource aspect: The government was reluctant to lose Biafra in large part owing to its rich deposits of oil

8. El Salvador–Honduran War of 1969

(a) Description: Invasion of sparsely populated Honduras by densely populated El Salvador, the latter evacuating Honduras following mediation by the Organization of American States (OAS)

(b) Location: Northern hemisphere; North America; tropical habitat

(c) Type and fatality class: Interstate war; 3

(d) Natural resource aspect: El Salvador (1969 population density, 158 persons per square kilometre; growth rate, 3.7 per cent, giving a doubling time of 19 years) invaded neighbouring Honduras (1969 population density, 22 persons per square kilometre) primarily to prevent Honduras from expelling its unauthorized El Salvadorian immigrants and to force it to accept immigrants in the future; El Salvador attained its first goal but not its second

9. Anglo-Icelandic Clash of 1972–1973

(a) Description: In 1972 Iceland unilaterally extended its coastal fishing rights from 22 to 93 kilometres; the UK (with the support of the International Court of Justice) refused to recognize this extension, but British trawlers and a frigate were driven away by Icelandic gunboats

(b) Location: Northern hemisphere; Atlantic Ocean island; arctic habitat

(c) Type and fatality class: Interstate war; 0

(d) Natural resource aspect: Iceland (which has been described as "a rock surrounded by fish") was protecting its access to a natural resource vital to its national economy. (In 1975 the fishing limits were once again extended, this time to 370 kilometres.)

10. Paracel Islands Clash of 1974

(a) Description: The Paracel (Hsi-sha) Islands (16° 30′ N 112° 15′ E) of the South China Sea were occupied by Japan during World War II but passed to China in 1945; the islands were also claimed by the South Vietnamese, who manned a small garrison there until 1974, when they were attacked and driven away by Chinese armed forces

(b) Location: Northern hemisphere; Pacific Ocean islands; tropical habitat

(c) Type and fatality class: Interstate war; 1

(d) Natural resource aspect: The islands are believed to be underlain by rich oil deposits, which is presumably one of the chief reasons for the interest shown in them

(e) References: SIPRI (1974 *b*: 133–135); see also the sources below

11. Western Sahara Revolt of 1976–

(a) Description: Ongoing attempt by insurgents (Frente Polisario) to create an independent nation out of the former Spanish (western) Sahara, which in early 1976 had been partitioned by Spain between Morocco (2/3) and Mauritania(1/3)

(b) Location: Northern hemisphere; Africa; desert habitat

(c) Type and fatality class: Civil war; 3

(d) Natural resource aspect: The region in question contains rich phosphate deposits—a major reason why Morocco and Mauritania are reluctant to relinquish it

---

Sources and notes:
[a]In addition to any special sources noted for individual wars, the information provided here has been derived primarily from Dupuy & Dupuy (1977), Harris & Levey (1975), Montross (1960), and Young & Calvert (1977). A number of these wars are further described in table 1.2.
[b]The wars are divided into one of three types: interstate, colonial, or civil (intrastate). Fatality classes are explained in appendix 1.1, note *b*.

Table 8.3. Oil consumption by the USA during the Second Indochina War period

Million cubic metres[a]

Fiscal year	Second Indochina War consumption[b]	Other military consumption	Total military consumption[c]	Civil consumption	Total consumption[d]
1961–62	?	?	45.8	548.1	593.9
1962–63	?	?	44.9	566.3	611.2
1963–64	?	?	45.5	587.5	633.1
1964–65	?	?	46.5	608.6	655.1
1965–66	2.2	48.5	50.8	633.8	684.6
1966–67	4.6	53.6	58.2	656.2	714.4
1967–68	6.5	55.9	62.4	692.7	755.2
1968–69	7.0	56.3	63.3	733.2	796.5
1969–70	6.4	47.0	53.4	789.3	842.7
1970–71	4.9	43.0	47.9	817.4	865.3
1971–72	3.3	42.9	46.3	864.7	910.9
1972–73	1.9	41.5	43.4	938.0	981.5
Total	**>36.9**	**>388.8**	**608.4**	**8 435.9**	**9 044.3**

Sources and notes:
[a]The average weight of oil is 855.4 kilograms per cubic metre (calculated from the *UN Statistical Yearbook 1976:* table 52).
[b]Second Indochina War data were supplied by the US Department of Defense (private correspondence of 6 February 1974).
[c]Total military data are taken from Pike (1974: 120).
[d]Total data are calculated from the monthly figures in *US Bureau of Mines Mineral Industry Surveys: Petroleum Statement Annual* 1961–1973: table 1.

Table 8.4. Multilateral environmental protection treaties of military significance[a]

1. Hague Declaration (IV, 2) concerning asphyxiating gases, 1899
   (a) *Entry into force:* 1900
   (b) *Parties as of December 1977[b]:* 27 or more, including China, France, the UK, and the USSR
   (c) *Environmental provisions:* The parties undertake to abstain from the use among themselves of projectiles, the sole object of which is the diffusion of asphyxiating or deleterious gases.

2. Hague Convention (IV) respecting the laws and customs of war on land, 1907
   (a) *Entry into force:* 1910
   (b) *Parties as of December 1977:* 33 or more, including China, France, the UK, the USA, and the USSR
   (c) *Environmental provisions:* The parties undertake not to employ poison or poisoned weapons. The attack or bombardment, by whatever means, of towns or villages which are undefended is prohibited. Pillage on the territory of a hostile state is forbidden.
   (d) *Note:* There is considerable overlap between this convention and Hague Convention (II) of 1899 (which has 46 or more parties); and some between this convention and Geneva Convention (IV) of 1949 (which has 134 parties).

3. Treaty regulating the status of Spitsbergen and conferring the sovereignty of Norway, 1920
   (a) *Entry into force:* 1925
   (b) *Parties as of December 1977:* 39 or more, including China, France, the UK, the USA, and the USSR

(c) *Environmental provisions:* Norway undertakes not to create nor to allow the establishment of any naval base in the Svalbard archipelago or on Bear Island and not to construct any fortification in the said territories, which may never be used for warlike purposes. Norway shall be free to maintain, take, or decree suitable measures to ensure the preservation and, if necessary, the reconstitution of the fauna and flora of the said regions, and their territorial waters.

4. Convention respecting the non-fortification and neutralisation of the Åland Islands, 1921

(a) *Entry into force:* 1922

(b) *Parties as of June 1978:* 9 or more, including France and the UK

(c) *Environmental provisions:* Finland undertakes not to fortify or use the Åland Islands for war purposes. Prohibited, *inter alia,* are all military (including naval and air) establishments, installations, and operations by Finland or any other state. In time of war, the islands are to be considered a neutral zone.

(d) *Note:* Russia had made a similar declaration in 1856, to which the USSR is perhaps bound.

5. Geneva Protocol for the prohibition of the use in war of asphyxiating, poisonous or other gases, and of bacteriological methods of warfare, 1925

(a) *Entry into force:* 1928

(b) *Parties as of December 1977:* 96 or more, including China, France, the UK, the USA, and the USSR

(c) *Environmental provisions:* The parties undertake not to use in war asphyxiating, poisonous, or other gases; all analogous materials, liquids, or devices; and bacteriological methods of warfare.

6. Convention on the prevention and punishment of the crime of genocide, 1948

(a) *Entry into force:* 1951

(b) *Parties as of December 1977:* 80, including France, the UK, and the USSR

(c) *Environmental provisions:* The parties undertake to prevent and to punish genocide, whether committed in time of peace or in time of war. Genocide is defined as meaning any of a series of specified acts committed with intent to destroy, in whole or in part, a national, ethnical, racial, or religious group.

7. International convention for the protection of birds, 1950

(a) *Entry into force:* 1963

(b) *Parties as of June 1978:* 9

(c) *Environmental provisions:* The parties undertake to protect birds in the wild state. With certain exceptions, protection is given to all birds, at least during their breeding season, and to migrants during their return flight to their nesting ground. Species which are in danger of extinction or which are of scientific interest are protected throughout the year.

8. Antarctic Treaty, 1959

(a) *Entry into force:* 1961

(b) *Parties as of December 1977:* 19, including France, the UK, the USA, and the USSR

(c) *Environmental provisions:* The parties undertake to use Antarctica for peaceful purposes only. Prohibited, *inter alia,* are any measures of a military nature, such as the establishment of military bases and fortifications, the carrying out of military manoeuvres, as well as the testing of any type of weapons. Any nuclear explosions in Antarctica and the disposal there of radioactive waste material is prohibited.

(d) *Note:* The parties undertake to meet at suitable intervals in order to consult, *inter alia,* on measures regarding preservation and conservation of living resources in Antarctica.

9. Treaty banning nuclear weapon tests in the atmosphere, in outer space and under water (Partial Test Ban Treaty), 1963

(a) *Entry into force:* 1963

(b) *Parties as of December 1977:* 106, including the UK, the USA, and the USSR

(c) *Environmental provisions:* The parties undertake to prohibit, to prevent, and not to carry out any nuclear weapon test explosion, or any other nuclear explosion, at any place under their jurisdiction or control: *(a)* in the atmosphere; beyond its limits, including outer space; or under water, including territorial waters or high seas; or *(b)* in any other environment if such explosion causes radioactive debris to be present outside the territorial limits of the state under whose jurisdiction or control such explosion is conducted.

10. Treaty on principles governing the activities of states in the exploration and use of outer space, including the moon and other celestial bodies (Outer Space Treaty), 1967

  (a) Entry into force: 1967

  (b) Parties as of December 1977: 75, including France, the UK, the USA, and the USSR

  (c) Environmental provisions: The parties undertake not to place in orbit around the Earth any objects carrying nuclear weapons or any other kinds of weapons of mass destruction, not to install such weapons on celestial bodies, or to station such weapons in outer space in any other manner. The Moon and other celestial bodies shall be used exclusively for peaceful purposes. The establishment of military bases, installations and fortifications, the testing of any type of weapons and the conduct of military manoeuvres on celestial bodies are forbidden. The parties also undertake to avoid the harmful contamination of outer space, including the Moon and other celestial bodies, and also to avoid causing adverse changes in the environment of the Earth resulting from the introduction of extraterrestrial matter.

11. Treaty for the prohibition of nuclear weapons in Latin America (Treaty of Tlatelolco), 1967

  (a) Entry into force: 1968

  (b) Parties as of December 1977: 27, including China, France, the UK, and the USA

  (c) Environmental provisions: The parties undertake to use exclusively for peaceful purposes the nuclear material and facilities which are under their jurisdiction, and to prohibit and prevent in their respective territories: *(a)* the testing, use, manufacture, production, or acquisition by any means whatsoever of any nuclear weapons; and *(b)* the receipt, storage, installation, deployment, and any form of possession of nuclear weapons.

12. Treaty on the non-proliferation of nuclear weapons (Non-Proliferation Treaty), 1968

  (a) Entry into force: 1970

  (b) Parties as of December 1977: 103, including the UK, the USA, and the USSR

  (c) Environmental provisions: The nuclear-weapon parties undertake not to transfer to any recipient whatsoever nuclear weapons or other nuclear explosive devices; and not in any way to assist, encourage, or induce any non-nuclear-weapon state to acquire them. The non-nuclear-weapon parties undertake not to receive the transfer from any transferor whatsoever of nuclear weapons or other nuclear explosive devices; not to manufacture or otherwise acquire them; and not to seek or receive any assistance in their manufacture.

13. Treaty on the prohibition of the emplacement of nuclear weapons and other weapons of mass destruction on the sea-bed and the ocean floor and in the subsoil thereof (Sea-Bed Treaty), 1971

  (a) Entry into force: 1972

  (b) Parties as of December 1977: 63, including the UK, the USA, and the USSR

  (c) Environmental provisions: The parties undertake not to emplant or emplace on the sea-bed and the ocean floor and in the subsoil thereof beyond the outer limit of a sea-bed zone of 22 kilometres any nuclear weapons or other types of weapons of mass destruction as well as structures, launching installations or any other facilities specifically designed for storing, testing, or using such weapons.

14. Convention on the prohibition of the development, production and stockpiling of bacteriological (biological) and toxin weapons and on their destruction, 1972

  (a) Entry into force: 1975

  (b) Parties as of December 1977: 74, including the UK, the USA, and the USSR

  (c) Environmental provisions: The parties undertake never in any circumstances to develop, produce, stockpile, or otherwise acquire or retain: *(a)* microbial or other biological agents, or toxins whatever their origin or method of production, of types and in quantities that have no justification for prophylactic, protective, or other peaceful purposes; and *(b)* weapons, equipment, or means of delivery designed to use such agents or toxins for hostile purposes or in armed conflict.

15. Convention concerning the protection of the world cultural and natural heritage, 1972

(a) *Entry into force:* 1975

(b) *Parties as of May 1978:* 36, including France and the USA

(c) *Environmental provisions:* The parties undertake to establish a list of world natural heritages selected from among many put forth by the individual parties. The parties undertake not to take any deliberate measures which might damage these directly or indirectly. The parties further undertake to establish a second list of endangered world natural heritages selected from among any put forth by the individual parties from among the first list. These shall include only those threatened by serious and specific dangers, such as the outbreak or the threat of an armed conflict. The parties shall publicize the natural heritages in danger and assist in their protection, conservation, preservation, or rehabilitation. Natural heritages are defined as : (a) natural features consisting of physical and biological formations or groups of such formations, which are of outstanding universal value from the aesthetic or scientific point of view; (b) geological and physiographical formations and precisely delineated areas which constitute the habitat of threatened species of animals and plants of outstanding universal value from the point of view of science or conservation; or (c) natural sites or precisely delineated natural areas of outstanding universal value from the point of view of science, conservation, or natural beauty.

16. Convention on the prohibition of military or any other hostile use of environmental modification techniques, 1977

(a) *Entry into force:* 1978

(b) *Parties as of December 1978:* 20, including the UK and the USSR

(c) *Environmental provisions:* The parties undertake not to engage in military or any other hostile use of environmental modification techniques having widespread, long-lasting, or severe effects as the means of destruction, damage, or injury to any other state party to the convention. The term 'environmental modification technique' refers to any technique for changing—through the deliberate manipulation of natural processes—the dynamics, composition, or structure of the Earth, including its biota, lithosphere, hydrosphere, and atmosphere, or of outer space.

17. Geneva Protocol additional to the Geneva Convention of 12 August 1949, and relating to the protection of victims of international armed conflicts (Protocol I), 1977

(a) *Entry into force:* 1978

(b) *Parties as of December 1978:* 3

(c) *Environmental provisions:* The parties undertake not to make civilian objects the object of attack or of reprisals. Attacks shall be limited strictly to military objectives. Starvation of civilians as a method of warfare is prohibited. It is prohibited to attack, destroy, remove, or render useless objects indispensable to the survival of the civilian population, such as foodstuffs, agricultural areas for the production of foodstuffs, crops, livestock, drinking-water installations and supplies, and irrigation wqrks, for the specific purpose of denying them for their sustenance value to the civilian population or to the adverse party, whatever the motive, whether in order to starve out civilians, to cause them to move away, or for any other motive. Objects indispensable for the survival of the civilian population shall not be made the object of reprisals. Care shall be taken to protect the natural environment against widespread, long-term, and severe damage. This protection includes a prohibition of the use of methods or means of warfare which are intended or may be expected to cause such damage to the natural environment and thereby to prejudice the health or survival of the population. Attacks against the natural environment by way of reprisals are prohibited. With certain exceptions, works or installations containing dangerous forces—namely, dams, dikes, and nuclear electrical generating stations—shall not be made the object of attack, even when these objects are military objectives, if such attack may cause the release of dangerous forces and consequent severe losses among the civilian population. Other military objectives located at or in the vicinity of these works or installations shall not be made the object of attack if such attack may cause the release of dangerous forces from the works or installations and consequent severe losses among the civilian population. It is prohibited to make any of the works, installations, or military objectives that may cause the release of these dangerous forces the object of reprisals. Indiscriminate attacks—those not directed at a specific military objective—are prohibited, including, *inter alia,* an attack by bombardment which treats as a single military objective a number of clearly separated military objectives located in a city, town, or village. It is prohibited to attack, by any means whatsoever, non-defended localities.

18. Geneva Protocol additional to the Geneva Conventions of 12 August 1949, and relating to the protection of victims of non-international armed conflicts (Protocol II), 1977

 (a) Entry into force: 1978

 (b) Parties as of December 1978: 3

 (c) Environmental provisions: The parties undertake not to make the civilian population as such the object of attack. Starvation of civilians as a method of combat is prohibited. It is therefore prohibited to attack, destroy, remove, or render useless, for that purpose, objects indispensable to the survival of the civilian population, such as foodstuffs, agricultural areas for the production of foodstuffs, crops, livestock, drinking-water installations and supplies, and irrigation works. Works or installations containing dangerous forces—namely, dams, dikes, and nuclear electrical generating stations—shall not be made the object of attack, even where these objects are military objectives, if such attack may cause the release of dangerous forces and consequent severe losses among the civilian population. The displacement of the civilian population shall not be ordered for reasons related to the conflict unless the security of the civilians involved or imperative military reasons so demand.

Sources and notes:
[a]For the texts (and discussions) of these treaties, see ACDA (1977); Dupuy & Hammerman (1973); Kristoferson (1975 a); Rosenblad (1974); Schindler & Toman (1973); SIPRI (1978 b); *UN Disarmament Yearbook 1977:* Supplement, Vol. II; and UNEP (1977–1978). See also appendix 8.3.
[b]The number of parties include all those nations that have ratified or acceded to the treaty and which are among the 159 nations in existence today (appendix 1.4). Any of the five permanent members of the UN Security Council—China, France, the UK, the USA, and the USSR—are listed by name.

Appendix 8.1

Sources for the relationship between natural resources and military activities

The fact that international instabilities—and thus wars—result from limited and unequally distributed natural resources (raw materials) has been examined in recent years by Brown (1972; 1978), Falk (1971), Heilbroner (1974), Kemp (1977–1978), Myrdal (1957), Schwab (1976), Shields & Ott (1974), Sprout & Sprout (1957; 1965), Ward (1962), and by many others. This relationship between war and raw materials has also been a subject of interest in the past, largely as a response to World War I. Among the studies of note are those by Clark (1931), Emeny (1934), Leith (1931), Leith *et al.* (1943), and Robbins (1939).

The importance to a nation's military might of having access to a forest (timber) resource has been examined for ancient times by Winters (1974), for the pre-twentieth century British Navy by Albion (1926), and for the early years of the USA by Dana (1956: chap. 1) and Ise (1920). The timber problems of the United Kingdom during World War II have been described by House (1965), and of the United States by Steen (1977: chap. 10).

Discussions of the *tactical* significance of forests include those by Army (1962), Clausewitz (1832–1834: 426–427, 530–531), Demorlaine (1919), Lesseux (1916), Mammen (1916), Peltier & Pearcy (1966), Ridsdale (1919 c), and Schultze (1915).

Appendix 8.2

Sources for nature conservation

1. *Justifications for nature conservation.* An immense literature is available on the conservation of nature. Brown (1978), Commoner (1971), Dasmann (1972), Eckholm (1976), Ehrenfeld (1972), and Ehrlich *et al.* (1977) provide a variety of excellent overviews. Perhaps the best brief review available on the necessity for conserving nature is the excellent recent essay by Ehrenfeld (1976). The specific problem of species in danger of extinction and justifications for attempting to save them—and thus their habitats—have been dealt with by Curry-Lindahl (1972), Fisher *et al.* (1969), Greenway (1967), Myers (1976), Ziswiler (1967), and others. Passmore (1974: Part 1) provides a succinct history of man's relationship to nature. Burr (1975), Lilly (1976), Stone (1972), and others explore the legal status of animals and of nature in general, Stone's work being a seminal exposition of the subject. Westman (1977) provides an interesting discussion of the economic values of natural ecosystems. Shepard (1978) develops the theme that wildlife is crucial to the development of the human psyche, and Ratcliffe (1976) that wildlife is needed for its continued well-being. Tunnard (1978) reaches a similar conclusion regarding the beauty of nature. Halliday (1978) justifies the conservation of species on the basis that animal extinctions are symptomatic of man's excessive exploitation of his own environment.

2. *Bases of the conservation crisis.* The historical, religious, and cultural roots of the conservation crisis have been ably illuminated by Moncrief (1970), Passmore (1974), Toynbee (1972), White (1967), and others.

Appendix 8.3

Sources for arms control as it applies to the environment

Contributions to the literature dealing with arms control as it applies to ecology or to the environment have been made by Bach (1971), Blix (1974), Falk (1973; 1974), Goldblat (1975 *b*; 1977), Israelyan (1974), Johnstone (1970–1971), Mudge (1969–1970), Ramberg (1978), Rosenblad (1973; 1977), Schneider (1976), *SIPRI Yearbook 1978*: chap. 13, Thorsson (1975), *UN Disarmament Yearbook 1976*: chap. 13, Verwey (1977), and Westing (1971–1972; 1974). For references to relevant documents, see table 8.4, note *a*. International environmental law in general has been covered by Bleicher (1972), Levin (1977), Taubenfeld (1973), Teclaff & Utton (1974), and others.

References

Aarkrog, A., 1971. Radioecological investigations of plutonium in an arctic marine environment. *Health Physics*, **20**: 31–47.

Aartsen, J. P. v., 1946. Consequences of the war on agriculture in the Netherlands. *Int. Rev. Agric.*, **37**: 5S–34S, 49S–70S, 108S–123S.

ACDA (Arms Control and Disarmament Agency, US), 1972. *Economic Impact of Reductions in Defense Spending*. Washington: US ACDA Publication No. 64, 31 pp.

ACDA (Arms Control and Disarmament Agency, US), 1976. *World Military Expenditures and Arms Transfers 1966–1975*. Washington: US ACDA Publication No. 90, 85 pp.

ACDA (Arms Control and Disarmament Agency, US), 1977. *Arms Control and Disarmament Agreements: Texts and History of Negotiations*. Washington: US ACDA Publication No. 94, 187 pp.

Ackefors, H., 1977. Production of fish and other animals in the sea. *Ambio*, **6**: 192–200, 294a.

Adams, S., 1975. Vietnam cover-up: playing war with numbers. *Harper's*, **250** (1500): 41–44, 62, 64, 65–66, 68, 70, 71–73.

Adams, W. A., 1972. Nerve gas—isopropyl methylphosphonofluoridate (GB)—decomposition and hydrostatic pressure on the ocean floor. *Environmental Science and Technology*, **6**: 928.

Agence Presse Gouvernement Provisoire, 1972. [War crimes by the U.S. and their puppets in the "Vietnamization" of the war: the crimes committed during 3 years of "rural pacification" by the U.S.] *Bull. d'Information du Gouvernement Révolutionnaire Provisoire de la République du Sud Viet Nam (Paris)*, **5** (165–166): 11–16. In French.

AID (Agency for International Development, US), 1977. *Selected Economic Data for the Less Developed Countries*. Washington: US AID Publication No. RC–W–136, 7 pp.

Air University Quarterly Review, 1953–1954. Attack on the irrigation dams in North Korea. *Air Univ. Quart. Rev.* (now *Air Univ. Rev.*), **6** (4): 40–61.

Albion, R. G., 1926. *Forests and Sea Power: The Timber Problem of the Royal Navy, 1652–1862*. (Harvard Univ. Press, Cambridge, Mass.), 485 pp. + pl.

Alland, A., Jr., 1967. War and disease: an anthropological perspective. *Natural History*, **76** (10): 58–61, 70.

Allee, W. C. and Schmidt, K. P., 1951. *Ecological Animal Geography*. 2nd Edn. (J. Wiley, New York), 715 pp.

Allen, D. L., 1962. *Our Wildlife Legacy*. Rev. ed. (Funk & Wagnalls, New York), 422 pp. + pl.

Allred, D. M., Beck, D. E. and Jorgensen, C. D., 1965. Summary of the ecological effects of nuclear testing on native animals at the Nevada test site. *Proc. Utah Acad. Scis., Arts and Ltrs.*, **42**: 252–260.

American Forestry, 1915. Forests in the war zone. *Amer. Forestry* (now *Amer. Forests*), **21**: 909–910.

Andreski, S., 1971. Evolution and war. *Science J.*, **7** (1): 89–92.

Anikouchine, W. A. and Sternberg, R. W., 1973. *World Ocean: An Introduction to Oceanography*. (Prentice-Hall, Englewood Cliffs, New Jersey), 338 pp.

Antonov, A. N., 1947. Children born during the siege of Leningrad in 1942. *J. Pediatrics*, **30**: 250–259.

Aplin, J. A., 1947. Effect of explosives on marine life. *Cal. Fish and Game*, **33**: 23–30.

Araldsén, O. P., 1967. Soviet Union and the Arctic. *U.S. Naval Inst. Proc.*, **93** (6): 48–57.

Arena, V., 1971. *Ionizing Radiation and Life*. (C. V. Mosby, St. Louis, Missouri), 543 pp.

Armed Forces Journal International, 1975. Culebra almost still. *Armed Forces J. Int., Washington, D.C.*, **112** (12): 6.

Army, US Dept. of the, 1956. *Law of Land Warfare*. US Dept. Army Field Manual No. 27–10, 236 pp.

Army, US Dept. of the, 1962. *Barriers and Denial Operations*. US Dept. Army Field Manual No. 31–10, 128 pp.

Army, US Dept. of the, 1975. *Scandinavia: A Bibliographic Survey of Literature*. US Dept. Army Pamphlet No. 550–18, 121 pp. + 6 maps.

Army and Air Force, US Depts. of the, 1967. *Military Chemistry and Chemical Agents*. US Dept. Army Technical Manual No. 3–215, 101 + 9 + 7 pp. + 2 tables.

Asimov, I., 1975. *Ends of the Earth: The Polar Regions of the World* (Weybright and Talley, New York), 363 pp.

AP (Associated Press), 1974. Old bomb kills 3 in Japan. *New York Times* (3 March 1974), p. 13.

Audy, J. R., 1948. Some ecological effects of deforestation and settlement. *Malayan Nature J.*, 4 (4): 178–189 + 3 figures.

Bach, M. 1975. [Machine-gunned forests in Lorraine.] *Rev. Forestière Française*. 27: 217–222. In French.

Bach, Pham Van, 1971. Law and the use of chemical warfare in Vietnam. *Scientific World*, 15 (6): 12–14.

Baes, C. F., Jr., Goeller, H. E., Olson, J. S. and Rotty, R. M., 1977. Carbon dioxide and climate: the uncontrolled experiment. *Amer. Scientist*, 65: 310–320.

Bahrenburg, B., 1971. *Pacific: Then and Now*. (G.P. Putnam's Sons, New York), 318 pp. + 32 pl.

Baines, G., 1970–1971. Nuclear games in the south Pacific. *Ecologist*, London, 1 (18): 9–11.

Baker, H. G., 1945. Late flowering of horse-chestnut. *Nature*, London, 156: 721.

Baker, R. H., 1946. Some effects of the war on the wildlife of Micronesia. *Trans. N. Amer. Wildlife Conf.*, 11: 205–213.

Banerjee, P. K. *et al.*, 1975. *Reduction of the Military Budgets of States Permanent Members of the Security Council by 10 Per Cent and Utilization of Part of the Funds thus Saved to Provide Assistance to Developing Countries*. (United Nations, New York), 40 pp.

Barrau, J. *et al.*, 1973. *Program on Man and the Biosphere (MAB). VII. Ecology and Rational Use of Island Ecosystems*. (UNESCO MAB Report, Ser. No. 11, Paris), 80 pp.

Baumann, G., 1962. The Arctic: strategic center of the world, *Military Rev.*, 42 (12): 85–97.

Baxter, S. B., 1966. *William III and the Defense of European Liberty 1650–1702*. (Harcourt, Brace & World, New York), 462 pp. + 8 pl.

Beck, N. L., 1970. Rice krispies nipped in bud. *Marine Corps Gaz.*, 54 (3): 50.

Beckwith, S. L., 1954. Ecological succession on abandoned farm lands and its relationship to wildlife management. *Ecological Monogr.*, 24: 349–376.

Becton, W. R. and Maunder, E. R., 1972–1973. Military forestry in France after 1944. *Forest History*, 16 (3): 38–43.

Behrens, W. W., Jr., 1971–1972. Environmental considerations in naval operations. *Naval War Coll. Rev.*, 24 (1): 70–77.

Bellamy, D. S., Clarke, P. H., John, D. M., Jones, D., Whittick, A. and Darke, T., 1967. Effects of pollution from the *Torrey Canyon* on littoral and sublittoral ecosystems. *Nature*, 216: 1170–1173.

Benoit, E., 1977–1978. Growth and defense in developing countries. *Economic Development and Cultural Change*, Chicago, 26: 271–280.

Bensley, C. J. F., 1951. Mollusca on the city bombed sites. *London Naturalist*, 31: 83–84.

Bensley, C. J. F., 1954. Fresh-water mollusca of the bomb-craters and gun-pits on Bookham Common. *London Naturalist,* **34:** 22–28.

Berger, C. (ed.), 1977. *United States Air Force in Southeast Asia, 1961–1973.* (US Air Force Office of Air Force History, Washington), 381 pp.

Berrill, M., 1966. Stillness on Eniwetok. *Natural History,* **75** (10): 20–25, 70.

Betts, R. and Denton, F., 1967. *Evaluation of Chemical Crop Destruction in Vietnam.* (Rand Corp. Memo. No. RM–5446–ISA/ARPA, Santa Monica, Cal.), 13 + 34 pp.

Bidinian, L. J., 1976. *Combined Allied Offensive Against the German Civilian 1942–1945.* (Coronado Press, Lawrence, Kansas), 284 pp. + 44 pl.

Bigelow, M. A., 1943. Are war marriages eugenic? *J. Heredity,* **34:** 123.

Biles, R. E., 1972. *Bombing as a Policy Tool in Vietnam: Effectiveness.* (US Senate Comm. on Foreign Relations, Pentagon Papers Staff Study No. 5), 29 pp.

Birch, H. G. and Gussow, J. D., 1970. *Disadvantaged Children: Health, Nutrition, & School Failure.* (Harcourt, Brace & World, New York), 322 pp.

Björnerstedt, R. *et al.,* 1973. *Napalm and Other Incendiary Weapons and All Aspects of Their Possible Use.* (United Nations, New York), 63 pp.

Blakesley, P. H. and Thompson, C., 1971–1972. Great white silence. *Int. J. Environmental Studies,* London, **2:** 153–159, 203–210.

Blanton, S., 1919. Mental and nervous changes in the children of the Volksschulen of Trier, Germany, caused by malnutrition. *Mental Hygiene,* **3:** 343–386.

Blechman, B. M., and Kaplan, S. S., 1977–1978. Use of the armed forces as a political instrument. *Naval War College Rev.,* **30** (4): 80–87.

Bleicher, S. A., 1972. Overview of international environmental regulation. *Ecology Law Quart.,* Berkeley, Cal., **2:** 1–90.

Bliss, L. C. and Wein, R. W., 1972. Plant community responses to disturbances in the western Canadian arctic. *Canad. J. Botany,* **50:** 1097–1109.

Blix, H., 1974. Current efforts to prohibit the use of certain conventional weapons. *Instant* [now *Current*] *Research on Peace and Violence,* **4:** 21–30.

Blok, P. J., 1907. *History of the People of the Netherlands. IV. Frederick Henry, John de Witt, William III* [translated from the Dutch by O. A. Bierstadt]. (G. P. Putnam's Sons, New York), 566 pp. + 3 maps.

Blumer, M., Sanders, H. L., Grassle, J. F. and Hampson, G. R., 1971. Small oil spill. *Environment,* **13** (2): 2–12.

Blumer, M. and Sass, J., 1972. Oil pollution: persistence and degradation of spilled fuel oil. *Science,* **176:** 1120–1122.

Bodart, G., 1916. *Losses of Life in Modern Wars: Austria–Hungary; France.* (Clarendon, Oxford), 156 pp.

Boesch, D. F., Hershner, C. H. and Milgram, J. H., 1974. *Oil Spills and the Marine Environment.* (Ballinger Publishing Co., Cambridge, Mass.), 115 pp.

Boffey, P. M., 1969. Biological warfare: is the Smithsonian really a "cover"? *Science,* **163:** 791–796.

Boldt, J. R., Jr. and Queneau, P., 1967. *Winning of Nickel: Its Geology, Mining, and Extractive Metallurgy.* (D. Van Nostrand, Princeton, New Jersey), 487 pp. + pl.

Bolin, B., 1977. Changes of land biota and their importance for the carbon cycle. *Science,* **196:** 613–615.

Bondar, B. and Bobey, P. J., 1974. Should we eat krill? *Ecologist,* **4:** 265–266.

Bouillenne, R., 1962. Man, the destroying biotype. *Science,* **135:** 706–712.

Boulding, K. E., 1962. *Conflict and Defense: A General Theory.* (Harper & Row, New York), 349 pp.

Bourneuf, A., 1958. *Norway: The Planned Revival*. (Harvard Univ. Press, Cambridge, Mass.), 233 pp.

Boxhall, P. G., 1966. Strategic use of islands in a troubled ocean. *J. Royal United Service Institution*, London, **111**: 336–341.

Branfman, F. (ed.), 1972. *Voices from the Plain of Jars: Life Under an Air War*. (Harper & Row, New York), 160 pp.

Bremer, S., Singer, J. D. and Luterbacher, U., 1973–1974. Population density and war proneness of European nations, 1816–1965. *Comparative Political Studies* **6**: 329–348.

Briggs, J. C., 1969. Sea-level Panama canal: potential biological catastrophe. *BioScience*, **19**: 44–47.

Brittain, V., 1944. *Seed of Chaos: What Mass Bombing Really Means*. (New Vision Publishing Co., London), 119 pp.

Broecker, W. S., Takahashi, T., Simpson, H. J. and Peng, T-H., 1979. Fate of fossil fuel carbon dioxide and the global carbon budget. *Science*, **206**: 409–418.

Brook, M., 1967. *Life of the Mountains*. (McGraw-Hill, New York), 232 pp.

Brookfield, H. C. and Hart, D., 1971. *Melanesia: A Geographical Interpretation of an Island World*. (Methuen, London), 464 pp. + 24 pl.

Brouillard, K. D., 1970. *Fishery Development Survey: South Vietnam*. (U.S. Agency International Development, Saigon), 41 pp.

Brown, L. R., 1972. *World Without Borders*. (Random House, New York), 395 pp.

Brown, L. R., 1978. *Twenty-ninth Day: Accommodating Human Needs and Numbers to the Earth's Resources*. (W. W. Norton, New York), 363 pp.

Brown, N. C., 1919 *a*. Forest losses on the Italian front. *Amer. Forestry* (now *Amer. Forests*), **23**: 1315–1328.

Brown, N. C., 1919 *b*. Forestry and the war in Italy. *J. Forestry*, **17**: 408–412.

Brown, R. W., Johnston, R. S. and Johnson, D. A., 1978. Rehabilitation of alpine tundra disturbances. *Journal of Soil and Water Conservation*, **33**: 154–160.

Browne, M. W., 1975. European bison, once near extinction, now a big herd in Polish–Soviet forest. *New York Times* (29 December 1975), p. 2.

Brünig, E. F., 1977. Tropical rain forest: a wasted asset or an essential biospheric resource? *Ambio*, **6**: 187–191.

Buchanan, R. E. and Gibbons, N. E. (eds), 1974. *Bergey's Manual of Determinative Bacteriology*. 8th Edn. (Williams & Wilkins, Baltimore), 1246 pp.

Buckman, H. O. and Brady, N. C., 1969. *Nature and Property of Soils*. 7th Edn. (Macmillan, New York), 653 pp. + 1 figure.

Budowski, G., 1956. Tropical savannas, a sequence of forest felling and repeated burnings. *Turrialba*, **6** (1–2): 23–33.

Bureau of Sport Fisheries and Wildlife, US, 1973. *Threatened Wildlife of the United States*. Rev. edn. (US Bureau of Sport Fisheries and Wildlife Resource Publication No. 114), 289 pp.

Burke, W. T., *et al.*, 1969. *Towards a Better Use of the Ocean: Contemporary Legal Problems in Ocean Development*. (Almqvist & Wiksell, Stockholm), 231 pp.

Burnet, M. and White, D. O., 1972. *Natural History of Infectious Disease*. 4th Edn. (Cambridge, England), 278 pp.

Burr, S. I., 1975. Toward legal rights for animals. *Environmental Affairs*, **4**: 205–254.

Buttrick, P. L., 1917. Forester at the fighting front. *Amer. Forestry* (now *Amer. Forests*), **23**: 710–716.

Cagle, M. W. and Manson, F. A., 1957. *Sea War in Korea.* (US Naval Inst., Annapolis), 555 pp. + photos.

Cairns, J., Jr., Dickson, K. L. and Herricks, E. E. (eds), 1977. *Recovery and Restoration of Damaged Ecosystems.* (Univ. Press of Virginia, Charlottesville), 531 pp.

Cameron, A. W., 1975–1976. Strategic significance of the Pacific islands: a new debate begins. *Orbis, Philadelphia,* **19**: 1012–1036.

Cameron, I., 1972. *Impossible Dream: The Building of the Panama Canal.* (Wm. Morrow, New York), 284 pp. + 8 pl.

Campbell, W. J. and Martin, S., 1973. Oil and ice in the Arctic Ocean: possible large-scale interactions. *Science,* **181**: 56–58; **186**: 843–846.

Canfield, C. J., 1972. Malaria in U.S. military personnel 1965–1971. *Proc. Helminthological Soc., Washington,* **39** (Special Issue): 15–18.

Carlozzi, C. A., 1972. Ecological overview of Caribbean development programs. In: Farvar, M. T. and Milton, J. P. (eds), *Careless Technology: Ecology and International Development.* (Natural History Press, Garden City, New York), 1 030 pp. + pl.: pp. 858–868.

Carlquist, S., 1965. *Island Life: A Natural History of the Islands of the World.* (Natural History Press, Garden City, New York), 451 pp.

Carlquist, S., 1974. *Island Biology.* (Columbia University Press, New York), 660 pp.

Carlson, W. S., 1962. *Lifelines Through the Arctic.* (Duell, Sloan & Pearce, New York), 271 pp. + 8 pl.

Carneiro, R. L., 1970. Theory of the origin of the state. *Science,* **169**: 733–738.

Carpenter, J. R., 1940. Grassland biome. *Ecological Monographs,* **10**: 617–684.

Carrier, J. M., 1974. *Effects of Herbicides in South Vietnam. B[4]. Estimating the Highlander Population Affected by Herbicides.* (National Acad. Sciences, Washington), 13 pp.

Carr-Saunders, A. M., 1928–1929. Biology and war. *Foreign Affairs,* **7**: 427–438.

Carson, R. L., 1961. *Sea Around Us.* Rev. edn. (Oxford Univ. Press, New York), 237 pp. + 16 pl.

Carter, V. G. and Dale, T., 1974. *Topsoil and Civilization.* Rev. edn. (Univ. Oklahoma Press, Norman), 292 pp. + pl.

Carthy, J. D. and Arthur, D. R. (eds), 1968. Biological effects of oil pollution on littoral communities. *Field Studies,* London, **2** (supplement): 1–198 + pl.

Cartwright, F. F. and Biddiss, M. D., 1972. *Disease and History.* (T. Y. Crowell, New York), 248 pp.

Casella, A., 1978 *a.* Dateline Vietnam: managing the peace. *Foreign Policy,* **1978** (30): 170-191.

Casella, A., 1978 *b.* Vietnam and Cambodia: basic incompatibility. *New York Times* (31 March 1978), p. A27.

Castell, C. P., 1944. Ponds and their vegetation. *London Naturalist,* **24**: 15–22.

Castell, C. P., 1954. Bomb-crater ponds of Bookham Common. *London Naturalist,* **34**: 16–21 + 2 figures.

Caterini, D. J., 1977. Repeating ourselves: the Philippine insurrection and the Vietnam war. *Foreign Service J.* Washington, **54** (12): 11–17, 31–32.

Caulfield, M. W. *et al.,* 1974. *Socio-economic Study of Tinian, Mariana Islands District, Trust Territory of the Pacific Islands.* (Univ. of Hawaii, Research Corp., Honolulu), 417 pp.

Ceres, 1975. Face of poverty. *Ceres,* Rome, **8** (3): 18–20.

Ceres, 1976. Seaweed and seaweed products. *Ceres,* Rome, **9** (6): 7, 9.

Chacko, M. E. *et al.,* 1972. *Economic and Social Consequences of the Arms Race and of Military Expenditures.* (United Nations, New York), 51 pp.

Chaliand, G., 1968. *Peasants of North Vietnam* [translated from the French by P. Wiles]. (Penguin Books, Middlesex, England), 244 pp. + 2 maps, 1969.

Chandler, D. G., 1966. *Campaigns of Napoleon*. (Macmillan, New York), 1 172 pp. + 1 map.

Chapman, V. J., 1976. *Mangrove Vegetation*. (J. Cramer, Vaduz), 447 pp. + 36 pl. + 3 maps.

Chapple, J. L., 1971–1972. Expedition to Bernier Island. *Oryx*, London, **11**: 273–274.

Charlier, R. H. and Vigneaux, M., 1974. Towards a rational use of the oceans. *US Naval Inst. Proc.*, **100** (4): 26–41.

Cheney, E. S., 1967. Mineral resources in national and international affairs. *Mining Engineering*, **19** (12): 47–49, 51, 54.

Chesapeake Biological Laboratory, 1948. *Effects of Underwater Explosions on Oysters, Crabs and Fish*. (Maryland Board of Natural Resources, Solomons Island, Chesapeake Bio. Lab. Publication No. 70), 43 pp.

Chevalier, A., 1948. [Biogeography and ecology of the dense ombrophilous forest of the Ivory Coast.] *Rev. Internationale de Botanique Appliquée et d'Agriculture Tropicale* (now *J. d'Agriculture Tropicale et de Botanique Appliquée*), **28**: 101–115. In French.

Child, G., 1970–1971. Wildlife utilization and management in Botswana. *Biological Conservation*, **3**: 18–22.

Chowdhury, A. K. M. A. and Chen, L. C., 1977. *Dynamics of Contemporary Famine*. Dacca, Bangladesh: Ford Foundation Report No. 47, 32 pp.

Christman, D. W. and Clark, W. K., 1978. Foreign energy sources and military power. *Military Rev.*, **58** (2): 3–14.

Clark, J. M., 1931. *Costs of the World War to the American People*. (Yale Univ. Press, New Haven, Conn.), 316 pp. + 1 table.

Clark, R. S. (ed.), 1947. Effect of the war on the stocks of commercial food fishes. *Conseil Permanent International pour l'Exploration de la Mer, Rapports et Procès-Verbaux des Réunions*, **122**: 1–62.

Clark, W. H., 1961. Chemical and thermonuclear explosives. *Bull. Atomic Scientists*, **17**: 356–360.

Clarke, R., 1968. *We All Fall Down: The Prospect of Biological and Chemical Warfare*. (Allen Lane, London), 201 pp. + 2 tables.

Clausewitz, [C.] v., 1832–1834. *On War* [translated from the German by O. J. M. Jolles]. (Infantry Journal Press, Washington), 641 pp., 1950.

Clinton, R. L., 1977. Never-to-be developed countries of Latin America. *Bull. Atomic Scientists*, **33** (8): 19–26.

Cloudsley-Thompson, J. L., 1971–1972. Recent expansion of the Sahara. *International J. Environmental Studies*, **2**: 35–39.

Cloudsley-Thompson, J. L., 1974. Expanding Sahara. *Environmental Conservation*, **1**: 5–13.

Cloudsley-Thompson, J. L., 1975. *Terrestrial Environments*. (Croom Helm, London), 253 pp.

Cloudsley-Thompson, J. L., 1977 *a*. Animal life and desertification. *Environmental Conservation*, **4**: 199–204.

Cloudsley-Thompson, J. L., 1977 *b*. Reclamation of the Sahara. *Environmental Conservation*, **4**: 115–119.

Cloudsley-Thompson, J. L., 1977 *c*. What is an ecodisaster? *Environmental Conservation*, **4**: 66–68.

Cloudsley-Thompson, J. L. and Chadwick, M. J., 1964. *Life in Deserts*. (G. T. Foulis, London), 218 pp. + 43 pl.

Clutterbuck, R. L., 1966. *Long, Long War: Counterinsurgency in Malaya and Vietnam*. (Praeger, New York), 206 pp.

Coast Guard, US, 1976. *Liquefied Natural Gas: Views & Practices, Policy and Safety*. (Washington: US Coast Guard Publication No. CG-478), 68 pp.

Coates, A., 1970. *Western Pacific Islands.* (Her Majesty's Stationery Office, London), 349 pp. + pl.

Cohen, C., 1973. Military engineering in the Sinai desert. *Military Engineer,* **65:** 379–381.

Coker, C. M. and Hollis, E. H., 1950. Fish mortality caused by a series of heavy explosions in Chesapeake Bay. *J. Wildlife Management,* **14:** 435–444 + 1 pl.

Colman, J. S., 1949. Newfoundland seal fishery and the second world war. *J. Animal Ecology,* **18:** 40–46.

Comar, C. L. *et al.,* 1972. *Effects on Populations of Exposure to Low Levels of Ionizing Radiation.* (National Acad. Sciences, Washington), 217 pp.

Commoner, B., *Closing Circle: Nature, Man, and Technology.* (A. A. Knopf, New York), 326 pp.

Conard, R. A. *et al.,* 1975. *Twenty-Year Review of Medical Findings in a Marshallese Population Accidentally Exposed to Radioactive Fallout.* (Brookhaven National Lab. Publication No. BNL50424, Upton, New York), 154 pp.

Cook, B. W., 1975. American justifications for military massacres from the Pequot War to Mylai. *Peace & Change,* **3** (2–3): 4–20.

Cooper, C. F., 1977–1978. What might man-induced climate change mean? *Foreign Affairs,* **56:** 500–520.

Cottrell, A. J. and Moorer, T. H., 1977. U.S. overseas bases: problems of projecting American military power abroad. *Washington Papers,* **5** (47), 67 pp.

Coulter, J. W., 1946. Impact of the war on South Sea Islands. *Geographical Rev.,* **36:** 409–419.

Council on Economic Priorities, 1970. *Efficiency in Death: The Manufacturers of Anti-personnel Weapons.* (Harper & Row, New York), 233 pp.

Council on Environmental Quality, US, 1970. *Ocean Dumping: A National Policy.* (Washington: US Council on Environmental Quality), 45 pp.

Courson, M., 1972. Kahoolawe: island of death. *Amer. Forests,* **78** (5): 16–19.

Croat, T. B., 1972. Role of overpopulation and agricultural methods in the destruction of tropical ecosystems. *BioScience,* **22:** 465–467.

Cross, J. P., 1971. Jungle warfare. *Army Quarterly & Defence J.,* London, **101:** 323–329.

Currie, P. W. E., 1949. Some notes on the birds of the bombed sites. *London Naturalist,* **29:** 81–84.

Currie, P. W. E., 1951. Sawflies of the Cripplegate bombed sites. *London Naturalist,* **31:** 89–91.

Curry-Lindahl, K., 1971–1972. War and the white rhinos. *Oryx,* London, **11:** 236–267.

Curry-Lindahl, K., 1972. *Let Them Live: A Worldwide Survey of Animals Threatened with Extinction.* (Wm. Morrow, New York), 394 pp.

Curry-Lindahl, K., 1974. Conservation problems and progress in equatorial African countries. *Environmental Conservation,* **1:** 111–122.

Cushing, D. H., 1975. *Marine Ecology and Fisheries.* (Cambridge University Press, Cambridge, England), 278 pp.

Czapowskyj, M. M., 1976. *Annotated Bibliography on the Ecology and Reclamation of Drastically Disturbed Areas.* (US Forest Service General Techn. Report No. NE-21), 98 pp.

Daalder, H., 1962. *Role of the Military in the Emerging Countries.* (Mouton, The Hague), 25 pp.

Dacre, J. C. and Rosenblatt, D. H., 1974. *Mammalian Toxicology and Toxicity to Aquatic Organisms of Four Important Types of Waterborne Munitions Pollutants: An Extensive Literature Evaluation.* (US Army Medical Research & Development Command Techn. Report No. 7403, Aberdeen Proving Ground, Maryland), 176 pp.

Dana, S. T., 1914. French forests in the war zone. *Amer. Forestry* (now *Amer. Forests*), **20**: 769–785.

Dana, S. T., 1956. *Forest and Range Policy: Its Development in the United States.* (McGraw-Hill, New York), 455 pp.

Darwin, C., 1859. *On the Origin of Species by Means of Natural Selection: Or the Preservation of Favoured Races in the Struggle for Life.* (John Murray, London), 490 pp. + 1 figure, (Harvard Univ. Press, Cambridge, Mass.), 502 pp. + 1 figure, 1964.

Dasmann, R. F., 1972. *Environmental Conservation,* 3rd Edn. (John Wiley, New York), 473 pp.

Dasmann, R. F., Milton, J. P. and Freeman, P. H., 1973. *Ecological Principles for Economic Development.* (John Wiley, New York), 252 pp.

Davis, G. M., 1974. *Effects of Herbicides in South Vietnam. B [6]. Mollusks as Indicators of the Effects of Herbicides on Mangroves in South Vietnam.* (US National Acad. Sciences, Washington), 29 pp.

Davis, J. H., Jr., 1939–1940. Ecology and geologic rôle of mangroves in Florida. *Papers Tortugas Lab.,* **32**: 303–412 + 12 plates + 2 maps.

Davis, K. P., 1966. *Forest Management: Regulation and Valuation.* 2nd Edn. (McGraw-Hill, New York), 519 pp.

Defense, US Dept. of, 1968. *United States–Vietnam Relations, 1945–1967.* US House Representatives Comm. on Armed Services, 12 vols, 1971.

Defense, US Dept. of, 1976. Maintaining defense efficiency with minimal impact on man and environment. *Commanders Digest,* **19** (23): 3–8.

Dellums, R. V. (ed.), 1972. Escalation, American options, and President Nixon's war moves. *US Congressional Record,* **118**: 16748–16836.

Demorlaine, J., 1919. [Strategic importance of forests and the war.] *Revue des Eaux et Forêts,* **57**: 25–30. In French.

Descheneau, T. E., 1977. New central front. *US Naval Inst. Proc.,* **103** (9): 38–46.

Desowitz, R. S., Berman, S. J., Gubler, D. J., Harinasuta, C., Guptavanij, P. and Vasuvat, C. 1974. *Effects of Herbicides in South Vietnam. B[7]. Epidemiological–ecological Effects: Studies on Intact and Deforested Mangrove Ecosystems.* (National Acad. Sciences, Washington), 54 pp.

Development and Resources Corp., 1969. *The Five Northern Provinces of the Republic of Vietnam: A Profile of Agriculture.* (Devel. & Resources Corp., New York), 168 + 14 pp.

DeVore, R. M., 1976. *Arab–Israeli Conflict: A Historical, Political, Social, & Military Bibliography.* (Clio Books, Santa Barbara, Cal.), 273 pp.

Diamond, J. M., 1974. Colonization of exploded volcanic islands by birds: the supertramp strategy. *Science,* **184**: 803–806.

Dirks, K. R., 1974. Infectious disease is large contributor to manpower losses in military operations. *Defence Management J.,* **10** (1): 10–13.

Dobbs, M., 1978. New Cambodia: phones, TV, cars on rubble heaps. *Washington Post* (23 March 1978), p. A20.

Dolgu, G. *et al.,* 1978. *Economic and Social Consequences of the Arms Race and of Military Expenditures.* Rev. edn. (United Nations, New York), 90 pp.

D'Olier, F. *et al.,* 1945 a. *Over-all Report (European War).* (US Strategic Bombing Survey, European War Report No. 2), 109 pp.

D'Olier, F. *et al.,* 1945 b. *Summary Report (European War).* (US Strategic Bombing Survey, European War Report No. 1), 18 pp.

D'Olier, F. *et al.,* 1946. *Summary Report (Pacific War).* (US Strategic Bombing Survey, Pacific Report No. 1), 32 pp + 2 maps.

D'Olier, F. *et al.*, 1947 *a. Index to Records of the United States Strategic Bombing Survey.* (US Strategic Bombing Survey), 317 pp.

D'Olier, F. *et al.*, 1947 *b. Statistical Appendix to Over-all Report (European War).* (US Strategic Bombing Survey, European War Report No. 2a), 166 pp.

Donaghho, W. R., 1950. Observations of some birds of Guadalcanal and Tulagi. *Condor,* **52** (3): 127–132.

Donaldson, G., Spears, J. S. Temple, G. P., Goering, T. J. and Dapice, D., 1978. *Forestry: Sector Policy Paper.* (World Bank, Washington), 65 pp.

Donlagić, A., Atanacković, Z. and Plenca, D., 1967. *Yugoslavia in the Second World War* [translated from the Serbo-Croat by L. F. Edwards]. (Medunarodna Stampa-Interpress, Belgrade), 245 pp. + maps.

Donovan, J. A., Jr., 1967. *United States Marine Corps.* (Fredk A. Praeger, New York), 246 pp. + pl.

Dorsman, C., 1947. [Damage to horticultural crops from inundation with seawater.] *Tijdschrift over Plantenziekten,* **53** (3): 65–86. In Dutch.

Drake, E. and Reid, R.C., 1977. Importation of liquefied natural gas. *Scientific American,* **236** (4): 22–29, 148.

Draper, S. E., 1971. Land clearing in the delta, Vietnam. *Military Engineer,* **63**: 257–259.

Drew, W. B., 1974. *Effects of Herbicides in South Vietnam. B [8]. Ecological Role of Bamboos in Relation to the Military Use of Herbicides on Forests of South Vietnam.* (National Acad. Sciences, Washington), 14 pp.

Duke, J. A. (ed.), 1971. Symposium on Amchitka Island bioenvironmental studies. *Bio-Science,* **21**: 593–711.

Dumas, S. and Vedel-Petersen, K. O., 1923. *Losses of Life Caused by War.* (Clarendon, London) 191 pp.

Dunbar, M. J., 1968. *Ecological Development in Polar Regions: A Study in Evolution.* (Prentice-Hall, Englewood Cliffs, New Jersey), 119 pp.

Dupuy, R. E. and Dupuy, T. N., 1977. *Encyclopedia of Military History: From 3500 B.C. to the Present.* Rev. edn.(Harper & Row, New York), 1 464 pp.

Dupuy, T. N., 1978–1979. Weapons lethality and the nuclear threshold. *Armed Forces Journal International,* **116** (2): 24, 26–27, 33.

Dupuy, T. N. and Hammerman, G. M. (eds), 1973. *Documentary History of Arms Control and Disarmament.* (R. R. Bowker, New York), 629 pp.

Durand, J. D., 1959–1960. Population statistics of China, A.D. 2–1953. *Population Studies,* London, **13**: 209–256 + 1 figure.

Dyer, R. S. *et al.*, 1975. *Survey of the Farallon Islands 500-Fathom Radioactive Waste Disposal Site.* (US Environmental Protection Agency), 74 pp.

Eckholm, E. P., 1975 *a.* Desertification: a world problem. *Ambio,* **4**: 137–145.

Eckholm, E. P., 1975 *b.* Deterioration of mountain environments. *Science,* **189**: 764–770.

Eckholm, E. P., 1976. *Losing Ground: Environmental Stress and World Food Prospects.* (W. W. Norton, New York), 223 pp.

Eckholm, E. and Brown, L. R., 1978. Spreading deserts: the hand of man. *Bull. Atomic Scientists,* **34** (1): 10–16, 44–51.

Eddie, G. O., 1977. *Harvesting of Krill.* (FAO Southern Ocean Fisheries Survey Programme Publication No. GLO/SO/77/2, Rome), 76 pp.

Egler, F. E., 1942. Indigene versus alien in the development of arid Hawaiian vegetation. *Ecology,* **23**: 14–23.

215

Ehrenfeld, D. W., 1972. *Conserving Life on Earth*. (Oxford Univ. Press, New York), 360 pp.

Ehrenfeld, D. W., 1976. Conservation of non-resources. *Amer. Scientist*, **64**: 648–656.

Ehrlich, P. R., Ehrlich, A. H. and Holdren, J. P., 1977. *Ecoscience: Population, Resources, Environment*. 3rd Edn. (W. H. Freeman, San Francisco), 1 051 pp.

Eichmann, E. and Gesenius, H., 1952. [Increases in birth malformations in Berlin and surroundings during the postwar years.] *Archiv f. Gynäkologie*, **181**: 168–184. In German.

Elepaio, 1942. Destruction of bird life on Rabbit Island. *Elepaio*, **3** (5): 16–17.

Ellender, A. J. and McClellan, J. L. (eds), 1972. *Department of Defense Appropriations for Fiscal Year 1973*. (US Senate Comm. on Appropriations, Pt. 5), 573 + 11 pp.

Eller, E. M., 1956-1957. Bibliography of sea power. *Ordnance* (now *National Defense*), **41**: 612–615.

Elton, C. S., 1958. *Ecology of Invasions by Animals and Plants*. (Methuen, London), 181 pp. + 50 photos.

Emeny, B., 1934. *Strategy of Raw Materials: A Study of America in Peace and War*. (Macmillan, New York), 202 pp. + 2 charts.

Engineer Agency for Resources Inventories & Tennessee Valley Authority, 1968. *Atlas of Physical, Economic and Social Resources of the Lower Mekong Basin*. (United Nations, New York), 257 pp.

Engineering News-Record, 1970. Land clearing emerges as a top tactic of the war. *Engineering News-Record*, **184** (3): 27.

Engineers, US Army Corps of, 1972. *Herbicides and Military Operations*. Washington: US Army Corps of Engineers, Engineer Strategic Studies Group Report No. TOPOCOM 9022300, 3 vols, 27 + [141] + 98 pp. Cf. *Science*, **177**: 776–779 (1972) and *Science & Govt. Report*, **2** (11): 1, 3–4 (1972).

Enthoven, A. C. and Smith K. W., 1971. *How Much is Enough? Shaping the Defense Program, 1961-1969*. (Harper & Row, New York), 364 pp.

Epstein, J., 1970. Rate of decomposition of GB in seawater. *Science*, **170**: 1396–1398.

Erfurth, W., 1951. *Warfare in the Far North*. Rev. edn [translated from the German by the US Army]. (US Dept. of the Army Pamphlet No. 20–292), 24 pp. + 1 map.

Estes, J. A. and Palmisano, J. F., 1974. Sea otters: their role in structuring nearshore communities. *Science*, **185**: 1058–1060.

Evans, D. R. and Rice, S. D., 1974. Effects of oil on marine ecosystems: a review for administrators and policy makers. *Fishery Bull.*, **72**: 625–638.

Everson, I., 1977. *Living Resources of the Southern Ocean*. (FAO Southern Ocean Fisheries Survey Programme Publication No. GLO/SO/77/1, Rome), 156 pp.

Falk, R. A., 1971. *This Endangered Planet: Prospects and Proposals for Human Survival*. (Random House, New York), 497 pp.

Falk, R. A., 1973. Environmental warfare and ecocide. *Bull. Peace Proposals*, **4**: 1–17.

Falk, R. A., 1974. Law and responsibility in warfare: the Vietnam experience. *Instant* [now *Current*] *Research on Peace & Violence*, **4**: 1–14.

Fall, B. B., 1965-1966. "This isn't Munich, it's Spain": a Vietnam album. *Ramparts*, **4** (8): 23–29.

Fay, J. A., 1973. Unusual fire hazard of LNG tanker spills. *Combustion Science and Technology*, **7**: 47–49.

Fay, J. A. and MacKenzie, J. J., 1972. Cold cargo. *Environment*, **14** (9): 21–22, 27–29.

Ferer, K. M., 1975. *Fifth Post-Dump Survey of the Chase X Disposal Site.* (US Naval Research Lab. Memo. Report No. 2996, Washington), 19 pp.

Fernando, V. A. and Thomas, M. P., 1977–1978. Role of technology in agriculture: a short ecological appraisal. *International Journal Environmental Studies,* 11: 35–38.

Ferry, B. W., Baddeley, M. S. and Hawksworth, D. L., 1973. *Air Pollution and Lichens.* (Athlone Press, London), 389 pp.

Fisher, H. I., 1966. Airplane-albatross collisions on Midway atoll. *Condor,* 68: 229–242.

Fisher, H. I. and Baldwin, P. H., 1946. War and the birds of Midway atoll. *Condor,* 48: 3–15.

Fisher, J., Simon, N. and Vincent, J., 1969. *Wildlife in Danger* (Viking, New York), 368 pp.

Fitch, J. E. and Young, P. H., 1948. Use and effect of explosives in California coastal waters. *Cal. Fish & Game,* 34: 53–70.

Fitter, R., 1973–1974. Most endangered mammals: an action programme. *Oryx,* London, 12: 436–449.

Fitter, R. S. R. and Lousley, J. E., 1953. *Natural History of the City.* (Corporation of London, London), 36 pp.

FitzGibbon, C., 1957. *Blitz.* (Allan Wingate, London), 272 pp. + 9 pl.

Fonda, J., 1974. Rebirth of a nation: a Vietnam journal. *Rolling Stone,* 1974 (164): 48–50, 52, 56–58.

Fosberg, F. R., 1959 *a.* Long-term effects of radioactive fallout on plants? *Atoll Research Bull.,* 1959 (61), 11 pp.

Fosberg, F. R., 1959 *b.* Plants and fall-out. *Nature,* 183: 1448.

Fosberg, F. R. (ed.), 1963. *Man's Place in the Island Ecosystem.* (Bishop Museum Press, Honolulu), 264 pp. + 1 map.

Fosberg, F. R., 1972. Man's effects on island ecosystems. In: Farvar, M. T. and Milton, J. P. (eds), *Careless Technology: Ecology and International Development.* (Natural History Press, Garden City, New York), 1 030 pp. + pl.: pp. 869–880.

Foster, M. S. and Holmes, R. W., 1977. Santa Barbara oil spill: an ecological disaster? In: Cairns, J., Jr. *et al.* (eds), *Recovery and Restoration of Damaged Ecosystems.* (Univ. Press of Virginia, Charlottesville), 531 pp.: pp. 166–190.

Francisco, L., 1973. First Vietnam: the U.S.–Philippine war of 1899. *Bull. Concerned Asian Scholars,* 5 (4): 2–16.

Franssen, H. T., 1973–1974. Oil and gas in the oceans. *Naval War Coll. Rev.,* 26 (6): 50–66.

Frawley, M. L., 1971. *Surface Mined Areas: Control and Reclamation of Environmental Damage: A Bibliography.* (US Dept. Interior, Office of Library Services Bibliography Ser. No. 27), 63 pp.

Fridriksson, S., 1975. *Surtsey: Evolution of Life on a Volcanic Island.* (Butterworths, London), 198 pp. + 20 pl.

Fuller, J., 1977. Dateline Diego Garcia: paved-over paradise. *Foreign Policy,* 1977 (28): 175–186.

Fullerton, B. and Williams, A. F., 1975. *Scandinavia,* 2nd Edn. (Chatto & Windus, London), 375 pp.

Funk, D. T., 1962. *Revised Bibliography of Strip-mine Reclamation.* (US Forest Serv., Central States Forest Experiment Station Misc. Release No. 35, Columbus, Ohio), 20 pp.

Furneaux, R., 1964. *Krakatoa.* (Prentice-Hall, Englewood Cliffs, New Jersey), 244 pp. + 16 pl.

Futrell, R. F., Mosely, L. S. and Simpson, A. F., 1961. *United States Air Force in Korea 1950–1953.* (Duell, Sloan & Pearce, New York), 774 pp. + pl.

Galbraith, J. K. *et al.,* 1945. *Effects of Strategic Bombing on the German War Economy.* (US Strategic Bombing Survey, European War Report No. 3), 286 pp.

Gans, B., 1969. Biafran relief mission. *Lancet,* **1969** (1): 660–665.

Garfield, B., 1969. *Thousand-Mile War: World War II in Alaska and the Aleutians.* (Doubleday, Garden City, New York), 351 pp. + 82 photos.

Garner, F., 1973. Mustard oil on troubled waters. *Environment,* **15** (2): 4–5.

Garwin, R. L., 1972. Antisubmarine warfare and national security. *Scientific American,* **227** (1): 14–25, 122.

Gaspin, J. B., 1975. *Experimental Investigations of the Effects of Underwater Explosions on Swimbladder Fish. I. 1973 Chesapeake Bay Tests.* (US Naval Surface Weapon Center, White Oak Lab. Techn. Report No. 75–58, Silver Spring, Maryland), 40 + 2 + 12 + 12 pp.

Gates, P. W., 1965. *Agriculture and the Civil War.* (A.A. Knopf, New York), 383 + 13 pp. + 8 pl. + 1 map.

Gavalas-Medici, R. and Day-Magdaleno, S. R., 1976. Extremely low frequency, weak electric fields affect schedule-controlled behaviour of monkeys. *Nature,* **261**: 256–259.

Gemmell, R. P., 1977. *Colonization of Industrial Wasteland.* (Edward Arnold, London), 75 pp.

Georgievski, A. S. and Gavrilov, O. K., 1975. [Public health problems and consequences of wars.] (*Medicina,* Moscow), 256 pp. In Russian.

Gerassi, J., 1968. *North Vietnam: A Documentary.* (Bobbs-Merrill, Indianapolis), 200 pp.

Ghabbour, S. I., 1971–1972. Some aspects of conservation in the Sudan. *Biological Conservation,* **4**: 228–229.

Gillett, J. D., 1972. *The Mosquito: Its Life, Activities, and Impact on Human Affairs.* (Doubleday, Garden City, New York), 359 pp. + pl.

Glasstone, S. (ed.), 1964. *Effects of Nuclear Weapons.* Rev. edn. (US Atomic Energy Commn.), 730 pp. + computer.

Glasstone, S. and Dolan, P. J., 1977. *Effects of Nuclear Weapons.* 3rd Edn. (US Depts. of Defense and Energy, Washington), 653 pp. + computer.

Goldberg, E. D., 1976. *Health of the Oceans.* (UNESCO Press, Paris), 172 pp.

Goldblat, J., 1973. Troubles in the Antarctic? *Bull. Peace Proposals,* **4**: 286–288.

Goldblat, J., 1975 a. Law of the sea and the security of coastal states. In: Christy, F. T., Jr. *et al.,* (eds), *Law of the Sea: Caracas and Beyond.* (Ballinger Publishing Co., Cambridge, Mass.), 422 pp.: 301–317.

Goldblat, J., 1975 b. Prohibition of environmental warfare. *Ambio,* **4**: 186–190.

Goldblat, J., 1977. Environmental warfare convention: how meaningful is it? *Ambio,* **6**: 216–221.

Gómez-Pompa, A., Vázquez-Yanes, C. and Guevara, S., 1972. Tropical rain forest: a non-renewable resource. *Science,* **177**: 762–765. Cf. ibid. **179**: 1147 (1973).

Goodman, D., 1975. Theory of diversity-stability relationships in ecology *Quart. Rev. Biol.,* **50**: 237–266.

Goodman, G. T. and Bray, S. A., 1975. *Ecological Aspects of the Reclamation of Derelict and Disturbed Land: An Annotated Bibliography.* (Geo Abstracts, Univ. of East Anglia, Norwich, England), 351 pp.

Gosnell, M., 1976. Island dilemma, *International Wildlife,* Washington D.C., **6** (5): 24–35.

Gowanloch, J. N., and McDougall, J. E., 1946. Biological effects on fish, shrimp and oysters of the underwater explosion of heavy charges of dynamite. *Trans. N. Amer. Wildlife Conf.,* **11**: 213–219.

Grantham, G. J., 1977. *Utilization of Krill.* (FAO Southern Ocean Fisheries Survey Program Publication No. GLO/SO/77/3, Rome), 61 pp.

Grassle, J. F., 1977. Slow recolonisation of deep-sea sediment. *Nature,* **265:** 618–619.

Gravel, M. *et al.* (eds), 1971–1972. *Pentagon Papers: The Defense Department History of United States Decisionmaking on Vietnam.* (Beacon Press, Boston), 5 vols (632 + 834 + 746 + 687 + [413] pp.).

Graves, H. S., 1918. Effect of the war on forests of France. *Amer. Forestry* (now *Amer. Forests*), **24:** 709–717.

Graymont, B., 1972. *Iroquois in the American Revolution.* (Syracuse Univ. Press, Syracuse, New York), 359 pp.

Greenway, J. C., Jr., 1967. *Extinct and Vanishing Birds of the World.* 2nd Edn. (Dover Publications, New York), 520 pp.

Grimmett, R. F., 1977. *United States Military Installations and Objectives in the Mediterranean.* (US House of Representatives Committee on International Relations), 95 pp.

Griswold, L., 1972. Cold front: USSR has strategic advantage above the Arctic Circle. *Sea Power,* Washington, D.C., **15** (11): 18–23.

Groff, J. B., 1977. Navy and the environment. *Military Engineer,* **69:** 103–105.

Gross, M. G., 1971. Pollution of the coastal ocean and the Great Lakes. *US Naval Inst. Proc.,* **97** (819): 228–243.

Groves, E. W., 1958. Some entomological records from the Cripplegate bombed sites, City of London. *London Naturalist,* **38:** 25–29.

Gulland, J. A., 1977. World fisheries and fish stocks. *Marine Policy,* **1:** 179–189.

Gundlach, E. R., 1977. Oil tanker disasters. *Environment,* **19** (9): 16–20, 25–27.

Györffy, I., 1948–1949. [On the colonized moss pioneers of bomb crater slopes at Salzburg.] *Mem. Soc. pro Fauna et Flora Fennica,* **25:** 107–114. In German.

Haan, D. S. de and Tinker, J. M., 1970. *Refugee and Civilian War Casualty Problems in Indochina* [report]. (US Senate Comm. on the Judiciary), 107 pp.

Halliday, T., 1978. *Vanishing Birds: Their Natural History and Conservation,* (Sidgwick & Jackson, London), 296 pp.

Hanning, H., 1967. *Peaceful Uses of Military Forces.* (Praeger, New York), 327 pp.

Hanson, W. C., 1967. Radioecological concentration processes characterizing ecosystems. In Åberg, B. and Hungate, F. P. (eds), *Radioecological Concentration Processes.* (Pergamon Press, Oxford), 1 040 pp.: pp. 183–191.

Hardin, G., 1968. Tragedy of the commons. *Science,* **162:** 1243–1248.

Hardy, E. P., Krey, P. W. and Volchok, H. L., 1973. Global inventory and distribution of fallout plutonium. *Nature,* **241:** 444–445.

Hare, F. K., 1977. Connections between climate and desertification. *Environmental Conservation,* **4:** 81–90.

Harrington, M., 1977. *Vast Majority: A Journey to the World's Poor.* (Simon & Schuster, New York), 283 pp.

Harris, D. R., 1962. Invasion of oceanic islands by alien plants: an example from the Leeward Islands, West Indies. *Inst. Brit. Geographers Trans. & Papers,* **1962** (31): 67–82 + 1 pl.

Harris, W. H. and Levey, J. S. (eds), 1975. *New Columbia Encyclopedia.* 4th Edn. (Columbia Univ. Press, New York), 3 052 pp.

Harrison, J. L., 1968. Effect of forest clearance on small mammals. In: Talbot, L. M. and Talbot, M. H. (eds), *Conservation in Tropical South East Asia.* (International Union Conservation Nature and Natural Resources Publ. N.S. No. 10, Morges, Switz.), 550 pp. + 2 pl.: pp. 153–156.

Hassanyar, A. S., 1977. Restoration of arid and semi-arid ecosystems in Afghanistan. *Environmental Conservation,* **4:** 297–301.

Hay, J. H., Jr., 1974. *Vietnam Studies: Tactical and Material Innovations.* (US Dept. Army), 197 pp.

Heady, H. F., 1975. *Rangeland Management.* (McGraw-Hill, New York), 460 pp.

Heede, B. H., 1976. *Gully Development and Control: The Status of our Knowledge.* (US Forest Serv. Research Paper No. RM–169), 42 pp.

Heilbroner, R. L., 1974. *Inquiry into the Human Prospect.* (W. W. Norton, New York), 150 pp.

Heintzelman, O. H. and Highsmith, R. M., Jr., 1973., *World Regional Geography.* 4th Edn. (Prentice-Hall, Englewood Cliffs, New Jersey), 432 pp.

Held, E. E., 1960. Land crabs and fission products at Eniwetok Atoll. *Pacific Science,* **14:** 18–27.

Henderson, G. R. G., 1955. Whirling wings over the jungle. *Air Clues,* **9** (8): 239–243.

Henderson, J. W., Barth, H. A., Heimann, J. M., Moeller, P. W., Soriano, F. S. and Weaver, J. O., 1971. *Area Handbook for Oceania.* (US Dept. Army Pamphlet No. 550–94, Washington), 553 pp. + maps.

Henniker, M. C. A., 1955. *Red Shadow Over Malaya.* (Wm. Blackwood, Edinburgh), 303 pp. + 8 pl.

Herbert, A. B. and Wooten, J. T., 1973. *Soldier.* (Holt, Rinehart & Winston, New York), 498 pp. + 16 pl.

Herbertson, A. J., 1905. Major natural regions: an essay in systematic geography. *Geographical J.,* London, **25:** 300–312.

Herbicide Policy Review Committee, 1968. *Report on the Herbicide Policy Review.* (US Embassy, Saigon), 80 pp. + 5 appendices (12 + 13 + 5 + 12 + 6 pp.)

Herodotus, ca. 430 B.C. *History* [translated from the Greek by G. Rawlinson and edited by E. H. Blakeney]. (J. M. Dent & Sons, London, 1910), 2 vols (366 + 353 pp.), 1910.

Hickey, G. C., 1973. Can South Vietnam make it on its own? *U.S. News & World Report,* **75** (7): 55–56.

Hickey, G. C., 1974. *Effects of Herbicides in South Vietnam. B [11]. Perceived Effects of Herbicides Used in the Highlands of South Vietnam.* (National Acad. Sciences, Washington), 23 pp.

Hiep, Nguyen Van, 1969. *Forestry Program for the Post-war Development of the Five Northern Provinces Constituting the I Corps Region of South Vietnam.* (Devel. & Resources Corp., Joint Devel. Group Working Paper No. 57, New York), 69 pp.

Hills, E. S. (ed.), 1966. *Arid Lands: A Geographical Appraisal.* (UNESCO, Paris), 461 pp.

Hines, N. O., 1962. *Proving Ground: An Account of the Radiobiological Studies in the Pacific, 1946–1961.* (Univ. Washington Press, Seattle), 366 pp.

Ho, P.-t., 1959. *Studies on the Population of China, 1368–1953.* (Harvard Univ. Press, Cambridge, Mass.), 333 + 32 pp.

Hobbs, W. H., 1945. *Fortress Islands of the Pacific.* (J. W. Edwards, Ann Arbor, Mich.), 186 pp.

Hoffmann, P. J., 1971. New world for which to war. *Military Rev.,* **51** (11): 67–76.

Hoffsommer, J. C. and Rosen, J. M., 1973. Hydrolysis of explosives in seawater. *Bull. Environmental Contamination & Toxicology,* **10:** 78–79.

Holdgate, M. W. and Woodman, M. J. (eds), 1978. *Breakdown and Restoration of Ecosystems.* (Plenum Press, New York), 496 pp.

Holm, D. A., 1960. Desert geomorphology in the Arabian peninsula. *Science,* **132:** 1369–1379.

Holmes, C. H., 1951. *Grass, Fern, and Savannah Lands of Ceylon, Their Nature and Ecological Significance.* (Brit. Imperial Forestry Inst. Pap. No. 28, Oxford), 95 pp. + 7 pl.

Holt, J. B., 1973. Pollution abatement: we do our part. *US Naval Inst. Proc.,* **99** (9): 69–75.

Horn, M. H., Teal, J. M. and Backus, R. H., 1970. Petroleum lumps on the surface of the sea. *Science,* **168**: 245–246.

Horne, A., 1977. *Savage War of Peace: Algeria 1954–1962.* (Macmillan, London), 604 pp. + 40 pl.

House, F. H., 1965. *Timber at War: An Account of the Organisation and Activities of the Timber Control, 1939–1945.* (Ernest Benn, London), 331 pp. + pl. + charts.

Howard, J. D., 1972. Herbicides in support of counterinsurgency operations: a cost-effectiveness study. (US Naval Postgrad. School, M.S. thesis, Monterey, Cal.), 127 pp.

Hubbard, C. E., Whyte, R. O., Brown, D. and Gray, A. P., 1944. *Imperata cylindrica: Taxonomy, Distribution, Economic Significance and Control.* (Brit. Imperial Agricultural Bur. Joint Publ. No. 7, Aberystwyth, UK), 63 pp.

Hubbell, T. H., 1968. Biology of islands. *Proc. National Acad. Sciences, Washington,* **60**: 22–32.

Hubbs, C. L. and Rechnitzer, A. B., 1952. Report on experiments designed to determine effects of underwater explosions on fish life. *Cal. Fish & Game,* **38**: 333–366.

Huisken, R. H., 1975. Consumption of raw materials for military purposes. *Ambio,* **4**: 229–233.

Huitfeldt, T., 1974. Strategic perspective on the arctic. *Cooperation & Conflict,* Oslo, **9**: 135–151.

Hulett, H. R., 1970. Optimum world population. *BioScience,* **20**: 160–161.

Hulse, F. S., 1961. Warfare, demography and genetics. *Eugenics Quart.,* **8**: 185–197.

Hunt, H. R., 1930. *Some Biological Aspects of War.* (Galton Publ. Company, New York), 118 pp.

Hurley, R. L., 1969. *Poverty and Mental Retardation: A Causal Relationship.* (Random House, New York), 301 pp.

Hutchison, F. W., 1958. Defoliation of *Hevea brasiliensis* by aerial spraying. *J. Rubber Research Inst., Malaya,* **15**: 241–274.

Hutnik, R. J. and Davis, G. (eds), 1973. *Ecology and Reclamation of Devastated Land.* (Gordon & Breach, New York), 2 vols (538 + 504 pp.).

IAEA (International Atomic Energy Agency), 1976. *Power Reactors in Member States.* (IAEA, Vienna), 84 pp.

Ibarrola, J., 1964. [Effects of the two world wars on French demographic evolution.] (Université de Grenoble, Faculté de Droit et des Sciences Économiques, doctoral thesis, Grenoble), 284 pp. In French.

Iklé, F. C., 1958. *Social Impact of Bomb Destruction.* (Univ. Oklahoma Press, Norman, Okla.), 250 pp. + 10 photos.

IMF (International Monetary Fund), 1977. Note on classification of countries. *IMF Survey,* Wash., D.C., **6**: 254.

Infield, G. B., 1971. *Disaster at Bari.* (Macmillan, New York), 301 pp. + 16 pl.

Ingersoll, J. M., 1965. *Historical Examples of Ecological Disaster: Famine in Russia 1921–22; Famine in Bechuanaland 1965.* (Hudson Inst. Rept. No. HI–518–RR/A1, Croton-on-Hudson, New York), 88 pp.

Irvine, B., 1970. Conditioning marine mammals to work in the sea. *Marine Technology Soc. J.,* **4** (3): 47–52.

Irving, L., 1972. *Arctic Life of Birds and Mammals: Including Man.* (Springer-Verlag, New York), 192 pp.

Ise, J., 1920. *United States Forest Policy.* (Yale Univ. Press, New Haven), 395 pp.

Israelyan, V., 1974. New Soviet initiative on disarmament. *International Affairs,* Moscow, **1974** (11): 19–25.

Jackson, W. B., 1969. Survival of rats at Eniwetok Atoll. *Pacific Science,* **23**: 265–275.

Jameson, S. C., 1975. Toxic effect of the explosive depth charge chemicals from the ship SANKISAN MARU on the coral reef fish *Dascyllus aruanus* (L). *Micronesia,* **11** (1): 109–113.

Jannasch, H. W., Eimhjellen, K., Wirsen, C. O. and Farmanfarmaian, A., 1971. Microbial degradation of organic matter in the deep sea. *Science,* **171**: 672–675.

Janzen, D. H., 1973. Tropical agroecosystems. *Science,* **182**: 1212–1219.

Jennings, F., 1975. *Invasion of America: Indians, Colonialism and the Cant of Conquest.* (Univ. N. Carolina Press, Chapel Hill, N.C.), 369 pp.

Jensen, A. J. C., 1948. [Changes in the fishery: war effects on the plaice *(Pleuronectes platessa)* fishery in the Skagerak, Kattegat, and Belt Sea.] *Fiskeeksportör-Bladet, Holbaek,* **14** (5): 7–9. In Danish.

Jett, S. C. (ed.), 1974. Destruction of Navajo orchards in 1864: Captain John Thompson's report. *Arizona & the West,* **16**: 365–378 + 2 pl.

Johnson, A., 1948. *Norway: Her Invasion and Occupation.* (Bowen Press, Decatur, Georgia), 372 pp.

Johnston, D. W. and Odum E. P., 1956. Breeding bird populations in relation to plant succession on the piedmont of Georgia. *Ecology,* **37**: 50–62.

Johnstone, L. C., 1970–1971. Ecocide and the Geneva Protocol. *Foreign Affairs,* **49**: 711–720.

Jones, A. W., 1954. Drone-fly visitors to the flowers on the City bombed sites. *London Naturalist,* **34**: 154–157.

Jones, A. W., 1957. Flora of the City of London bombed sites. *London Naturalist,* **37**: 189–210 + 1 map.

Josephy, A. M., Jr., 1968. *Indian Heritage of America.* (A.A. Knopf, New York), 384 + 15 pp. + pl.

Judd, F., 1975. Security of offshore resources. *RUSI Journal, London,* **120** (3): 3–9.

Kanegis, A. *et al.,* 1970. *Weapons for Counterinsurgency: Chemical/Biological, Anti-Personnel, Incendiary.* (Amer. Friends Service Comm., Philadelphia), 104 pp.

Kellogg, S. C., 1903. *Shenandoah Valley and Virginia, 1861–1865: A War Study.* (Neale Publishing Co., New York), 247 pp.

Kellogg, W. W. , 1978. Is mankind warming the earth? *Bull. Atomic Scientists,* **34** (2): 10–19.

Kemp, G., 1977–1978. Scarcity and strategy. *Foreign Affairs,* **56**: 396–414.

Kende, I., 1972. *Local Wars in Asia, Africa and Latin America, 1945–1969.* (Hung. Acad. Sciences, Ctr. Afro-Asian Research, Studies on Developing Countries, No. 60, Budapest), 86 pp.

Kennedy, E. M. (ed.), 1967. *Civilian Casualty, Social Welfare, and Refugee Problems in South Vietnam.* (US Senate Comm. on the Judiciary), 332 pp.

Kennedy, E .M. (ed.), 1974. *Relief and Rehabilitation of War Victims in Indochina: One Year After the Ceasefire.* (US Senate Comm. on the Judiciary), 399 pp.

Kennedy, E. M. (ed.), 1975 *Humanitarian Problems in South Vietnam and Cambodia: Two Years After the Cease-fire*. (US Senate Comm. on the Judiciary), 178 pp.

Kennedy, E. M. (ed.), 1976. *Aftermath of War: Humanitarian Problems of Southeast Asia*. (US Senate Comm. on the Judiciary), 589 pp.

Kernan, H. S., 1945. War's toll of French forests. *Amer. Forests*, **51**: 442.

Kerver, T. J., 1974. To clear the way. *National Defense*, **58**: 454–455.

Kieffer, F. V., 1972. *Bibliography of Surface Coal Mining in the United States to August, 1971*. (Forum Associates, Columbus, Ohio), 71 pp.

Kiernan, J. M., 1967. Combat engineers in the Iron Triangle. *Army*, **17** (6): 42–45.

Kimble, G. H. T. and Good, D. (eds), 1955. *Geography of the Northlands*. (J. Wiley; Amer. Geographical Soc. Spec. Publ. No. 32, New York), 534 pp. + 1 map.

King, F., 1977. Cold weather warfare: what would happen? *Military Rev.*, **57** (11): 86–95.

Kinney, G. F., 1962. *Explosive Shocks in Air*. (Macmillan, New York), 198 pp.

Kipp, R. M., 1967–1968. Counterinsurgency from 30,000 feet: the B-52 in Vietnam. *Air Univ. Rev.*, **19** (2): 10–18.

Kirby, R. C. and Prokopovitsh, A. S., 1976. Technological insurance against shortages in minerals and metals. *Science*, **191**: 713–719.

Klare, M. T., 1975–1976. Superpower rivalry at sea. *Foreign Policy, New York*, **1975–1976** (21): 86–96, 161–167.

Klein, D. R., 1971. Reaction of reindeer to obstructions and disturbances. *Science*, **173**: 393–398.

Klein, D. R., 1971–1972. Problems in conservation of mammals in the north. *Biological Conservation*, **4**: 97–101.

Klingberg, F. L., 1966. Predicting the termination of war: battle casualties and population losses, *J. Conflict Resolution*, **10**: 129–171.

Kolko, G., 1968. Report on the destruction of dikes: Holland 1944–45 and Korea 1953. In Duffet, J. (ed.), *Against the Crime of Silence: Proceedings of the Russell International War Crimes Tribunal: Stockholm, Copenhagen*. (O'Hare Books, Flanders, New Jersey), 662 pp.: pp. 224–226.

Krepon, M., 1973–1974. Weapons potentially inhumane: the case of cluster bombs. *Foreign Affairs*, **52**: 595–611.

Kristoferson, L. (ed.), 1975. Selection of documents . . . pertaining to war and the environment. *Ambio*. **4**: 234–244.

Kruszewski, C., 1940. Germany's *Lebensraum*. *Amer. Political Science Rev.*, **34**: 964–975.

Kryuchkova, M. I., Lagunov, L. L., Lestev. A. V., Makarov, R. R. and Tsareva, L. D., 1971. [Krill as a food resource.] *Proc. All-Union Research Inst. Marine Fisheries & Oceanography)*, **79**: 153–157. In Russian.

Kukla, G. J. and Kukla, H. J., 1974. Increased surface albedo in the northern hemisphere. *Science*, **183**: 709–714.

Kutger, J. P., 1960–1961. Irregular warfare in transition. *Military Affairs*, **24**: 113–123.

LaFarge, H. (ed.), 1946. *Lost Treasures of Europe*. (Pantheon, New York), 39 pp. + 427 pl.

Lafont, P.-B., 1967. [Shifting agriculture of the proto-Indochinese of the plateaus of central Viet Nam.] *Cahiers d'Outre-Mer*. **20** (77): 37–48. In French.

Lamb, D., 1977. Conservation and management of tropical rain-forest: a dilemma of development in Papua New Guinea. *Environmental Conservation*, **4**: 121–129.

Lamb, H., 1927. *Genghis Khan: The Emperor of All Men*. (R. M. McBride, New York), 270 pp.

Lance, J., 1965. Commentaries on jungle warefare. *Infantry*, 55 (1): 52–59.

Lang, A. *et al.*, 1974. *Effects of Herbicides in South Vietnam. A. Summary and Conclusions.* (National Acad. Sciences, Washington), [398] pp. + 8 maps.

Lapage, G., 1950. Parasites and war. *Endeavour*, 9: 134–137.

Lapp, R. E., 1958. *Voyage of the Lucky Dragon.* (Harper & Bros., New York, 200 pp. + photos.

Larkin, P. R. and Sutherland, P. J., 1977. Migrating birds respond to Project Seafarer's electromagnetic field. *Science*, 195: 777–779.

Laurie, M. V., 1974. *Tree Planting Practices in African Savannas.* (Food & Agriculture Org. Development Pap. No. 19, Rome), 185 pp. + 3 maps.

Lavergne, M., 1970. Emission by underwater explosions. *Geophysics*, Tulsa, 35: 419–435.

Lawrence, G. H. M., 1951. *Taxonomy of Vascular Plants.* (Macmillan, New York), 823 pp.

Leahy, W. D., 1950. *I Was There: The Personal Story of the Chief of Staff to Presidents Roosevelt and Truman Based on His Notes and Diaries Made at the Time.* (McGraw-Hill, New York), 527 pp. + 17 pl.

LeBarron, R. K. and Walker, R. L., 1971. Kahoolawe. *Aloha Aina, Honolulu,* 2 (2): 16–20.

Leckie, R., 1962. *Conflict: The History of the Korean War, 1950–53.* (G. P. Putnam's Sons, New York), 448 pp. + pl.

Leckie, R., 1967. *Battle for Iwo Jima.* (Random House, New York), 173 pp.

LeGros, A. E., 1948. Notes on the spiders of the bombed sites. *London Naturalist*, 28: 37–39.

Leider, R., 1973. Strategies for an environmental decade. *Orbis,* 16: 881–891.

Leith, C. K., 1931. *World Minerals and World Politics: A Factual Study of Minerals in Their Political and International Relations.* (McGraw-Hill, New York), 213 pp.

Leith, C. K., Furness, J. W. and Lewis, C., 1943. *World Minerals and World Peace.* (Brookings Institution, Washington), 253 pp.

Lemons, H. and Wood, L. E., 1967. Environmental research on high elevations. *Military Rev.*, 47 (6): 45–50.

Leopold, A., 1933. *Game Management.* (Chas. Scribner's Sons, New York), 481 pp. + 3 pl.

Leopold, A. S., 1950. Deer in relation to plant successions. *J. Forestry,* 48: 675–678.

Leopold, A. S., 1961. *Desert. (Time,* New York), 192 pp.

Leslie, A., 1977–1978. Where contradictory theory and practice co-exist. *Unasylva,* 29 (115): 2–17.

Lesseux, C. de., 1916. [Forests of France and the war.] *Revue des Eaux et Forêts,* 54: 110–115. In French.

Levin, A. L., 1977. *Protecting the Human Environment: Procedures and Principles for Preventing and Resolving International Controversies.* (UN Inst. for Training & Research, New York). 131 pp.

Lewallen, J., 1971. *Ecology of Devastation: Indochina.* (Penguin, Baltimore), 179 pp.

Lewis, A., 1970. Rickets on rise, Vietcong report. *New York Times* (15 March 1970), p.4.

Libber, L. L. and Rozzell, T. C., 1972. Study of the possible biological effects of SANGUINE. *Naval Research Revs.,* 25 (2): 1–11.

Library of Congress, US, 1971. *Impact of the Vietnam War.* US Senate Comm. on Foreign Relations, 36 pp.

Liddell-Hart, B. H., 1929. *Sherman: Soldier, Realist, American.* (Dodd, Mead, New York), 456 pp. + 11 maps.

Liddell-Hart, B. H., 1970. *History of the Second World War.* (G. P. Putnam's Sons, New York), 766 pp.

Life Magazine, 1964. First world war. VI. Scarred face of Verdun. *Life Mag.,* 56 (23): 68–83.

Life Magazine, 1971. 'Dozer pilot who digs peace. *Life Mag.,* **71** (1): 72.

Likens, G. E., Bormann, F. H., Pierce, R. S., Eaton, J. S. and Johnson, N. M., 1977. *Biogeochemistry of a Forested Ecosystem.* (Springer-Verlag, New York), 146 pp.

Lilly, J. C., 1976. Rights of cetaceans under human laws. *Oceans,* **9** (2): 66–68.

Lindsey, G. R., 1976–1977. Strategic aspects of the polar regions. *Behind the Headlines,* Toronto, **35** (6), 24 pp.

Littauer, R. and Uphoff, N. (eds), 1972. *Air War in Indochina.* Rev. edn. (Beacon Press, Boston), 289 pp.

Livingstone, F. B., 1967. Effects of warfare on the biology of the human species. *Natural History,* **76** (10): 61–65, 70.

Lloyd, T., 1969–1970. Canada's arctic in the age of ecology. *Foreign Affairs,* **48**: 726–740.

Loftas, T., 1970. Fishery boom for South Vietnam? *New Scientist,* **46**: 280, 282–283.

Loftas, T., 1976. Eldorado of the deep. *Ceres,* Rome, **9** (6): 22–26.

Lubow, R. E., 1977. *War Animals.* (Doubleday, Garden City, New York), 255 pp.

Luce, D., 1974. Vietnam eyewitness: rebuilding underway. *Guardian,* New York, **26** (15): 13.

Luce, D. and Sommer, J., 1969. *Vietnam: The Unheard Voices.* (Cornell Univ. Press, Ithaca, New York), 336 pp.

Lucey, M. N., 1972. Resources of the sea. *Brassey's Annual* (now *R.U.S.I. and Brassey's Defence Yrbk),* London, **83**: 161–174.

Lumsden, M., 1972. Politics of reconstruction in Indochina, *Instant* [now *Current*] *Research on Peace & Violence,* **2** (1): 17–33.

Lumsden, M., 1975. "Conventional" war and human ecology. *Ambio,* **4**: 223–228.

Lund, D. H., 1947 Revival of northern Norway. *Geographical J.,* **91**: 185–197 + 4 pl.

Lutz, H. J. and Chandler, R. F., Jr., 1946. *Forest Soils.* (J. Wiley, New York), 514 pp.

Lyons, A. R., Coblentz, T. H. and Waterstradt, W., 1971. *Effectiveness of Defoliation Operations for Temperate Zone Vegetation.* (US Army Desert Test Ctr. Techn. Report No. 71–116, Ft. Douglas, Utah).

Lyons, R. D., 1978. G.A.O. warned the White House of satellite hazards. *New York Times* (7 February 1978), p. 4.

Maass, W. B., 1975. *Years of Darkness: The Austrian Resistance Movement, 1938–1945* [translated from the German by J. Wilde]. (Federal Press Serv., Vienna), 68 pp.

MacArthur, R. H. and Wilson, E. O., 1967. *Theory of Island Biogeography.* (Princeton Univ. Press, Princeton, New Jersey), 203 pp.

MacIsaac, D. (ed.), 1976. *United States Strategic Bombing Survey.* (Garland Press, New York), 10 vols (ca. 3 400 pp.).

Macnae, W., 1968. General account of the fauna and flora of mangrove swamps and forest in the Indo-West-Pacific region. *Advances Marine Biology,* **6**: 73–270 + 1 figure.

Mahon, G. H. (ed.), 1972. *Department of Defense Appropriations for 1973.* (US House Representatives Comm. on Appropriations, Pt. 4), 1 248 pp.

Major, R. H., 1941. *Fatal Partners: War and Disease.* (Doubleday, Doran, Garden City, New York), 342 pp. + 8 pl.

Mammen, F. V., 1916. [Significance of the forest particularly in war.] ("Globus", Wissenschaftliche Verlagsanstalt, Dresden), 96 pp. In German.

Marine Pollution Bulletin, 1976. World War II poisons. *Marine Pollution Bull.,* Oxford, **7**: 179.

Markham, J. M., 1975. Heavy psychological toll is half-hidden but shattering result of the long Vietnam war. *New York Times* (22 January 1975), p.8.

Marriott, J., 1974–1975 *a*. Defence of North Sea oil and gas. *NATO's fifteen Nations,* **19** (5): 72–79, 82–84.

Marriott, J., 1974–1975 *b*. Mine warfare. *NATO's Fifteen Nations,* **19** (5): 44–50.

Marshall, J. D., Ouy, D. V., Gibson, F. L., Dung, T. C. and Cavanaugh, D. C., 1967. Ecology of plague in Vietnam: commensal rodents and their fleas. *Military Medicine,* **132**: 896–903.

Martin, L., 1973. *Arms and Strategy: An International Survey of Modern Defence.* (Weidenfeld & Nicolson, London), 320 pp.

Marwick, A., 1974. *War and Social Change in the Twentieth Century: A Comparative Study of Britain, France, Germany, Russia and the United States.* (St. Martin's Press, New York), 258 pp. + 6 pl.

Massey, D., 1970. Land clearing team: Rome plows on the border. *Hurricane,* **1970** (35): 34–37.

Maude, H. E. and Doran, E., Jr., 1966. Precedence of Tarawa atoll. *Annals Assn. Amer. Geographers,* **56**: 269–289.

Mayer, J., 1969. Famine in Biafra. *Postgraduate Medicine,* **45** (4): 236–240.

Mayer, J., Axinn, G. H., Brown, R. E. and Orick, G. T., 1969. Report of the Biafra study mission. *US Congressional Record,* **115**: 4371–4382.

McClintock, M., Rissman, P. and Scott, A., 1971. Talking to ourselves. *Environment,* **13** (7): 16–19, 42–45.

McClintock, M. and Scott, A., 1974. Sanguine. *Environment,* **16**: (6): 27–34.

McCullough, D., 1977. *Path Between the Seas: The Creation of the Panama Canal, 1870–1914.* (Simon & Schuster, New York), 698 pp.

McDonald, V. P., 1975. Panama Canal for Panamanians: the implications for the United States. *Military Rev.,* **55** (12): 7–16.

McEachern, J. and Towle, E. L., 1974. *Ecological Guidelines for Island Development.* (International Union Conservation Nature & Natural Resources Publication N.S. No. 30, Morges, Switz.), 65 pp.

McGinnies, W. G., Goldman, B. J. and Paylore, P. (eds), 1968. *Deserts of the World: An Appraisal of Research into their Physical and Biological Environments.* (Univ. Arizona Press, Tucson), 788 pp.

McHale, J. and McHale, M. C., 1978. *Basic Human Needs: A Framework for Action.* (Transaction Press, New Brunswick, New Jersey), 249 pp.

McIndoe, K. G., 1969. *Preliminary Survey of Rubber Plantations in South Vietnam.* (Devel. & Resources Corp. Vietnam Working Pap. No. 3, New York), 41 + 13 pp.

McNeill, W. H., 1976. *Plagues and Peoples.* (Doubleday, Garden City, New York), 371 pp.

Meid, P. and Yingling, J. M., 1972. *U.S. Marine Operations in Korea, 1950–1953. V. Operations in West Korea.* (US Marine Corps, Washington), 643 pp. + photos.

Meijer, W., 1970. Regeneration of tropical lowland forest in Sabah, Malaysia, forty years after logging. *Malayan Forester,* **33**: 204–229.

Meijer, W., 1973. Devastation and regeneration of lowland dipterocarp forests in southeast Asia. *BioScience,* **23**: 528–533.

Melman, S. (ed.), 1968. *In the Name of America.* (E. P. Dutton, New York) 421 pp.

Menzies, R. J., 1968. Transport of marine life between oceans through the Panama Canal. *Nature,* **220**: 802–803.

Mercer, J. H., 1978. West Antarctic ice sheet and CO_2 greenhouse effect: a threat of disaster. *Nature,* **271**: 321–325.

Meyerhoff, A. A., 1976. Economic impact and geopolitical implications of giant petroleum fields. *Amer. Scientist,* **64:** 536–541.

Mihaly, E. B., 1972–1973. Micronesia: a US strategic pawn of 2000 South Sea islands. *War/Peace Report,* New York, **12** (6): 17–21.

Mihaly, E. B., 1973–1974. Tremors in the western Pacific: Micronesian freedom and US security. *Foreign Affairs,* **52:** 839–849.

Mill, J. S., 1871. *Principles of Political Economy: With Some of their Applications to Social Philosophy.* 7th Edn. (Univ. Toronto Press, Toronto), 2 vols (1 166 pp. + 2 pl.), 1965.

Miller, D. S., Peakall, D. B. and Kinter, W. B., 1978. Ingestion of crude oil: sublethal effects in herring gull chicks. *Science,* **199:** 315–317.

Miller, S. C., 1969–1970. Our Mylai of 1900: Americans in the Philippine insurrection. *Trans-action* (now *Society),* **7** (10): 19–28.

Milne, L. J. and Milne, M., 1962. *Mountains. (Time,* New York), 192 pp.

Milward, A. S., 1977. *War, Economy and Society 1939–1945.* (Allen Lane, London), 395 pp.

Mirsky, J., 1967. Tombs of Ben Suc: 'too blind stupid to see'. *Nation,* **205:** 397–400.

Mitchell, B., 1977. Resources in Antarctica: potential for conflict. *Marine Policy,* Surrey, England, **1:** 91–101.

Mohr, E. C. J., Baren, F. A. v. and Schuylenborgh, J. v., 1972. *Tropical Soils: A Comprehensive Study of their Genesis.* 3rd Edn. (Mouton, Ichtiar Baru, van Hoeve, Hague), 481 pp. + pl.

Moncrief, L. W., 1970. Cultural basis for our environmental crisis. *Science,* **170:** 508–512.

Montross, L., 1960. *War Through the Ages.* 3rd Edn. (Harper & Bros., New York), 1 063 pp.

Morgan, G. T., Jr., (ed.), 1961. Forester at war: excerpts from the diaries of Colonel William B. Greeley, 1917–1919. *Forest History,* **4** (3–4): 3–15.

Morris, R., 1974. Triumph of money and power. *New York Times* (3 March 1974), p. E13.

Morrow, M., 1972. Unexploded bombs: Laotians face continuous threat. *Amer. Report,* **2** (15): 10.

Morton, L., 1963. North Pacific: 1941–43. *Military Rev.,* **43** (1): 34–47.

Moser, R. H., 1965. Of plagues and pennants. *Military Rev.,* **45** (5): 71–84.

Moulton, J. M. and Backus, R. H., 1955. *Annotated References Concerning the Effects of Man-made Sounds on the Movements of Fishes.* (Maine Dept. of Sea and Shore Fisheries, Circ. No. 17, Augusta, Maine), 9 pp.

Mudge, G. A., 1969–1970. Starvation as a means of warfare. *International Lawyer,* **4:** 228–268.

Mumford, L., 1934. *Technics and Civilization.* (Harcourt, Brace, New York), 495 pp. + 16 pl.

Murphy, J. M., Murfin, G. D., Jamieson, N. L., III, Rambo, A. T., Glenn, J. A., Jones, L. P. and Leighton, A .H., 1974. *Effects of Herbicides in South Vietnam. B [12]. Beliefs, Attitudes, and Behavior of Lowland Vietnamese.* (National Acad. Sciences, Washington), [299] pp.

Murray, S. C., 1975. Marianas: new outpost of empire. *Nation,* New York, **220:** 459–461.

Murrmann, R. P. and Reed, S., 1972. *Military Facilities and Environmental Stresses in Cold Regions.* (US Army Corps of Engineers Cold Regions Research & Engineering Lab. Spec. Report No. 173, Hanover, New Hampshire), 20 pp.

Myers, N., 1976. Expanded approach to the problems of disappearing species. *Science,* **193:** 198–202.

Myrdal, A. 1976. *Game of Disarmament: How the United States and Russia Run the Arms Race.* (Pantheon Books, New York), 397 pp.

Myrdal, A. *et al.,* 1972. *Disarmament and Development.* (United Nations), New York, 37 pp.

Myrdal, G., 1957. *Rich Lands and Poor: The Road to World Prosperity.* (Harper & Bros., New York), 168 pp.

National Bureau of Standards, U.S., 1977. *International System of Units (SI).* 4th Edn. (US Natl Bur. Standards, Washington, Special Publication No. 330), 41 pp.

Neel, S., 1973 *Vietnam Studies: Medical Support of the U.S. Army in Vietnam, 1965–1970.* (US Dept. Army), 196 pp.

Nef, J. U., 1950. *War and Human Progress: An Essay on the Rise of Industrial Civilization.* (Harvard Univ. Press, Cambridge, Mass.), 464 pp.

Neilands, J. B., Orians, G. H., Pfeiffer, E. W., Vennema, A. and Westing, A. H., 1972. *Harvest of Death: Chemical Warfare in Vietnam and Cambodia.* (Free Press, New York), 304 pp.

Nelson, K. L. (ed.), 1971. *Impact of War on American Life: The Twentieth-Century Experience.* (Holt, Rinehart & Winston, New York), 395 pp.

Netzén. G. *et al.,* 1976. [Spent nuclear fuel and radioactive waste. II]. (Swedish Ministry Industry Report No. SOU 1976: 31, Stockholm), 222 pp. In Swedish.

Newcombe, K., Kalma, J. D. and Aston, A. R., 1978. Metabolism of a city: the case of Hong Kong. *Ambio,* **7**: 3–15.

Ngan, Phung Trung, 1968. Status of conservation in South Vietnam. In: Talbot, L. M. and Talbot, M. H. (eds), *Conservation in Tropical South East Asia.* (International Union of Conservation Nature & Natural Resources Publication N.S. No. 10, Morges, Switz.), 550 pp. + 2 pl.: pp. 519–522.

Nicolai, G. F., 1918. *Biology of War* [translated from the German by C. A. & J.Grande]. (Century, New York), 553 pp.

Nier, A. O. C. *et al.,* 1975. *Long-Term Worldwide Effects of Multiple Nuclear-Weapons Detonations.* (National Acad. Sciences, Washington), 213 pp.

Novicow, J., 1911. *War and Its Alleged Benefits* [translated from the Russian by T. Seltzer]. (Henry Holt, New York), 130 pp.

Nowak, R. M., 1976. Wildlife of Indochina: tragedy or opportunity? *National Parks & Conservation Mag.,* **50** (6): 13–18.

Nye, P. H. and Greenland, D. J., 1960. *Soil under Shifting Cultivation.* (Brit. Commonwealth Bur. Soils Techn. Communication No. 51, Harpenden, England), 156 pp. + 16 pl.

O'Ballance, E., 1966. India-Pakistan campaign, 1965. *J. Royal United Service Institution,* **111**: 330–335.

Odum, E. P., 1971. *Fundamentals of Ecology.* 3rd Edn. (W.B. Saunders, Philadelphia), 574 pp.

Odum, H. T., Sell, M., Brown, M., Zucchetto, J., Swallows, C., Browder, J., Ahlstrom, T. and Peterson, L., 1974. *Effects of Herbicides in South Vietnam. B[13]. Models of Herbicide, Mangroves, and War in Vietnam.* (National Acad. Sciences, Washington), 302 pp.

Okada, S., Hamilton, H. B., Egami, N., Okajima, S., Russell, W. J. and Takeshita, K. (eds), 1975. Review of thirty years study of Hiroshima and Nagasaki atomic bomb survivors. *J. Radiation Research,* Chiba, **16** (supplement): 1–164.

Oliver, D. L., 1961. *Pacific Islands.* Rev. edn. (Harvard Univ. Press, Cambridge, Mass.), 456 pp.

Oliver, F. W., 1945–1946. Dust-storms in Egypt and their relation to the war period, as noted in Maryut, 1939–45. *Geographical Journal,* London, **106**: 26–49 + 4 pl.; **108**: 221–226 + 1 pl.

Olzendam, R. M., 1918. France at war. *Amer. Forestry* (now *Amer. Forests)*, **24**: 201–203.

Opler, P. A., Baker, H. G. and Frankie, G. W., 1977. Recovery of tropical lowland forest ecosystems. In: Cairns, J., Jr. *et al.* (eds), *Recovery and Restoration of Damaged Ecosystems.* (Univ. Press of Virginia, Charlottesville), 531 pp.: pp. 379–421.

Orians, G. H. and Pfeiffer, E. W., 1970. Ecological effects of the war in Vietnam. *Science*, **168**: 544–554.

Orvin, A. K., 1951–1953. Twenty-five years of Norwegian sovereignty in Svalbard, 1925–50. *Polar Record*, **6**: 179–184 + 1 pl.

Østreng, W., 1977. Strategic balance and the arctic ocean: Soviet options. *Cooperation & Conflict*, **12**: 41–62.

O'Sullivan, A. J. and Richardson, A. J., 1967. *Torrey Canyon* disaster and intertidal marine life. *Nature*, **214**: 448, 541–542.

Otterman, J., 1974. Baring high-albedo soils by overgrazing: a hypothesized desertification mechanism. *Science*, **186**: 531–533. Cf. ibid., **189**: 1012–1015 (1975); and **194**: 747–749 (1976).

Otterman, J., Waisel, Y. and Rosenberg, E., 1975. Western Negev and Sinai ecosystems: comparative study of vegetation, albedo and temperatures. *Agro-Ecosystems*, **2**, 47–59.

Owen, D. F., 1949. Macrolepidoptera of the Moorgate, London, bombed sites. *Entomologist*, **82**, 59–62.

Owen, D. F., 1951 *a*. Bombed site Lepidoptera. *Entomologist*, **84**: 265–272.

Owen, D. F., 1951 *b*. Lepidoptera of Cripplegate. *London Naturalist*, **31**: 84–88.

Owen, D. F., 1954. Further analysis of the insect records from the London bombed sites. *Entomologist's Gaz.*, **5**: 51–60.

Palmer, H. E., Hanson, W. C., Griffin, B. I. and Braby, L. A., 1965. Radioactivity measured in Alaskan natives, 1962–1964. *Science*, **147**: 620–621.

Palumbo, R. F., 1962. Recovery of the land plants at Eniwetok Atoll following a nuclear detonation. *Radiation Botany*, **1**: 182–189.

Parmenter, L., 1953. Flies of the Cripplegate bombed site, City of London. *London Naturalist*, **33**: 89–100.

Passmore, J., 1974. *Man's Responsibility for Nature: Ecological Problems and Western Traditions.* (Duckworth, London), 213 pp.

Pavlov, D. V., 1965. *Leningrad 1941: The Blockade* [translated from the 2nd Russian edn by J. C. Adams]. (University of Chicago Press, Chicago), 186 pp + 15 pl.

Payne, R., 1973. *Massacre.* (Macmillan, New York), 168 pp. + 8 pl.

Payne, R. M., 1944. Notes on the distribution of dragonflies on Bookham Common. *London Naturalist*, **24**: 23–31.

Pearl, R., 1940–1941. Some biological considerations about war. *Amer. J. Sociology*, **46**: 487–503.

Pearson, W., 1961. Alaska: Gibraltar of the north. *Military Rev.*, **41** (2): 44–56.

Peel, R. F., 1960. Some aspects of desert geomorphology. *Geography*, **45**: 241–262.

Peltier, L. C. and Pearcy, G. E., 1966. *Military Geography.* (D. Van Nostrand, Princeton, New Jersey), 176 pp. + 8 maps.

Perlmutter, A., 1977. *Military and Politics in Modern Times: On Professionals, Praetorians, and Revolutionary Soldiers.* (Yale Univ. Press, New Haven), 335 pp.

Peterson, B. C., 1942–1943. War's threat to bird species. *Frontiers*, **7** (5): 133–135.

Peterson, I., 1971. Giant U.S. 'plows' clear scrub along foe's route, *New York Times* (7 May 1971), p. 5.

Peterson, R. T., 1968. Plea for a magic island. *Audubon Mag.*, **70** (1): 50–51.

Petrow, R., 1974. *Bitter Years: The Invasion and Occupation of Denmark and Norway, April 1940–May 1945.* (Wm. Morrow, New York), 403 pp.

Pike, O. G. (ed.), 1974. *Department of Defense Energy Resources and Requirements.* US House Representatives Comm. on Armed Services, 390 pp.

Pincus, W., 1975. Visiting Kwajalein: missile-age Stonehenge. *New Republic*, Washington, *D.C.*, **172** (19): 12–14.

Pincus, W., 1978 *a.* Pacific experience shows difficulty of cleaning up radiation. *Washington Post* (18 April 1978), p. A2.

Pincus, W., 1978 *b.* US errs: Bikini island still isn't safe. *Washington Post* (19 March 1978), pp. A1, A16.

Pincus, W., 1978 *c.* US to relocate Bikinians, cites radiation effect. *Washington Post* (13 April 1978), pp. A1, A13.

Ploger, R. R., 1968. Different war: same old ingenuity. *Army*, **18** (9): 70–75.

Ploger, R. R., 1974. *Vietnam Studies: U.S. Army Engineers, 1965–1970.* (US Dept. Army), 240 pp.

Polinière, J.-P., 1967. [Phytopathological situation in different *Hevea brasiliensis* culture sites in relation to probable exposure to defoliants.] (Rubber Research Inst. of Vietnam Report No. 5/67, Saigon), 7 pp. In French.

Pollitt, R. L., 1971–1972. Wooden walls: English seapower and the world's forests. *Forest History*, **15** (1): 6–15.

Poor, C. L., 1969. Disposal of chemical agents. *Ordnance*, **54** (295): 30, 32.

Popper, R. D. and Lybrand, W. A., 1960. *Inventory of Selected Source Materials Relevant to Integration of Physical and Social Effects of Air Attack.* (Human Sciences Research Publication No. HSR-RR-60/4–SE, Arlington, Virginia) 1 vol. (unpaginated).

Preston, A., Woodhead, D. S., Mitchell, N. T. and Pentreath, R. J., 1971–1972. Impact of artificial radioactivity on the oceans and on oceanography. *Proc. Royal Soc., Edinburgh, Sect. B.*, **72**: 411–423.

Prina, L. E., 1974. Tale of two islands. *Sea Power*, Washington, D.C., **17** (3): 36–38.

Prinzing, F., 1916. *Epidemics Resulting from Wars.* (Clarendon, Oxford), 340 pp.

Prokosch, E., 1972. *Simple Art of Murder: Antipersonnel Weapons and their Developers.* (Amer. Friends Service Comm., Philadelphia), 88 pp.

Prokosch, E., 1976. Antipersonnel weapons. *International Social Science J.*, **28**: 341–358.

Prud'homme, R., 1969. *[Economy of Cambodia.]* (Presses Univ. France, Paris), 299 pp. In French.

Ramberg, B., 1978. *Destruction of Nuclear Energy Facilities in War: A Proposal for Legal Restraint.* (Princeton Univ. World Order Studies Program Occ. Pap. No. 7, Princeton, New Jersey), 32 pp.

Ramseier, R. O., 1974. Oil on ice. *Environment*, **16** (4): 6–14.

Rao, V. P., Ghani, M.A., Sankaran, T. and Mathur, K. C., 1971. *Review of the Biological Control of Insects and Other Pests in South-East Asia and the Pacific Region.* (Brit. Commonwealth Inst. Biological Control Techn. Communication No. 6, Trinidad, W.I.), 149 pp.

Rapp, A., LeHouérou, H. N. and Lundholm, B. (eds), 1976. *Can Desert Encroachment be Stopped?: A Study with Emphasis on Africa.* (Swedish Natural Science Research Council Ecological Bull. No. 24, Stockholm), 241 pp.

230

Ratcliffe, D. A., 1976. Thoughts towards a philosophy of nature conservation. *Biological Conservation,* **9**: 45–53.

Ray, C., 1970–1971. Ecology, law, and the 'marine revolution'. *Biological Conservation,* **3**: 7–17.

Rayner, J. F., 1957–1958. Studies of disasters and other extreme situations: an annotated selected bibliography. *Human Organization,* **16** (2): 30–40.

Red Cross, International Committee of the, 1973. *Weapons that May Cause Unnecessary Suffering or Have Indiscriminate Effects.* (International Comm. Red Cross, Geneva), 72 pp.

Rees, D., 1964. *Korea: The Limited War.* (St. Martin's, New York), 511 pp. + 15 pl.

Revelle, R. and Munk, W., 1977. Carbon dioxide cycle and the biosphere. In: Revelle, R. R. *et al., Energy and Climate.* (US National Acad. Sciences, Washington), 158 pp.: pp. 140–158.

Revelle, R., Wenk, E., Ketchum, B. H. and Corino, E. R., 1971. Ocean pollution by petroleum hydrocarbons. In: Matthews, W. H., Smith, F. E. and Goldberg, E. D. (eds), *Man's Impact on Terrestrial and Oceanic Ecosystems.* (MIT Press, Cambridge, Mass.), 540 pp.: pp. 297–318.

Richard, W. E. and Brown, J., 1974. Effects of vehicles on arctic tundra. *Environmental Conservation,* **1**: 55–62.

Richards, P. W., 1952. *Tropical Rain Forest: An Ecological Study.* (Cambridge Univ. Press, London), 450 pp. + 15 pl. + 4 figures.

Richards, P. W., 1970. *Life of the Jungle,* (McGraw-Hill, New York), 232 pp.

Richards, P. W., 1971. Some problems of nature conservation in the tropics. *Bull. Jardin Bot. Natl. Belg.,* **41**: 173–187.

Richards, P. W., 1973. Tropical rain forest. *Scientific Amer.,* **229** (6): 58–67, 148.

Richardson, D., 1977. Missiles in the sun. *Flight International,* London, **112**: 397–400.

Richardson, L., F., 1969. *Statistics of Deadly Quarrels.* (Boxwood Press, Pittsburgh), 373 pp. + 2 tables.

Rickard, W. H. and Shields, L. M., 1963. Early stage in the plant recolonization of a nuclear target area. *Radiation Botany,* **3**: 41–44.

Ridsdale, P. S., 1916. Shot, shell and soldiers devastate forests. *Amer. Forestry* (now *Amer. Forests),* **22**: 333–340.

Ridsdale, P. S., 1919 *a.* Belgium's forests blighted by the Hun. *Amer. Forestry* (now *Amer. Forests),* **25**: 1250–1258.

Ridsale, P. S., 1919 *b.* Forest casualties of our allies. *Amer. Forestry* (now *Amer. Forests),* **25**: 898–906.

Ridsdale, P. S., 1919 *c.* French forests for our army. *Amer. Forestry* (now *Amer. Forests),* **25**: 962–972.

Ridsdale, P. S., 1919 *d.* War's destruction of British forests. *Amer. Forestry* (now *Amer. Forests),* **25**: 1026–1040.

Ripley, S. D. *et al.,* 1964. *Land and Wildlife of Tropical Asia.* (Time-Life Books, New York), 200 pp.

Rissanen, T. I., 1977. Finland, from a geopolitical perspective. *Military Rev.,* **57** (10): 56–64.

Robbins, L., 1939. *Economic Causes of War.* (J. Cape, London), 124 pp.

Robinson, J. P., 1977. Neutron bomb and mass-destruction conventional weapons. *Bull. Peace Proposals, Oslo,* **8**: 321–327.

Rogers, B. W., 1974. *Vietnam Studies: Cedar Falls–Junction City: A Turning Point.* (US Dept. Army), 172 pp.

Rollet, B., 1962. [Forest inventory east of the Mekong.] (Food & Agriculture Org. Report No. 1500, Rome), 184 pp. + [14] pl. In French.

Rosenblad, E., 1973. Starvation as a method of warfare: conditions for regulation by convention. *International Lawyer,* 7: 252–270.

Rosenblad, E., 1974. *Prohibited Weapons: Treaties and Bibliography.* (Royal Swedish Library, Bibliographical Inst. Documentation & Data Ser. No. 6, Stockholm), 50 + 2 pp.

Rosenblad, E., 1977. International humanitarian law of armed conflict: some aspects of the principle of distinction and related problems. (Stockholm Univ. doctoral dissertation), 200 pp.

Rosson, W. B., 1966. *Combat Operations: Economic Warfare.* (US Military Assistance Cmd Vietnam, Directive No. 525–7, Saigon), 7 + [11] pp.

Rosswall, T. and Heal, O. W. (eds), 1975. *Structure and Function of Tundra Ecosystems.* (Swedish Natural Science Research Council Ecological Bull. No. 20, Stockholm), 450 pp.

Roush, J. H., Jr., 1975. Norway's significance from a military point of view. *Military Rev.,* 55 (7): 18–27.

Rowe, T. E., 1971. More precious than bullets. *Army,* 21 (3): 38–44.

Rubinoff, I., 1968. Central American sea-level canal: possible biological effects. *Science,* 161: 857–861.

Rubinoff, I., 1970–1971. Sea-level canal controversy. *Biol. Cons.,* 3: 33–36.

Rubinoff, R. W. and Rubinoff, I., 1968. Interoceanic colonization of a marine goby through the Panama Canal. *Nature,* 217: 476–478.

Ruivo, M. (ed.), 1971. *Pollution: An International Problem for Fisheries.* (Food & Agriculture Org., World Food Problems Report No. 14, Rome) 85 pp.

Rumsfeld, D. H., 1977. *Annual Defense Department Report FY 1978.* (US Dept. Defense), [386] pp.

Russell, D., 1973. How many Indians were killed?: White man versus Red man: the facts and the legend. *American West,* Palo Alto, Cal., 10 (4): 42–47, 61–63.

Russell, R. S. *et al.,* 1966. *Evaluation of Risks from Radiation.* (Pergamon Press; International Commn. on Radiological Protection Publication No. 8, Oxford), 60 pp.

Russo, A. J., 1967. Statistical analysis of the U.S. crop spraying program in South Vietnam. (Rand Corp. Memo. No. RM–5450–ISA/ARPA, Santa Monica, Cal.), 15 + 34 pp.

Ryan, P. B., 1977. Canal diplomacy and U.S. interests. *US Naval Inst. Proc.,* 103 (1): 43–53.

Ryther, J. H., 1969. Photosynthesis and fish production in the sea. *Science,* 166: 72–76; 168: 503–505.

Salisbury, E. J., 1943 *a.* Flora of bombed areas. *Nature,* 151: 462–466.

Salisbury, E. J., 1943 *b.* Flora of bombed areas. *North Western Naturalist,* 18: 160–169.

Salisbury, H. E., 1969. *900 Days: The Siege of Leningrad.* (Harper & Row, New York), 635 pp.

Sanchez, P. A. and Buol, S. W., 1975. Soils of the tropics and the world food crisis. *Science,* 188: 598–603.

Sauer, C. O., 1950. Grassland climax, fire, and man. *J. Range Mgt.,* 3: 16–21.

Saunders, D. N., 1967. Bari incident. *US Naval Inst. Proc.,* 93 (9): 35–39.

Schaller, F. W. and Sutton, P. (eds), 1978. *Reclamation of Drastically Disturbed Lands.* (American Society of Agronomy, Madison, Wisconsin), 742 pp.

Schell, J., 1967. *Village of Ben Suc.* (A. A. Knopf, New York), 132 pp.

Schell, J., 1968. *Military Half: An Account of Destruction in Quang Ngai and Quang Tin.* (A. A. Knopf, New York), 212 pp.

Schell, W. R. and Watters, R. L., 1975. Plutonium in aqueous systems. *Health Physics*, **29**: 589–597 + 1 figure.

Schindler, D. and Toman, J., 1973. *Laws of Armed Conflict: A Collection of Conventions, Resolutions and Other Documents*. (A. W. Sijthoff, Leiden), 795 pp.

Schlich, W., 1915. Forestry and the war. *Quart. J. Forestry*, **9** (1): 1–7.

Schneider, M. M., 1976. [Against the military misuse of the environment.] *Deutsche Aussenpolitik*, E. Berlin, **21**: 578–601. In German.

Schultz, V., 1966. References on Nevada test site ecological research. *Great Basin Naturalist*, **26** (3–4): 79–86.

Schultz, E., 1915. [French forests and the war.] *Z. f. Forst- und Jagdwesen*, **47**: 497–512. In German.

Schwab, D. E. (ed.), 1976. *Raw Materials & Foreign Policy*. (International Economic Studies Inst., Washington), 416 pp.

Scoville, H., Jr., 1972. Missile submarines and national security. *Scientific American*, **226** (6): 15–27, 136.

Scrimshaw, N. S. and Gordon, J. E., (eds), 1968. *Malnutrition, Learning, and Behavior*. (MIT Press, Cambridge, Mass.), 566 pp.

Scullard, H. H., 1961. *History of the Roman World from 753 to 146 B.C.* 3rd Edn. (Methuen, London), 480 pp. + 4 maps.

Sekora, P., 1973. *Aleutian Islands National Wildlife Refuge Wilderness Study Report*. (US Bureau of Sport Fisheries & Wildlife, Aleutian Islands National Wildlife Refuge, Adak, Alaska), 409 pp.

Seymour, A. H. *et al.* (eds), 1971. *Radioactivity in the Marine Environment*. (US National Acad. Sciences, Washington), 272 pp.

Shapiro, C. S., 1974. Effects on humans of world-wide stratospheric fall-out in a nuclear war. *Bull. Peace Proposals*, **5**: 186–190.

Shawcross, W., 1978–1979. Third Indochina War. *New York Rev. Books*, **25** (5): 15–22.

Shawcross, W., 1979. *Sideshow: Kissinger, Nixon and the destruction of Cambodia*. (Simon & Schuster, New York), 467 pp. + 16 pl.

Shelford, V. E., 1963. *Ecology of North America*. (Univ. of Illinois Press, Urbana, Ill.), 610 pp.

Shepard, P., 1978. *Thinking Animals: Animals and the Development of Human Intelligence*. (Viking, New York), 274 pp.

Sheridan, P. H., 1888. *Personal Memoirs*. (Chas. L. Webster, New York), 2 vols (500 + 486 pp. and 4 + 7 maps).

Sherrod, R., 1944. *Tarawa: The Story of a Battle*. (Duell, Sloan & Pearce, New York), 183 pp.

Shields, L. M. and Rickard, W. H., 1961. Preliminary evaluation of radiation effects at the Nevada test site. In: Bailey, D. L. (ed.), *Recent Advances in Botany*. (Univ. Toronto Press, Toronto), 1 766 pp.: pp. 1 387–1390.

Shields, L. M. and Wells, P. V., 1962. Effects of nuclear testing on vegetation. *Science*, **135**: 38–40.

Shields, L. M. and Wells, P. V., 1963. Recovery of vegetation on atomic target areas at the Nevada test site. In: Schultz, V. and Klement, A. W., Jr. (eds), *Radioecology*. (Reinhold Publ. Corp., New York), 746 pp.: pp. 307–310.

Shields, L. M., Wells, P. V. and Rickard, W. H., 1963. Vegetational recovery on atomic target areas in Nevada. *Ecology*, **44**: 697–705.

Shields, L. P. and Ott, M. C., 1974. Environmental decay and international politics: the uses of sovereignty. *Environmental Affairs*, **3**: 743–767.

Shipler, D. K., 1973. Villagers lingering in misery in 'safe' site near Saigon. *New York Times* (13 November 1973), p. 2.

Shulenherger, E., 1977. Contaminants in the Navy medium. *Naval Research Reviews,* **30** (9): 1–18.

Sidorenko, A. A., 1970. *Offensive* [translated from the Russian by the US Air Force]. (US Air Force, Washington; originally Military Publishing House, Moscow), 228 pp., 1973.

Siegel, L., 1977. Diego Garcia. *Pacific Research,* **8** (3): 1–12.

Siegenthaler, U. and Oeschger, H., 1978. Predicting future atmospheric carbon dioxide levels. *Science,* **199**: 388–395.

Silva, A. de and Simson, O. v., 1963. *Man Through His Art. I. War and Peace.* (Educational Productions, London), 64 pp. + 20 pl.

Simpson, L. L., 1976. Alaska's north slope oil fields: energy asset or defense liability? *Military Rev.,* **56** (9): 33–44.

Singer, J. D. and Small, M., 1972. *Wages of War, 1816–1965: A Statistical Handbook.* (J. Wiley, New York), 419 pp.

SIPRI (Stockholm International Peace Research Institute), 1971. *The Problem of Chemical and Biological Warfare. I. The Rise of CB Weapons.* (Almqvist & Wiksell, Stockholm), 395 pp.

SIPRI (Stockholm International Peace Research Institute), 1972 *a. Prospects for Arms Control in the Ocean.* (SIPRI Research Report No. 7), 25 pp.

SIPRI (Stockholm International Peace Research Institute), 1972 *b. Resources Devoted to Military Research and Development: An International Comparison.* (Almqvist & Wiksell, Stockholm), 112 pp.

SIPRI (Stockholm International Peace Research Institute), 1974 *a. French Nuclear Tests in the Atmosphere: The Question of Legality.* (SIPRI, Stockholm), 38 pp.

SIPRI (Stockholm International Peace Research Institute), 1974 *b. Oil and Security.* (Almqvist & Wiksell, Stockholm), 197 pp.

SIPRI (Stockholm International Peace Research Institute), 1974 *c. Tactical and Strategic Antisubmarine Warfare.* (Almqvist & Wiksell, Stockholm), 148 pp.

SIPRI (Stockholm International Peace Research Institute), 1975 *a. Delayed Toxic Effects of Chemical Warfare Agents.* (Almqvist & Wiksell, Stockholm), 60 pp.

SIPRI (Stockholm International Peace Research Institute), 1975 *b. Incendiary Weapons.* (Almqvist & Wiksell, Stockholm), 255 pp. + 12 pl.

SIPRI (Stockholm International Peace Research Institute), 1976. *Ecological Consequences of the Second Indochina War.* (Almqvist & Wiksell, Stockholm), 119 pp. + 8 pl.

SIPRI (Stockholm International Peace Research Institute), 1977. *Weapons of Mass Destruction and the Environment.* (Taylor & Francis, London), 95 pp.

SIPRI (Stockholm International Peace Research Institute), 1978. *Arms Control: A Survey and Appraisal of Multilateral Agreements.* (Taylor & Francis, London), 238 pp.

SIPRI (Stockholm International Peace Research Institute), 1979. *Anti-personnel Weapons.* (Taylor & Francis, London), 299 pp. + 14 pl.

Skagestad, G., 1975. Frozen frontier: models for international cooperation. *Cooperation & Conflict,* Oslo, **10**: 167–187.

Skogen, 1943. [War damage in Finnish forests.] *Skogen,* **30**: 268. In Swedish.

Small, S. H. (ed.), 1963. *Nuclear Detonations and Marine Radioactivity.* (Norwegian Defence Research Establishment, Kjeller, Norway), 221 pp.

Smith, D. M., 1962. *Practice of Silviculture.* 7th Edn. (J. Wiley, New York), 578 pp.

Snow, D. W., 1970. *Eastern Indian Ocean Islands: A Summary of their Geography, Fauna and*

Flora. (International Union Conservation Nature & Natural Resources Publication No. 17, Morges, Switz.), 282 pp.: pp. 212–223.

Soerjani, M., 1970. Alang-alang: *Imperata cylindrica* (L.) Beauv. (1812): pattern of growth as related to its problem of control. (Univ. Gadjah Mada, Ph.D. thesis, Bogor, Indonesia), 88 pp. Also: *Biotrop Bull.,* **1970** (1): 88 pp.

Sollie, F., 1974. New development in the polar regions. *Cooperation & Conflict,* Oslo, 9:75-89.

Sorokin, P. A., 1942. *Man and Society in Calamity: The Effects of War, Revolution, Famine, Pestilence Upon Human Mind, Behavior, Social Organization and Cultural Life.* (E. P. Dutton, New York), 352 pp.

Sorokin, P., 1957. *Social & Cultural Dynamics.* Rev. & abr. (Porter Sargent, Boston), 718 pp.

Southern, W. E., 1975. Orientation of gull chicks exposed to Project Sanguine's electro-magnetic field. *Science,* **189:** 43-145.

Spedding, C. R. W., 1971. *Grassland Ecology.* (Clarendon Press, Oxford), 221 pp.

Speller, J. P., 1972. *Panama Canal: Heart of America's Security.* (Robert Speller & Sons, New York), 164 pp. + 8 pl.

Spoehr, A., 1954. Saipan: the ethnology of a war-devastated island. *Fieldiana: Anthropology,* **41:** 1–383.

Sprout, H. and Sprout, M., 1957. Environmental factors in the study of international politics. *J. Conflict Resolution,* **1:** 309-328.

Sprout, H. and Sprout, M., 1965. *Ecological Perspective on Human Affairs: With Special Reference to International Politics.* (Princeton Univ. Press, Princeton, New Jersey), 236 pp.

Spurr, S. H. and Barnes, B.V., 1973. *Forest Ecology.* 2nd Edn. (Ronald Press, New York), 571 pp.

Stackpole, E. J., 1961. *Sheridan in the Shenandoah: Jubal Early's Nemesis.* (Stackpole Co., Harrisburg, Pa.), 413 pp.

Stahler, L. M. and Whitehead, E. I., 1950. Effect of 2,4-D on potassium nitrate levels in leaves of sugar beets. *Science,* **112:** 749-751.

Stamp, L. D. (ed.), 1961. *History of Land Use in the Arid Regions.* (UNESCO Arid Zone Research No. 17, Paris), 388 pp.

Steele, J. H., 1974. *Structure of Marine Ecosystems.* (Harvard Univ. Press, Cambridge), 128 pp.

Steen, H. K., 1977. *U.S. Forest Service: A History.* (Univ. Washington Press, Seattle), 356 pp. + pl.

Stein, Z., Susser, M., Saenger, G. and Marolla, F., 1972. Nutrition and mental performance. *Science,* **178:** 708-713.

Stein, Z., Susser, M., Saenger, G. and Marolla, F., 1975. *Famine and Human Development: The Dutch Hunger Winter of 1944-1945.* (Oxford Univ. Press, New York), 284 pp.

Stephens, M. M., 1973. *Vulnerability of Total Petroleum Systems.* (US Dept. Interior, Office of Oil & Gas), 160 pp.

Stoddart, D. R. (ed.), 1967. Ecology of Aldabra atoll, Indian ocean. *Atoll Research Bull.,* **1967** (118): 141 pp. + pl.

Stoddart, D. R., 1968 *a.* Catastrophic human interference with coral atoll ecosystems. *Geography,* **53:** 25–40.

Stoddart, D. R., 1968 *b.* Isolated island communities. *Science J.,* **4** (4): 32–38.

Stoddart, D. R. and Taylor, J. D. (eds), 1971. Geography and ecology of Diego Garcia atoll, Chagos archipelago. *Atoll Research Bull.,* **1971** (149): 237 pp. + figures + plates.

Stoddart, D. R. and Wright, C. A., 1967. Ecology of Aldabra atoll. *Nature,* **213:** 1174-1177.

Stoddart, L. A., Smith, A. D. and Box, T. W., 1975. *Range Management*. 3rd Edn. (McGraw-Hill, New York), 532 pp.

Stone, C. D., 1972. Should trees have standing?: toward legal rights for natural objects. *Southern California Law Rev.*, **45**: 450–501.

Stott, D. H., 1962. Cultural and natural checks on population-growth. In: Montagu, M. F. A. (ed.), *Culture and the Evolution of Man*. (Oxford Univ. Press, New York), 376 pp.: pp. 355–376.

Strahler, A. N., 1975. *Physical Geography*. 4th Edn. (J. Wiley, New York), 643 + 39 + 17 pp. + pl. + maps.'

Stuiver, M., 1978. Atmospheric carbon dioxide and carbon reservoir changes. *Science*, **199**: 253–258; **202**: 1109.

Summerhays, S., 1973. Galapagos: islands in the balance. *Ecologist*, London, **3**: 144–146, 148–149.

Svensson, G. K. and Lidén, K., 1965. Transport of ^{137}Cs from lichen to animal to man. *Health Physics*, **11**: 1393–1400.

Sverdrup, H. U., Johnson, M. W. and Fleming, R. H., 1942. *Oceans: Their Physics, Chemistry, and General Biology*. (Prentice-Hall, Englewood Cliffs, New Jersey), 1 087 pp. + 7 charts.

Swann, R., 1971. Culebra: island besieged. *Nation*, **212**: 262–265.

Swanson, C. R. and Shaw, W. C., 1954. Effect of 2,4-dichlorophenoxyacetic acid on the hydrocyanic acid and nitrate content of sudan grass. *Agronomy J.*, **46**: 418–421.

Sylva, D. P. de and Michel, H. B., 1974. *Effects of Herbicides in South Vietnam B [15]. Effects of Mangrove Defoliation on the Estuarine Ecology and Fisheries of South Vietnam.* (National Acad. Sciences, Washington), 126 pp.

Synhorst, G. E., 1973. Soviet strategic interest in the maritime Arctic. *US Naval Inst. Proc.*, **99** (843): 88–111.

Talbot, L. M. and Talbot, M. H. (eds), 1968. *Conservation in Tropical South East Asia*. (International Union Conservation Nature & Natural Resources Publication N.S. No. 10, Morges, Switz.), 550 pp. + 2 pl.

Tân, Phan Huy, 1971. [Defoliation with chemicals.]. (Directorate of Waters & Forests, Saigon), [6] pp. In Vietnamese.

Tanter, R., 1976–1977. Military situation in East Timor. *Pacific Research*, Mt. View, Cal., **8** (2): 1–6. Cf. ibid., 7 (1): 7–9.

Tate, M. and Hull, D. M., 1964. Effects of nuclear explosions on Pacific islanders. *Pacific Historical Rev.*, **33**: 379–393.

Taubenfeld, H. J., 1973. International environmental law: air and outer space. *Natural Resources J.*, **13**: 315–316.

Taylor, B. W., 1957. Plant succession on recent volcanoes in Papua. *J. Ecology*, **45**: 233–243 + 1 pl.

Teal, J. J., Jr., 1950–1951. Europe's northernmost frontier. *Foreign Affairs*, **29**: 263–275.

Teal, J. J., Jr., 1953–1954. Rebirth of north Norway. *Foreign Affairs*, **32**: 123–134.

Teal, J. J., Jr., 1955. Aboriginal populations. In: Kimble, G. H. T. and Good, D. (eds), *Geography of the Northlands*. (J. Wiley; Amer. Geographical Soc. Spec. Publication No. 32, New York), 534 pp. + 1 map; pp. 139–162.

Teclaff, L. A. and Utton, A. E. (eds), 1974. *International Environmental Law*. (Praeger, New York), 271 pp.

Thomas, W. L., 1974. *Effects of Herbicides in South Vietnam. B[16]. Economic Stress and Settlement Changes.* (National Acad. Sciences, Washington), 61 pp.

Thornton, I., 1971. *Darwin's Islands: A Natural History of the Galápagos.* (Natural History Press, Garden City, New York), 322 pp. + 36 pl.

Thorsson, I., 1975. Disarmament negotiations: what are they doing for the environment? *Ambio,* **4**: 199–202.

Thucydides, ca. 411 B.C. *History of the Peloponnesian War* [translated from the Greek by C. F. Smith]. (Harvard Univ. Press, Cambridge, Mass.), 4 vols (461 + 445 + 375 + 459 pp. + maps), 1921–1930.

Tickell, C., 1977. *Climatic Change and World Affairs.* (Harvard Univ. Studies in International Affairs, No. 37, Cambridge, Mass.), 75 pp.

Times, 1977. *Times Atlas of the World: Comprehensive Edition.* 5th Edn. (Times Books, London), 40 + 224 pp. + 123 pl.

Times, New York, 1970. Departing division leaves its mark in Vietnam. *New York Times* (5 April 1970), p. 7.

Times, New York, 1972. Text of intelligence report on bombing of dikes in North Vietnam issued by State Department. *New York Times* (29 July 1972), p. 2.

Tirelli, M., 1949. [Invisible damage of the war to Italian agriculture.] *Notiziario sulle Malattie delle Piante,* Pavia, **1949** (3): 9–12. In Italian.

Tolmer, L., 1947. [Marine fauna of Calvados and the disembarkment of 6 June 1944.] *Feuille Naturalistes, N.S.,* **2**: 90. In French.

Tont, S. A. and Delistraty, D. A., 1977. Food resources of the oceans: an outline of status and potentials. *Environmental Conservation,* **4**: 243–252.

Topp, R. W., 1969. Interoceanic sea-level canal: effects on the fish faunas. *Science,* **165**: 1324–1327.

Toumey, J. W. and Korstian, C. F., 1947. *Foundations of Silviculture Upon an Ecological Basis.* 2nd Edn. (J. Wiley, New York), 468 pp.

Toynbee, A., 1972. Religious background of the present environment crisis: a viewpoint. *International J. Environmental Studies, London,* **3**: 141–146; **4**: 157–158.

Travers, W. B. and Luney, P. R., 1976. Drilling, tankers, and oil spills on the Atlantic outer continental shelf. *Science,* **194**: 791–796; **199**: 125, 127–130, 132.

Tregaskis, R., 1943. *Guadalcanal Diary.* (Random House, New York), 263 pp. + 16 pl.

Tremayne, P., 1977–1978. Falkland Islands. *R.U.S.I. and Brassey's Defence Yrbk, 1977/78*: 156–170.

Tunnard, C., 1978. *World with a View.* (Yale Univ. Press, New Haven), 196 pp.

Turbiville, G. H., 1974. Soviet desert operations. *Military Rev.,* **54** (6): 40–50.

Turner, N., 1975. Nuclear waste drop in the ocean. *New Scientist,* **68**: 290.

Ukens Nytt fra Norge, 1943. [Plague of predators gaining ground: Germans refuse to distribute hunting rifles.] *Ukens Nytt fra Norge, Washington,* **1** (298): 8. In Norwegian.

Umbricht, V., Bourcier, P., Lankester, C., Pantalu, R. and Arnaud, A., 1978. *Report of the Special Mission on International Assistance for the Reconstruction of Viet Nam Appointed by the Secretary-General in Accordance with General Assembly Resolution 32/3.* (United Nations General Assembly Document No. 78–02689, New York), 278 pp. + 1 map.

Umbricht, V., Wagner, K., Boumendil, H. and Cheang, A., 1976. Report of the United Nations mission to North and South Viet Nam. In: Kennedy, E. M. (ed.), *Aftermath of War: Humanitarian Problems of Southeast Asia.* (US Senate Comm. on the Judiciary, Washington), 589 pp.: pp. 143–234.

UN (United Nations), 1945. Charter. In: Russell, R. B., *History of the United Nations Charter.* (Brookings Institution, Washington), 1 140 pp.: pp. 1035–1053.

UNEP (United Nations Environment Programme), 1977–1978. *Register of International Conventions and Protocols in the Field of the Environment.* (UNEP Governing Council Information Paper No. 5, with supplement, Nairobi), 96 + 37 pp.

Union of Rubber Planters in Vietnam *et al.,* 1969. *Rubber in Vietnam.* (Union of Rubber Planters in Vietnam, Saigon), 57 pp. + pl.

Unna, W., 1974. Diego Garcia. *New Republic, Wash., D.C.,* **170** (10): 7–8.

UNSCEAR (United Nations Scientific Committee on the Effects of Atomic Radiation), 1972. *Ionizing Radiation: Levels and Effects.* (United Nations, New York), 2 vols 447 pp.

UN War Crimes Commission, 1948. *History of the United Nations War Crimes Commission and the Development of the Laws of War.* (His Majesty's Stationery Office, London), 592 pp.

Urlanis, B., 1971. *Wars and Population* [translated from the Russian by L. Lempert]. (Progress Publishers, Moscow), 320 pp.

VanCleve, K., 1977. Recovery of disturbed tundra and taiga surfaces in Alaska. In: Cairns, J., Jr. *et al.* (eds), *Recovery and Restoration of Damaged Ecosystems.* (Univ. Press of Virginia, Charlottesville), 531 pp.: pp. 422–455.

VanderEls, T., 1971. Irresistible weapon. *Military Rev.,* **51** (8): 80–90.

Väyrynen, R. (ed.), 1978. *Review of Research Trends and an Annotated Bibliography: Social and Economic Consequences of the Arms Race and Disarmament.* (UNESCO Reports & Papers in the Social Sciences No. 39, Paris), 44 pp.

Velimirovic, B., 1974. [Investigations on the epidemiology and control of plague in South Vietnam.] *Zentralblatt f. Bakteriologie, Parasitenkunde, Infektionskrankheiten & Hygiene, Sect. I, Pt. A,* **228**: 482–508. In German.

Vellodi, M. A. *et al.,* 1968. *Effects of the Possible Use of Nuclear Weapons and the Security and Economic Implications for States of the Acquisition and Further Development of these Weapons.* (United Nations, New York), 76 pp.

Verwey, W. D., 1977. *Riot Control Agents and Herbicides in War: Their Humanitarian, Toxicological, Ecological, Polemological, and Legal Aspects.* (A. W. Sijthoff, Leyden), 377 pp.

Vincendon, P., 1965. Far north. *Military Rev.,* **45** (9): 39–44.

Voevodsky, J., 1970. Quantitative analysis of nations at war. *Peace Research Revs.,* **3** (5): 1–63.

Vorren, Ø. (ed.), 1960. *Norway North of 65.* (Oslo Univ. Press, Oslo), 271 pp. + 2 maps.

Vos, A. de, 1977–1978. Game as food. *Unasylva,* **29** (116): 2–12.

Wait, J. R., 1972. Project Sanguine. *Science,* **178**: 272–275.

Walker, E. P. *et al.,* 1975. *Mammals of the World.* 3rd Edn. (Johns Hopkins Press, Baltimore), 2 vols (1 500 pp.).

Wall, P., 1976–1977. Defence of North Sea energy sources: the military aspects of the problem. *NATO's Fifteen Nations,* **21** (2): 78–83.

Wallace, A. R., 1880. *Island Life: Or, The Phenomena and Causes of Insular Faunas and Floras, Including a Revision and Attempted Solution of the Problem of Geological Climates.* (Macmillan, London), 526 pp. + 3 maps.

Wallace, B., 1973. Conscription at sea. *Saturday Rev. Sciences* (now *Saturday Rev.*), **1** (2): 44–45.

Walsh, J., 1967. Aldabra. I. Biology may lose a unique ecosystem. II. Reprieve for an island. *Science,* **157:** 788–790; **158:** 1164.

Walter, H., 1971. *Ecology of Tropical and Subtropical Vegetation* [translated from the German by D. Mueller-Dumbois]. (Van Nostrand Reinhold, New York), 539 pp. + 1 figure + 1 pl.

Walters, J. B., 1973. *Merchant of Terror: General Sherman and Total War.* (Bobbs-Merrill, Indianapolis), 267 pp.

Ward, B., 1962. *The Rich Nations and the Poor Nations.* (W. W. Norton, New York), 159 pp.

Ward, H. B., 1943. Warfare and natural resources. *Science,* **98:** 289–292.

Warner, O., Bennett, G., Macintyre, D., Uhlig, F., Jr., Wettern, D. and Preston, A., 1975. *Encyclopedia of Sea Warfare from the First Ironclads to the Present Day.* (Thos. Y. Crowell, New York), 256 pp.

Warren, W. F., Henry, L. H. and Johnston, R. D., 1967. *Crop Destruction Operations in. RVN During CY 1967.* (US Dept Defense, Commander-in-chief Pacific, Scientific Advisory Group Working Pap. No. 29–67, Honolulu), 12 + [32] pp.

Washington, G., 1788. [Letter to Arthur Young of 4 December 1788.] In: Washington, G., 1803, *Letters from His Excellency George Washington, to Arthur Young, Esq. F.R.S. and Sir John Sinclair, Bart., M.P.* (Cotton & Stewart, Alexandria, Virginia), 128 pp.: pp. 13–17.

Weast, R. C. (ed.). 1974. *Handbook of Chemistry and Physics.* 55th Edn. (CRC Press, Cleveland), [2 279] pp.

Webster, C. and Frankland, N., 1961. *Strategic Air Offensive Against Germany 1939–1945.* (Her Majesty's Stationery Office, London), 4 vols (1 705 pp.) + maps.

Weeks, W. F. and Campbell, W. J., 1973. Icebergs as a fresh-water source: an appraisal. *J. Glaciology,* **12:** 207–233.

Wells, P. V., 1965. Scarp woodlands, transported grassland soils, and concept of grassland climate in the Great Plains region. *Science,* **148:** 246–249.

West, G. C., 1976. Environmental problems associated with arctic development especially in Alaska. *Environmental Conservation,* Geneva, **3:** 218–224.

Western, K. A., 1969. Report . . . on nutritional and health conditions in Biafra, October-November 1969. In: Kennedy, E. M. (ed.), 1969–1970, *Relief Problems in Nigeria–Biafra.* (US Senate Comm. on the Judiciary), 291 pp.: pp. 212–272.

Westing, A. H., 1970. Arrogance of power. *New Republic,* **162** (13): 28–29.

Westing, A. H., 1971. Forestry and the war in South Vietnam. *J. Forestry,* **69:** 777–783. Cf. ibid., **70:** 129 (1972).

Westing, A. H., 1971–1972. Herbicides as agents of chemical warfare: their impact in relation to the Geneva Protocol of 1925. *Environmental Affairs,* **1:** 578–586.

Westing, A. H., 1972 a. Herbicidal damage to Cambodia. In: Neilands, J. B. *et al., Harvest of Death.* (Free Press, New York), 304 pp.: pp. 177–205.

Westing, A. H., 1972 b. U.S. food destruction program in South Vietnam. In: Browning, F. and Forman, D. (eds), *Wasted Nations.* (Harper & Row, New York), 346 pp.: pp. 21–25.

Westing, A. H., 1973. Postwar visit to Hanoi. *Boston Globe* (23 September 1973), p. A6.

Westing, A. H., 1974. Proscription of ecocide: arms control and the environment. *Bull. Atomic Scientists,* **30** (1): 24–27.

Westing, A. H., 1975. Unexploded munitions problem: an American legacy to Indochina that still wounds and kills. *Sunday Rutland [Vt.] Herald & Times Argus* (14 December 1975), Sect. 4, p. 3.

Westing, A. H., 1978 *a*. Ecological considerations regarding massive environmental contamination with 2,3,7,8-tetrachlorodibenzo-*para*-dioxin. In: Ramel. C. (ed.), *Chlorinated Phenoxy Acids and their Dioxins.* (Swedish Natural Science Research Council Ecological Bull. No. 27 [Vol. I], Stockholm), 302 pp.: pp. 285–294.

Westing, A. H., 1978 *b*. Military expenditures and their reduction. *Bull. Peace Proposals*, **9**: 24–29.

Westing, A. H., 1978 *c*. Neutron bombs and the environment. *Ambio*, **7**: 93–97.

Westing, A. H. and Lumsden, M., 1979. Threat of modern warfare to man and his environment: an annotated bibliography. (UNESCO Reports and Papers in the Social Sciences No. 40, Paris), 25 pp.

Westing, A. H. and Pfeiffer, E. W., 1972. Cratering of Indochina. *Scientific Amer.*, **226** (5): 20–29; **138** (6): 7.

Westman, W. E., 1977. How much are nature's services worth? *Science*, **197**: 960–964.

Wet, C. R. de, 1902. *Three Years War (October 1899–June 1902)* [translated from the Dutch]. (Archibald Constable, Westminster, England), 520 pp. + 1 map.

Wharton, C. H., 1966. Man, fire and wild cattle in north Cambodia. *Proc. Tall Timbers Fire Ecology Conf.*, **5**: 23–65.

Wharton, C. H., 1968. Man, fire and wild cattle in southeast Asia. *Proc. Tall Timbers Fire Ecology Conf.*, **7**: 107–167.

Whitaker, D. P. *et al.*, 1973. *Area Handbook for the Khmer Republic (Cambodia).* 3rd Edn. (US Dept. Army Pamphlet No. 550–50), 387 pp.

White, L., Jr., 1976. Historical roots of our ecologic crisis. *Science*, **155**: 1203–1207.

White, P. T., 1965. Saigon: eye of the storm. *National Geographic Mag.*, **127**: 834–872.

Whitehead, E. I., Kersten, J. and Jacobsen, D., 1956. Effect of 2,4-D spray on the nitrate content of sugar beet and mustard plants. *Proc. S. Dakota Acad. Science*, **35**: 106–110.

Whitmore, T. C., 1975. *Tropical Rain Forests of the Far East.* (Oxford Univ. Press, New York), 282 pp.

Whittaker, R. H. and Likens, G. E., 1973. Carbon in the biota. In: Woodwell, G. M. and Pecan, E. V. (eds), *Carbon and the Biosphere.* (U.S. Atomic Energy Commission, Washington, Symposium Series No. 30), 392 pp.: pp. 281–302.

Whittaker, R. H. and Likens, G. E., 1975. Biosphere and man. In: Lieth, H. and Whittaker, R. H. (eds), *Primary Productivity of the Biosphere.* (Springer-Verlag, W. Berlin), 339 pp.: pp. 305–328.

WHO (World Health Organization), 1968. *Epidemiological Situation in Viet Nam.* (World Health Org. Publication No. EB41/42, Geneva), 19 + 6 + 15 pp.

WHO (World Health Organization), 1973. Plague in 1972. *W.H.O. Weekly Epidemiological Record*, **48**: 141–142.

WHO (World Health Organization), 1976. [Reports on Vietnam of February 1976.] In: Kennedy, E. M. (ed.), *Aftermath of War: Humanitarian Problems of Southeast Asia.* (US Senate Comm. on the Judiciary, Washington), 589 pp.: pp. 98–142.

Wilcke, J., 1971. [The underwater explosion: processes, consequences, problems.] *Soldat u. Technik, Frankfurt-am-Main*, **14**: 74–77. In German.

Williams, H., 1967. Bikini nine years later. *Science J.*, **3** (4): 48–53.

Wilson, R. D., Monaghan, P. H., Osanik, A., Price, L. C. and Rogers, M. A., 1974. Natural marine oil seepage. *Science*, **184**: 857–865.

Wimpenny, R. S., 1953. *Plaice.* (Edward Arnold, London), 145 pp.

Windholz, M., Budavari, S., Stroumtsos, L. Y. and Fertig, M. N., 1976. *Merck Index: An Encyclopedia of Chemicals and Drugs.* 9th Edn. (Merck & Co., Rahway, New Jersey), [1 937] pp.

Winick, M., Meyer, K. K. and Harris, R. C., 1975. Malnutrition and environmental enrichment by early adoption. *Science,* 190: 1173–1175.

Winters, R. K., 1974. *Forest and Man.* (Vantage Press, New York), 393 pp.

Won, W. D., DiSalvo, L. H. and Ng, J., 1976. Toxicity and mutagenicity of 2,4,6-trinitrotoluene and its microbial metabolites. *Applied & Environmental Microbiology,* 31: 576–580.

Wong, C. S., Green, D. R. and Cretney, W. J., 1974. Quantitative tar and plastic waste distributions in the Pacific Ocean. *Nature,* 247: 30–32.

Wood, D., 1968. *Conflict in the Twentieth Century.* (International Inst. for Strategic Studies, Adelphi Paper No. 48, London), 27 pp.

Wood, F. G., 1973. *Marine Mammals and Man: The Navy's Porpoises and Sea Lions.* (Robert B. Luce, Washington), 264 pp.

Woodwell, G. M., Whittaker, R. H., Reiners, W. A., Likens, G. E., Delwiche, C. C. and Botkin, D. B., 1978. Biota and the world carbon budget. *Science,* 199: 141–146. Cf. ibid. 204: 1345–1346 (1979).

Wright, Q., 1965. *Study of War: With a Commentary on War Since 1942.* 2nd Edn. (Univ. Chicago Press, Chicago), 1 637 pp.

Wright, R. A. (ed.), 1978. *Reclamation of Disturbed Arid Lands.* (Univ. New Mexico Press, Albuquerque), 196 pp.

Wrighton, F. E., 1947. Plant ecology at Cripplegate, 1947. *London Naturalist,* 27: 44–48.

Wrighton, F. E., 1948. Plant ecology at Cripplegate, 1948. *London Naturalist,* 28: 29–44.

Wrighton, F. E., 1949. Plant ecology at Cripplegate, 1949. *London Naturalist,* 29: 85–88.

Wrighton, F. E., 1950. Plant ecology at Cripplegate, 1950. *London Naturalist,* 30: 73–79 + 2 pl.

Wrighton, F. E., 1952. Plant ecology at Cripplegate, 1951–52. *London Naturalist,* 32: 90–93.

Young, P. and Calvert, M., 1977. *Dictionary of Battles: 1816–1976.* (New English Library, London), 606 pp.

Zamenhof, S., Marthens, E. v. and Grauel, L., 1971. DNA (cell number) in neonatal brain: second generation (F_2) alteration by maternal (F_0) dietary protein restriction. *Science,* 172: 850–851.

Zander, I. and Araskog, R., 1973. *Nuclear Explosions 1945–1972: Basic Data.* (Swedish National Defence Research Inst. Report No. A 4505–A1, Stockholm), 56 pp.

Ziemke, E. F., 1959. *German Northern Theater of Operations, 1940–1945.* (US Dept Army Pamphlet No, 20–271, Washington), 342 pp. + 10 maps.

Zinsser, H., 1935. *Rats, Lice and History.* (Little, Brown, Boston), 301 pp.

Ziswiler, V., 1967. *Extinct and Vanishing Animals: A Biology of Extinction and Survival* [translated from the German and rev. by F. & P. Bunnell]. (Springer-Verlag, New York), 133 pp.

Index